A SHEARWATER BOOK

Politics, Pollution, and Pandas

Politics, Pollution, and Pandas

An Environmental Memoir

Russell E. Train

Island Press / SHEARWATER BOOKS

Washington • Covelo • London

A Shearwater Book
Published by Island Press

Copyright © 2003 Russell E. Train

All rights reserved under International and Pan-American Copyright
Conventions. No part of this book may be reproduced in any form or
by any means without permission in writing from the publisher: Island
Press, Suite 300, 1718 Connecticut Ave., NW, Washington, DC 20009.

Shearwater Books is a trademark of The Center for Resource Economics.

Library of Congress Cataloging-in-Publication Data
Train, Russell E., 1920-
Politics, pollution, and pandas : an environmental memoir /
Russell E. Train.
p. cm.
Includes bibliographical references and index.
ISBN 1-55963-286-0 (acid-free paper)
1. Train, Russell E., 1920- 2. Environmental policy — United States —
History — 20th century. 3. Conservation of natural resources — United
States — History — 20th century. 4. Environmentalists — United States —
Biography. 5. Cabinet officers — United States — Biography. I. Title.
GE56.T73A3 2003
333.72'092 — dc22   2003016275

British Cataloguing-in-Publication Data available.

Printed on recycled, acid-free paper.

Manufactured in the United States of America

09 08 07 06 05 04 03 02   8 7 6 5 4 3 2 1

Dedicated to

Al Alm, Tim Atkeson, Bob Cahn,

Fitz Green, Jack Horton,

Gordon MacDonald, Marian O'Connell,

Lee Rogers, and Steffen Plehn

Contents

Preface

The Richard M. Nixon and Gerald R. Ford presidencies (1969–1977) saw concern for the environment explode as a public issue. While largely lost today in the shadows of Watergate, the fact is that Nixon seized the political moment to enable an extraordinary array of environmental initiatives, both domestically and internationally to be taken. That environmental agenda was so wide-ranging, and yet so comprehensive, as to be without precedent in the history of the United States.

None of that is intended to belittle the vital contributions in the environmental area made by the Democratic Congresses of those years, or the importance of bipartisan support in Congress for environmental programs, or the significant environmental work begun in the years preceding. But the fact is that we would never have moved so far nor accomplished so much without presidential leadership in that period.

I do not for a moment suggest that Nixon himself was an environmentalist. He understood the political importance of environmental issues but had little understanding of or interest in their complexities. He let others carry the environmental ball on his behalf. Personally, he was often ambivalent about environmental issues, increasingly so as time went on.

In the closing years of the Nixon administration, as the energy "crisis" began to bite and as the Watergate fiasco increasingly distracted the White House, the environmental bloom began to fade. Then, as Ford succeeded to the presidency in August 1974, environmental programs became more and more embattled over energy and economic concerns. Though that battle was not decisively won by either side — nor, perhaps, should it have been — environmental programs remained largely intact and on track during those critical years. In subsequent years, of course, the U.S. government's environmental performance has fluctuated with both the political currents and the personalities involved. Today, George W. Bush and his White House appear determinedly negative on environmental matters, both nationally and internationally.

This book, in no small part, is designed to tell the environmental story of the Nixon and Ford years and their aftermath from the perspective of one who was privileged to have a central role in both the formulation of environmental policy and its implementation.

As under secretary of the Department of the Interior, as the first chairman of the Council on Environmental Quality in the Executive Office of the President, and as the second administrator of the Environmental Protection Agency, I played a major part in the environmental developments within the federal government during the late 1960s and the 1970s as well as, before and after that time, in the private nongovernmental environmental community, most notably as head of the World Wildlife Fund in the United States.

This book is not intended to provide a history of the environmental movement nor a comprehensive compendium of environmental policy making during the years I was active in these affairs. It is, rather, an account of my personal involvement in those matters: how I came to be there, my experience at the time, and what that experience subsequently led to. For excellent, well-researched accounts of the Nixon administration's environmental record in particular, I recommend John Whitaker's *Striking a Balance*[1] and J. Brooks Flippen's *Nixon and the Environment*.[2] I have used both of these books to refresh my own memory.

In 2000, I published privately a memoir, which covered lightly both my public career and my private life,[3] the latter ranging from my childhood through my education and my military service in World War II. The volume also contains an extensive account of our family farm on the Eastern Shore of Maryland and accounts of my various travels around the world, among other noncareer subjects. Of necessity, to keep the volume within reasonable bounds, the treatment of my public career was not extensive. Thus, *A Memoir* was essentially a book written for family and friends.

Some of the material, particularly of an anecdotal nature, that appeared in *A Memoir* is also present here, often in expanded form. While the earlier book depended primarily upon memory, not always a highly reliable source at my age, for this book I have made use of extensive personal files.

These include copies of memoranda written for my own files or addressed to the president of the United States or members of the White House staff, occasional notes made contemporaneously about particular events, published proceedings of congressional committees, speeches I delivered, and diaries I kept. Some of the latter are very detailed, but for much of the period involved I unfortunately kept no diary at all. For the present volume, I personally researched all these materials without the help of an assistant. As a result, any errors of fact are my responsibility.*

I have discovered that, in some cases, my very clear current recollection of an event does not jibe with an account I wrote at the time of the event. Where that situation arose in the writing of this book, I let the written record prevail. I have made extensive use of newspaper articles and editorials in the pages that follow and do not hesitate to quote statements favorable to myself from these sources. To do so may be tasteless of me, but if I don't, who will? (Actually, I have made an effort to quote unfavorable comments as well.)

At several points in this book, I describe changes being made in the way the U.S. government handled environmental factors in decision making as truly revolutionary. Since I also describe myself as having played a central role in those changes, I should make clear that I advance no claim to being a revolutionary. At the time in question, I was a moderate conservative in a Republican administration.

In 1969, while serving as under secretary of the Interior Department, I was interviewed by John McPhee for his book *Encounters with the Archdruid*, about David Brower, then the charismatic head of the Sierra Club. In response to one of McPhee's questions, I am quoted as having said: "Thank God for Dave Brower. He makes it so easy for the rest of us to be reasonable."[4] Some years later, at a lecture in Lexington, Kentucky, Brower is reported to have said, after quoting my remark: "Well, it took me seven years to think of a reply. Finally, I said, 'Thank God for Russell Train — he makes it so easy for anyone to appear outrageous.'"[5]

And that's probably as good a place as any to leave the matter.

*Now that this book is complete, my papers, primarily those related to my public service, are being deposited in the Library of Congress.

Two roads diverged in a wood, and I —
I took the one less traveled by,
And that has made all the difference.

<small>Robert Frost, "The Road Not Taken"</small>

With the end of the Cold War and the
Communist threat, the bond that held
the United States and its allies together
for half a century has loosened. The
international community is breaking into
national or (at best) regional groupings
pursuing their own narrow self-interests.
Prospects for sustainable development
could shatter in such a divided world. We
are convinced that the urgent need to put
the world on the road to sustainability
provides a common purpose that can
and must unite the global community.

Choosing a Sustainable Future:
The Report of the National Commission
on the Environment, 1993

Politics, Pollution, and Pandas

Prologue

How One Thing Leads to Another

IT WAS A COLD, wet winter's night in New York City, with rain blowing in gusts down Fifth Avenue. I pulled the collar of my overcoat higher around my neck and trudged into the rain, keeping a tight grip on my umbrella. There were few other pedestrians, but dinnertime traffic jammed the avenue. Despite the miserable weather, I was excited, and not a little nervous, about what lay a few blocks ahead.

It was January 11, 1969, and Richard M. Nixon was nine days away from becoming the thirty-seventh president of the United States. Just after his election in November, he had asked Paul McCracken[1] to set up advisory task forces on a broad range of public policy issues, including taxes, agriculture, housing, space, and health — but not on conservation and the environment. Fatefully for me, McCracken's deputy in the task force effort was a friend, Henry Loomis, who had for several years been a trustee of The Conservation Foundation, the small, ecologically oriented policy organization of which I was president. Henry called to tell me about the task force enterprise and pointed out that there was no environmental group. "Russ, don't you think there *should* be a task force on the environment?" he asked. "And, if your answer is yes, would you be willing to chair it?" I thought deeply for a nanosecond and then replied, "Yes — on both counts!" Henry had evidently cleared all this in advance.

Here was a remarkable opportunity, I thought, to help shape an environmental policy for the country. Aside from one radio talk of Nixon's in the fall, the subject of the environment had received little attention in the campaign. It seemed a good omen that at least it was now being considered part and parcel of the new administration's planning.

Looking back on my task force participation, I can only be amazed by the combination of events, personal associations, and plain dumb luck that brought it all about. Whatever the explanation, that involvement was to become a major determinant of my life's future course, and its timing couldn't have been better. My career was already in full transition toward environmental interests. Following graduation from law school in 1948, I had embarked on a career as a government tax attorney and subsequently became a judge of the United States Tax Court. Two hunting safaris in East Africa in those years with my wife, Aileen, however, inspired a deeply felt commitment to the conservation of African wildlife. While still a judge, I had become the principal founder of the African Wildlife Leadership Foundation (now simply the African Wildlife Foundation) and a founding director of the World Wildlife Fund. Then, in 1965, I made a major change in course: I resigned from the Tax Court to become the full-time president of The Conservation Foundation. From my vantage point, the task force assignment constituted a further step, potentially a significant one, along the road I had chosen just a few years earlier.

In selecting members for the task force, I had a free hand. The Nixon people made no effort to dictate or even suggest members, and I saw to it that the task force makeup was bipartisan. Given the haste with which it was put together, it was an extraordinarily good group, representative of environmental organizations, state governments, business, science, and academia, as well as different geographic areas of the country.[2]

Officially titled the Task Force on Natural Resources and Environment, our group met in Washington over one lengthy dinner and again during most of the following day. We quickly reached agreement on the central thrust of our recommendations. "Evidence of progressive environmental deterioration is incontrovertible," we wrote, and we went on to cite the "poisoning of our lakes and rivers," air pollution, the increasing carbon dioxide content of the atmosphere, the harmful effects of pesticides and other toxic chemicals, "visual ugliness and urban sprawl," and "the rising tide of human numbers." "We now possess the knowledge and technology to begin the job of remediation," we declared. The question was, "Do we possess the will?"

We saw strong evidence of growing citizen concern over environmental problems and increasing interest among members of Congress, which gave some grounds for optimism. "Internationally," we wrote, "these problems constitute an extraordinary opportunity for United States lead-

ership and new initiatives." At home, we reported, "environmental quality is a unifying goal that cuts across economic and racial lines, across
political and social boundaries. It is a goal that provides a new perspective
to many national problems and can give a new direction to public policy.
Its values and support come not from the divisions that plague our society but from the common aspirations of all for a life of dignity, health, and
fulfillment."

We were able to come together so quickly on the general thrust of the
report because all members of the group had a positive environmental
orientation, some from the standpoint of traditional conservation-of-
nature concerns and some from the more recent antipollution concerns.
Without making an issue of the matter, we, in effect, brought the two
areas together under the single concept of "the environment."

We quickly realized, however, that were we to try to address in the task
force report the many issues that came under that broad heading, we
would become bogged down. Thus, we avoided trying to make our report
a lengthy wish list of environmental actions. We emphasized instead two
broad areas in which the new administration could act without delay. First,
we recognized that there were already a number of environmental laws in
place—such as early efforts to address air and water pollution—and we
recommended that, before embarking on a lot of new environmental
initiatives, the Nixon administration focus its energies at the outset on
making existing environmental laws work effectively and on seeing to it
that they were adequately funded. Second, and most important, we urged
that a focal point for environmental policy be established in the White
House. We recommended that the president appoint a special assistant
for environmental affairs and reconfigure the existing Council on
Recreation and Natural Beauty as an interagency Council on the Environment, with the special assistant as its chair. All this could be accomplished quickly by presidential action and without legislation. And we left
no doubt that prompt action on an environmental agenda would pay
political dividends. We attached tables to our report that showed a rising
tide of environmental concern as reflected in polls.

Our report was only four pages long. It avoided potentially divisive
rhetoric and was strongly pragmatic in its approach. With the hindsight
of more than thirty years, I still think that was the right strategy. The
report was adopted unanimously by our task force, and there were no
minority or supplemental views.

FOLLOWING HIS election, Nixon had established his transition head-quarters at the Hotel Pierre in New York, and it was there I was heading on that rainy January evening. Earlier in the day, our task force had met with members of the new administration. We had been crowded into a small room at the Pierre and had sat around a horseshoe-shaped table with people — mostly unknown to me at the time — jammed against the walls and in the doorway. By my side sat Clifford Hardin, who had been announced as secretary of the Department of Agriculture. Missing was Walter J. Hickel, former governor of Alaska and Nixon's controversial nominee for the environmentally critical Department of the Interior post.

Hickel's absence was plainly a disappointment to some of the more aggressive members of my task force who had looked forward to an opportunity for direct give-and-take with him. Some believed he was simply ducking a face-to-face meeting, but this was unfair to Hickel. His first responsibility at the moment was to deal with his looming confirmation problems in the United States Senate. Moreover, whatever faults Hickel may have had, lack of guts or combativeness was not one of them.

The members of the task force all had copies of our report, but otherwise we had distributed it only to the president-elect. I summarized our work, several of our members expanded on various points, and this was followed by some exchange with Hardin and others. No objections were raised. The well-known nuclear physicist Lee DuBridge, sitting in a far corner, said he was to be the president's science advisor and that his responsibilities would include the environment. It was not a particularly substantive session, and the image it left in my mind of crowded confusion, hasty comings and goings, and uncertain identities was probably a fair and largely unavoidable reflection of the entire transition process.

Back in December, when the president-elect announced Walter Hickel as a Cabinet choice, I had volunteered to the transition office to put together briefing materials on natural resource and environmental issues that I thought he would need, both during his confirmation hearings and after he took office, assuming he would be confirmed. I had never met Hickel, but it seemed obvious that he would need such materials, and I did not know where else he would get them. It was unlikely that he would feel comfortable turning to a Department of the Interior still at least nominally responsible to Lyndon B. Johnson, with the top management posts filled by Johnson appointees.

Even by that time it was apparent that, while most of the Nixon nom-inees would go sailing through the confirmation process, Hickel had been singled out as a vulnerable target of political opportunity by the Demo-cratic leadership in the Senate. Hickel was known as a land developer, a characterization that largely stemmed from the fact that as governor of Alaska he had often sided with those interests that sought access to fed-eral lands in the state for oil and gas and similar development. Given that Alaska was largely undeveloped, Hickel's record as governor in this regard does not seem unusual. It was also in my mind that it might do a lot of long-term good to get a solid — and, I hoped, fair-minded — analy-sis of environmental issues into the hands of the man who was probably going to be the next secretary of Interior.

In any event, at The Conservation Foundation we put together an extensive set of materials in a large loose-leaf notebook — much of it focusing on the Federal Water Pollution Control Act, which at that time was administered by Interior. I was invited to bring the briefing materials to Hickel's apartment at Washington's Sheraton Park Hotel. It was our first meeting, and it lasted a couple of hours, in the presence of Hickel's political advisor, Carl McMurray, and other members of his staff from Alaska. Hickel was a short, feisty sort of a guy who bounced in and out of the room where we met, a bundle of energy and nerves.

Hickel was friendly, but we hardly had a real conversation at the time. Discussion centered on his Alaskan record and his own business affairs. I was simply a listener. While I felt some disappointment over the lack of substantive discussion of environmental matters, subsequent events made clear that this group had its priorities absolutely right insofar as the con-firmation hearings were concerned. The Senate Interior Committee showed far less interest in Hickel's position on Interior Department issues than in his various business investments.

The real reason I had been invited that afternoon, I later realized, was to give Hickel and his associates a chance to look me over — presumably at the suggestion of Nixon's transition staff. It was only a few days later, while my family and I were at our farm on Maryland's Eastern Shore, that McMurray phoned to say the governor wanted to see me again as soon as possible. It was New Year's Eve, and we had old friends staying with us. I chartered a small plane and flew to Washington. I went directly to the Sheraton Park and up to Hickel's apartment. After the barest of prelimi-naries, he came straight to the point: he would like me to be his under secretary. I expressed surprise and said I was flattered by his confidence. After some conversation, I said I would need the weekend to think it over. Given that this was Friday and New Year's Eve at that, I was committing myself to making a decision involving a major change of life for myself and my family within just a couple of days. At the same time, considering the other problems Hickel faced, it seemed only right that I give him a prompt answer.

I returned to the farm that afternoon in time to spend a couple of hours before dark duck-shooting with my houseguest, E. U. Curtis "Buff" Bohlen. We never fired a shot; instead we talked in confidence about the decision I had to make. Later, I talked with Aileen about it far into the night. Of course — and we both knew it — there was really no way I could say no and look at myself in the mirror in the future. At least, that was how we rationalized the matter. After all, a prime objective of my three years at The Conservation Foundation had been to get serious consideration of ecological factors and environmental values built into public policy making. To turn down a chance to be directly involved in the government policy-making process at a high level, and in a key spot involving environmental factors, was unthinkable. I had only one qualm — I did not want a job that was simply window dressing for the incoming administration. I felt in some danger of being used in that fashion, given that I was both a Republican and an environmentalist — not a common bird by any stretch of the imagination. However, I had secured Hickel's assurance that he wanted me to be a full participant in his top management team, a commitment he lived up to fully in the first months of our association.

Sunday evening, I flew to New York and spent the night at Laurance and Mary Rockefeller's apartment. Laurance was vice chairman of the board of The Conservation Foundation, and over the past three years I had come to like and respect him immensely. He fully supported my decision to take the under secretary job. Finally, I lunched with my friend and mentor Fairfield Osborn, president of the New York Zoological Society (later renamed the Wildlife Conservation Society) and founder, chairman, and longtime guiding spirit of The Conservation Foundation.

Fair was then well into his eighties and increasingly frail. My leaving the Foundation would be, I knew, a heavy blow, not so much because of me personally but because it would leave in an unsettled state one of his own prime projects. But after I described my situation, he was game as always. "Let's drink to it!" he said, and, when the martinis came — very cold, very dry, and straight up, as he liked them—he raised his glass and said "To the future!" There was no question that he meant both of our futures. "You will never regret doing this," he later wrote to me, *"never."* And he was right.

Before boarding the shuttle for Washington that afternoon, I called Hickel to accept his offer. I felt both excited by the prospect ahead and fortunate in the circumstances that had brought about this turn of events. Though I was not sure what all those circumstances had been, I certainly was not going to waste time worrying about them. I knew that as under secretary of Interior, I would have an extraordinary opportunity to promote environmental values in government decision making. Besides, on a less visionary note, the chance of occupying such a prominent government position doubtless had an appeal of its own.

In retrospect, I don't think there was much mystery in my selection by the new administration. As a result of my task force involvement, I had become known to the transition team as an environmentalist and as a Republican. As a former federal judge, I had already held a substantial public position. I also had good contacts in Congress. When Hickel ran into confirmation problems, therefore, it is likely that my name quickly surfaced as a way to balance his development record. John Ehrlichman may have played a key role in my selection, even though I did not know him at the time. As Nixon's choice for his assistant for domestic affairs, Ehrlichman seems the most likely of those around Nixon to have involved himself in the matter. Moreover, until he was fired during the Watergate scandal a few years later, it was clearly Ehrlichman who dealt directly with the president in getting the go-ahead on environmental initiatives.

It was only a week later that I found myself at that January 11 Hotel Pierre meeting presenting our report to members of the incoming administration. There was to be a banquet that night for the several hundred members of the various task forces. Late that afternoon, I learned that I was to sit next to the president-elect. I sat in my hotel room for a couple of hours wondering what in the world I should talk to him about, and my mind continued on this train of thought as I walked uptown to the Pierre.

When I arrived, the reception room was already incredibly crowded. Nixon stood on one side, shaking hands and exchanging pleasantries with those who filed by. When I finally got through the crowd and introduced myself, he said, "I think we have plans for you!"

At dinner in the Grand Ballroom, I was indeed seated on the dais at Nixon's immediate left, with the other task force chairmen arrayed on either side. (They were all men, as were the members of my task force.) Nixon was in good humor, relaxed, waving to friends in the crowd, and attentive in conversation. The man to his right chaired a space program task force, and at first I despaired of getting a word in as he talked to Nixon of moon shots, planetary landings, and space probes. This was heady stuff, even for a president-elect. Toward the end of the dinner, Nixon stood and talked to the crowd for about fifteen minutes. It was an impressive performance. He spoke entirely without notes and with considerable humor. He expressed appreciation for all the work the task forces had put in and spoke of his aspirations for his new administration, though steering clear of any programmatic specifics.

Earlier, when he had turned to me after his excursions into space, I had confessed, "Mr. President, I am embarrassed to say that when I heard I was going to sit next to you, I spent the next couple of hours stewing over what I should talk about. I thought to myself that this might be my one and only chance to speak directly to the next president of the United States and that I should decide in advance what was the single most important idea to try to get across. I am afraid that is a hell of a way to approach a dinner conversation." Nixon turned to look me squarely in the eyes and said, "That is just exactly what you should have done!"

I had decided to talk with Nixon about the politics of the environment, a matter with which, so far as I was aware, he had little or no previous experience. I knew I couldn't talk him into becoming an instant environmentalist, but it seemed entirely possible that he could become an effective proponent of environmental programs if it seemed to him good politics to do so. I have never for a moment doubted the wisdom of that decision.

I spoke of the fact that environmental issues were of importance across a broad spectrum of economic and social groups and in all parts of the country. An environmental program could be a unifying, not a divisive, issue. "Quality of life" would increasingly be a concern of the American people, I predicted, and the environment would be a key element of that quality. Nixon was a good listener. He certainly seemed to pay close attention, and, when he did ask a question, it was very much to the point.

When I had finished a particularly positive appraisal of the political appeal of environmental issues, Nixon said, "I am sure you are right in the suburbs and among much of the middle and upper classes. But what about the blacks and the poor in the cities? What is the appeal of the issue to them?"

He had gone right to the heart of the matter, on the very grounds I had myself chosen. He had put his finger squarely on the problem of elitism, which has always been a danger in the environmental movement. Of course, it usually is in fact the central city residents who suffer the most from environmental degradation, particularly through adverse health effects, and I said as much to Nixon. Industrial pollution, sulfur emissions from power plants, lead in paint, automobile emissions, water pollution, noise, and other environmental contaminants are most concentrated in and around the inner city. It is the inhabitants of the city — most often the poor and the minorities, about whom Nixon was asking — who undoubtedly have the most to gain from a cleaner, healthier environment. Yet, for understandable reasons, their own priorities tend to stress jobs, equal opportunity, decent housing, crime reduction, education, and so forth. It is hard to worry about pollution when you're out of work and your kids are on dope.

Obviously, I could not cover all that ground at dinner. However, I like to think that in the years immediately ahead, as Nixon became the sponsor of an extraordinary array of environmental initiatives, our conversation that evening served, in at least some small way, to persuade him of the benefits of such action.

When I headed back to my hotel after dinner, the rain had stopped, the skies were clearing, and the wind was now at my back. I, of course, had no real clue of what was to come — that I would spend the next eight years in government and that during this time protection of the environment would become a national priority, both domestically and internationally, and a major focus of public policy; that the issue would then become embroiled in controversy over energy and economic concerns; and that I would play a central role in those events. Nor, of course, could I see even farther down the road to where, after leaving government, I would continue to pursue equally vital but more conservation-oriented environmental goals in the private, nonprofit sector with the World Wildlife Fund. I did not have the gift of prophecy to see all this, but I sensed that important developments lay ahead, and that I could help shape them.

Chapter 1

Washington Beginnings

I WAS FORTY-EIGHT years old on that fateful day in New York when my meeting with President-Elect Nixon marked the imminent beginning of my career as an environmentalist in government. Though I had resigned a judgeship on the United States Tax Court to become president of The Conservation Foundation three years before, in 1965, one would look in vain for any discernible influences in my early life that would steer me into an environmental career. I had occasional hunting, fishing, and other outdoor experiences as a youth, but, while nature was enjoyed, it was also taken for granted. What did stand me in very good stead in later years, it now strikes me, was the fact that I grew up in the social and political world of Washington, D.C., and always felt reasonably at home in that complex and challenging environment.

Though I grew up in Washington as the son and grandson of naval officers, I was born, in June 1920, in Jamestown, Rhode Island. The U.S. Atlantic Fleet, of which the destroyer squadron my father commanded was a part, was spending that summer in Narrangansett Bay, and this had led my parents to rent a house there.

My father, Charles Russell Train, had also grown up in Washington. He was a graduate of the U.S. Naval Academy and rose to the rank of rear admiral before heart problems forced him to retire to our D.C. home, just before World War II. It was a crushing blow to him to miss the combat for which he had trained all his adult life.

His father, Charles Jackson Train, was the son of a man elected to the United States Congress in 1858 as a Republican, the first year there were such. Also a graduate of the Naval Academy, my grandfather had built his family home at Connecticut Avenue and R Street in Northwest Washington, D.C., where a movie theater stood until recently. He was commander in chief of the U.S. Asiatic fleet when he died, in 1906, of a sudden illness in Chinese waters. Of course, I never knew him, and I wish it were otherwise. He loved opera and played the piano, flute, and violin. He visited the major art galleries all over Europe, read widely in French and German, and, full of fun, loved poker and other games. He also loved duck-hunting, a passion passed on to my father and, later, to me. The two of them would get together in China, where my father commanded a gunboat on the Yangtze River, and hunt ducks and shorebirds in the riverside marshes and pheasants in the rice fields. On a more serious note, my grandfather played a role in the strategic planning for the Spanish-American War;[1] in a less strategic role, he reportedly was responsible for introducing mint to the Philippines. Clearly, he was a man with a balanced approach to life.

My Train forebears in America extend back to John Trayne, who emigrated in 1635 from Scotland and settled in the Massachusetts Bay Colony, where he and his descendants for some generations were mainly farmers. Since about 1800, though, my forebears have largely been professionals, including clergy, lawyers, and naval officers. After the Revolutionary War, for example, Charles Train, my great-great-grandfather, departed his family's Puritan-Congregationalist tradition to become a Baptist minister after his graduation from Harvard University in 1805. Until shortly before his death, in 1849, he was pastor of a beautiful Christopher Wren–inspired church in Framingham Center, and he served several terms in the Massachusetts legislature, where he was known as a strong proponent of public education and the separation of church and state. He was also a dedicated proponent of temperance, a persuasion that was not shared by his constituents and that he did not pass on to his descendants.

John Trayne's descendants fought in the various wars of the time, including King Philip's War and the French and Indian Wars. Indeed, military service was probably the most broadening event in their lives. Baptist pastor Charles's own father, Samuel, fought the British at Saratoga during the Revolutionary War, and his grandfather, also Samuel, was a Minuteman at Concord Bridge. While the American Trains were all New Englanders by background, my maternal grandmother's family, from the Sea Islands of South Carolina, were plantation owners; their way of life disappeared with the onset of the Civil War. Surprisingly, out of that aristocratic, slave-owning background emerged another Baptist clergyman, my great-grandfather James Hazzard Cuthbert. Following his graduation from Princeton University in 1843, he got caught up in the religious ferment of the time and departed his family's Anglican tradition to join the Baptist ministry.

It was my mother's Brown family that provided my earliest roots in Washington. A young man with the memorable name of Obadiah Bruen Brown came to Washington in 1807 from Newark, New Jersey, of which his New England Puritan forebears had been among the founders in 1666. He, too, had become a Baptist pastor, and he built a large church on Tenth Street in 1833 — later, it would be the site of Ford's Theater, where Abraham Lincoln was assassinated. He was an unusual man in many ways — he served as chief contract officer of the Post Office Department for many years, a job that evidently provided the financial wherewithal for his ministry; chaplain of the U.S. House of Representatives and of the United States Senate at various times; cofounder with Luther Rice of what later became George Washington University; a director of one of Washington's leading banks; and, with his wife, Elizabeth, keeper of a boarding house that became a gathering place for Jacksonian politicians.[2]

My grandparents Train and Brown built houses, about 1880, only a few doors apart on Connecticut Avenue near R Street in Northwest Washington. My mother and father thus knew each other from childhood. Washington life was certainly a lot simpler and more personal then. Horse-drawn trolleys ran up Connecticut Avenue in those days as far as Florida Avenue, a block to the north, where the driver would unhitch the horse from one end of the trolley and move it to the other end before starting the return journey. When my grandmother Train wanted to go downtown, she would hang a signal of some sort on the outside doorknob of her house; the trolley driver would see it on his way uptown and then either stop on his way back to pick her up or take a package for delivery along his route. On Sundays, the Train family would walk to St. John's (Episcopal) Church, across Lafayette Square from the White House,* about twenty minutes away by foot but perhaps more with children. My aunt Sue, then a little girl, recalled on at least one such occasion

---

*St. John's remained my family's church, and my wife, Aileen, and I were married there in 1954. I served for a number of years on the vestry, including terms as junior and senior warden.

passing William Henry Harrison and his wife walking up Connecticut to their own church, at the corner of N Street. My grandfather tipped his hat as they passed and said, "The President of the United States and no one paying the slightest notice of him." How times have changed!

In 1924, my parents bought a large Victorian house in the Georgetown area of Washington. This was their home for the rest of their lives, and it was where I grew up. I walked from there to the Potomac School, a private school (then located on California Street, about a block from where I now live) that I attended through the fourth grade. Following Potomac, I went to St. Albans School, which I reached by bus and streetcar. St. Albans was a private preparatory school operated by the Episcopal Diocese of Washington and located on the Washington Cathedral Close. I stayed there through the twelfth grade (sixth form). I was an unexceptional student and a poor athlete, but I did become managing editor of the school newspaper, which regularly won prizes in national scholastic competitions.

Some of the times I remember best were summer vacations. For a number of years, I regularly spent summers at Elizabethtown in the Adirondack Mountains with my father's sister Susan Hand and her husband, Augustus Noble Hand. He was a distinguished federal judge, first of the District Court for the Southern District of New York and later of the United States Court of Appeals for the Second Circuit, where he joined his first cousin, Learned Hand. Uncle Gus was a large man of serious mien, but among family and close friends he had a fund of stories, poetry, and songs with which to regale the company. My small bedroom was next to his and Aunt Sue's, and I remember as a small boy climbing into their four-poster bed with them in the morning. Uncle Gus had a large, bristly moustache, and it was, I imagined, a bit like getting into bed with a bear. Aunt Sue would soon depart, and Uncle Gus would tell me stories of his own growing up, of camping in the Adirondack wilderness with his cousin Learned, of huddling around the campfire while panthers screamed in the dark forest around them. When I was a bit older, there was climbing among the high peaks of the Adirondacks.

My summer as a ten-year-old was spent on Cape Cod with another sister of my father, Grace, and her husband, Myron Whitney. They had a wonderful old farmhouse, south of Sandwich, that had been in the Whitney family since the early eighteenth century. There I learned to swim, fish, crab, ride a horse, and, without much success, milk a cow. The farm had no electricity; in the evening we read and played games by the light of an oil lamp in the living room.

When Herbert Hoover was elected president in 1928, he and Mrs. Hoover made a "good will" trip around South America. My father, as commanding officer of the battleship USS *Utah*, was detailed to pick up the Hoovers at Montevideo, Uruguay, and bring them back to Norfolk, Virginia. The trip home took seventeen days, and by its end there was mutual liking and respect between the Hoovers and my father. Two years later, when I was ten, my father became Hoover's naval aide at the White House. The job had a pronounced ceremonial side, which provided my parents with opportunities to meet such people as Charles and Anne Lindbergh, Rear Admiral Richard Byrd, and Amelia Earhart and to develop lasting friendships with members of the Hoover administration such as Charles Francis Adams, secretary of the Navy. The job imposed a heavy social burden on my parents, and it seemed to me at the time that they were out for dinner almost every night, at either the White House, some embassy, or another official function. There was no National Security Council at the White House in those days, so my father found himself providing a major link between the president and the Navy Department. This circumstance led to my father's close involvement in such matters as ratification of the London Naval Treaty on battleship construction and planning for a new Department of Defense.

I spent several Christmas Eves with the Hoover family at the White House and was also aboard the presidential yacht on the Potomac River on several occasions. Finally, when my father was ordered to the Naval War College at Newport, Rhode Island, in 1932, the Hoovers invited my two brothers and me to stay at the White House the night before we left Washington, thus relieving my mother of the necessity of dealing with us while she closed the Georgetown house. We stayed in the Andrew Jackson bedroom; my brothers shared the big double bed, and I slept in a small connecting bedroom. In the morning, the three of us breakfasted on the South Portico with the Hoovers, who were warm and chatty with their young guests.

Following his year at the Naval War College, my father was given command of a division of light cruisers on the West Coast. That summer, my mother, brothers, and I drove from Washington to Seattle to join my father for the summer; my mother expected to remain on the West Coast for the next two years while my father was on duty there. The trip took about twelve days and was a great adventure for all of us. We took a boat on the Great Lakes from Cleveland to Duluth, drove across the Great Plains on mostly gravel roads to Glacier National Park, and then continued on to Seattle. It was a tremendous opportunity for a youngster to experience at first hand the sheer physical size of the country as well as some of its extraordinary diversity. After a brief time in the Seattle area, my brother Mid and I had the thrill of accompanying Father for several days aboard his flagship, the USS *Concord*, as it moved down the West Coast to San Francisco. It was an exciting adventure, and I suspect my father had hopes that it would help lead me into a naval career.

A set of experiences that were particularly memorable in my teenage years were four summertime trips to Europe with my childhood friend Orme Wilson, whose father was in the Foreign Service and stationed in Europe. We spent the summer of 1934 in Berlin as Adolf Hitler and the Nazi Party gathered power. I felt the tension when the supposed uprising that summer by the "brownshirts" was ruthlessly put down by Hitler. We joined a great crowd one night to watch the Reichstag, the German parliament, burn, an act quickly pinned on a half-witted Jew. The growing plight of the Jewish people was evident. The large house the Wilsons had rented belonged to a prominent Jewish banking family who felt they could no longer live openly there. I believe they died in the Holocaust.

Almost fifty years later, when in Berlin, I took a street map and walked to the site of the house, on Drakestrasse. Damage from World War II was still very evident in the neighborhood. It was all very quiet. I found the location of the house by the numeral 10 set in a mosaic in the sidewalk. Beyond the sidewalk were two steps. They rose to nothing. A metal fence, as I recall, surrounded the large lot, now a cratered wilderness of weeds.

Orme and I were in Prague during the summers of 1935 and 1936, when the threat of German expansion loomed over the country, a threat soon to be fulfilled. We traveled to Berlin for the 1936 Olympic Games and had the experience of being in the midst of 100,000 people standing, raising their arms in the Nazi salute, and shouting "*Sieg heil!*" repeatedly as Hitler arrived in the stadium. Orme and I remained seated, silent, hands in our pockets. Aside from a few curious glances, there was no reaction to our behavior. And there we watched Hitler ignore the great African American track star Jesse Owens when he won a gold medal. In 1939, we were in Brussels as the war clouds were gathering. In fact, it was then that Hitler launched his invasion of Poland, and Britain and France declared war on Germany just after we left a French port for home. The British passenger ship *Athenia* was torpedoed and sunk by a U-boat in the mid-Atlantic while we were at sea, a fact we learned at the time.

My four years of college at Princeton that followed were unremarkable. I majored in political science and was generally a poor student but, once again, rallied at the end, in 1941, to graduate with honors. Having disappointed my father by not attending the Naval Academy, and there being no U.S. Navy Reserve Officers' Training Corps (ROTC) program at Princeton, I had entered the Army ROTC in my freshman year. As a result, immediately after graduation I was ordered to active military duty as a second lieutenant in the field artillery.

My five-year military career was unheroic. I trained recruits for both the field artillery and tank destroyer units. I helped form and train a heavy field artillery battalion of eight-inch howitzers and about 500 men as the training and operations officer, and we finally went overseas, to Okinawa. The island had been largely secured by the time of our arrival, but we did take part in clearing out Japanese soldiers holed up in caves at the island's southern end. We were slated to take part in the invasion of the Japanese home islands, an event we assumed was inevitable if the war was to end. The atomic bombs dropped on Hiroshima and Nagasaki changed all that, of course, for which I and my fellow soldiers were very grateful at the time. Several years ago, I returned to Okinawa on World Wildlife Fund business and found the exact location where my battalion had camped fifty years before. The site had been returned to agriculture, and where our tents had stood there were small, neat fields. The rocky ridge where the Japanese soldiers had holed up was still there, strangely unmenacing. No people were visible, and all was quiet. The wartime scene and the men with whom I had shared it were still vivid in my mind, yet it was now as if none of that had ever happened. I felt oddly detached.

When I returned home from the Pacific, I was almost twenty-six, and choosing a career was much on my mind. For some while, I had seriously considered the Foreign Service. However, for various reasons I had given that up, and, once home, I decided to pursue a legal career. In truth, I really was not sure what I wanted to do, but I believed that training in the law would provide a professional base from which I could move in a number of directions. Doubtless, the example of my uncle, Judge Augustus Hand, was also a factor in my choice. One thing was certain: no thought of a conservation or environmental career ever entered my head.

In any event, I was accepted by Columbia Law School. Like most of my classmates just out of military service, I opted to complete the program in two years instead of the customary three, which necessitated a full course schedule in the summers. I became a student member of the staff of the Legislative Drafting Research Fund, a law school program. The Fund had been established on the reasonable premise that the drafting of effective legislation required professional training and skill. Indeed, over its period of existence, the Fund had done a good bit of legislative drafting for the New York legislature and had been the progenitor of the Offices of Legislative Counsel of the House of Representatives and the Senate.

One research project I undertook at the Fund involved the institution of congressional joint committees, such as the Joint Committee on Atomic Energy and the Joint Committee on the Economic Report, which include both House and Senate members. During spring break in 1948, while I was at home in Washington with my parents, I took advantage of the opportunity to meet with the staff directors of several of these committees. I had an introduction from personal friends to Gordon Grand, clerk (chief of staff) of the powerful House Committee on Ways and Means, who in turn introduced me to Colin Stam, longtime chief of staff of the Joint Committee on Internal Revenue Taxation.

Stam and I seem to have hit it off reasonably well; later that spring, I was offered a position on the staff of the Joint Committee after I graduated from law school. When I accepted the offer at $4,200 per year, I became one of the highest-paid members of my law school class. Thus began my career as a tax lawyer — a career for which my rather mediocre performance in the law school's taxation course had given little advance indication.

Chapter 2

From Clerk to Judge

I N RETROSPECT, my job with the congressional Joint Committee on Internal Revenue Taxation was a kind of apprenticeship in government. The job was to give me a familiarity with the workings of the United States Congress and an acquaintance with some of the major personalities involved that would stand me in good stead in my later career. I was brought into regular contact with the executive agencies, particularly the Department of the Treasury, as well as with the many private sector interest groups concerned with tax policy.

The Joint Committee, established by the Revenue Act of 1926, was made up of the three senior members of the House Committee on Ways and Means and of the Senate Committee on Finance. It met formally only occasionally, and then principally to review and approve all income tax refunds over a certain size. In practice, the real function of the Joint Committee was to provide staff support to the two legislative committees, neither of which had any professional tax staff of their own at the time.

In my years on the Joint Committee staff, I sometimes worked on special research projects, such as a legislative history of the percentage depletion allowance for oil (an arbitrary percentage of the gross income from oil production, intended to compensate for depletion of the resource). More often, I was engaged in meetings with members of the Treasury staff to discuss specific legislative issues and to hammer out differences between us. The issues tended to be complex, as anyone with even a passing acquaintance with the Internal Revenue Code will appreciate. Then there were the committee "markup" of draft legislation in executive session, the drafting of the committee report on any bill it reported, action by the full House of Representatives, and then the shift of the action to the Senate Finance Committee and the full United States Senate. The last stage, assuming favorable action by the House and Senate, would be the convening of a conference committee to iron out differences. I was regularly engaged in every step of this process.

Clerk of Ways and Means

The Republican Party swept the 1952 elections, putting Dwight D. Eisenhower in the White House and capturing control of both houses of Congress. Daniel Reed, from upstate New York, became chairman of the Ways and Means Committee, and my friend Gordon Grand became clerk (chief of staff). Not long afterward, Grand was offered the presidency of the Olin Mathieson Chemical Corporation (now simply the Olin Corporation) and persuaded Reed to offer me the position of clerk in his stead. I accepted with alacrity and found myself catapulted into one of the senior staff positions on Capitol Hill at the astronomical salary of $14,800 per year.

The job was interesting and surprisingly fun. Reed was an old-timer, first elected to Congress during the William McKinley administration, and he boasted—a bit tongue in cheek—that his opinions, particularly on tariff matters, had been formed then and that his mind had been closed ever since. Indeed, he was an old-fashioned protectionist and proud of it. White-haired, ruddy-faced, and square-jawed, Reed was an imposing figure. He was by no means a brilliant man, but he was decent, straightforward, and thoughtful, if at times stubborn.

Substantive tax work was provided largely by Colin Stam and his Joint Committee staff. When it came to tariff and social security issues, however, Reed and the Republican majority looked to me and the Ways and Means staff, small as it was. In any event, my responsibilities as clerk had less to do with substantive issues and more to do with organizing the work of the committee, scheduling and running hearings, providing liaison with Stam and the Treasury, interfacing with the press, dealing with the countless lobbyists, replying to the voluminous mail, and spending time with the chairman on a daily basis to discuss both near- and long-term plans. In addition, I was responsible for dealing with all correspondence from Reed's home district concerning matters within the committee's jurisdiction. The committee had no subcommittees in those days, so my office dealt with the full scope of its jurisdiction: taxes; tariffs, including trade agreements; and social security.

The staff totaled ten: an assistant clerk, two other (nontax) professionals, four secretaries, two messengers, and me.

Aileen

It was while I was serving as clerk of the committee that I married Aileen Bowdoin Travers of New York and my private life changed dramatically for the better.* Moreover, Aileen has played an important role in my public career, as will be apparent in these pages from time to time. We bought a house on Woodland Drive in Washington, D.C., on a hillside with ancient oaks that were part of the original forest of the area. There our children grew up and we lived until 1977, when I left the government.

Aileen has always had her own interests and has served on the boards of a variety of nonprofit organizations, particularly educational and environmental. At the same time, she has not tried to pursue an independent career of her own but has always been strongly supportive of mine, for which I am profoundly grateful. It has helped that she has shared enthusiastically my career interests, especially after I moved into the environmental field. Aileen's natural common sense has made her a wonderful source of wisdom on problems I have faced from time to time. Naturally gregarious, she has many friends and enjoys cultivating new ones. These cut across the full spectrum of Washington life — private sector, government, diplomatic, media, and others. As a result, we have always had an active social life.

Minority Advisor

When the Republicans lost the House in the 1954 midterm election — they would not regain it until 1994 — I lost the clerkship and moved one

*Aileen had been previously married and was recently divorced (1951) when we married, in 1954. She had two small daughters, Nancy and Emily, by the earlier marriage, whom I adopted that same year. Her Bowdoin family was prominent in the affairs of New York and, earlier, of Massachusetts, where her ancestor James Bowdoin II had been the second governor after independence (1785–1787). Alexander Hamilton was another direct ancestor. The two children of our marriage, both born in Washington, were our son, Bowdoin (Bowdy), born in 1955, and daughter Errol, born in 1959, and named for my mother.

door down the hall to become minority advisor. Reed, of course, became the ranking minority member and thus continued as my boss. While I no longer had responsibility for the committee agenda or for organizing hearings, much of the work remained about the same.

Having estimated that the Ways and Means Committee's staff structure, including both majority and minority functions, totaled thirteen at the time of my tenure, I took a look at a recent *Congressional Directory* and counted sixty-five people on the committee payroll. (Of course, each committee member has his or her own office staff as well.) I cannot help but wonder what all these people do. Granted, the U.S. population and economy have grown substantially over the forty years since I was on the committee staff. However, the jurisdiction of the committee has not changed; the tax laws have always been complicated, and I doubt that added complexity explains added bureaucracy. Indeed, it is probably the other way around — the more bureaucracy, the greater the complexity. The one thing that has changed is the number of lobbyists, which appears to have grown exponentially.

Even if lobbyists have greatly increased in number, there were plenty of them in my years with the committee and they provided a principal link with the outside world. Lawyers, doctors, retired persons, farmers, labor unionists, truckers, railroads, airlines, state governments, trade associations, churches, insurance companies, sugar producers, and on and on — representatives of such interests were constantly at one's doorstep. I found most of them informative, and they certainly helped me appreciate the diversity of interests involved in almost every legislative issue. So far as I was personally concerned, I never found the lobbying fraternity particularly sinister, although I have no doubt some of them could have been. I do not recall being invited to expenses-paid conventions or other get-togethers — perhaps that says more about my perceived influence than about the purity of the lobbyists — and I did not attend receptions given by lobbying organizations. When I met with a lobbyist — and I did so constantly — it was normally in my small office and with the close presence of my secretary. In fact, I made a practice of being "busy" for lunch, which often consisted of a sandwich eaten in solitude at a drugstore counter several blocks up Pennsylvania Avenue, SE.

While I was still on the staff of the Joint Committee, I concocted a scheme for the taxation of gambling that in due course became part of the Internal Revenue Code. The concept was relatively simple, and it largely evolved out of my own experience as a bettor on horse races. Many billions of dollars were wagered every year — most of this illegally, as in the "numbers" game or with bookies — and most of the money represented cash transactions that totally escaped taxation.

I proposed what was essentially an excise tax on slot machines and a flat tax of 10 percent on all other wagers, paid by the receiver of the bet — the bookmaker, for example. I even called up a bookie for professional advice. The Ways and Means Committee report on the legislation thus reflected an expertise on gambling that raised a few eyebrows. My boss, Colin Stam, was delighted with the whole idea and sold it to the Senate Finance Committee as well. It became law and constituted my only completely original contribution to the field of tax legislation.

When the wagering tax was eventually challenged in the courts, the case ended up in the United States Supreme Court. A fellow staffer and I went over to the Court to hear oral argument. By pure coincidence, I was wearing a rather loud checked tweed jacket that day, and, as I entered the crowded courtroom and slid my way down a row to an empty seat, I plainly saw and heard Justice Felix Frankfurter lean over and say in a stage whisper to his neighbor on the bench, while nodding in my direction, "There's one now!" Not a few heads turned in my direction, some of which I would suppose belonged to real bookies in unobtrusive dark attire. The law has remained on the books for years, but it has never really been enforced.

Flat Tax Proposal

One cumulative effect of my years with the tax committees on the Hill, and later with the Treasury and the United States Tax Court, was impatience and frustration on my part with the ever-growing complexity of the Internal Revenue Code. Our income tax law and regulations had become so complicated that it was next to impossible for the average citizen to make out his or her tax return. It took an army of lawyers and accountants to shepherd people through the Byzantine maze of the tax law. And the situation is worse today.

In the fall of 1976, when I was in my waning days as administrator of the Environmental Protection Agency and should have had other things on my mind, I read in the press of the progress of that year's principal revenue bill through Congress — doubtless named something like the "Tax

Reform and Simplification Act of 1976." I read that the House of Representatives had adopted an amendment providing an income tax credit for the cost of purchasing home garden tools. I could hardly believe my eyes. I was outraged that anyone should even suggest, let alone that the House should approve, an amendment providing that the federal government, and thus the American people, should bear the entire expense of an individual's purchase of garden tools.

It was the proverbial straw that broke the camel's back. I sat down and wrote an article titled "Real Tax Reform," which proposed scrapping much of the existing tax code as beyond fixing and substituting a relatively simple flat income tax with essentially no deductions. The article was lengthy for an op-ed piece, but the *Washington Post* carried it in its Sunday editorial section,[1] and Senator Claiborne Pell inserted the article in the *Congressional Record*.[2]

While the flat tax is a relatively familiar concept today, it was a pretty novel idea in 1976, and I, at least, had never seen it seriously proposed before. Be that as it may, the idea did not generate much excitement at the time. Since then, Congressman Bill Archer of Texas, chairman of the Ways and Means Committee at the time, has proposed such a reform, and in 1996 Steven Forbes made a flat tax the centerpiece of his unsuccessful campaign for the Republican nomination for the presidency. This book is not the place to argue the merits of a flat tax; I simply wish to put on the record my proposal of the idea in 1976.

During my time on the Hill, I gained considerable respect for the legislative process. I served under both Democratic and Republican majorities and saw little evidence of raw partisanship in the operation of the tax committees. Members worked together with courtesy and respect. Civility and comity were the norm. Seniority was the unquestioned rule, and, while it may have led at times to leadership that was past its prime, on the whole it worked well and promoted stability and orderly process. There was only one real power base in the Ways and Means Committee, and that was the chairman. There were no subcommittees in my time; there are now several, and that situation exists with respect to most committees of the House. Today, each member of the House, no matter how junior, wants his or her place in the public eye, which is understandable, but it leads to fragmentation and lack of cohesion within the parties.

———

Assistant to the Treasury Secretary

When I became minority advisor to the Ways and Means Committee in 1955, I set my sights on appointment as a judge of the United States Tax Court. At the age of thirty-five, I saw a judicial appointment as an extraordinarily attractive prospect. I doubt it ever occurred to me to ask whether that was what I wanted to do for the rest of my life. Indeed, for most relatively young people, the concept of "the rest of your life" has little reality. In any event, I went to work on the matter and managed to enlist the support of just about every member of the Ways and Means Committee, both Republican and Democratic, as well as others with political influence. Finally, H. Chapman Rose, the under secretary of Treasury, came to see me and offered a suggestion. The feeling was that I was not quite ready for a judgeship, he said, but, if I were willing to come to Treasury as head of the Legal Advisory Staff, I could have a judgeship the next time a vacancy on the Tax Court arose. It was a good deal, and I took it. (Tax Court judges were appointed by the president, subject to Senate confirmation, but by custom the secretary of Treasury had the deciding voice in the initial selection.)

The Legal Advisory Staff reviewed all Treasury regulations proposed by the Internal Revenue Service, worked on tax legislation, and represented the department before the congressional committees on tax matters. While I had a top-notch professional staff at the Treasury, all lawyers, the job was a hard one and entailed long hours. Proposed regulations were almost always lengthy and usually were highly complex, and, though attorneys on my staff were the ones who had to go through them with a fine-tooth comb, I had to sign off on them. I shared the legislative work with Dan Throop Smith, head of the Office of Tax Analysis, and my easy relationship with the members of both the Ways and Means and Finance Committees and their staffs was always helpful.

Judge of the U.S. Tax Court

As it turned out, I was at the Treasury little more than a year before a vacancy opened up at the Tax Court. The Treasury secretary—then George Humphrey, probably the most powerful member of the Eisenhower administration on domestic policy—was as good as his word, and my nomination by President Eisenhower to fill the unexpired term vacancy soon went to the Senate. A year later, in 1958, Eisenhower nominated me to a full twelve-year term.

The U.S. Tax Court had been created by Congress in 1926 to help ease the tax litigation burden on the district courts and also to provide taxpayers with a less burdensome process for adjudicating tax issues — and, presumably, a more expert forum for considering such issues. Under the old English common law, a subject (citizen) could never sue the sovereign. Therefore, when a citizen claimed that he had been wrongfully taxed, he was permitted only to bring a personal action against the tax collector for "monies wrongfully had and received." He was entitled to trial by jury if he wanted it. This is essentially the nature of a taxpayer's case in the federal district court today. The hitch is that, in order to avail himself or herself of that potential remedy, the taxpayer must pay the tax in question and then sue to get it back. Under the alternative Tax Court process, the taxpayer need not pay the tax in advance but simply must file a claim within ninety days of receiving a deficiency notice from the Internal Revenue Service. There is no jury trial in the Tax Court.

During my time on the court, the chief judge was J. Edgar Murdock, an able jurist and a warm friend. Considerably older than I was, Ned Murdock had a quick mind and a fine sense of humor. During one court session in Washington, D.C., a taxpayer representing himself — as was permitted under Tax Court rules but very seldom availed of — closed his case by declaring, "Your honor, as God is my judge, I do not owe this tax." Judge Murdock, who was presiding, responded without a moment's pause as follows: "He's not. I am. You do." The *Washington Post* wrote a lead editorial on the decision, praising it as a model of judicial brevity and clarity.[3]

Since one purpose of the Tax Court is to provide greater convenience to taxpayers who want to dispute a tax assessment, the court conducted trial calendars throughout the country. In some major population centers, such as New York, Chicago, and Los Angeles, court sessions were essentially continuous. In other places, such as Boise, Idaho, or Helena, Montana, a calendar might be an annual occurrence at best. Each calendar was assigned to an individual judge. Thus, we "rode circuit" in the traditional sense, presiding over the calendars in the various locations, assisted by an experienced court clerk.

About six calendars per year made up a normal schedule for each judge. I spent the rest of my time in my chambers at the court's Washington headquarters, working on the cases I had heard, deciding them, and writing my opinions. In this regard, at any given time I had the invaluable help of two law clerks, who studied the transcripts of the trials, reviewed the briefs filed by the parties, and researched the law involved.[4]

I soon found that I enjoyed the trials and that, despite my lack of court-room experience, I handled most evidentiary and procedural issues with confidence. I brushed up on the law of evidence and learned that, when in doubt, plain old common sense usually provided a pretty good guide. In any event, I was never criticized on appeal for rulings on evidence.[5]

There were some amusing incidents. Once, when I went to Hunting-ton, West Virginia, I understood that a case on the docket involved the alleged underpayment of taxes by a brothel operator and that a pillar of the government's case was a count of the towels that the brothel sent to the laundry. Naturally, I was looking forward to what promised to be a somewhat colorful trial.

I checked into my hotel shortly before dinner, and no sooner had I settled in my room than there was a knock on the door. I opened the door and was confronted by a rather gaudy blonde. "Hello!" she said archly, batting her eyes at me. "I heard that you were looking for company." "No, thanks!" I said hastily and shut the door. She swore and let fly a kick at the door panel. The next day, when the brothel case was called, it had been settled earlier that morning without a trial. It was hard not to con-clude that I had been targeted for a setup.

We did not set calendars during July and August, and that period was open for vacations, subject, of course, to the backlog of cases each of us had in the office—usually quite large. On the whole, however, judges were free to set their own work schedules. This arrangement allowed Aileen and I, in the late summer of 1958, to go on our second African safari, the first having been two years earlier, when I was still working with Congress.

Taken together, those two safaris were fateful events in my life, leading inexorably (or so it seems in retrospect) but utterly unexpectedly to my leaving a tax law career and the bench and embarking on a new career in conservation and the environment.

Chapter 3

Africa: Land of the Soul

I N A PROFILE of me written in early 1970, when I was announced by
President Richard Nixon as chairman of the newly created Council
on Environmental Quality, the *New York Times* put it this way: In
1956, "Russell Errol Train shot an elephant and was chased by a
rhinoceros. Life was never the same after that. For the safari that Mr.
Train took to Africa turned him into a conservationist and led him down
a path that convinced him to give up the secure life of a judge of the
Federal Tax Court to devote full time to saving the environment."[1] While
that was a bit of an oversimplification, it was pretty much on target.
Certainly, my life was never the same. The two safaris in East Africa on
which Aileen and I went in 1956 and 1958 played, without a doubt, a central role in the future course of my life and work.

Aileen is fond of recounting that, when we married, in May 1954, I
came to our new home in Washington, D.C., with a cook named Gloria,
two suitcases of clothes, my black Labrador, Swift, and about two hundred books about hunting in Africa. With due allowance for some embel-
lishment on her part, she has it essentially right. How this fascination
started, I am not sure. My parents' library contained a few books on
African travel and hunting, which I had read. The first movie I ever saw
was *Simba*, in 1928, a film made by Martin and Osa Johnson in East
Africa. About two years later, I read a book about three Boy Scouts who
went on safari in Africa with the Johnsons. I envied them the experience.
Apparently, I talked of Africa to Aileen from time to time because about
six months after our marriage she said to me with her usual directness,
"Why don't we stop talking about it and go!" The upshot was that we

arranged a one-month, tented hunting safari in Kenya with the premier outfitting firm, Ker & Downey.

And so, in the late summer of 1956, Aileen and I flew to Rome and then overnight to Nairobi via stops at Benghazi on the Libyan coast and Khartoum on the Nile River. We flew at relatively low altitude, and the blackness below was broken only by the silver ribbon of the Nile reflecting the light of the moon. We were met at Nairobi by our professional hunter, George Barrington. We camped and hunted in Kenya along the Athi River, southeast of Nairobi, in thick, dry bush country, mostly flat but with occasional hills; then near Lake Magadi, close to the border with Tanganyika (now Tanzania), a soda lake with bare, stony hills and some open savanna; and finally in the Northern Frontier District (NFD) northwest of Isiolo. The NFD was dry, remote country, with Mount Kenya rising to the southeast and mountains stretching north toward the Ethiopian border. Most of the area in which we hunted was tribal land where hunting was controlled by the British colonial government in Nairobi.

In addition to our hunter, the safari was made up of about ten Africans, all referred to in those days both individually and collectively, irrespective of age, as "boys." Of course, when talking to them, we used their given names. There was the headman, Molo, who served the meals, took care of our tents, washed and ironed our clothes daily, and generally ran the camp. There were the cook and a cook's helper, who turned out three excellent meals a day. There were two gun bearers — one for George and one (Kimuya) for me. There were two skinners, who prepared both trophies and game meat for the camp. There were two drivers — one for the large lorry that carried all the camp gear and most of the staff and one for the Land Rover in which we rode. Our hunter, George, normally drove the latter, and the "driver" usually sat in the back. His principal duty was really to keep the vehicle clean and in good operating order. When we moved camp, a tarp was pulled down over the small mountain of camp gear in the lorry; three of the staff sat in the front seat with the driver, and about five perched on top of the load.

Camping arrangements were simple: a double tent for Aileen and me, a single for the professional hunter (usually some distance away), a kitchen tent, and a mess tent. Each tent had a fly stretched over it, which helped deflect the midday sun. The staff had more makeshift arrangements: basically, bedrolls near the fire. In our tent, a compartment at the back held a canvas tub into which buckets of piping hot water (*magi moto*) were poured in the evening before dinner. We had our own toilet, consisting of an open pit with a folding toilet seat above it, a pile of dirt alongside for kicking into the pit as needed, and canvas sides all around. This convenience was usually referred to in British fashion as the "loo" and occasionally as "the House of Parliament." It always seemed to be located quite a distance away in the bush, a somewhat daunting destination in the dark.

I remember vividly our first night in the African wild; we camped along the high banks of the Athi River, our tent pitched beneath the spreading branches of an enormous wild fig. When we finally left the campfire and crawled into our cots, it was to lie awake listening to the strange night sounds. We could hear animals coming to drink from the river just below our tent. There were sudden snorts and startled rushes through the nearby bush. In the black, moonless night, it was impossible to identify the source of the sounds, but we fully expected a lion or, at the very least, a leopard to invade our tent by morning. Of course, none did, and we soon grew reasonably accustomed to the African night.

It was there along the Athi, in dry, thick "bush" country, that we were in fact chased by several rhinos. They were plentiful then, though they have since vanished from that locale. They tended to charge out of the bush unexpectedly, holding their heads down and snorting like a steam engine. Fortunately, rhinos' eyesight is poor, so they usually blundered past. On several occasions when we chanced upon one, we climbed up a thorn tree—not the most comfortable of operations, particularly when attempted in some haste—until the beast wandered off.

After our hunt along the Athi, we went first to hunt near Lake Magadi and then traveled north past Mount Kenya, whose forested slopes were closed to visitors because of government operations against the remnants of Mau Mau gangs, and into the NFD, a land of bare brown and red soil, distant purple hills, and vast spaces reminiscent of parts of the American West. (Mau Mau was a secret society, drawn mostly from the majority Kikuyu tribe, that engaged in bloody attacks, usually at night, on white farmer-settlers. Although the colonial authorities finally suppressed the movement, it hastened the coming of independence in Kenya.)

Mount Kenya dominated the landscape. Its base of rolling hills stretched a hundred miles in each direction, its lower slopes cloaked by a dense rain forest giving way at higher altitude to bamboo, which in turn gave way to alpine moorland and finally to the spectacular Gothic spires of rock and ice of the 17,000-foot peak.

George Adamson was game warden of this district, which included our hunting area, and was headquartered at Isiolo. He and his wife, Joy, became famous as the foster parents of Elsa the lioness, the subject of several books and a popular movie.[2] We called on Adamson at his small office to present our licenses and discuss our plans. George Barrington already knew him from previous occasions, and Adamson invited us to visit him and Joy at their home outside town. We met Elsa first on that occasion and then again in the bush one evening when the Adamsons came to our camp for supper. They arrived in an open jeep, Elsa sitting in the back seat with a small African boy, who was about ten years old, tightly gripping her slender leash. Elsa was then not much bigger than a Great Dane but already a powerful animal. I remember trying to play with her and quickly finding myself flat on the ground, entangled with her and her leash, wondering if she might suddenly become annoyed and make a meal of me.

The safari experience was everything of which I had dreamt. It was a wonderful adventure in wild, remote country, and we spent most of our time hunting on foot with a local tribesman as tracker. The experience of a first African hunting safari, like that of a first love, can never be duplicated. But that doesn't keep one from enjoying a second. We returned to East Africa in 1958, soon after I became a judge of the Tax Court, for a second safari, which was also memorable. Again, we spent a month on a tented safari and hunted in Kenya, though in different areas than on the previous trip, including two weeks spent in the forests of Mount Kenya.

We traveled to Kenya this time via Athens; Stanleyville (now Kisangani), in the old Belgian Congo; Lake Kivu; the Virunga volcanoes, in Rwanda; and Uganda's Queen Elizabeth National Park. In the Virunga volcanoes we tracked and finally caught up with small bands of mountain gorillas, an extraordinary experience and years before the gorillas became habituated to visiting tourists. We had quietly followed the gorillas' trail along a steep mountainside, communicating among ourselves by sign or by whisper. We realized that we were very close to our quarry when we felt their still-wet saliva on half-chewed nettles and other plants beside the trail. Suddenly, the silence was shattered by a roar ahead of us as a dominant male made a threatening demonstration, bursting through the bushes, shaking them violently, and roaring at us. Aileen and I and our lone African tracker, Reuben, were unarmed, and encounters such as these — the first for Aileen and me — were heart-stopping events. We had been assured that an attack was unlikely, particularly if we avoided any appearance of being threatening, so, at the first sight of a gorilla, we sank to our knees on the trail and kept very still. In each case when this occurred, the old male broke off the encounter quite quickly and followed after his family, whose silent departure into the forest he had been covering. After one such encounter, as I was still crouching on the ground, Aileen said that I looked very pale. "It must be the altitude," I replied.

We saw little of the Congo, but Lake Kivu and the lakes and mountains of Rwanda and Uganda were breathtaking in their beauty. Even though these areas were on the brink of independence, they seemed peaceful and stable. Their more recent record is depressing, to say the least — tribal genocide in Rwanda, with more than 800,000 slaughtered; the bloody tyranny of Idi Amin in Uganda; and the ongoing warfare in the Belgian Congo (which later became Zaire, then the Democratic Republic of the Congo), where almost the entire infrastructure of that very large country — highways, schools, hospitals, and the like — has been destroyed. Only Uganda has recovered a modicum of political stability.

The mountain gorilla still maintains its precarious existence in the Parc National des Volcans. Poaching and the incursions of armed bands threaten them, but their biggest threat has been from loss of habitat as the cutting of forests and the cultivation of crops creep inexorably up the mountainsides. The park guards — often unpaid and unprovisioned — have been heroic in their fight to protect the gorillas. Many years ago, the World Wildlife Fund (WWF), the African Wildlife Foundation, and the Fauna and Flora Preservation Society of Britain joined together in a cooperative effort to help ensure their survival. Given the extreme political instability around them, their future continues to be at risk.

Although Aileen tried hunting on one occasion, she did not enjoy it. However, she thoroughly enjoyed going along on the hunts and was always right with me as we followed up our quarry. On both trips, we also collected for the Smithsonian Institution's National Museum of Natural History — insects (*dudus* in Swahili) in 1956 and small mammals, such as rats, squirrels, and bats, in 1958. A senior scientist at the museum had encouraged us to make such collections and suggested how we could be useful in this regard. He outfitted us with collecting bottles and other paraphernalia and we carried all this to Africa. Somewhere in the museum files is a record of our collections. They were pretty amateurish, I am afraid.

We loved every minute of those safaris. We were enthralled by the strangeness and beauty around us—Masai warriors leaning on their spears, the early morning chill, the quiet breeze that flowed through the camp at first light, the sibilant calling of the doves in the dawn, the heat of midday spent in the shade of an acacia, the hot, dry smell of the African earth, the spoor of the passing game, the sight of the game itself, elephants bathing in a stream below, the gentle grace of giraffes browsing through the thorn trees, the tension and concentration of the hunt, the beauty and incredible variety of the birds, the sundowner beside the fire and the tales told at such a time, the soft sound of African voices, the nights full of stars, the occasional roar of a distant lion, the call of a hyena.

It was heady stuff and we ate it up. There were harshness and brutality, thirst, and fear, and pain, and sudden death, but also peace and innocence. It was the earth in the springtime of life, when all seemed fresh and young. For us, it was romance pure and simple.

Of course, there was a good deal of naiveté in all this and we doubtless were exposed to very little of the reality of modern Africa—all too often characterized by poverty, disease, political tyranny, corruption, and overpopulation. Never mind, I was in love with Africa, and I still am—the old Africa of the early hunters, explorers, and settlers, of golden landscapes and immense skies, of wildlife, of Isak Dinesen, Ernest Hemingway, and Elspeth Huxley. Truly, in the phrase of my South African friend Ian Player, Africa is the "land of the soul."*

I have returned to Africa again and again over the years—about twenty times, I would guess. After those first two safaris, I never hunted there again, not because I am opposed to hunting but because my interest waned; I had done that. And I had other things to do, primarily involving the conservation of wildlife.

Kenya has been closed to hunting for many years now; the closure was ostensibly an effort to conserve wildlife but certainly, in part, a domestic political act, since most licensed big game hunting in colonial days was done by white foreigners and closed to Africans. Whatever the motivations, the wildlife populations outside of parks and other protected areas have declined dramatically. Well-regulated hunting such as we did took

---

*The complete story of these two safaris is told in two mimeographed books, both unpublished: *African Safari* (1956) and *Back to Africa* (1958), which Aileen and I distributed to family and friends at Christmastime those years. Each was written by me with suggestions from Aileen and was based on a daily diary that I kept. The keeping of such a diary became a habit, followed on most trips after that.

an insignificant number of animals but ensured the presence in remote areas of safari operations that monitored wildlife populations and helped control poaching. On our first safari, for example, George, Aileen, and I, together with our two gun bearers, were walking through the bush when we came upon the camp of a large poaching operation. The poachers fled at our approach, and we confiscated a large number of steel snares and poisoned arrows. In more recent times, with the widespread availability and relatively low cost of automatic weapons, poachers tend to be well armed and ready to fight government game patrols.

In contrast to the situation in Kenya, hunting is still permitted in many African countries, and, if properly managed, can provide a significant income for local peoples. Simply closing a country to hunting without a parallel effort to engage local communities in wildlife protection by creating benefits, such as from tourism, will usually mean the disappearance of the wildlife. When no one has an incentive to protect the game, it will go, often as the result of organized poaching carried out to supply commercial markets. Be that as it may, I realize that hunting is a controversial matter on which opinions vary widely, and I also am aware that my perceptions were formed almost a half century ago, when conditions were quite different from those that may exist today.

In more recent years, particularly as I became closely identified with wildlife conservation, it sometimes came as a shock to people to learn that I have hunted and killed wild animals.* There are two fundamental and quite different questions involved here. The first is the very basic: "How *could* you do such a thing?" That is a rational but often a very emotional question, and there is no simple answer. It depends, in part, I think, on how you were brought up. In my family, hunting and fishing were a fact of life when I was young—primarily duck- and quail-hunting. Even my clergy ancestors wrote of the joys of a day spent in the field with rod or gun. Early Train forebears in New England doubtless hunted deer, wild turkeys, squirrels, and rabbits on their farms to protect their crops and help feed their families. Gradually, such activities evolved into a sport rather than a necessary subsistence activity. However, few ever paused for a philosophical self-analysis of the whole matter.

My father brought up his three sons to hunt, just as he had been raised by his own father. My eldest brother never participated because his eye-

*When I lunched with Averell Harriman some years ago in Florida, he expressed surprise that I could have hunted. I apparently replied that, like Nixon, "I have my light side and my dark side!" RET, Diary, January 7, 1978.

sight was poor; therefore, his children have never hunted and doubtless abhor the whole idea. My elder brother and I loved it. As a result, our children and grandchildren enjoy hunting. And so it seems to go. To a great extent, I think sport hunting in its various manifestations is a cultural phenomenon. As such, I tend to have little sympathy with those who want to ban hunting because it is foreign to their own culture. I no longer have any interest in big game hunting, but I have no argument with those who do.

The second question often raised with regard to hunting is "How can you reconcile hunting with the conservation of wildlife?" That is an easier one. Assuming there is no hunting of endangered species and assuming that the hunting in question is managed and controlled so that the "take" is kept at sustainable levels, hunting can be beneficial to both the wildlife and the human communities associated with it. My farm on the Eastern Shore of Maryland is home to a herd of twenty to thirty white-tailed deer. While I do not hunt them, I invite a neighbor to do so with local friends, and about a half dozen deer are taken every year. The herd remains stable and healthy, does little damage to our crops, and does not invade the vegetable or flower gardens. One or more of the animals are frequently visible when we walk or ride around the property, which gives us great pleasure. In the absence of wolves and cougars, it is hard to know how else deer numbers would be kept in balance with their habitat except by controlled hunting.

There are far more deer today in the eastern states than there were at first settlement in the seventeenth century. Subsequently, deer had been all but exterminated in a state such as Pennsylvania by the early 1900s as the result of overhunting. The abundance of deer today, while partially the result of habitat changes, is primarily the result of wildlife management policies and practices aimed at maintaining a renewable resource for hunting.

As an example, in several areas of Africa where hunting has been legal for many years, the revenue from such hunting had never accrued to the local communities but instead had gone to outside safari firms and to a distant government. Typically in such areas, the local people did nothing to stop illegal poaching because the loss of wildlife meant nothing to them. In several such areas, the WWF has succeeded in having the government change the fee structure so that a significant part of the revenue from hunting now goes to the local community. Once the wildlife is perceived as having a positive economic benefit, local people typically organize to stop poaching and help protect and manage the wildlife resource.

From time to time, an argument is made to me that the only true conservationists are hunters. That is nonsense. Many hunters are, indeed, wonderful conservationists. Theodore Roosevelt is perhaps our best-known example of that tradition, but many others come to mind in this regard. On the organizational side, Ducks Unlimited, an organization supported principally by waterfowlers, is a major force for the protection and restoration of wetlands in North America. Trout Unlimited and the Izaak Walton League of America, supported principally by fishermen, are important protectors of fish habitat. The National Wildlife Federation has many hunters in its membership. The small but prestigious Boone and Crockett Club, an organization of North American big game hunters founded by Theodore Roosevelt (to which I have belonged for many years), has been a significant force in advocating the conservation of big game and "fair chase" rules. These are a few of many examples.

On the other side of the coin are major nonprofit organizations dedicated to the conservation of wildlife and wildlife habitat irrespective of whether these are important for hunting. Examples include the WWF, the preponderance of whose support doubtless comes from nonhunters, and The Nature Conservancy, the National Audubon Society, the Wildlife Conservation Society, and Conservation International, among others. The supporters of such organizations are the large number of Americans who love wildlife for its own sake, not only in their own backyards but also, increasingly, in remote parts of the globe that they will probably never have the opportunity to visit except in spirit. In addition, conservation efforts are motivated more and more by the scientific rationale of the desirability — indeed, the vital necessity, for the health of the planet and our own human future — of maintaining biological diversity wherever possible.

Hunters and nonhunters alike can justifiably take pride in and credit for many fine conservation accomplishments. Both are important to our conservation objectives. I would make two pleas in this regard. The first is that each side be tolerant and accepting of the other's interests and motivations. Second, I hope that more hunters will espouse the cause of conservation more broadly than dictated by their interest in particular game species. Overall, we must face the fact that the conservation challenge worldwide is far greater than the resources and efforts that any of us have been able to mobilize to date. We must all pitch in, and we must all work together.

To return, after the foregoing detour, to the subject of my own African experience, I have found that the most spectacular and accessible views of African wildlife are usually found in national parks and other protected areas. There, under reasonably complete protection and without competition from human settlement, wildlife concentrates in its greatest numbers and variety and shows the least fear of human presence — particularly in a vehicle. In most such areas, weapons of any sort are usually prohibited and visitors are confined to their vehicles and forbidden to leave them in the normal course of events. This policy makes for incomparable game-viewing, birding, and photography. On the other hand, to move on foot through the hot, still bush produces an intensity of experience and a knife-sharp awareness of one's surroundings that are altogether different. It is in part the difference between being a mere spectator and being, at least to some extent, a participant.

In more recent years, Aileen and I have done nonhunting safaris on foot with an armed guide in the great Selous Game Reserve of Tanzania, in the South Luangwa National Park of Zambia, in the Okavango Delta of Botswana, and, in particular, with our good friend and guide John Stevens along the Zambesi River in Zimbabwe. These have all been wonderful experiences that seem only to whet the appetite for yet another return to Africa.

Whatever the circumstances, those first African safaris in 1956 and 1958 were life-changing events for me. It wasn't that I was suddenly turned into a conservationist. Out of my own upbringing, I carried with me to Africa a sense of the importance of conserving wildlife, of hunting in a controlled, responsible fashion, of practicing good sportsmanship, of protecting habitat. While on safari, we often talked to our professional hunter of these matters and of specific African conservation problems, of poaching and the pressures of ever-growing human populations. With the countries of British East Africa in transition from colonial to independent rule, he, like many other colonials, was highly skeptical of the future of the wildlife under African management. Beyond all these considerations, however, the sheer wonder of what I saw and experienced in Africa gripped my imagination as had nothing before in my life. I was fertile ground for the development of ideas and plans for saving African wildlife and, eventually, for undertaking conservation on a larger scale.

Chapter 4

First Steps for Wildlife

SOMETIME AFTER Aileen and I returned to Washington, D.C., from our second safari in 1958, Maurice Stans, then deputy postmaster general, invited us to join the African Safari Club of Washington, an organization newly formed by a group of local businessmen who had gone on a hunt together in Mozambique.* The main purpose of the club was to provide a venue for the exchange of African hunting experiences.

You can talk only so long about your hunting experiences before it all begins to get pretty boring—or so it seemed to me. As a result, after Aileen and I attended a couple of evenings of that sort, I suggested that the group develop a conservation mission. As I look back on it all, my guess is that ever since returning from our latest trip, I had been turning over in my mind what I could do to help promote conservation in Africa. Here seemed an opportunity made to order. I certainly had no grand strategy or plan in mind but was simply groping for ideas as to how to be useful in what seemed a pretty dire situation.

My view of the conservation future in East Africa was primarily the product of our two safaris, a pretty limited exposure. Our stops in Nairobi,

---

*Stans later became director of the Bureau of the Budget and then secretary of the Department of Commerce in the Nixon administration. He had made several hunting safaris in Africa, and he was my principal advisor when Aileen and I planned our first safari. Stans, who died in 1998, ran into legal difficulties in the aftermath of Watergate when he was charged with, and pled guilty to, improper handling of campaign funds. As I knew him, Maury was a fine person who set high standards in both public and private life.

Kenya's capital, were always brief and mostly spent in getting licenses, items of safari wear, or other equipment. Once in the field, the native Africans we met, other than our safari crew, were living at a bare subsistence level, without access to health care, with little or no formal education, and finding shelter in the simplest huts.

Of course, the native Kenyans were a very diverse lot, made up of many tribes and different cultures that did not lend themselves to generalization. The largest tribe, the Kikuyu of highland Kenya, and the Luo, based near Lake Victoria, were agriculturists who lived in fairly dense farm communities and had little tolerance for the wildlife that invaded their fields. The Nderobo people of the mountain forests were hunter-gatherers, and the Wakamba of southeastern Kenya were hunters who also farmed. The pastoralist tribes, such as the Masai and the Samburu, tended to be nomadic and more warlike, raiding their neighbors for cattle, women, or both, and were usually fairly tolerant of wildlife, except for the lions that attacked their herds. The tribes of Uganda and Tanzania and other areas demonstrated comparable diversity. Poaching was chronic in all areas except in the grazing lands of the pastoral tribes.

Whether tolerant or intolerant of wildlife, few Africans were "nature lovers." People living on the edge of survival seldom are. Subsistence hunting is an ongoing war against nature, or so it often seems. In North America, our forebears showed little concern about conserving wildlife and succeeded in exterminating the passenger pigeon; almost wiping out the bison; hunting deer populations down to a tiny fraction of what they are today; eliminating panthers, grizzly bears, and wolves from most of their range; and so on.

Few Africans showed any interest in visiting national parks, nor, indeed, were they encouraged to do so. Under colonial rule, game-viewing and legal hunting were reserved, in practice, for whites. Even if other forces had not been at work, it is small wonder that the average African had little interest in wildlife conservation. Even today, the overwhelming majority of visitors to national parks and other protected areas in Africa are white tourists.

My principal source of information on all such matters while on safari was our professional hunter, George Barrington, with whom we spent almost every waking moment. His experiences, attitudes, and values were those of a typical colonial settler — and this is not said to disparage those settlers. George was pessimistic about the future of wildlife with the coming of political independence. That Kenya's population was increasing at close to 4 percent per year, one of the highest birthrates in the world, was another discouraging factor.

All these factors were cause for concern and provided the motivation for my proposal that the African Safari Club develop a conservation mission. My suggestion met with a reasonably positive response, and, as so often happens in such situations, I was asked to head a committee to explore what might be done. In addition to me, the committee consisted of Arthur "Nick" Arundel, Jim Bugg, Kermit "Kim" Roosevelt, Maury Stans, and Ed Sweeney (later president of the Explorers Club). Kim was Theodore Roosevelt's grandson; his father, also named Kermit, had accompanied TR on his famous African safari in 1910–1911. In turn, Kim, together with his own son, had recently retraced the route of his grandfather's safari.[1]

Early in our committee's meeting, held in my office at the United States Tax Court, we decided that the most important wildlife conservation task in Africa was to help Africans equip themselves with the knowledge and skills that would enable them to manage their own wildlife resources, to run game departments and national parks. Today, we would be apt to call this "capacity building." The forces of independence were sweeping through Africa, and European powers were turning over political control of the colonies to their African inhabitants. While the Europeans had done a fair job of training Africans in a variety of administrative areas, they had done little or nothing to train them as natural resource managers. In the British colonies in particular, the management of game departments and national parks had mostly been the bailiwick of gifted and dedicated amateurs, often retired British and Indian army officers. What these men may have lacked in professional training they made up for with a passionate love of nature — birds, animals, and plants. It seemed unlikely that many Africans, with different priorities, would be similarly motivated. Thus, not only was training a high priority; the need was urgent, and it was not being addressed by any other conservation group. We decided that the focus, initially at least, should be on British East Africa, in large part because we were most familiar with that area.

Such a mission would require money in significant amounts. To raise funds of that magnitude would in turn require not only a non-profit organization that was tax exempt but also one for which contributions would be tax deductible. That ruled out the African Safari Club of Washington itself as the vehicle because it was a social, not a charitable, organization. Finally, having decided to launch a new organization, we decided on a name: the African Wildlife Leadership Foundation, the word "leadership" intended to convey the sense of Africans developing the capacity to manage their own wildlife resources.

We informed the Safari Club membership of what we were doing, but any real association between the organizations soon evaporated. One of my law clerks, Lee Rogers,* drew up incorporation papers under the laws of the District of Columbia; I gave him the $15 filing fee to take with the papers to the District offices, and AWLF was in business. That was early 1961.[2]

We established a board and elected members; I was elected chairman and chief executive officer, positions I held until 1969. At the outset, the AWLF headquarters was essentially my office supplemented by a postal box at the Benjamin Franklin Station, across the street. Subsequently, I rented a small office in the National Press Building and hired a secretary, Betty Spacek. Judge or not, I was the chief cook and bottle-washer of AWLF in those early days. I raised essentially all the money, designed our program and projects, communicated with the public at home, and kept in touch with those doing conservation on the ground in Africa. Later on, others came on board to share the responsibilities.

We soon had several young Africans at U.S. universities studying wildlife management. The first of these, Perez Olindo, went on to become the first African director of national parks in Kenya, and a loyal friend.[†] Thanks to the late Paul Mellon and his Old Dominion Foundation plus matching funds of our own, we were able to provide the initial funding for the College of African Wildlife Management at Mweka, Tanzania. Later, we did the same for a similar institution headed by Andrew Allo, another early AWLF wildlife management student, for French-speaking Africans at Garoua, Cameroon, thanks in that instance to help from Laurance S. Rockefeller and the Rockefeller Brothers Fund.[3] We also established educational programs at Nairobi National Park in Kenya and at Murchison Falls National Park in Uganda. I was able to enlist the help of the African-American Institute in New York to screen and process

---

*Edward Lee Rogers, one of my first law clerks, went on to a distinguished career in the law, including environmental law. He died tragically in an auto accident in 1998.
†When Kenya combined its national parks and game departments into the Kenya Wildlife Service, Olindo became the new agency's first director.

scholarship applicants in Africa and to administer to the students who came to the United States.

We initiated a summer course to provide an introduction to the management of national parks and wildlife for some of the many African students studying in other disciplines at American universities at the time. These students tended to be an elite group selected because of their academic records, and when they returned to Africa it would presumably be to positions of some influence. We hoped that a brief exposure to the management of wildlife, parks, and other protected areas would demonstrate the importance of conservation matters to a nation such as the United States and would help influence the students in their future careers. Each summer we recruited about twenty of these students for a six-week course based at the School of Natural Resources of the University of Michigan, Ann Arbor. Secretary of Interior Stewart Udall was an enthusiastic supporter, and the Department of the Interior made its personnel available as guides and instructors. The Department of Defense lent us buses for travel. The university's School of Natural Resources made its instructors available. Thus, we patched together on the proverbial shoestring a fairly impressive effort.

To help ensure that our program had a firm intellectual base, AWLF convened a small meeting in Berkeley, California, of experienced academicians to explore educational alternatives for Africans being trained to take part in the conservation of wildlife. The group was chaired by A. Starker Leopold, a professor at the University of California, Berkeley, and son of Aldo Leopold, who is often called the father of the science of wildlife management, and it included internationally known ecologist Frank Fraser Darling of The Conservation Foundation and Ian McTaggart Cowan of the University of British Columbia, among others. A major effort went into developing the *African Wildlife News*, printed in tabloid format and modeled after the *St. Albans News*, of which I had been managing editor during my school days. The *African Wildlife News* went out free to all donors as well as to others who had been on safari or otherwise were thought to have an interest in African wildlife. I wrote the copy, including the editorials, took some of the photographs, wrote the heads, corrected the galleys, and did the layout in the evenings. I don't believe the operation really impinged on my official duties, but it certainly did on my personal life. However, Aileen was understanding and, indeed, shared my enthusiasm for AWLF.

Friends and collaborators from Africa, such as Major Bruce Kinloch, chief game warden of Tanzania; Major Ian Grimwood, chief game warden of Kenya; and John Owen, director of Tanzania's national parks, visited us in Washington. Rennie Bere and Mervyn Cowie, national parks directors of Uganda and Kenya, respectively, I knew and worked with on their home grounds. A particularly valued associate from Africa was distinguished wildlife scientist Hugh Lamprey, who became the first principal of the College of African Wildlife Management.* All of these men made great contributions to the future of African wildlife, and they and their wives became close friends of Aileen's and mine, friends with whom we shared a deep commitment to conservation in Africa as well as many experiences in the African wilds.

I made a number of trips to Africa on AWLF business over a half dozen years starting in 1961, sometimes on my own and sometimes accompanied by Aileen. I believed we were really accomplishing things in Africa, and I was having great fun. A small organization in which one personally does almost all the work—and AWLF could not have been much smaller —can be enormously satisfying. There is little question that larger organizations with larger bureaucracies can have the potential for great accomplishment, but, at the same time, the personal satisfaction factor may decrease as size increases. Of course, the principal factor in my enjoyment of my AWLF involvement was a compelling belief in our mission to help save African wildlife for the future. My associates and I were deeply committed to that goal. It is gratifying that, under a succession of able leaders, the African Wildlife Foundation, as it is now known, today continues stronger than ever.†

A special friend in those years was Bill Eddy, an inspired and gifted teacher. Eddy had received a Ford Foundation grant to initiate a program in Tanzania to introduce African students to their wildlife and national

*Subsequently, Lamprey became the first director of the Serengeti Research Institute and then head of the WWF office in Nairobi.
†Robinson McIlvaine was an outstanding AWLF president for several years. A career Foreign Service officer, he served as U.S. ambassador to Kenya and then, on retirement, headed AWLF in Nairobi. He was followed by Robert Smith, also a career Foreign Service officer, and Paul Schindler. More recently, Michael Wright, formerly a vice president of the World Wildlife Fund, did a fine job as chief executive officer for several years. When he joined the John D. and Catherine T. MacArthur Foundation as head of its Conservation and Sustainable Development program, his place at AWF was taken by Patrick Bergin, who for several years has directed AWF's operations in Africa.

parks. Although I could never persuade him to become a regular member of the AWLF staff, we worked together on a number of enterprises in Africa.

I was to have many more associations with Africa in later years, particularly with WWF, but it all began with those two safaris and the start of AWLF.* Though I did not fully appreciate the fact at the time, it is plain in retrospect that the center of my interests had begun to shift substantially. Whether I knew it or not, my days as a judge of the Tax Court were numbered.

---

*A hobby I have pursued with enthusiasm for many years is the collecting of books, letters, diaries, maps, photographs, and art concerning the early exploration of Africa and travel, natural history, and big game hunting on that continent. The collection comprises several thousand items. As of 2003, the Russell E. Train Africana Collection is becoming part of the Joseph F. Cullman 3rd Library of Natural History in the National Museum of Natural History of the Smithsonian Institution in Washington, D.C.

Chapter 5

From Judge to Conservationist

IN 1961, I was forty, a federal judge, and becoming known in the international conservation world, primarily because of the African Wildlife Leadership Foundation. In midyear, shortly after the establishment of AWLF, a group of international conservationists, mostly European and including such luminaries as Sir Julian Huxley, organized the World Wildlife Fund (WWF), with international headquarters in Switzerland. WWF's purpose was to raise funds to support international conservation efforts, which were woefully underfunded at the time. H.R.H. Prince Bernhard of the Netherlands was named international president. In September, WWF-UK was established in the United Kingdom, with H.R.H. the Duke of Edinburgh as president, and in December, WWF-US was launched in the United States.

I was asked to be a founding director of WWF-US and also vice president (in a nonexecutive capacity), and I accepted both positions with enthusiasm, thus beginning an association that continues to the present, covering a span of more than forty years.[1] WWF had a natural appeal for me because it brought a broader, worldwide dimension to my commitment to African conservation and also provided an international network of organizations to help further the conservation effort. The association also lent additional legitimacy to my own role in the conservation world. A fund-raising dinner at the Waldorf Astoria in New York in June 1962, with Prince Bernhard and Prince Philip as the guests of honor, helped promote WWF to the public.

An early member of the WWF board was Fairfield Osborn, president of the New York Zoological Society (NYZS), which included the Bronx

Zoo, and chairman of the board of The Conservation Foundation (CF). Osborn had started the Foundation to further his environmental interests that went beyond the normal concerns of the zoo, such as the control of human population growth and regulation of pesticides.

Fair, as he was known by his friends, was a good deal older than I; he was probably at least seventy when we first met. He was a strong personality and a power in his field. The Osborns were an old New York-Hudson River valley family, and Fair's father, Henry Fairfield Osborn, had for many years been head of the American Museum of Natural History. Fair had established a small African wildlife conservation program under the auspices of NYZS, and he began to look with a somewhat jaundiced eye on the growing visibility of AWLF. After all, I was raising funds from some of his longtime supporters in the New York area, and he was definitely not used to being challenged on his own turf.

One day, Fair called me at my office at the United States Tax Court. He opened the conversation by complimenting me on the growing success of AWLF. It was wasteful to have several organizations doing the same thing, he said, emphasizing that NYZS already had an African program and planned to expand it. The message was plain: we should either fold up and quit or join up with NYZS. After thanking him for his kind words about AWLF, I retorted that the reason why NYZS was planning an expanded African program was that "we have lit a fire under you!" There was a pause at the other end of the line, and then, "Train, you son-of-a-bitch!" I took those words not as an insult but as an expression of admiration, which became mutual. Fair was a great man, an effective and articulate spokesman for conservation, and he had done a splendid job of building NYZS and The Conservation Foundation. We became good friends.

In early 1964, Fair proposed that I leave the Tax Court and become president of CF, taking the place of Sam Ordway, who wanted to retire. I had been on the court about six years and was beginning to feel restless. Shortly after I had gone on the court, a friend had asked how I liked my judicial role. "It's fine," I said, "except that the phone never rings!" That was a bit of an exaggeration, but life on the court was fairly secluded, certainly as compared with my jobs on Capitol Hill, where one worked in a constant turmoil of lobbyists and politicians. That may have been one reason why I had gravitated into so many nonjudicial activities, particularly conservation, which by this time had become something of an overarching interest. Aileen, always one to face reality, finally said to me, "Russ, it seems to me that you are going to have to decide to be either a judge or a conservationist." I knew she was right, but I had avoided coming to grips with the issue. Plainly, two career paths lay ahead of me. At the moment, I was trying to travel down both simultaneously, but the time had come to choose. One road—the judicial, tax law career—was a known quantity, secure and steady. The other road—a conservation/ environmental career—led into uncharted territory with no signposts whatsoever. I lunched with Fair in New York to discuss the possibility of my resigning from the court and becoming president of CF.

Founded in 1948, The Conservation Foundation at the time was a small nonprofit organization that had been housed for years on an upper floor of an old building on Forty-third Street in New York, reached by a rickety cage elevator. It had considerable prestige in the ecological world, in great part derived from the stature of Fairfield Osborn himself, who had written two well-received and pioneering books that warned of environmental disaster unless such problems as human population growth were addressed.[2]

The stated purposes of CF were ones to which I was highly sympathetic: "to promote public knowledge about the earth's resources—its waters, soils, minerals, plant and animal life; to initiate research and education concerning these resources and their relation to each other; to ascertain the most effective methods of making them available and useful to people; to assess population trends and their effect upon environment; finally, to encourage human conduct to sustain and enrich life on earth." Those modest goals were underwritten by an annual budget of about $400,000. CF, however, had no endowment and no membership; funds came from a few foundations and a few major individual donors.

I indicated that I would need a salary at least equal to what I was receiving as a judge, namely, $50,000 per year. Fair was somewhat taken aback. The CF tradition was to have gentlemen of wealth at the top who would serve without compensation. A more difficult issue was the future location of CF. I had no intention of moving my life to New York. Not long after, Laurance S. Rockefeller and I had lunch in Washington and pursued these issues as well as his perspectives on CF. Laurance was vice chairman of the board and had been a generous supporter since CF's inception. He was also a devoted admirer of Fair. He was less interested in ecological research than Fair and more interested in linking environmental policy to human needs. He was a strong supporter of open space protection, for example, not just for the sake of preservation but also because of the opportunities open space provided for outdoor recreation. He wanted to be assured that, if I became head of CF, I would not devote all my efforts to esoteric studies and would give appropriate attention to his more pragmatic approach. His orientation was fully compatible with my own and Laurance and I became good friends over the years. He has been a major force in conservation, particularly in the United States but also internationally.[3]

In due course, Fair and I reached agreement on all issues, and I agreed in principle to leave the bench and take on the presidency of CF. A difficult problem was the timing of the move. It was a point of honor for me to decide all the cases I had heard. In the event, this took about a year. To this day, I am amazed at how understanding Fair and his associates on the CF board were on the matter. In late July 1965, President Lyndon B. Johnson accepted my resignation in a letter that expressed regret at my leaving the court but then went on to say, "I am gratified to learn, Russell, that you will be applying your great gifts to the conservation effort—an endeavor which, more than ever before, is crucial to the future of our Nation."[4] Both Wilbur Mills, chairman of the House Committee on Ways and Means, and ranking Republican member John Byrnes made generous remarks about me in the House.[5] Aileen and I spent that August with our children at "Barney's Joy" in South Dartmouth, Massachusetts, a marvelous farm property we rented from a friend with a mile or more of dunes and ocean beach. Effective the day after Labor Day 1965, I became president of The Conservation Foundation.

My first public exposure in the new job was a speech given the following weekend at Jackson Lake Lodge in Grand Teton National Park before a joint conference of the American Forestry Association and the National Council of State Garden Clubs. It was quite a high-profile affair, with both Laurance Rockfeller and Lady Bird Johnson present. The theme of the conference was "Natural Beauty"; it was a follow-up to the recently completed White House Conference on Natural Beauty, which they had cochaired, and the emphasis was on conservation with a public enjoyment orientation.

I was introduced by Wyoming's governor (later senator), Clifford P. Hansen. I had spent days composing the speech while at Barney's Joy, recognizing the importance of the event for myself. I emphasized that "natural beauty" was not a simplistic, cosmetic approach to conservation but one that helped put conservation issues into a context that could be understood by a wide public. It was a long speech, and in it I covered many aspects of conservation. Laurance Rockefeller said many years later that when, at the time, he commented to me on the speech's length, I replied that I wanted to include everything on my mind because the speech might turn out to be my last. Actually, the speech seemed to be a success and received good press coverage around the country. It got me off to a good start as a full-time environmentalist.*

It is interesting to note, in light of the creation in 1970 of the Council on Environmental Quality as part of the National Environmental Policy Act of 1969 (NEPA), that in my Jackson Hole speech I had recommended the creation of just such a high-level policy group:

> I propose that the President establish a Council of Ecological Advisors, or alternatively, an interdisciplinary group of environmental advisors having a strong ecological orientation. And let me make it clear that I am not just talking about an interdepartmental committee. With one such bold stroke, concern for the quality of the environment would be given important new status in planning and policy-making at the highest level of government.[6]

Whatever the stature and purposes of CF, or the early favorable publicity I received, my family and Aileen's were nonplussed by my leaving the bench and entering an environmental career. To give up the prestige of a federal judgeship was strange enough. To do so to head an environmental organization was inexplicable. None of them had a clue about environmental issues. When I tried to explain, they listened politely, but it was plain that they simply did not understand what I was doing or why. Sadly, they really never did. I have to say, however, that most of our friends at the time didn't, either. Times have changed in that regard.

It is hard to appreciate today how little public concern there was in 1965 for environmental problems. If they were recognized at all, there was little or no sense of urgency in dealing with them. Although the envi-

---

*At about the same time, I joined the board of the American Conservation Association (ACA), which was chaired by Laurance and funded by him through Jackson Hole Preserve, another nonprofit philanthropic entity he had founded and chaired. With the exception of my time in government, I served on ACA's board until 1996, by which time Laurance's son, Larry, had taken on its chairmanship. Through relatively small grants, ACA has been an important source of seed money for young conservation organizations and new initiatives.

ronmental awakening was not far off, at the time there were essentially no effective federal controls on industrial air and water pollution; automobile emissions and fuel economy were unregulated; toxic chemicals were introduced freely into the environment; the use of DDT and other persistent pesticides was uncontrolled; the discharge of toxic wastes onto the land was unregulated; there were no effective federal rules governing noise pollution and safety of drinking water; ocean dumping of wastes was unregulated, as was the discharge of wastes by vessels at sea; there were no controls on the international trade in endangered species; there was no national effort to protect endangered species, except in the case of a few species important to hunters; there were no requirements on either state or federal governments that adverse environmental effects be taken into account in the planning of new projects and programs; there was no Environmental Protection Agency; and so on.

I served as president of CF until the end of 1968. We had a small but able staff of about sixteen. British ecologist Frank Fraser Darling was vice president; he kept his base in England but spent extended periods in Washington, D.C. On Darling's retirement in 1966, an American ecologist, Raymond Dasmann, joined CF on a full-time basis as director of environmental studies. Frank Gregg was also a vice president, as was Sidney Howe, who later became CF's president. Once CF was established in Washington, in a modern office building at 1250 Connecticut Avenue, AWLF moved in with us. At first, I continued to operate the latter pretty much single-handedly, but this soon became impractical. Janet Bohlen joined us as editor of the *African Wildlife News* and Gordon Wilson became executive director.

With my assumption of its presidency and its move to Washington, CF became focused principally on bringing environmental values into decision making generally, particularly developmental decision making. Our emphasis became less on research and more on practical applications and demonstrations, primarily in the United States. Thus, we undertook a project at Rookery Bay, south of Naples on Florida's western coast, to demonstrate how real estate development could be designed to protect heron rookeries and mangroves along the shoreline, which were vital to fish populations. With CF's financial support, Ian McHarg, professor of landscape architecture at the University of Pennsylvania, wrote a seminal book on ecologically sensitive landscape planning titled *Design with Nature*.[7] I felt a strong personal commitment to these efforts because I

was convinced of the need to bring ecological principles and environmental values into the everyday life of our society. This became an endur-
ing interest of mine that later would be reflected in such efforts as that to
enact national land-use planning legislation during the Richard M. Nixon
administration.

With our own new concern for government policy and programs at
CF, we worked closely with like-minded congressional staff and played a
role in developing what became NEPA, enacted at the close of 1969 (and
which will receive considerable attention later in these pages). Indeed,
when the Senate Committee on Interior and Insular Affairs, which developed the legislation, wished to hire as a consultant Lynton Keith Caldwell, professor of political science at the University of Indiana, CF was
asked to pay his compensation. Caldwell had been a member of CF's
Advisory Council for some years, and we were happy to cooperate in that
fashion. As it turned out, Caldwell was responsible for developing the
environmental impact statement process, which became central to the
NEPA legislation and an integral part of decision making by all federal
agencies.[8] Of course, CF's focus on bringing environmental values into
decision making was what NEPA was all about.*

In 1966, while I was president of CF, President Johnson appointed
and the Senate confirmed me as a member of the National Water Commission, which was charged by Congress with reviewing national water
policies, including such matters as the criteria for establishing the economic viability of dams and other water projects, mostly in the West. It
was a small group, chaired by Charles Luce, under secretary of Interior,
and its staff was headed by Ted Tchad. I was expected to represent the
environmental side of the water policy equation as, it was hoped, a balance to the industrial and agricultural interests represented. We filed a
strong report that pointed out such facts as that the interest rate assumptions used in the economic analysis of federal water projects were often
wildly unrealistic. Unfortunately, reform of such matters would have
drastically reduced the number of water projects, which were so dear to
congressional hearts. As might have been predicted, Congress did not act
on our report, though some of our recommendations were incorporated
in legislation over the years. It was an interesting endeavor, and I gained
a high regard for Chuck Luce in the process.

*Some fifteen years later, when CF merged with WWF, it brought a vital public policy
dimension to the latter's conservation program.

In the fall of 1968, as recounted in the prologue to this book, soon after Nixon's first presidential election, I was asked by his transition team to chair the Task Force on Natural Resources and Environment. The very fact that the incoming Nixon administration accepted the idea of a task force on the environment, even if a bit belatedly, was a telling one. The "environment" as a public policy concept was still not widely recognized in 1968, although conservation in terms of national parks, national forests, and fish and wildlife refuges had long been accepted. Selected pollution problems, such as air and water pollution, had begun to be addressed in a fairly rudimentary way by the federal government. But there was little integration of policies or planning. Jurisdiction over air pollution was in the Department of Health, Education, and Welfare, for example, while that over water pollution was in the Department of the Interior. (There was some support at the time for moving the air quality program to Interior, but it met with opposition on the Hill, notably from Ed Muskie, who was concerned that Interior's developmental responsibilities with regard to water, energy, and mineral resources would create serious conflicts of interest in which air quality could lose out.)

If little or no thought was given to the interconnectedness of all these matters under the concept of "environment," that was exactly the thrust of the simple act of creating a task force on the environment. Moreover, our task force's key recommendation, establishing a focal point for environmental policy making in the White House, recognized not only that environmental issues were interrelated but also that they could be brought together effectively and integrated with the other concerns of government at only one point, namely, the presidency. I remain strongly of that view. At the time, I would soon have opportunities to put that principle into practice.

Chapter 6

To Interior as Under Secretary

THE DEMOCRATS in the United States Senate in early 1969 selected Walter Hickel, Richard Nixon's choice as secretary of the Department of the Interior, out of all the Cabinet nominees as their target of political opportunity and chose to make his environmental record—or lack of one—their point of attack. That they did so says a lot about how the environment as an issue had, by the end of the 1960s, finally begun to attract wide public concern and be perceived as politically significant.

Congressional Democrats, led by Senator Ed Muskie of Maine, had already seized the initiative on pollution issues. What they did not anticipate was that Nixon would also prove sensitive to popular concern over the environment and would move quickly, once in office, to establish his own environmental record and, in so doing, trump Muskie's likely presidential ambitions.

On January 21, prior to the vote on Hickel's nomination, the Republican minority leader, Senator Everett Dirksen of Illinois, took the unusual step of announcing on the Senate floor that Russell Train, "known from one end of the country to another as a great conservationist," would be nominated as under secretary of Interior.[1] While there had been some press speculation on my appointment, Dirksen's announcement was the first hard news on the subject. Under secretarial appointments seldom get much notice in the press. Here, it was plain I was being nominated as a pro-environment Republican to balance the Hickel nomination, and that was the way the media treated the matter. Hickel's nomination had become such a center of political controversy that my nomination also received quite a lot of press attention, generally quite favorable. Some of the attention I could have done without, such as being described variously as an "eastern elitist," an "Ivy Leaguer," and a "white-shoe conservationist"—whatever that is. These descriptions must have raised the hackles of a self-made frontiersman like Hickel, but he did not comment—at least not to me.

Nomination and Confirmation

President Nixon sent my nomination to the Senate on January 28. Coincidentally, earlier that day one of the defining events of the environmental crisis had occurred. A blowout on an offshore oil well—actually a leak from a drill site on the ocean bottom—in the Santa Barbara Channel, off California, produced a mammoth oil slick that soon fouled miles of coastal beaches, killing a large number of seabirds and damaging marine life. Apparently having heard of my impending nomination, a senior Interior official on the West Coast called me at home at the crack of dawn that day to brief me on the event. Given the difference in time, he must have been up all night. I made sure that Hickel was alerted to the spill, and he visited the site in the next few days. He called for a voluntary halt to drilling operations in the channel, but, when several companies ignored the call, the White House insisted that he order a shutdown. Meanwhile, the media seized on the event, with televised pictures of seabirds fatally covered with oil. The public was incensed, and the Santa Barbara oil spill became one of the events that helped fuel the environmental ferment of the time. The public reaction was triggered not so much by any particular regulatory failure at Santa Barbara as by the stark images, which served as a sort of visual metaphor for perceived environmental outrages throughout the country.

The full committee hearing on my nomination on February 4 lasted about ninety minutes. It was followed by a closed session on my finances. There were no problems, and the committee voted unanimously to approve my nomination. I was confirmed by the Senate without difficulty on February 7 and was sworn in on the same day by U.S. Supreme Court justice Potter Stewart, with Aileen holding the Bible. The ceremony was held in Hickel's office at Interior with the secretary standing at my elbow.

During Hickel's confirmation hearing, the members of the Interior Committee had aimed their questions at ensuring that he would give appropriate weight to environmental values. Somewhat ironically but understandably, my hearing reflected the reverse side of the coin. Western senators in particular wanted to be sure that I would not be biased against development. For example, Senator Frank Church of Idaho wanted to know if I would oppose the building of dams planned and constructed by Interior's Bureau of Reclamation, usually for irrigation and flood control purposes, and usually in the West. "I have frequently defined conservation as meaning, to me, the rational—and I emphasize 'rational'—use of the earth's resources to produce the highest quality of living for mankind," I said in reply.

Some 100 million more people were expected in the United States over the next three decades or so, and our challenge would be to do a better job of development while increasingly taking environmental factors into account in our planning. "This does not mean you won't build a dam," I continued. "But it means when you build a dam you carefully select the site, and you build multiple-use factors into your plan and design."[2]

Senator Frank Moss of Utah pressed me on the issue of preservation versus use in the national parks. "Preservation" would mean, for example, setting aside large areas as wilderness to protect their natural value, while "use" could put emphasis on building roads and other facilities for tourists. I said that we needed to pursue a dual objective of making parks available for use, enjoyment, and education while at the same time maintaining the exceptional areas of the American landscape in as natural a condition as possible. I conceded that these two objectives might come into conflict. Too few roads or facilities could result in an area not really being available for public use and enjoyment, while too many roads or facilities could threaten the natural quality of an area and thus undermine "the very values which the people have come to see in the first place." I concluded, "So I think here, as in so many things, what we need is a good balance."

Easier said than done, I think as I write this more than thirty years later, with all the accumulated experience of those years. The fact is that "balance" is a very subjective concept, differing radically according to one's particular interest and perspective. Moreover, "public use and enjoyment" tends readily to find a political constituency, particularly in the local communities affected, while "protection of natural values" is more amorphous and unfortunately does not attract the same focused support. Snowmobiles are a case in point today. A relatively small percentage of the visitors to Yellowstone National Park use snowmobiles, but these machines intrude on the natural values of the area and cause noise and other forms of pollution on a scale out of all proportion to the numbers involved. Local people and some visitors presumably enjoy the use of snowmobiles, and the latter are economically attractive to the communities surrounding Yellowstone. Politically, therefore, these people tend to bring to bear far more clout than the "natural values" supporters. The latter point was brought home recently when the George W. Bush administration lifted the ban imposed by President Bill Clinton, which would have started in 2003, on snowmobiles in Yellowstone. A stated reason for this action was that the "gateway" communities around the park oppose the ban. To give such weight to local preferences is to negate the very concept that brought Yellowstone and the National Park System into being—namely, that these areas are truly part of the national heritage of *all* Americans everywhere and are of such outstanding natural value that their fate cannot be left to local determination or transitory political considerations. The continued integrity of that concept, however, requires a presidency that puts the interest of the nation as a whole above local political considerations.

One other important question raised at my confirmation hearing was whether as under secretary of Interior I expected to confine my duties to program areas of primary environmental significance, such as parks, fish, and wildlife. I replied unequivocally that my duties would extend to the full range of Interior's responsibilities and that I had received the assurance of the secretary-designate in that regard. Indeed, Hickel entirely lived up to that assurance in the months ahead.

An Early Challenge

My tenure as under secretary was short, lasting just a year. It did not begin propitiously. When Hickel made his courtesy calls on key members of the Senate, he made the mistake of visiting Senator Muskie accompanied by James Watt, a lobbyist for the U.S. Chamber of Commerce (and a future Interior secretary under Ronald Reagan), who was an opponent of legislation to protect water quality. Since Muskie was the Senate's leading proponent of clean water legislation and also was sensitive to political opportunities, he went through the proverbial roof and issued a blast against Hickel that made all the papers. Hickel's mistake in this case was doubtless due to a certain amount of political naiveté as well as to his general unfamiliarity with the Washington, D.C., scene.

With that background, and after I had physically moved into an office at Interior but before the Senate had acted on my nomination as under secretary, I received a call from Hickel's immediate assistant, Carl Mc-Murray, who announced that the secretary wanted me to appoint Jim Watt as my deputy under secretary. Alarm bells immediately rang in my head. The secretary had hundreds of positions that he could fill, I replied, but I only had about three or four in my immediate office and believed that he should leave those for me to choose. McMurray took that message to the secretary and soon called me back: "The secretary orders you to appoint Watt!" "In that case," I said, "I will carry out the secretary's order but will ask that the White House immediately withdraw my nomination from the Senate." A few moments later, McMurray called back: "The secretary says to forget all about it!"

I really had no choice but to take the position I did. My credibility and usefulness as under secretary would have been fatally compromised had I acceded to Hickel's wishes. Hickel later found a spot in the department for Watt, but we never had any contact.

I heard no more of my refusal to appoint Watt. Hickel may even have respected me for hanging tough. In any case, I quickly recruited Boyd Gibbons, a young attorney and legislative assistant to Senator Paul Fannin of Arizona, as deputy under secretary.

Interior Duties

Once the Watt issue was behind us, my relationship with the secretary became surprisingly good. Hickel had little interest in the nuts and bolts of managing the diverse programs of Interior, ranging from Indian affairs, mineral policy, water pollution control, and fish, wildlife, and parks to offshore oil leasing, the building of dams, management of the public lands, and oversight of the Trust Territory of the Pacific Islands. His management style was simple: he wanted to be decisive. At the same time, he had little interest in details or lengthy briefings. He wanted to be shown the levers to push or pull. He dealt directly with most political issues, including those that involved personnel in the department. That suited me just fine. The secretary gave me responsibility for putting together the departmental budget and for all legislative matters — a very large portfolio.

The budget responsibility put me in touch with every bureau and office in the department and necessarily involved policy considerations. The legislative responsibility involved the initiation of legislative proposals as well as testimony and other responses to congressional requests. Whenever significant policy questions arose or when opinion within the department was sharply divided on some issue, I tried to ensure that the secretary was informed and had an opportunity to make the decision.

When I first moved into my office at Interior, every table and chair was stacked two or three feet deep with folders containing matters for decision at the secretarial level. Hickel's immediate staff must have directed all this material to me in order to keep decisions out of the hands of "holdovers" from the Lyndon Johnson administration. Buff Bohlen,* my administrative assistant, organized all this material, and we gradually worked our way through it.

To cover all this ground, my immediate office had a professional staff of four: Gibbons, Bohlen, Jack Horton, and John Quarles. Of course, I was able to call on additional staff, as needed, from around the department. For example, Frank Bracken, legislative counsel in the Office of the Solicitor, worked with me regularly on legislative matters.† In those days, before creation of the Environmental Protection Agency, the Federal Water Pollution Control Administration was part of Interior and its head, David Dominick, kept in frequent touch with us. Some idea of the scope of what I was dealing with is conveyed by the topics in a memorandum I prepared for my files after meeting with Hickel in midyear to brief him on matters being handled in my office: coal mine health and safety, wastewater treatment financing, the trans-Alaska pipeline, dredge and fill permits, oil drilling permits, Outer Continental Shelf (OCS) oil leasing, the underwater TEKTITE research program, waste treatment at federal facilities, seabed issues (Law of the Sea), a dam on the Rappahannock

*E. U. Curtis "Buff" Bohlen was later a deputy assistant secretary of Interior for fish and wildlife and parks, and then a senior vice president of the World Wildlife Fund and subsequently assistant secretary of the Department of State for oceans and international environmental and scientific affairs (1990–1993). He was recently chairman of The Ocean Conservancy and a consultant to the secretary of Interior on land issues.

†Frank Bracken became under secretary of Interior in the George H. W. Bush administration.

River in Virginia, the Hudson River Expressway, and, of course, the department's budget and appropriations.[3]

The listing by no means covered the full range of our activities. For example, staff of my office, especially deputy under secretary Gibbons, developed the Coastal Zone Management Act of 1972, still in effect today, which encourages Great Lakes and coastal states to manage and protect their coastal resources, including, in cooperation with local governments, the development of land-use plans for their coastal zones. With Buff Bohlen taking the lead, we developed a comprehensive plan for reorganizing federal civil functions relating to the oceans. Naturally, our plan involved centralizing those functions in the Department of the Interior, which already included the Bureau of Commercial Fisheries, the largest unit involved. One of my last acts at the department was sending a memorandum to John Ehrlichman urging that the marine programs be placed in Interior. I stressed the need to recognize the interrelationships of land and ocean resources and to manage them in a coordinated fashion.[4] We lost that one when Hickel lost favor in the White House and the functions were consolidated in the Department of Commerce as the National Oceanic and Atmospheric Administration (NOAA).

While many of those issues had environmental implications, there were several others, such as the proposal to construct an oil pipeline across Alaska, in which environmental factors became the dominant consideration and the work of our office was a trailblazing effort.

Trans-Alaska Pipeline Plans

In 1968, oil was discovered in recoverable quantities on the North Slope of Alaska. The area lies to the west of the present Arctic National Wildlife Refuge on the coastal plain abutting Prudhoe Bay, an arm of the Beaufort Sea, which in turn opens into the Arctic Ocean. At the time, there was no great controversy over oil development in the area, given that it was legally open to leasing.

The protracted controversy that did develop arose over the various plans for moving oil from the Alaskan wells to market in the lower forty-eight states. Since the Beaufort Sea was frozen over for a good part of the year, transport of the oil by ship was not practical. A pipeline to a year-round port became the principal alternative. (Another route, across Canada to midwestern U.S. markets, an enormous undertaking, was proposed after I left Interior. The route was rejected by Nixon on national security grounds, but the decision was motivated, at least in part, by Nixon's dislike of Prime Minister Pierre Trudeau — or so I understood.)

My office coordinated the department's and later the administration's response to the proposal to build a 789-mile trans-Alaska oil pipeline from Prudhoe Bay on the Beaufort Sea to Valdez on Prince William Sound and the Gulf of Alaska. Hickel quite correctly avoided any day-to-day contact with the pipeline issue because of his Alaska associations. On my staff, Jack Horton, a young Wyoming rancher and geologist by training, took charge of the issue on a day-to-day basis.

I have vivid memories of my first trip to the North Slope. Horton and I flew north in a TAPS (Trans-Alaska Pipeline System) plane along the route of the proposed pipeline, gaining some sense of the rugged terrain it would have to traverse. On the vast coastal plain, north of the Arctic Circle, I visited the construction facilities and one of the oil rigs. From the platform of the latter, I looked out over the snow-covered landscape, dimly lit by the twilight sky, with snow swirling in the gusty winds. As far as I could see, there were scattered low mounds, each with a ghostly white figure standing motionless upon it — snowy owls, I was told, waiting with endless patience for lemmings to seize as prey.

With the secretary's agreement, I organized an Interior-wide task force to help deal with the complex issues presented by the pipeline project. The task force included representatives of the U.S. Fish and Wildlife Service, National Park Service, Bureau of Land Management, Bureau of Commercial Fisheries, U.S. Geological Survey, Bureau of Indian Affairs, and Federal Water Pollution Control Administration, all of which had statutory responsibilities potentially affected by the pipeline. Later, the White House broadened this effort to include agencies outside of Interior, such as the U.S. Army Corps of Engineers and the U.S. Coast Guard, and designated me as the task force head. It was a dramatic introduction for all of us to the complexities inherent in environmental management.

It deserves emphasizing that all of the environmental analyses that were to prove so critical to the ultimate resolution of the pipeline issue were initiated and organized prior to enactment of the National Environmental Policy Act of 1969 (NEPA). We were, in fact, pioneering the entire environmental impact process, and doing so with respect to what was being called the largest private construction project in history.

I don't think I had any serious doubts about the pipeline's eventual feasibility. I was determined, however, that we not simply accept the assurances of the oil companies but identify the range of potential problems and try to find solutions. Possible adverse environmental effects included oil spills in the numerous rivers crossed by the pipeline, damage to fish spawning gravel beds by the removal of gravel for construction, oil spills from tankers in Prince William Sound, hazards associated with the disposal of oil drums and other wastes, and disruption of wildlife habitat, including, in particular, caribou migration routes, among other potential consequences. Obviously, my small staff was not capable of addressing such issues, but we assigned responsibility to the appropriate agencies and oversaw their performance and results. And, of course, there were other kinds of adverse effects to be addressed, such as those on the way of life of the native peoples of Alaska. In a sense, we were determined that the federal government, in carrying out its permitting responsibility, exercise due diligence.

The pipeline consortium, whose principal members were the Atlantic Richfield Company (ARCO), Standard Oil of Ohio (SOHIO—later merged into the British Petroleum Company), and Exxon, announced their pipeline plan on February 10, 1969, and these companies' representatives came to see me about a construction permit not long after. They insisted that the permit had to be issued no later than June of that year, or a whole construction season would be lost. (The permit application was formally filed on June 10, with a request for a favorable response "by July.")5 As we began to look into the plan, we learned that a great deal of the proposed pipeline right-of-way lay across permafrost, ground that remained frozen not far below the surface throughout the year. The consortium proposed to bury the pipeline for its entire length. When the oil in the North Slope field reached the surface, its temperature was at about 150 degrees Fahrenheit; such heat would permit the oil to flow with relative ease through the pipeline. The problem was, as I described it then, that burying a hot oil pipeline in permafrost was much like laying a red-hot poker on a cake of ice. The permafrost would melt beneath and around the pipe and turn into essentially a bottomless mush, leaving the pipeline with no structural integrity in such areas. (Today, the effect on permafrost of global warming would be a significant issue, but I do not recall the question being raised in 1969.)

That August, I chaired a hearing in Fairbanks, Alaska, to explore the problem, and we required the consortium to take drillings along the entire proposed route and to map with accuracy the location of permafrost. Ultimately, the consortium was required to install the pipeline above ground wherever the route crossed permafrost. In addition, where the line crossed traditional migration routes for caribou herds, underpasses were required so as not to impede the movement of the animals.

The construction permits for the pipeline were not issued for several years, long after I had left Interior. In 1970, the Sierra Club and the Environmental Defense Fund filed a suit in federal court to require Interior to file an environmental impact analysis under NEPA, which by that time had gone into effect. There was a move in Congress to exempt the pipeline from NEPA requirements, but it was defeated, and Interior eventually did the required analysis. While there was the inevitable claim of unnecessary delay, it was basically time well spent. In an April 1970 interview, I commented: "If we had accepted the companies' assurances, we could have been in a hell of a mess. I think the companies themselves will be the major beneficiaries of the fact that we have proceeded with some care."[6] And Thornton Bradshaw, president and chief operating officer of ARCO at the time, told me privately after the pipeline was in operation that, had it been built according to the original specifications, the result would have been a disaster, environmentally and economically.

The Miami Jetport Controversy

My office also led Interior's successful opposition to the effort to build a mammoth new Miami international airport in Dade County, Florida, a development project of a quite different kind from the Alaska pipeline and one that would have significantly damaged Everglades National Park. The jetport was to be constructed about fifty miles west of Miami and would have covered almost forty square miles of wetlands, part of the Everglades drainage system. The Department of Transportation had the principal federal permitting authority, and its secretary, John Volpe, strongly favored the project. However, he had agreed with Hickel in early June to establish a joint task force derived from the two departments, with me as chairman, to study the issue and make recommendations. Boyd Gibbons led our staff effort in this case and enlisted the assistance of Luna Leopold, a senior scientist with the U.S. Geological Survey and, like his brother Starker, a son of Aldo Leopold. After a comprehensive study, Leopold was able to show quite convincingly the potentially devastating ecological consequences of the project on Everglades National Park.

Nat Reed,* at that time environmental advisor to Florida's governor, Claude Kirk Jr., had persuaded Kirk to oppose the jetport, and the two of them came to Washington to work against the project. The ultimate decision to kill the jetport was made almost entirely on environmental grounds and was announced by the White House in January 1970.

In both the Alaska pipeline and the Miami jetport issues, I developed an excellent working relationship with John Ehrlichman, Nixon's powerful assistant for domestic policy, who was interested in and supportive on both issues. In the case of the jetport, for example, while the authority to grant or deny the necessary permits belonged to the Department of Transportation, it was Ehrlichman's clout, pure and simple, that ultimately resolved the issue in Interior's favor. It was our environmental analysis that provided Ehrlichman with the scientific rationale for that decision.[7]

I also succeeded in having Interior support strong coal mine health and safety legislation on Capitol Hill despite White House opposition led by Arthur Burns, counselor to the president and, later, chairman of the Federal Reserve Board. (I recall no other pressure on this issue from the White House, including from John Ehrlichman.) The conservative mining industry was strongly opposed to the legislation, as one might expect. Even in the face of such opposition, however, Hickel was supportive of our position favoring the legislation. He had pronounced populist leanings, which later got him into serious difficulty with the White House. On another politically charged issue, we joined with the Army Corps of Engineers to condition the permits for the Marco Island housing development, off the western coast of Florida, to protect a substantial amount of wetlands, including bald eagle nesting sites and heron rookeries. Former Florida senator George Smathers lobbied me hard on behalf of the developers. In my office, John Quarles took the lead on this as well as on other dredge and fill permit issues, and he worked closely with Robert Jordan, general counsel of the Department of the Army.

The friendships I made at the Cabinet level while I was at Interior were part of the fun of my job, and they stood me in good stead over the years.

*Nathaniel P. Reed served as assistant secretary of Interior for fish and wildlife and parks (1971–1976) and has been a major force for conservation, particularly in Florida.

The under secretaries, in particular, were a fairly close-knit group. I suppose being number two provided us with a common bond! We lunched together two or three times that year, and the occasions were mostly social. The group was informally chaired by my old friend Elliot Richardson, then under secretary of the Department of State, the senior department. There were also Dave Packard at Defense (cofounder with Bill Hewlett of the Hewlett-Packard Company), Charls Walker at Treasury, Dick Van Dusen at Housing and Urban Development, Rocco Siciliano at Commerce, Jim Hodgson at Labor, Phil Campbell at Agriculture, Jack Veneman at Health, Education, and Welfare,[8] Jim Beggs at Transportation, and Dick Kleindeinst at Justice, among others.

During that year I also had the rewarding experience of getting to know and work with some of the top career people in the department, such as Bill Pecora, director of the U.S. Geological Survey, and George Hartzog Jr., director of the National Park Service. These were individuals of great ability, integrity, and dedication to the public interest. I was always unhappy when partisan politics intruded on the tenure of such people. I do not recall ever being consulted by the secretary on decisions to remove bureau heads, but on several occasions I was given the unhappy task of firing them. It has become politically fashionable in recent years to attack Washington and "bureaucrats," but this has been cheap politics that, in my view, has been largely self-defeating in that it keeps a lot of good people from entering public service. We should be promoting public service, not denigrating it.

A Meeting with Nixon

I hoped to attend a Cabinet meeting that year as Interior's representative but never did, for the simple reason that Hickel never missed a session. The only substantive meeting with President Nixon that I recall was held in the Oval Office on Christmas Eve 1970, when I presented Interior's appeals on the budget decisions. Much to his unhappiness, Hickel was sick with flu in Alaska and unable to be there. At the meeting were the president; budget director Robert Mayo; the latter's deputy, James Schlesinger; and John Ehrlichman. I was on my own. The president came to the door to greet me. When we had sat down, he said, referring to what was then called the Bureau of the Budget, "Well, I guess you agree with all of BOB's[9] decisions on your budget." "Absolutely not!" I replied. The president put his feet up on his desk and tilted back in his chair, and the meeting got under way.

The discussion centered primarily on financing for wastewater treatment and funding for open space acquisition, both big-ticket items. Since our department could appeal only a few budget items, we had selected those that were of major importance to Interior and that we hoped would also be attractive to the president. He said he was strongly in favor of moving ahead aggressively on open space funding. I urged that he approve the full $200 million authorized by the Land and Water Conservation Fund legislation for open space acquisition and, in addition, release all the unspent funds — amounting to about $138 million — for that purpose carried over from prior years. Nixon agreed and made the point that price escalation and increasing development made it important not to defer open space acquisition. I added that, if he put up only minimum amounts, he would never be able to do more than liquidate Lyndon Johnson's land acquisition commitments and would never be able to have his own open space program.

The discussion was very relaxed. Nixon said he knew something about real estate because it was about the only thing in which he could invest. No effort was made to put me on the defensive, and I felt completely at ease during the discussion. When the president decided to end the meeting, he did so, saying it was not necessary to talk about the remaining issues. He took me across the room to see the instrument the astronauts had used to pick up rocks on the moon. I wished him a merry Christmas and left.

Cabinet Visit to Japan

I also represented the Interior Department at a regular joint U.S.-Japan Cabinet meeting in Tokyo, an assignment that gave Aileen and me our first of several visits to Japan. It had once been the practice for the entire Cabinet to participate in these meetings. However, after the full U.S. Cabinet was found to be airborne over the mid-Pacific at the time of President John F. Kennedy's assassination, it was decided that thereafter only about half the department heads would participate in meetings, with the other departments represented by their under secretaries — fortunately for me.

Aside from a stop for refueling at Elmendorf Air Force Base at Fairbanks, Alaska, we flew in a converted cargo plane straight from Andrews Air Force Base, outside Washington, to Nagasaki and then bused to Kyoto, where we were supposed to rest and recuperate after the twenty-four-hour trip. After arriving at our hotel in Kyoto, we attended a lengthy dinner, replete with geishas and rounds of saki. Toward the end of dinner, our host, the Japanese ambassador to the United States, Nobuhiko Ushiba, sang a lengthy song in Japanese. (We knew Ushiba in Washington, and Aileen played tennis with his wife.) At his song's conclusion, he indicated that it was now the U.S. contingent's turn to respond in kind. I looked around the group and did not see any American who seemed up to the challenge. Secretary of Agriculture Clifford Hardin practically had his head on the table, and I could not blame him. We hadn't been to bed in more than twenty-seven hours. I looked across the table at Maury Stans, secretary of Commerce. He seemed at least semi-awake. He and I quickly agreed to try a duet, and in a moment we were singing "A Bicycle Built for Two." It was not much, but American honor was saved.

Neither country at that time had any individual at the ministerial level with responsibility for environmental matters (although that was soon to change). I met with Minister of Fisheries Hasegawa, and we signed a northern Pacific fisheries agreement. Later, there was a stiffly formal reception for our party at the Imperial Palace to introduce us to Emperor Hirohito and Empress Nagako. By that time, Secretary of State Bill Rogers and his wife, Adele, had joined us. A knife-wielding assailant had attempted, unsuccessfully, to attack Rogers at the airport, and as a result, the Japanese put tight security around all of us. One evening, free of official obligations, Aileen and I went with another American couple to a crowded restaurant. If unobtrusiveness is the norm in Japanese social behavior, this night was different. We were kept at the door while two security guards with submachine guns at the ready swept through the restaurant. When they signaled that all was clear, we proceeded to our table, preceded by two other guards with weapons in hand.

Other International Affairs

Aside from the trip to Japan, I had little contact with overseas matters, although a number of Interior's bureaus carried out international activities. The National Park Service and the Fish and Wildlife Service, for example, provided advisory services to other nations. I considered these activities to represent a useful extension of U.S. experience and influence in an area of peaceful cooperation, normally at very modest cost. The department's Office of International Affairs, headed by Myron Sutton (whose son, Mike, was on the World Wildlife Fund staff with me many years later), oversaw and coordinated these activities. Hickel took little interest in these matters, and I will have to say that I never knew any subsequent secretary who did, either. Years later, when I was out of government, I made a practice of calling on new secretaries of Interior. Each time, I would describe these various international activities and urge the secretary to invite his director of the Office of International Affairs to provide him with a briefing on Interior's role and opportunities in the world. Sadly, so far as I am aware, none of them ever did. Recently, when I raised the issue with Bruce Babbitt after he left office as Interior secretary in the Clinton administration, he blamed in large part Congress and its negative attitude toward international matters for this sorry state of affairs.

Man-in-the-Sea Program

One small program at Interior in which I took a special interest was called TEKTITE, a pioneering effort to develop and test new underwater technologies in an underwater habitat constructed in the Virgin Islands. A number of other agencies such as the Departments of Transportation and the Navy, in addition to Interior, as well as a number of universities, participated in the project, which was also known as the Man-in-the-Sea Program. I found it quite fascinating but badly in need of funds and with none of the interested agencies in charge. I succeeded in rounding up the necessary funds from the several agencies, thereby rescuing the program, and Interior then became the lead agency. It was through this program that I first met Sylvia Earle, who later served as a director of the World Wildlife Fund and senior scientist at NOAA.

National Environmental Policy Act of 1969

The National Environmental Policy Act of 1969 (NEPA) legislation, which The Conservation Foundation had helped develop when I was its president, reached the public hearing stage in 1969. The dual focus of the legislation was the creation of a Council on Environmental Quality (CEQ) in the Executive Office of the President and the requirement of an environmental impact statement (EIS) with respect to all federal actions significantly affecting the environment. Secretary Hickel, accompanied by me, presented the official administration position. Under instruction from the White House, we testified against the legislation before the Senate Interior Committee on the ground that it was unnecessary since the administration had already established the interagency Environmental Quality Council (EQC).[10] Chairman Henry "Scoop" Jackson and his staff and, I suspect, every other member of the committee were well aware that this position was directly contrary to my personal convictions. The White House had set up the EQC in response to the recommendation of the Task Force on Natural Resources and Environment, which I had chaired. However, our task force had called for a focal point for environmental policy development in the White House; the EQC was a very imperfect response to that proposal. The EQC had met several times but had proven ineffectual, as do most such interagency groups. The very nature of such an institution guarantees that it will reach decisions that offend none of its members and that generally represent the lowest common denominator of their interests. Since Hickel was determined to establish his own environmental credentials, he always represented Interior at meetings of the council. I was never informed of those meetings or their agenda and never attended a meeting. Nor did Hickel ever say a word to me about the council's activities. Of course, that was pretty much par for the course.

Subsequently, I (along with others, I am sure) was able to persuade the administration to change its position on NEPA. Aside from the self-evident inadequacy of the EQC, one of my main arguments with the White House in support of NEPA was the fact that the legislation was going to pass overwhelmingly. I was authorized to testify in favor of the legislation in the House, where Representative John Dingell of Michigan had introduced a companion bill. Dingell was chairman of the Fish and Wildlife Subcommittee of the House Committee on Merchant Marine and Fisheries and had a reputation for being difficult to deal with. He and I always got along well, however, and remain friends today, possibly because of our mutual interest in duck-hunting and also because his father had been a senior member of the House Committee on Ways and Means back in the days when I worked on its staff. Meanwhile, Senator Ed

Muskie introduced similar legislation establishing not a three-member council but an Office of Environmental Quality with a single head. There were other major differences. In any event, the Muskie bill was referred to the Senate Committee on Public Works, which in due course reported on it favorably, and the bill passed through Congress and became law. It remained on the books but was never really implemented, although it actually provided additional authorization for staffing CEQ, which proved helpful.

Trouble with Hickel

In mid-1969, my relatively high visibility led to tension with Hickel and our relationship began to deteriorate. While it was easy to blame Hickel's considerable ego, the fault was not all on one side. He was not the only one with an ego! I had not learned that a "number two" in an agency should keep a low profile, and I was doubtless a bit insensitive to the situation.

The event that sparked the unraveling of our relationship, however, was the publication of a long front-page profile of Hickel in the *Wall Street Journal.*[11] After the main headline about Hickel, which credited his "zeal for conservation effort," a subhead declared, "Leaning on a Powerful Aide." The article appeared to have been written by two or more reporters. The second half mocked Hickel for his malapropisms and general lack of polish. The first part of the article concerned the management of the department and quoted one of the assistant secretaries as saying that, when you need a decision, you go to Train. Quite understandably, Hickel blew his top. I had not seen the article, and neither I nor anybody else in my office had been interviewed for it or was aware that it was being written. No matter.

I was informed through Hickel's assistant, Carl McMurray, and assistant secretary for administration Larry Dunn that my authority in the area of the budget would be shifted elsewhere. I was given the same message two or three times in the ensuing weeks, but nothing happened. Finally, an event brought matters to a head. The Miami jetport issue had been drifting along without resolution. I kept Hickel informed of the work of our task force and the general status of the issue, but he never gave me an inkling of his own thinking and never asked me any questions. The word to me through McMurray was that the decision would be made at the secretarial level, that Hickel and Volpe would work it out — hardly very reassuring. On September 4, Walter Cronkite reported on the *CBS Evening News* that a decision had effectively been made against the jetport. I did not hear the newscast but had calls from the *Chicago Tribune*, the *Miami Herald*, and the *New York Times*. I had to say I knew nothing about a decision. Hickel was at the presidential retreat at San Clemente, California, for a Cabinet meeting, and I could only speculate that he had made some statement.

In fact, the issue continued to drift. As I look back at it all, it seems clear that while Hickel wanted to remove authority from me, he was not satisfied with the alternatives and did not want a public blowup in the department. On September 15, Stan Benjamin, a reporter for the Associated Press, came in to see me at lunchtime while I was eating a hamburger at my desk. Some of what I said to Benjamin was on the ticker the next day — that I planned to go to Florida and talk to Dade County officials and that it was time that Interior took some initiatives. In the context of my conversation with Benjamin, the statement had been unobjectionable, but on the ticker it came across as a little abrupt. The secretary sent for me in midmorning. He was with McMurray and another assistant. The news reports were read to me, and the secretary's declaration that "this shit has to stop!" pretty well captures the tone of the meeting.[12] Whatever the merits of the matter, it ended the secretary's indecision about my role in the department. Orders were issued the next day shifting the budget function to the assistant secretary for administration and the legislative function to the department's solicitor, thus stripping me of my most visible responsibilities. Nevertheless, much of the day-to-day business of the department continued to flow through my office.

To be fair to Hickel, I do not recall his ever being supportive of the jetport or in any way antagonistic toward the hard line against it developed in my office. About six weeks after the meeting just described and after Volpe issued a press release that was positive about the jetport, I called Hickel, who was in the Virgin Islands at the time, to report on Volpe's statement. Hickel authorized me to say that he was "damned unhappy" and that "unless additional data has been developed which has not been presented to us, we have as much concern as we ever have [had]."[13]

Plainly, Hickel's unhappiness with me was not over the substance of my position on the jetport — nor over any other position, for that matter — but over the fact of my being out front publicly on the issue. While I had not shirked media opportunities that came my way, the fact was that the jetport issue had considerable public interest, and it would have been unthinkable to allow the pro-jetport interests to monopolize the media. At the same time, Hickel had little or no interest in discussing such matters with the press. Given this situation, it's remarkable that our relationship remained as amicable as it did for so long.

Ehrlichman's Involvement

The next afternoon, September 17, I went to the White House for a meeting with John Ehrlichman at his office in the West Wing and told him the whole sorry story.[14] We talked for about forty-five minutes. I saw no alternative but to leave Interior, I said, but I did not want simply to resign because that could be politically damaging to the president. I mentioned the interagency Environmental Quality Council and Hickel's failure to communicate with me in any way about it. This led Ehrlichman to mention his own lack of confidence in the way Lee DuBridge, director of the Office of Science and Technology in the Executive Office of the President, was running the council.

Ehrlichman suggested I "come over and run the council." I said I could not do that because it would in effect make me secretary to a group of Cabinet members. However, I said, I had an idea: Congress was about to pass legislation establishing a statutory Council on Environmental Quality; make me chairman of the new council and also executive director of the old interagency group. (I have no recollection of the latter part of my suggestion, but my diary of that period clearly so states.) Ehrlichman thought the idea was plausible and suggested that I leave the matter to him to run down.

As the autumn went by, I simply sat tight in the Department of the Interior. Despite the official transfer of the legislative function, I continued to handle legislative matters pretty much as before. The press occasionally carried reports of strained relations between Hickel and me. I never commented on these, and my staff was instructed to keep off the subject with the press. I was determined to avoid a break and believed that any public showdown or confrontation — while temporarily gratifying to me — would weaken me personally by making me a problem in the administration. If my suggestion to the White House were to work out, it would be important to leave the department on as friendly a note as possible.

White House Invitation

On December 19, there was a meeting at the White House of all Cabinet members, under secretaries, assistant secretaries, and so on. Each department head gave a five-minute year-end report. We met at 3:00 P.M. in the East Room, with Vice President Spiro Agnew introducing each of us in turn. The president sat in the center and observed the proceedings. Since Hickel was in Alaska, I gave the report for the Department of the Interior, which I had written myself. Naturally, I thought it was good!

I noted that Interior's year had opened with the Santa Barbara oil spill and that the latter had underlined how critical it was that the development of resources go hand in hand with the protection of environmental quality. I said that we had pursued these twin goals in the case of the Alaska oil pipeline and the proposed Miami jetport. I called attention to the coastal zone management legislation proposed by Interior, and I referred to Hickel's call for a "massive effort to clean up the nation's waters *now*." I said that Interior's traditional emphasis on parks and recreation had shifted to urban areas, and I cited the new Gateway National Recreation Area, serving New York City and northern New Jersey. (New York's mayor, John V. Lindsay, an old friend, had visited me to promote the concept.) I referred to coal mine health and safety issues, tighter regulations governing leasing and drilling on the Outer Continental Shelf, and the settlement of land claims of Alaskan natives, among other accomplishments. I said there was a "new look" at Interior, citing the Man-in-the-Sea Program and our work on lunar mapping for the Apollo program. In all of this, I should add, I made numerous references to Hickel's leadership.

Our families had been invited to join us after the meeting, and we moved on to a crowded reception in the State Dining Room. There was a mob around the president, and our children Bowdy and Errol both met him twice. Nixon executed one of his typical crowd-meeting gestures, throwing both his arms into the air, and succeeded in hitting Bowdy on the end of his nose. A bit later, when the crowd around the president had thinned, Aileen and I went back to speak with him. He flabbergasted me by saying that someone had to take charge of environmental matters for all the executive agencies and that I was the man for the job! He had talked to Ehrlichman about the matter, he said. I don't remember saying much more than "Yes, sir!"

On January 1, 1970, the president signed into law the National Environmental Policy Act of 1969 (NEPA), which mandated the environmental impact analysis process in federal decision making and established the Council on Environmental Quality (CEQ). Aileen and I were in Hobe Sound, Florida, at the time. Ned Kenworthy of the *New York Times* reported that I was to be chairman. I called Ehrlichman at San Clemente, and he told me that he was to see Hickel immediately on his return on January 5. Up to this point, there had been no discussion whatsoever with the secretary about any of this.

I think it was on January 8 that Ehrlichman finally saw Hickel. I received no report on that meeting, so I called John, and he filled me in on the conversation. He said he had told the secretary that the president wanted me on the CEQ; that Hickel had replied he did not want to lose me; that he, Ehrlichman, had said it was his impression that I would not stay in the department for long anyway; and that Hickel had expressed surprise over the latter suggestion. I asked Ehrlichman whether he had told Hickel that I was to be chairman of the CEQ or simply a member. He replied that he had not specified, and he went on to say that this aspect of the CEQ arrangement was not certain. Anything less than the chairmanship would be a demotion, I responded, and, should that turn out to be the offer, I might have to "rethink my entire situation." Ehrlichman said he would get back to me. Later, I worried that I had not made myself entirely clear. I called John Whitaker, Cabinet secretary (later Ehrlichman's assistant on the Domestic Council's staff for natural resources, energy, and the environment). I told him flat out that I could not accept anything less than the chairmanship. I said I knew that sounded as if I were trying to use leverage on the president and that I did not intend it that way. I simply could not leave my present job — particularly under the circumstances, which had become fairly widely known outside the department — for a demotion.

Several days later, Whitaker called to say that I was to be chairman and that the president had signed off on the matter. The announcement was made at the White House on January 29, the anniversary of my nomination as under secretary of Interior.

Departure from Interior

Before the announcement, I had finally had a long, very friendly, very frank talk with Hickel. It was as if, with my departure a reality, the chemistry between us had radically changed. He was worried about running the department. I encouraged him to develop a truly competent, professional staff to assist him if he wanted to run the department himself. He had made a start in that direction. With my concurrence, John Quarles had already left my office to head the secretary's program staff, and Buff Bohlen was to become an assistant in his office after I left. Hickel himself finally came to odds with the White House—where he had never been popular—and was fired the day before Thanksgiving 1970. (The event that led to Hickel's firing was the so-called Kent State massacre, in which four students protesting the Vietnam War were shot to death by members of the Ohio National Guard. The White House issued a statement dismissive of the student protest, and the next morning Hickel wrote a letter to the president declaring, in part, that the dissent of youth should be heard. Hickel evidently leaked the letter to a reporter within twenty minutes of sending it. The story was a worldwide sensation and Hickel an instant hero. The president waited until after the midterm elections and picked the slow news day of the Thanksgiving holiday to fire him.) Whatever his faults might have been, from the outset of his time as secretary of Interior, Hickel did his best to burnish his environmental credentials. In fact, I do not recall ever having a disagreement with him on an environmental issue—or really, for that matter, on almost anything else of a programmatic nature.

It had been an exciting year as under secretary, and I had had the satisfaction of being given major responsibilities in the department and carrying them out with, I believed, considerable success. Of key importance to those activities and such achievements as my office had was my own immediate staff—Boyd Gibbons, Buff Bohlen, John Quarles, Jack Horton, and Marian O'Connell, my longtime secretary. Frank Bracken was also very much part of the team. They were a wonderful group of talented, highly motivated people. I had developed positive relationships, and in many cases strong personal friendships, with key individuals in other agencies, in the White House, and on Capitol Hill, relationships that would prove of immense value and pleasure in the years immediately ahead.

Of great importance was that I had established very positive and easy working relationships with members of the press, many of which continued into the years that immediately followed.[15] I kept myself accessible to members of the press and tried to be open and straightforward in our contacts. I do not think I was ever treated unfairly by any of them.

Despite all these positive factors, the fact remained that my position at Interior had become increasingly frustrating as my relationship with Hickel deteriorated. I left the department with considerable sadness, as I had enjoyed dealing with the wide-ranging functions of Interior. However, I also felt a strong sense of relief at getting out of what had become an impossible situation. It was time to move on.

And what I was moving on to seemed promising indeed. I must admit that the whole concept of NEPA, which was passed by Congress with broad sponsorship and bipartisan support, was enormously satisfying to me personally. Its creation of a focal point for White House environmental policy, the Council on Environmental Quality, of which I now would be a part, was itself the fruition—at least, I looked at it that way—of the recommendation we on the Task Force on Natural Resources and Environment had put forward in early December 1968 for the incoming president.

Chapter 7

The CEQ Years

THE COUNCIL on Environmental Quality (CEQ) came into existence just as the environment as an issue was bursting full force onto the public stage. The National Environmental Policy Act of 1969 (NEPA), which created CEQ, declared it now to be national policy to "prevent or eliminate damage to the environment and stimulate the health and welfare of man."[1] The passage of the act brought about a historic change in the priority given to environmental considerations in federal decision making, and CEQ became the focal point for an extraordinary array of environmental initiatives, both domestic and international.

President Richard M. Nixon seized on the issue of the environment as a priority of his administration and he was determined to get as much public credit for doing so as he could. He chose to sign NEPA into law on January 1, 1970, while at the presidential retreat at San Clemente, California, as his first official act of the new decade, a symbolic move but one that presaged the explosion of environmental initiatives that followed. Three weeks later, he devoted the largest single portion of his State of the Union Address to the environment, once again taking his opponents by surprise. In the address, he mentioned not only air and water pollution problems but also broader issues of quality of life brought about by population growth and demographic shifts. He declared, in part:

> The great question of the seventies is, shall we surrender to our surroundings, or should we make our peace with nature and begin to make reparations for the damage we have done to our air, our land, and our water? . . .

77

Clean air, clean water, open spaces—these should once again be the birthright of every American. If we act now—they can be.

We still think of air as free. But clean air is not, and neither is clean water. The price tag on pollution control is high. Through our years of past carelessness we incurred a debt to nature, and now that debt is being called.

The program I shall propose to Congress will be the most comprehensive and costly program in this field ever in the nation's history.[2]

After referring to the country's rapid population growth combined with a substantial decline in its rural population, he continued:

The violent and decayed central cities of our great metropolitan complexes are the most conspicuous area of failure in American life.

I propose that before these problems become insoluble, the nation develop a national growth policy. Our purpose will be to find those means by which Federal, state and local government can influence the course of urban settlement and growth so as positively to affect the quality of American life.[3]

These were remarkable words to hear from a president of the United States in 1970 and his call for a national growth policy would be almost as remarkable today, more than thirty years later. In any case, on February 10, Nixon followed his State of the Union Address with his Special Message to the Congress on Environmental Quality, outlining an ambitious thirty-seven-point program including twenty-three major legislative proposals. The environmental cause, he declared, was "as fundamental as life itself."

Nixon's Environmental Politics

While I doubt that this sort of rhetoric reflected Nixon himself, the message itself was no flash in the pan. A year later he again gave emphasis to the environment in his State of the Union Address,[4] declaring, "[Our] third great goal is to continue the effort so dramatically begun last year: to restore and enhance our natural environment." This was again followed by an extensive message on the environment,[5] this time drafted in detail by me and my colleagues at CEQ.

The emphasis the White House was giving to the environment was led by John Ehrlichman and his staff and cleared by Ehrlichman with the president. Initially, and before the advent of CEQ, Ehrlichman had set up a working group in the White House, first under the direction of Egil "Bud" Krogh and later under John Whitaker, to put together a package of environmental initiatives for the president to submit to Congress early in 1970.* The working group was made up mostly of younger staffers from the various agencies, such as Christopher DeMuth and Roger Strelow from the Department of Health, Education, and Welfare (HEW) and Alvin Alm from the Bureau of the Budget (Alm was soon to be chief of staff at CEQ). I had no involvement with the group whatsoever, with its recommendations, or with the message transmitting those recommendation to Congress.

There can be little doubt that Ehrlichman was responding to clear signals from Nixon and that Nixon was determined to get out in front of the Democratic Congress on the issue. I have no direct knowledge of these signals, but one can assume with confidence that any such major policy commitment, sustained over several years, would have had the full agreement of the president.

There is no evidence of which I am aware that Nixon had any real personal interest in environmental matters. I certainly never heard him express any. His reaction to these issues was that of a highly political animal. He read the polls and he had to be aware that concern for the environment was rapidly rising among the American people. His political instincts told him that he and the Republican Party could not afford to be seen as anti-environment.[6] Moreover, with the 1972 presidential election rapidly approaching, it was understandable that he would want to seize the environmental high ground from the Democrats, particularly from one of the leading contenders for the Democratic nomination, Maine's senator, Ed Muskie. In this context, it is equally understandable that once the Muskie candidacy was destroyed and the 1972 election was won overwhelmingly, Nixon's interest in the environment would begin to wane.

In the course of writing *President Nixon: Alone in the White House*,

---

*When the Domestic Council was established later that year with Ehrlichman as director, Whitaker was deputy director for natural resources, energy, and the environment, a large and complicated portfolio, which he handled extremely well. He had a personal commitment to the environment, and I know he was an advocate for our cause within the limits of his position. I attribute much of what we accomplished to his support. We were in almost daily contact with him then. In 1972, Whitaker became under secretary of Interior and Richard Fairbanks took his place on the Domestic Council staff.

Richard Reeves had access to both the Nixon tapes and the many memos, often written on yellow legal pads, that Nixon apparently liked to compose while in seclusion. In March 1970, Nixon dictated a memo about organizing his own time, which he clearly recognized as a valuable commodity. He listed various domestic issues in which he wanted to be kept directly involved, such as crime, school integration, and the economy, but he consciously excluded the environment from that group. "I consider this [the environment] to be important," he said, "[but] I don't want to be bothered with the details. Just see that the job is done."[7]

My interaction with Nixon on the substance of environmental issues was indeed limited, both at CEQ and later at the Environmental Protection Agency (EPA). The very fact that Nixon delegated almost complete responsibility for dealing with environmental policy to his staff may well explain how we were able to put together such a comprehensive and far-reaching set of environmental initiatives over the ensuing few years. Moreover, there is no question of Nixon's success in upstaging the Democrats on the issue. Of the 1971 State of the Union Address, a year later, Reeves says: "Nixon had indeed stolen some of the Democrats' clothes, particularly on health care and the environment."[8]

Council Formation

My two fellow members of CEQ and I were nominated by the president on January 29, 1970, and confirmed by the United States Senate on February 6 after a public hearing the day before by the Senate Interior Committee. At Chairman Jackson's invitation, sitting with the committee on that occasion were Senator Warren Magnuson, chairman of the Senate Commerce Committee, and Senator Ed Muskie of the Senate Public Works Committee, the Democratic leader on pollution matters. In my remarks to the committee, I indulged in a bit of high-flown rhetoric, but the words still ring true to me more than thirty years later:

> Public anxiety over environmental deterioration has reached a high level — and rightly so. Yet the problems with which we must deal have been years in the making. They will not be cured overnight. It is important that the public, as well as government agencies, understand that the road ahead will be long and hard. Even were we to eliminate all forms of environmental pollution, we would still not have guaranteed a high quality environment. Environmental

quality is a far more complex, more subtle objective. It involves the development of new attitudes and new values. Thus, while we must make the investments and achieve the technological breakthroughs necessary to clean up our environment, we must at the same time develop a new perception of man's relation to nature, learn to control our numbers, develop effective land-use policies, and find new measures of public and private success which emphasize quality rather than mere quantity.[9]

In addition to myself as chairman, a position I was to hold from that February until September 1973,[10] the council consisted of Gordon Mac-Donald, a gifted geophysicist and member of the National Academy of Sciences, and Robert Cahn, a Pulitzer Prize–winning newspaperman with the *Christian Science Monitor* who had strong credentials with the environmental community.* MacDonald provided us with important linkages to the scientific and academic communities and made major contributions on international environmental matters. Cahn took the lead in putting together CEQ's annual report to Congress, mandated by NEPA. Following our confirmation by the Senate, we were sworn in by Chief Justice Warren Burger in his chambers at the Supreme Court.

Getting Under Way

Nixon introduced the new council to the press on January 29 at the White House in what is now called the Roosevelt Room, next to the Oval Office.[11] I would be his "chief officer in the effort to protect and restore the American environment," he said, and he declared that CEQ would act as the environmental conscience of the nation. That description, of course, implied that CEQ would be occupying a sort of bully pulpit— hardly practical, given the fact that CEQ was part of the Executive Office of the President.

Implicit in our situation at CEQ was an understanding that our recommendations to the president were for him (and his staff) only. Likewise, if we had disagreements with White House policy, we would not normally go public with them. Nor would we go public with recommendations for specific legislative or executive actions that had not already

---

*Both Cahn and MacDonald resigned from the council at the close of 1972 and their places were taken by Beatrice Willard and John Busterud. Bob Cahn's wife, Pat, became my public affairs assistant at EPA.

been given a general go-ahead by the White House. To make certain we had no misunderstandings on this score, John Ehrlichman joined us in John Whitaker's office immediately after our introduction to the press and described our role as he saw it—to advise and assist the president and not take an independent line.[12] We agreed, and I believe we quite faithfully adhered to this modus operandi, although there were those on the outside, including members of the press, who never understood or accepted these self-imposed strictures on our behavior. Nor, to be honest, did we hesitate to diverge from those rules on occasion.

My own natural style was probably ideally suited to the method of operation I have described. I had no illusions of being a charismatic leader or evangelist for the environmental cause. At the same time, I would not have given up a federal judgeship and the security and prestige that went with it for an environmental career and all the uncertainties involved unless I felt deeply about the significance of the environmental issue to our future. I think I sensed from the outset of my time at The Conservation Foundation, and then at the Department of the Interior, that I was in the forefront of a revolution in the way government and society as a whole perceived the environment and made decisions affecting it. That sense came into full bloom at CEQ. However, I have to admit to being, at best, a quiet revolutionary. In the aftermath of the 1960s, at a time when the public perception of an environmentalist was often that of a longhaired individual in blue jeans, I normally wore a conservative business suit, often a gray pinstripe, and had had a fairly recent haircut. In retrospect, I suspect that members of Congress, members of the business community, and the heads of other government agencies, many of whom were uneasy with environmental issues, were probably reassured and perhaps at times a bit disarmed by my conservative demeanor. Moreover, a former judge (and a United States Tax Court judge at that), one who was at home in the Washington, D.C., community, was hardly the stuff of which revolutions normally were made. Of course, I suspect that the inevitable downside of all that was that some in the environmental community never really accepted me as one of their own.

CEQ met first in my office at Interior, which I had not yet vacated. Our chief of staff was Al Alm, most recently a senior examiner at the Bureau of the Budget for water pollution and water resources programs. Boyd Gibbons, who had been my deputy at Interior, joined CEQ as council secretary.* Al explained to us that there were traditionally two modes of operation among the various councils in the federal government: the strong chairman mode and the weak chairman mode. Naturally, I opted for the former. My associates agreed, and we adopted the resolutions necessary to that approach, such as those dealing with personnel management and other administrative functions. As a result, while we three members frequently met informally and worked in close proximity to one another, I do not recall that we ever again met formally as a council. The staff that Alm would lead reached fifty-four at its peak. He was an old government hand and proved to be a master in dealing with the intricacies of the issues and, even more important, with the competing bureaucracies involved. He was one of the most skilled public servants I have ever known.[†]

The president had announced at our introduction to the press that the new CEQ would have offices in the Executive Office Building (EOB), "just like the Council of Economic Advisors." H. R. (Bob) Haldeman, Nixon's chief of staff, disabused me of this prospect the next day. There was simply no room at EOB. However, he assured me of excellent quarters, and, after a few weeks in temporary quarters, we ended up at 722 Jackson Place, half a block from the White House and looking out on Lafayette Square. It was a fine location; it did not have the security complications of EOB, and it gave us a sense and the appearance of at least some independence from the taut control of the White House.

Earlier, as First Lady, Jacqueline Kennedy had taken a keen interest in preserving and restoring the historic quality of Lafayette Square and its immediate surroundings. She secured the services of noted architect John

---

*Gibbons left CEQ in early 1973 to join the staff of the nonprofit Resources for the Future, where he wrote a widely acclaimed book on land use, *Wye Island* (Baltimore: published for Resources for the Future by Johns Hopkins University Press, 1977). During 1979–1991, he was on the senior editorial staff of *National Geographic*. In 1991, he became director of the California Department of Fish and Game. Since 1997, he has been president of the Johnson Foundation (Wingspread Conference Center, Racine, Wisconsin).

[†]Al Alm left CEQ early in 1973 to become EPA assistant administrator for planning and management, a position he held throughout my time as administrator of EPA (1973–1977). In the Carter administration he became an under secretary of the new Department of Energy. After a stint of teaching at Harvard, he returned to EPA as deputy administrator during Ruckelshaus's second term as administrator. Following the Reagan administration, he left government and became a senior vice president of the Science Applications International Corporation in McLean, Virginia. He died suddenly in 2000.

Warnecke to preserve at least the facades of most of the old houses, largely Victorian, along Jackson Place on the west side of the square. CEQ's location was in a section that had been torn down and replaced with three Federal style three-story brick buildings that connected with one another. (I have recently concluded that 722 Jackson Place is in the exact location of the old 22 Jackson Place, occupied by the conservation-minded Theodore Roosevelt and his family in 1902–1903 as both home and office while the White House was being extensively renovated.)[13]

According to a newspaper report, CEQ had "Colonial chandeliers and Williamsburg reproduction wallpaper to inspire thoughts of clean living, but no antiques."[14] In my own office, I had taken on loan from the Smithsonian Institution several splendid George Catlin paintings of American Indian scenes, including buffalo hunting on the Great Plains. Behind my desk hung an oil painting, owned by me, of an orangutan by the Swiss artist Hug. The painting made front pages all over the country when a photographer from the Associated Press took a picture of me standing in front of it during a press conference. I sometimes referred to the painting as being of "our first chairman." My office ran along the front of the building, and from my windows I could see the White House off to the right and St. John's Church, where I had been baptized and married and later served as a vestryman and senior warden, diagonally across the square on the north side. Jackie Kennedy had interested Bunny Mellon, wife of philanthropist Paul Mellon, in helping to restore the park landscape, and it now had broad brick walks with benches, on which I would give several press interviews in the years ahead.

One of the most unsettling times I spent with Nixon was just as I became CEQ chairman. I had been in the job just one day when I flew on Air Force One to Chicago with the president, Bob Haldeman, John Ehrlichman, and others for a meeting at the Field Museum with the governors of the five Great Lakes states to discuss the environment. While I was still at Interior, the White House had been drafting amendments to the Clean Air Act about which I knew absolutely nothing. I had not been involved in their development and had not been briefed on them. Nor had anyone told me the agenda at the Field Museum. I suspected I was invited along largely as window dressing. I quickly learned otherwise.

There we were in the grand boardroom of the museum: on one side of the large oval table were seated the president and his staff; on the other side, facing them, were the five governors; Laurance Rockefeller, in his capacity as chairman of the Citizens' Advisory Committee on Environmental Quality; and me. After a few introductory remarks, the president introduced me as the new head of environmental matters at the White House and then asked me to summarize the new Clean Air Act amendments for the governors. Thank God for John Ehrlichman. He knew I knew nothing of the matter and stepped in to fill the breach. I had been totally blindsided — probably not intentionally at all, I later concluded, but as a result of a dropped ball. In any case, I was mortally embarrassed. When I walked out with the president, I tried to interest him in the sculptures we passed, created by Carl Akeley, who had helped arrange Theodore Roosevelt's 1910 safari in East Africa, but Nixon would have none of it.

The next morning I helicoptered with Nixon to Hammond, Indiana, near the Illinois border, where a tertiary sewage treatment plant had been built. In the plant, we gathered around the top of a large tank full of clear water — treated effluent. An employee on the far side of the tank held a long pole with a glass set in the end. He dipped the glass down into the pool and then swung the full glass over to Nixon. The president was urged to have a drink but shook his head politely and said, "I am sorry, but I never take a drink before lunch."

Traveling back to Chicago on the helicopter, Nixon and I sat knee-to-knee facing each other. Haldeman sat on a bench to one side, and Ehrlichman sat toward the back of the small craft. Nixon was quiet, tired, and seemingly dispirited. As he stared glumly down into the backyards of Chicago's slums, he shook his head slowly and said: "Lyndon Johnson will be remembered for [saving] the redwoods. I will be remembered for sewage treatment plants." I thought later: you should be so lucky!

As if that Chicago trip were not sufficiently traumatic, at about the same time, I managed to inject myself uninvited into the supersonic transport (SST) issue. The president had asked Congress to appropriate funds for the development of two prototype commercial SSTs, and at the time the British and French were also seeking landing rights for the Concorde. Cahn, MacDonald, and I were invited to a press breakfast at the National Press Club. Alan L. Otten of the *Wall Street Journal* asked my opinion of the SST. I said I thought it had serious environmental problems that had not been solved. On the national Sunday talk show *Face the Nation,* I warned of greatly increased (by two to five times) airport noise, excessive use of energy, as well as climate warming and ozone layer depletion from the operation of a fleet of SSTs. I testified on the subject before the Joint Committee on the Economic Report on May 12. All of these concerns I set out later in a memorandum to Nixon, making clear that I had stated them in public testimony and that CEQ had conveyed them directly to the Department of Transportation.[15] The White House was considerably annoyed and I can understand the reaction. My public pronouncements on the SST do seem in retrospect to have violated CEQ's own rules of behavior as outlined here earlier. On the other hand, the whole affair certainly dispelled any concern that we were just presidential rubber stamps.[16]

Pollution Controls and the CEQ

While air and water pollution were among the hottest environmental issues of the time, CEQ had little to do with them initially. Both the Clean Air Act Amendments of 1970 and the Federal Water Pollution Control Act Amendments of 1972 were originally proposed by the president before CEQ came into existence. However, we would become involved in many related matters.

The Clean Air Act amendments mandated national ambient air standards and, as they finally passed the Congress, a stringent schedule for meeting auto emission standards. I was to deal with the latter when I became EPA administrator (as did William Ruckelshaus in 1972). The courts also added the requirement that there could be no significant deterioration in ambient air quality in any state where air quality was already better than federal standards, a requirement that would result in something of a crisis for me during the Ford administration.

While Nixon was not very happy with the clean air legislation as it passed in Congress, he signed the act on December 31, 1970, before invited members of Congress and the administration involved in the legislation—with one exception: Ed Muskie, who had not been invited. When I was later asked by the press whether omission from the ceremony of the legislation's principal architect on Capitol Hill was not unusual, I had to agree that it was. I was not privy in any way to the exclusion of Muskie. It came across as an act of pettiness on the part of Nixon and probably served to highlight the role of Muskie — the exact opposite of what Nixon must have intended.

Legislation involving the Federal Water Pollution Control Act amendments dragged on for the better part of two years. Without going into all the ramifications, suffice it to say that the bill that finally passed in Congress contained vastly more money for municipal sewage treatment plants than Nixon had proposed. The new EPA head, William Ruckelshaus, chairman Paul McCracken of the Council of Economic Advisors, and I had all testified against the Senate bill, largely on budgetary grounds, before the House Public Works Committee.[17]

I supported the administration's concept of requiring the "best practicable" technology by 1976 but testified against the committee's proposed goal of "no discharge or best available technology" by 1981 on the ground that it "would either be very costly compared to the benefits or ineffective." I added: "If we insist that the public pay—through . . . increased prices for manufactured goods—many billion dollars for water cleanup beyond the point where added benefits can be demonstrated . . . we will hurt the environmental cause." Nixon ended up vetoing the legislation on October 17, 1972, largely on the ground of cost, despite contrary advice from Ruckelshaus. His veto was subsequently overridden overwhelmingly by both houses of Congress.[18]

Refuse Act of 1899 Strategy

During the period 1970–1972, while congressional consideration of the water pollution legislation dragged on, a sudden breakthrough occurred that put the clean water initiative back in the hands of the president. The Refuse Act of 1899, which prohibited the deposit of refuse into the navigable waters of the United States, had been on the books since the days of President William McKinley. Following a Supreme Court decision that held "refuse" to include liquid wastes, the Department of the Interior in 1970 brought an action under the act against the Florida Power and Light Company for discharging wastes into navigable waters. All of a sudden, a door was opened to using executive authority under existing law to put into place a comprehensive permit program governing the discharge of wastes into the nation's waters, without waiting for Congress to take action on the pending water pollution legislation.

I announced my support for using the Refuse Act and, in early December 1970, convened a meeting at CEQ of all the interested agencies to explore the matter further. Bill Ruckelshaus, who would run the program at EPA, sat next to me. We met in CEQ's high-ceilinged conference room, which doubled as a reference library. Shelves of books, most of which I had personally selected, reached the ceiling. The meeting developed a strong consensus in favor of proceeding with a permit plan under the Refuse Act. On December 23, 1970, on behalf of the president, I announced the new program before the White House press. I was accompanied by Ruckelshaus and Robert Jordan, general counsel of the Department of the Army, which had a major interest in the program through the U.S. Army Corps of Engineers. This executive initiative helped goad Congress into action, and the Federal Water Pollution Control Act Amendments of 1972, as finally enacted, embodied much of the permit program.[19]

Seizing the Environmental Initiative

The president had wasted no time in assigning responsibilities directly to CEQ. In his environmental message to Congress of February 10, 1970, he had directed attention to the need for recycling of natural resources and asked the council to develop recommendations for a "bounty payment or other system to promote the prompt scrapping of all junk automobiles." I was also directed as chairman to work with other federal agencies, industries, and consumer groups to develop incentives and other proposals to submit to Congress "to encourage the re-use, re-cycling or easier disposal of other commonly used goods."[20]

The president appointed me a member of the new Property Review Board, which was charged with identifying surplus federal properties that could be converted to parks and recreation areas, an understandably popular program. In addition to working with the board itself, much of the time under the chairmanship of Anne Armstrong, a counselor to the president and later ambassador to Great Britain, and subsequently under the chairmanship of Donald Rumsfeld, now in his second tour as secretary of Defense, I also officiated at ceremonies turning over properties to state and local governments. Among these, I represented the federal government in turning over an old coastal artillery site in Narragansett Bay on the southern tip of Acushnet Island, Rhode Island (the site of Jamestown, where I was born), for dedication as a state park.

The president also established in his 1970 environmental message a goal of producing an "unconventionally powered virtually pollution-free automobile within five years," and he ordered the start of an extensive federal research and development program for that purpose "under the general direction" of CEQ. We appointed an Advisory Committee on Alternative Automotive Power Systems, made up of private sector scientists and engineers. However, with the advent of EPA, the latter took over the program before transferring it, in 1975, to the Federal Energy Administration.

A few days before presenting his environmental message to Congress, the president issued an executive order, which CEQ had drafted, directing all federal agencies and their facilities to be in compliance by December 31, 1972,[21] with the air and water quality standards established by the Clean Air Act and the Federal Water Pollution Control Act. Such compliance was notoriously lacking, particularly on the part of defense agencies. I briefed the White House press on February 3 on the extent of the problem and on the details of the president's order.[22] The president directed CEQ to "maintain continuing review of the implementation" of the order and to report to him thereon from time to time. Almost three decades later, the task is still ongoing. In 2003, for example, the Department of Defense was urging legislation to exempt military facilities in the United States from much environmental regulation.

The actions I have just outlined tended to require little study and could be put forward quickly at the beginning of 1970 as part of Nixon's effort to seize the environmental initiative. CEQ continued to be responsible for coordinating the development of new environmental policy initiatives, both domestically and internationally, and often was responsible for the initiatives themselves, as in the case of the Toxic Substances Control Act (TOSCA). The latter empowered EPA to restrict or ban the use or marketing of chemicals if necessary to the protection of health or the environment and to require the testing of certain new chemicals before they could be marketed. In addition to TOSCA, there were new legislative proposals to regulate pesticides, fungicides, and herbicides; to provide controls on surface mining and ocean dumping; to protect marine mammals; to protect water and air quality; to manage solid waste; to ensure safe drinking water; to provide noise controls; to institute a tax on sulfur oxide emissions; to inaugurate a national land-use policy; and much else. Many other initiatives were of an executive nature, such as a ban on the use of DDT on federal lands. Progress was not made overnight. For example, it was not until late in 1976 that TOSCA finally became law.

The Environmental Impact Statement Process

The same sweeping executive order that required the cleanup of air and water pollution at federal facilities gave CEQ, among other authorities, the responsibility for monitoring and overseeing agency compliance with the environmental impact statement (EIS) process mandated by NEPA. That process went to the heart of CEQ's authority, and we gave particular attention to the drafting of that portion of the executive order. The EIS process became enormously influential in federal decision making and has been the subject of extensive legal and scholarly attention. NEPA required, with respect to "major Federal actions significantly affecting the quality of the human environment," a detailed statement on the environmental effects of such proposed actions as well as on alternatives to them. The initial reaction to this requirement within the executive branch was, to say the least, confused. A number of agencies, such as the Federal Highway Administration, did their best to avoid compliance. Others argued that the environmental impact analysis should be conducted not by the agency in question but by CEQ itself. We maintained successfully and, after all, with the support of the statute, that the environmental impact analysis process had to be an *integral* part of the agencies' *own* decision making and not something imposed from outside.

A number of congressional committees asked CEQ to testify with respect to particular environmental impact analyses. We would have been swamped had we tried to do so and we managed to refuse such requests. We designed guidelines for compliance under the executive order and were successful over time in securing the conformance of the various federal agencies with the law. Citizen suits, authorized by NEPA and brought by public interest law firms, were also influential in reaching this result. Thus, the Natural Resources Defense Council (NRDC) sued the U.S. Agency for International Development (USAID) and succeeded in getting the courts to reject USAID's argument that NEPA and the requirement for environmental impact statements did not apply to its projects abroad.

Securing compliance was a continuing process requiring day-by-day supervision on our part, including meetings with thirty or more operating agencies, interested members of the public, and the congressional committees with jurisdiction over the agencies, the functions involved, or both. Using as a model the practice at the Bureau of the Budget, we established a system of CEQ "examiners" for each program area who monitored the EIS performance of the agencies concerned and interacted with the responsible staff members of those agencies. The CEQ examiners had no hesitancy in criticizing and making suggestions as to agency performance. Thus, over time we achieved not only more responsible consideration of adverse environmental effects but also a new level of transparency in government decision making. Our requirement that a draft EIS be made fully available to the public well in advance of final action represented a significant opening of the processes of government to private citizens and citizen organizations.

The strength of the EIS process mandated by NEPA took the White House, as well as the administration generally, by surprise. One cannot help but speculate as to whether Nixon would have signed the legislation had he been aware of the extent of its influence on decision making by federal agencies. My guess is that he still would have signed, given his determination at that particular time to be viewed as strongly pro-environment.

The whole EIS process and CEQ's role in that process were extraordinary, even though it all may sound matter-of-fact, even commonplace, as I recount it today. However, it really did represent a radical change in the way the government did business. The very idea that one small agency of the government could have the authority, by legislation and with the president's backing, to monitor, review, and comment on the projects of all other executive agencies was almost inconceivable. Yet that was exactly the authority CEQ had. It is not surprising that initially we ran into a great deal of resistance, and it is a remarkable tribute to the skill and diplomacy of the CEQ staff that they were able to deal with and ultimately overcome that resistance with a minimum of open conflict. CEQ had no real veto power over projects. However, I think it was pretty widely accepted that, if we strongly opposed a project, the White House would support us.

Of course, bureaucracy being what it is, environmental impact statements could become so lengthy and time-consuming that the process could seem almost ludicrous. The press was happy to point this out, of course. In 1976, a press report noted: "A press conference questioner asked the tax court judge-turned-environmentalist whether parents-to-be should have to file his agency's infamous environmental impact statements. His reply: 'I don't know if they'd be able to complete it in the requisite nine months.'"[23]

A highly publicized project known as the Tocks Island Dam helped establish the potency of the EIS process and CEQ's pivotal role in it. The project was an Army Corps of Engineers proposal for damming of the Delaware River at the Delaware Water Gap. Several hundred million dollars and four states were involved. The proposed dam would create a thirty-seven-mile-long lake, which would receive runoff from the agricultural areas upstream. In April 1971, CEQ returned the Corps' EIS, noting that it had inadequately addressed the issue of rapid eutrophication of the lake as a result of nutrient loading from agricultural wastes. These nutrients, when dissolved in the lake water, would lead to a dense growth of algae and other plant life, which would in turn decay, depleting the water of oxygen. The Corps replied simply with assurances that the states concerned would take measures to control the agricultural runoff. As we know today, the control of agricultural runoff is a highly complex matter involving political, economic, scientific, and technological issues, and the Corps' mere assurances were inadequate for the problem.

A year and a half later, the *New York Times* declared, in a lead editorial, "A condition demanded by the Council on Environmental Quality for proceeding with the dam is adequate assurance from the four affected states that they will undertake whatever antipollution measures are necessary to prevent the otherwise inevitable eutrophication of the resulting 37-mile lake." [24] We had again returned the EIS to the Corps for further study, and the whole project eventually died, with Congress taking such funds as had already been appropriated for the project and diverting them to open space acquisition.

It was significant that CEQ never viewed its role in this case as being either for or against the Tocks Island project; rather, it saw its role as ensuring that adequate environmental safeguards and commitments were obtained prior to construction. Interestingly, there was never the slightest suggestion of White House interference with us in the Tocks Island review process.

An even more dramatic example of CEQ influence was another Army Corps of Engineers project, the Cross-Florida Barge Canal, for the simple reason that the project, originally authorized in 1942 and with construction begun in 1964, was so far advanced when it was killed. Reportedly, President John F. Kennedy had given the go-ahead on construction as a favor to his loyal supporter Senator George Smathers. Our analysis showed that the canal not only had very questionable economics but also could have a devastating effect on the ecology of northern Florida.

We had looked at a number of large water projects around the country

— some promoted by the Corps and some by the Bureau of Reclamation (part of the Interior Department) — and had identified a number as having adverse environmental effects, including the Cross-Florida Barge Canal. In a memorandum to John Whitaker, probably written after a preliminary discussion with him, I recommended that further funding for the Cross-Florida Barge Canal be frozen.[25] Whitaker was a strong supporter of our recommendation and Ehrlichman became one. The Corps was naturally very much opposed to our view, as was the entire Florida congressional delegation. In any event, the president accepted our arguments and, on January 19, 1971, ordered "a halt to further construction to prevent potentially serious environmental damage," effectively killing the project. The president directed the Corps and CEQ to develop recommendations for the future of the area. Nixon's action in this regard received a great deal of positive public attention throughout the country.[26] The following year, I announced an administration proposal to make the Oklawaha River in Florida (where the barge canal was to have been built) part of the National Wild and Scenic Rivers System. (To this day, that proposal has not been carried out because a dam constructed by the Corps on the river has never been removed.)

Poison, Predators, and Public Lands

Most of our efforts at CEQ, however, were directed not toward single projects, such as the Tocks Island Dam and the Cross-Florida Barge Canal, but toward broader policy issues. In practice, CEQ led the administration's policy response to environmental issues — broadly defined, a process that required quiet, behind-the-scenes staff work. In all cases, it was essential to involve in the process all those executive agencies that had an interest in the subject matter of a particular initiative.

For example, in 1971 we initiated, in partnership with the Department of the Interior, an advisory committee headed by former assistant secretary of Interior Stanley Cain and including Nathaniel P. Reed, the current assistant secretary, to study the problem of predator control on public lands.* It had become common practice to use highly toxic chemicals on public lands in the West to control coyotes and other predators. Large

---

*Reed worked closely with us on this and a number of other issues, including the ban on the use of DDT on public lands, regulation of clear-cutting along streams, protection of Alaskan lands (including native claims), establishment of the Big Cypress National Preserve in Florida, review of wetland permits, and others.

numbers of nontarget species, such as hawks and eagles, were being killed in the process as well. Our advisory committee documented the facts and concluded that control of coyotes and other predators could be carried out without the use of poisons, a position that led William Poage, chairman of the House Committee on Agriculture, to say to Reed and me, "You love coyotes more than sheep!" On the basis of this report and our recommendation, the president issued an executive order barring the use of poisons on all public lands except in emergencies.[27]

Taconite Tailings

An unusual example of CEQ functioning in a hands-on, operational manner rather than simply in a policy role occurred in early 1973 with a highly publicized threat to the drinking water supply of Duluth, Minnesota, posed by the Reserve Mining Company's daily discharge of 67,000 tons of taconite mine tailings into Lake Superior. The taconite tailings contained particles of asbestos, a suspected carcinogen. The White House designated me, as CEQ chairman, to be the person in charge of organizing and overseeing the federal government's response.

I sent a member of the CEQ staff, Warren Muir, to Duluth to be my on-site representative and I recall telephoning the chief of the Army Corps of Engineers one morning and directing him to deliver a water purification unit to Duluth by 5:00 that afternoon. In 1974, Reserve Mining was ordered by a federal district court to halt all discharges of taconite tailings into Lake Superior. After another round of appeals, the company decided to shift to on-land disposal of its wastes.

Citizen Action and the Politics of the Environment

Citizen concern and citizen action were key ingredients both of our nation's rapid development of environmental protection policies and of the effective implementation of those policies. April 20, 1970, marked the first observance of Earth Day, an event that galvanized many young people around the United States, particularly at the university level. Organized by Denis Hayes, Earth Day was celebrated on campuses and elsewhere throughout the country. There was, of course, a definite anti-establishment bias to much of the proceedings and a certain amount of nonsense, such as the burial of an automobile at Ann Arbor, Michigan.

While government officials were generally not welcomed, we few environmental types in government provided appropriate window dressing for some of these occasions. I took part in a meeting at Harvard University[28] on Earth Day, participated in a nationwide National Education Network program that evening, and gave an environmental speech two days later at the inauguration of a new chancellor at the University of California, Davis.[29] On that occasion I spoke outdoors, and I have a vivid memory of the proceedings being interrupted for a considerable period by a line of chanting and dancing half-clothed students.

Overall, I thought Earth Day was a great success. It really did call attention to environmental issues, and it had a considerable influence on our political leaders, although I recall no particular response from the White House. It helped build that high tide of public concern for the environment that made possible the policy initiatives we undertook at the time.[30]

More generally, many established citizen environmental organizations played an active and effective role, indeed a crucial one, in monitoring and promoting the enforcement of environmental laws, especially in the early 1970s during initial implementation of the EIS process in federal decision making.

On October 9, 1970, Randolph Thrower, commissioner of the Internal Revenue Service (IRS), announced a formal review of the tax-exempt status of organizations that file lawsuits against alleged polluters. Ralph Nader's Center for Study of Responsive Law was rumored to be the special target of the IRS review. Several days previous to this announcement, I had written to Thrower urging that the tax-exempt status of such organizations be retained. "Litigation brought by private groups that must rely on contributions for their support," I stated, "[has] strengthened and accelerated the process of enforcement of antipollution laws." I quoted CEQ's Legal Advisory Committee[31] to the effect that "private litigation before courts and administrative agencies has been and will continue to be an important environmental protection technique supplementing and reinforcing Government environmental protection programs."[32]

Copies of my letter were circulated quite widely, and there was considerable press coverage of the issue. The IRS finally announced that it was halting its review and in effect it withdrew its proposal. I was very pleased to get a letter from a former IRS commissioner, Mortimer M. Caplin, congratulating me and CEQ's general counsel, Timothy Atkeson, for our "crucial" role in turning back the IRS proposal. "[Y]our participation was *the* key factor," he wrote.[33]

CEQ's initiative in this case is a good example of the role it was able to play in significant environmental matters. I remain convinced that no other agency could have filled such a role so appropriately and effectively. Legally, our authority extended wherever the environment was a factor in the federal government, and that was essentially everywhere. Most important, we spoke with the authority of the White House and had its backing.[34]

We Americans tend to take for granted the relative openness of our government and private institutions, but my consistent experience abroad suggests that we are almost unique in this regard. The NEPA requirement of public hearings as part of the EIS process is unusual, to say the least. Most other nations seem to adhere to the principle that the less their citizens know about how decisions are made, the better. The very fact that occasional apparent departures from openness in our government tend to cause a public hullabaloo in Congress, the media, and elsewhere, as in the case of Vice President Richard Cheney's task force on energy policy early in the George W. Bush administration, serves only to reinforce the point.

Public interest law firms play a pivotal role in maintaining our tradition of openness as well as in calling to account government agencies that may be failing to implement the laws under which they are operating. This is just one of the ways in which the integrity and independence of the nonprofit sector are vital to the strength of our democracy. Nonprofit institutions are an important source of innovation in our society — critical to the nation's growth and development. The ability of those institutions to play at least a limited role in the public arena without penalty is one of our system's strengths.

The Campaign against Ocean Dumping

At CEQ, we developed what appears to have been an effective strategy for advancing policy objectives. Because of CEQ's central position and its presidential support, we were able to orchestrate a multitude of events and key players that enabled us to achieve some notable environmental policy successes on both the domestic and international fronts. For example, convinced that dumping of wastes into the oceans was an increasingly critical problem, we undertook a study at the president's direction that resulted in a CEQ report titled *Ocean Dumping: A National Policy* in early October 1970. The study and the report were the product of a joint effort, led by CEQ, involving staff from the Departments of the Interior, the Army, HEW, State, and Transportation as well as from the Bureau of the Budget, the Smithsonian Institution, the National Council on Marine Resources and Engineering Development, and the National Science Foundation.[35] The president released our report with his endorsement on October 7 and simultaneously urged legislation to deal with the problem, including measures on municipal sewage, industrial debris, and chemical wastes. Our proposal also included analysis of the disposal of chemical and biological weapons and radioactive wastes. I announced that legislation to control ocean dumping would be submitted early in the next session of Congress. I also took the opportunity to say that the president's recommendations on ocean dumping were a worldwide first, hailed them as an "important opportunity for international leadership," and suggested that we encourage similar action by other governments as well as inclusion of the issue on the agenda of the United Nations Conference on the Human Environment, to be held in Stockholm in 1972.

Subsequently, in his 1971 environmental message, the president recommended a national policy banning unregulated ocean dumping and placing strict limits on the ocean disposal of any harmful materials. He submitted legislation put together by CEQ providing the newly formed EPA with the specific authority to regulate dumping of any wastes into the oceans, estuaries, and the Great Lakes and to ban the dumping of wastes harmful to the marine environment. As pollution in the air, in the rivers, and on the land became increasingly strictly regulated, the oceans had become an all-too-convenient alternative, with potentially disastrous consequences for marine life. The president called for international action and said that he was "instructing the Secretary of State, in coordination with the Council on Environmental Quality, to develop and pursue international initiatives" designed to promote the adoption of similar measures by other nations.

The June 1972 United Nations Conference on the Human Environment, at which I led the U.S. delegation, did in fact, on our initiative, vote unanimously to endorse the concept of an international convention governing ocean dumping. Later that autumn, a conference on the subject was convened at Lancaster House on the Mall in London, with ninety-two nations participating. After much discussion and debate, we finally succeeded in adopting the international Convention on the Prevention of Marine Pollution by Dumping of Wastes and Other Matter (Ocean Dumping Convention), thanks in significant part to the leadership of the conference chairman, Martin Holdgate of the United Kingdom. The convention constituted a major environmental achievement in the international arena.

We were able to get considerable U.S. press attention for the London conference and I like to think that the coverage helped light a fire under Congress, which then did finally pass the Marine Protection, Research, and Sanctuaries Act of 1972, commonly known as the Ocean Dumping Act.[36]

An interesting sidelight on the London conference had been the participation of the Soviets. I had gone to the USSR in mid-September 1972 to begin implementation of the US-USSR environmental agreement that Nixon had signed that June in Moscow. My Soviet counterpart at the time, Yevgeny F. Fyodorov, and I had discussed the Stockholm Conference at some length because the Soviets had not attended as a result of Western opposition to accepting East Germany as a national participant, and we also discussed the upcoming ocean dumping conference. In any event, in the negotiations in London the Soviet delegation supported the United States at every turn. It was as if they had been instructed by Moscow to follow the U.S. lead. It was an excellent example of how cooperative international work in broad areas can have positive effects in other areas of involvement. Today, I think we need to face the reality that the reverse is also true.

Some Setbacks

Of course, while it is fun to write about our successes, we had our failures as well. One that comes to mind was our effort to secure an executive order from the president limiting the clear-cutting of trees in the national forests. We had developed the proposal in 1971 with the idea that it could be included in the president's environmental message of the following January. Our forward pass was intercepted in midair, however, by a very effective lobbying effort mounted by the forest products industry. They insisted to White House staff that our proposal would raise the cost of timber operations, driving up the cost of lumber and creating a "price and supply crunch" in the spring home-building season—just before the 1972 presidential election. That was the end of our initiative and it was dropped from the 1972 environmental message. A *New York Times* editorial saw to it that our discomfiture did not go unnoticed.[37]

Another setback, although of a more personal nature, involved my attendance at Cabinet meetings. When CEQ was first created, I had been invited to Cabinet meetings on a regular basis. I usually sat along the wall facing the president, together with the chairman of the Council of Economic Advisors, the director of the Central Intelligence Agency, the national security advisor, and the like. But beginning sometime in the fall of 1970, I was no longer invited on a regular basis. My disinvitation may have been triggered by a *Life* magazine article that described me as an eastern elitist and a "high priest of American conservationism." [38] A more likely cause was a presentation I had made to a full Cabinet meeting early that fall, at John Whitaker's suggestion, on the operation of the EIS process.

Whitaker had developed a fairly complex chart to show the various steps in the process, and the chart was set up on a tripod at the end of the Cabinet room. The federal action I chose to use as my example of the working of the process was the proposed five-megaton test of the Spartan antiballistic missile's nuclear warhead, to be conducted on the island of Amchitka in the Aleutian Islands, off Alaska. The test, code-named Cannikin, was public knowledge and was a controversial matter. I made several mistakes. One was that the responsibility for the test lay with the Atomic Energy Commission, which was chaired by James Schlesinger (who was not at the meeting), rather than with the Department of Defense (DOD), to which I attributed responsibility. DOD's secretary, Mel Laird, seemed understandably startled by my presentation. My second mistake was to assume that the Cannikin test would even be subject to an EIS. (A court decision soon held that national security matters were exempt from the EIS process.) But my major mistake was simply choosing such a high-profile, controversial matter for my example of the EIS operation rather than a hypothetical dam or highway or some other, more mundane example. When another Cabinet meeting was scheduled and I did not receive an invitation, I called Bob Haldeman, and he simply told me that I was not being invited as a regular matter anymore.

Aside from the Cabinet meeting, I managed to inject myself into the

Cannikin project. I wrote a confidential letter to the under secretary of State, Jack Irwin, warning of the possible earthquake and tsunami (tidal wave) that could result from such a test, and the letter got into the press with front-page coverage.[39] As it turned out, the test went off as scheduled in November 1971, with Schlesinger and his family in attendance as observers, and there were no untoward results.

A third setback was possibly more serious in its long-term implications. While CEQ was demonstrating successfully its ability to carry out its mandates under NEPA and to address effectively a wide range of current and near-term policy issues, it was plain that we did not possess the capability to do long-range analytical work. CEQ was both too small and too close to the policy-making process to carry out such a function. At the same time, the federal government badly needed access to some agency or institution that had the capability for long-term analysis of environmental policies; of their interrelation with other policy areas, such as energy and agriculture; and, in particular, of their economic implications. The continued burgeoning of environmental initiatives in both the executive and legislative branches of the government gave added urgency to this need.

In the spring of 1970, we started exploring the idea of setting up a quasi-independent environmental policy institute, and I consulted with MacGeorge Bundy, president of The Ford Foundation and former national security advisor to Presidents Kennedy and Johnson,* on the possibility of an institution that would be jointly funded by the federal government and private institutions. At CEQ, Al Alm headed a staff group to examine the idea and the available options.[40] There was a good deal of support for the idea among members of the administration, including George Schultz, who was then director of the Office of Management and Budget (OMB), John Whitaker, and John Ehrlichman. Schultz was particularly interested in seeing environmental programs and proposals subjected to intense economic analysis. The White House, of course, was anxious that such an institute not become a loose cannon and a political embarrassment to the president.

In his 1971 message on the environment, Nixon also espoused the concept, however, and Senator Jackson introduced a bill in the Senate

---

*Both Bundy and his wife, Mary, were longtime friends of my wife, Aileen, and me. We shared a number of vacations, usually with Peter and Deborah Solbert, in the Caribbean region and once in the French Dordogne.

that would amend NEPA to add a new title III establishing a National Environmental Policy Institute. We even reached agreement on a candidate to head the institute—Alain Enthoven, a brilliant economist who had been one of Robert McNamara's inner group at the Defense Department and who was then with the Rand Corporation. Unfortunately, when Ehrlichman put Enthoven's name before Nixon, the latter vetoed him on the ground that he was too liberal.

At this point, all hands agreed to let the matter rest until after the 1972 presidential election. We at CEQ then resubmitted a proposal, but there the matter lay and essentially died. A combination of circumstances had derailed it. I have already mentioned several: concern over the directorship and nervousness about an independent, freestanding institution that might not prove controllable. Growing disarray in the White House resulting from the Watergate scandal doubtless played its part, however.[41]

The idea remained on my mind. In early 1975, during the Ford administration, I suggested to the White House the establishment of a new agency in the Executive Office of the President that would combine a scientific advisory function and a long-range policy analysis function. I suggested that such an agency might be called the Office of Research and Analysis.[42] Nothing came of the proposal.

The Birth of EPA

The Environmental Protection Agency (EPA) and the National Oceanic and Atmospheric Administration (NOAA) both were created in late 1970 by reorganization plans President Nixon submitted to Congress. I was the administration's lead witness on the issue before congressional committees. Following approval of the reorganization plans, EPA became the focal point for the implementation and enforcement of environmental laws (as NOAA did for the management of marine fisheries and for oceanographic and atmospheric research).

The White House had originally favored establishment of a Department of Natural Resources (a greatly expanded Department of the Interior), which would have included the environmental regulatory functions that ultimately went to EPA. The President's Advisory Council on Executive Organization—the Ash Council, so called for its chairman, Roy Ash, former head of the Litton Corporation—leaned in the same direction. As a result, the question of how best to organize major environmental functions within the executive branch became an important focus for the council, and for me personally, in early 1970.

I urged in testimony before the Ash Council that the government's environmental responsibilities be concentrated in a single, independent agency (such as EPA became) rather than submerged in a new Department of Natural Resources. I believed strongly that environmental issues needed a sharp, cutting edge in government, one that had high visibility to the public.

I also addressed these issues in a memorandum to John Ehrlichman.[43] I argued that the proposed Department of Natural Resources would be "excessively unwieldy and exceedingly difficult to administer." Speaking from some experience, I added: "The present Department of the Interior is difficult enough to manage. The new organization would be far more so." Furthermore, combining environmental regulatory functions with the welter of natural resource authorities of Interior, including (at that time) oil and gas, minerals, and electric power, would lead to inevitable conflicts of interest. "Any reorganization plan as complex and controversial as that being proposed by the Ash Council will generate a great deal of Congressional heat," I continued. "I believe that the present proposal would simply add Muskie to the opposition and give him an issue. Proposal of a separate environmental protection agency would neutralize his position in this regard. . . . All members of the Council on Environmental Quality concur in recommending a separate agency." (I believe I was the principal proponent within the executive branch of making EPA a separate, independent agency.) This was the view that ultimately prevailed, despite opposition to the EPA proposal from Secretaries Clifford Hardin of Agriculture, Robert H. Finch of HEW, and Walter Hickel of Interior. I suspect that my point with respect to Muskie might have been my most persuasive argument with the Nixon White House, where Muskie was already being seen as a possible opponent to Nixon in 1972.[44]

Today, I remain convinced that establishing EPA as an independent agency was the right course of action at the time. Twenty years later, when the issue arose again in the George H. W. Bush administration, I wrote a letter to the president urging him to give EPA departmental status.[45] I pointed out that most foreign governments had given ministerial status at Cabinet level to their environmental agencies and that, in terms of the number of its employees and the size of its budget, EPA was already larger than most existing departments. "More importantly," I said, "its mission critically affects all parts of the nation, all areas of the economy, and all segments of our society. It is really an anomaly today that it is not already a department." I am not sure whether I was simply jumping on a bandwagon or the timing was fortuitous. In any case, only three days later the president announced at a press conference that he had decided to make EPA a department.[46] The legislation did not pass the Congress, however.

I testified before the House Judiciary Committee in favor of the proposal, although I had some misgivings then about my testimony. I continue to have them today. I am all in favor of raising the stature of our principal environmental agency, but I am concerned about making it more political while so doing. After all, EPA is strongly regulatory in nature. I am not at all comfortable today with what appears to be the constant involvement of the George W. Bush White House in EPA decision making.[47] In any event, making EPA as such a department is far different from merging the EPA functions into a much larger Department of Natural Resources. In my opinion, the latter course — which, as described earlier, I helped derail in the Nixon administration — would have been a disaster, pure and simple.

When EPA came into being in early December 1970, William Ruckelshaus was named its first head. He was a splendid choice. I had not known him until a mutual friend told me of his likely nomination and we arranged to have lunch together. An assistant attorney general at the time, he had previously served in the Indiana legislature, where he had accrued an impressive record on environmental issues and then made an unsuccessful run for the Senate seat of Birch Bayh. Thus, he combined a strong political, legal, and environmental background, all of which he would need in full measure. As I got to know him over time, I learned to appreciate his keen intelligence, practical approach, good judgment, and fine sense of humor, the latter being an invaluable asset in government.

I realize that readers may have been struck by the modesty and self-effacement that characterizes this account of my involvement in the environmental events of the time. However, I believe that history should be aware that I was not above ambition and was not loath to push myself forward on occasion. While EPA was still in gestation, I sent a formal recommendation to John Ehrlichman that the chairman of CEQ also be named administrator of EPA.[48] Needless to say, nothing came of this creative suggestion. I put it forward again, albeit informally, in 1973, with the same result. No one wanted an environmental czar. It was also a rotten idea.

Nixon and CEQ's First Annual Report

Nixon called CEQ's first annual report (August 3, 1970) the "first time in the history of nations that a people has paused, consciously and systematically, to take comprehensive stock of the quality of its surroundings." The *New York Times* was more critical. A lead editorial[49] characterized the report as too easygoing and not strong enough in its recommendations. The *Times* declared that CEQ should provide "more forceful leadership in defining priorities and establishing effective strategies for realizing them." There was no question but that the report was short on specific proposals and long on the description of problems — actually, not a bad approach, given the circumstances. More to the point, the president had submitted a comprehensive thirty-seven-point program in his first environmental message to Congress only about six months earlier, and essentially none of those recommendations had been acted upon as yet.

We placed major emphasis in that first report on the need to develop a national land-use policy and a national energy policy. With regard to land use, which was to become a CEQ priority, the report identified a number of areas in which action was needed, without spelling out what the action should be. Given the high level of controversy associated with the land-use issue in the United States, I still believe our approach was probably the right one. We hoped to provoke some public dialogue on the issue before becoming more specific.

We gave a good deal of attention in the report to the economic aspects of correcting pollution. "Our price system fails to take into account the environmental damage that the polluter inflicts on others," we declared. "If there were a way to make the price structure shoulder these external costs . . . then the price for the goods and services produced would reflect these costs. . . . A price structure that took environmental degradation into account would cause a shift in prices, even a shift in consumer preferences and, to some extent, would discourage buying pollution-producing products." These pronouncements were certainly not unfamiliar to economists, but they bore emphasizing in a political world that tended to rely almost exclusively on command-and-control approaches to pollution reduction. They helped pave the way for our subsequent proposals for taxes on sulfur emissions and lead in gasoline.

CEQ and the President

That report was the first of what was an annual CEQ effort. It is not my intent to detail here all the environmental initiatives and achievements of CEQ from February 1970 to September 1973, the period during which I was chairman. A fairly full history of those eventful years is to be found in the annual reports of CEQ, the first having been submitted to Congress in August 1970.[50] These annual reports not only chronicle current legislative and administrative actions on environmental issues but also lay out some of the philosophical underpinnings of issues such as land use, as well as some of the evidence (in the 1970 report) of "man's inadvertent modification of weather and climate." More than thirty years later, while scientific evidence continues to accumulate as to the reality of the climate change problem, the world community and, most notably, the United States, still appear unable to reach agreement on how to deal with the issue. Indeed, the George W. Bush White House appears to be in a state of denial on the problem of climate change.

The submission of CEQ's annual report to the president for his transmittal to Congress was the only occasion for the meeting of the council's three members with the president. These were usually fairly nonsubstantive occasions. Once, I recall, he told us he had just seen the musical *Hair* in New York. I said, "That has a lot of nudity in it, doesn't it?" He looked up at me and replied, "What's wrong with a little nudity?"

I had practically no substantive meetings with Nixon while I was head of CEQ. About twice a year, I would have what the White House staff described as a "stroke session" with him. (I was the one being "stroked.") I recall one such meeting at which the president sat in a chair to the right of the fireplace and I sat on the end of a sofa to the left. As usual, there was a fire going, regardless of the outside temperature. I took the opportunity to try to interest him in land-use planning.

I described the differences between the English countryside landscape and the strip development and urban sprawl that tends to afflict so much of our own landscape. I did not get much of a reaction to that, but he did pick up on the overall subject. He said, more or less, as follows: "You know, when I play golf at Key Biscayne with Bebe [Rebozo], there are mangroves growing along the water's edge, which block the view. We wanted to cut just a few vistas through the mangroves, but we were not allowed to. Yet those mangroves aren't good for anything except gooney birds!"

As he said this, his longtime valet, Manuel Sanchez, entered the room with a fresh cup of coffee for the president. "Isn't that right, Manuel?" said Nixon, looking up at him. "No, Mr. President," said Manuel, "that's not right. You know that when I have my day off down there I go fishing. I know that the fish I catch need those mangroves to grow up in. If you cut down those mangroves, there won't be any more fish." Manuel picked up the empty cup and turned and walked out of the room while Nixon stared at him.[51] From then on, whenever I saw Manuel around the West Wing of the White House, I would ask him whether he had given the president any more ecology lessons.

I have mentioned that I had few really substantive meetings with Nixon. I was not alone in this regard. I believe Nixon avoided direct face-to-face discussion of specific issues with his agency heads and confined most such contacts to his immediate staff. I recall Caspar (Cap) Weinberger (at different times director of OMB, counselor to the president, secretary of HEW, and secretary of DOD) telling me that he almost never had had a substantive meeting with Nixon. Vice President Spiro Agnew told me the same thing.

Toward a National Land-Use Policy

Nixon never did become a personal proponent of land-use planning, although he twice submitted to Congress a proposed National Land Use Policy Act, which CEQ had drafted. Our group had become interested in land use policy early on. Boyd Gibbons, who had led the development of the Coastal Zone Management Act of 1972 in my office at Interior, brought that interest with him to CEQ. The report of the Task Force on Natural Resources and Environment, which I had chaired for the president-elect in 1968, had touched on the issue, and CEQ's first annual report in 1970, as noted earlier, emphasized the "need to begin shaping a national land use policy." While the latter report's recommendations were couched in fairly general terms, we included some pointed statements. For example:

The Federal Government should encourage, through project approval under existing programs, widespread use of devices such as cluster zoning and timed development.

Comprehensive metropolitan planning should identify flood plains, wetlands, aquifer recharge areas, unstable surface and subsurface characteristics, and areas of value for scenic, wildlife, and recreational purposes. Development in these areas should be controlled.

Federal grants for sewer and water projects and open space acquisition should be directed toward communities or project areas which will use them to control development rather than to those which merely respond to uncontrolled growth.

In early 1970, Gibbons recruited William K. Reilly, whose specialty was land use, and he in turn secured the help of Fred Bosselman and David Callies as consultants under contract with CEQ. They produced a report[52] in late 1971 that we hoped would influence debate on the issue. In his 1971 environmental message, prepared by CEQ, the president recognized that while most land-use decisions are made at the local level and should continue to be made there, "we must draw upon the basic authority of State government to deal with land use issues which spill over local jurisdictional boundaries." He called for reform of the institutional framework in which land-use decisions are made. He proposed legislation "to establish a National Land Use Policy which will encourage the states, in cooperation with local government, to plan for and regulate major developments affecting growth and the use of critical land areas. This should be done by establishing methods for protecting lands of critical environmental concern, methods for controlling large-scale development, and improving use of land around key facilities and new communities."[53] He asked for $100 million over a period of five years to assist the states in this effort, certainly an inadequate amount when spread over fifty states but probably enough to get the program started. There was disappointingly little public response to the president's proposal.

Which agency should be designated to have jurisdiction over the legislation wasn't clear. George Romney, secretary of Housing and Urban Development, and Rogers Morton, secretary of Interior, came to my office along with John Whitaker to decide the issue. Neither department had a very good claim to executive responsibility over land use. However, HUD had essentially no environmental credentials, and the nod finally went to Interior. Land-use legislation sponsored by Senator Jackson passed the Senate in September 1972. The bill had many similarities to the administration's proposal. It did not disturb the basic authority of local governments to make land-use decisions having primarily local effects, but it called for a state role in decisions having effects outside the local area, particularly in critical environmental areas. The House Interior Committee reported a bill that was bottled up in the Rules Committee (with the encouragement of the Nixon White House), and the legislation died with the Ninety-second Congress. In the next Congress, Jackson reintroduced the legislation that had previously passed the Senate, and in June 1973 it passed there a second time. The story in the House was much more complicated, as recounted in detail in Whitaker's book.[54] Conservative opposition within Republican ranks, combined with John Ehrlichman's departure from the White House in the wake of Watergate, sounded the death knell of the legislation, and it died in Congress the next year. It has never been revived. Without Ehrlichman's persuasive counsel on the land-use issue, Nixon simply had not the strength of interest or personal conviction to withstand conservative complaints about the legislation.[55] In his 1972 environmental message, Nixon had also proposed a set of special income tax incentives and disincentives to help protect coastal wetlands from development. However, this excellent proposal likewise went nowhere in Congress.[56]

I have touched at some length on the subject of land use because I consider CEQ's effort in that regard both adventuresome and farsighted. Urban sprawl, the loss of environmentally critical areas such as wetlands, and the concentration of people along sensitive estuaries such as Chesapeake Bay—to name but a few of the problems—cry out for attention around the country. The American tradition is to leave such decisions to local communities rather than to the states. More often than not, local decision makers either go along with development pressures or do nothing. The very idea of the federal government playing a role in the matter is, to many, a revolutionary one—not to say anathema. Yet the federal government makes decisions all the time with regard to highways and the siting of federal facilities that have a significant effect on the quality of local land use. The land-use legislation that the Nixon administration proposed was designed not to create a federal planning process but to energize the states to do so. It laid out certain broad criteria for state land-use planning in "areas of critical environmental concern," it provided some funds to assist in undertaking the process, and it carried a penalty—loss of certain funds—for nonparticipation. It was a start.

The land-use program proposed was an idea that was probably ahead of its time, and in retrospect it is surprising that the legislation got as far as it did, including passage in the Senate twice. John Ehrlichman, with his background as a land-use lawyer in Seattle, was the major force in the White House in enlisting Nixon's support. Aside from a rather traditional bias against federal intrusion into what he considered the states' business, Nixon's view of land-use problems was quite unsophisticated. He saw the challenge as simply one of "protecting natural beauty" but then added, "Christ, I wouldn't want to live on a farm."[57] In addition, I have no doubt that some Republican real estate developers took strong exception to the language in the president's 1971 environmental message to Congress, which supported the need for such legislation. I understood that Nixon said at some point, in reference to that language, "Who is the son-of-a-bitch who wrote this stuff for me?"

Environmentally sound land use is a concept that badly needs revisiting. Many regions in the United States are experiencing major demographic pressures, particularly coastal areas and estuaries such as Chesapeake Bay and its watershed. In the Chesapeake Bay area, which covers several states, decisions on new housing developments, for example, are made today by local governments, yet those decisions can have a significant effect on water quality and associated marine resources throughout the bay. Moreover, not only is a broader perspective needed, but also local governments frequently lack the financial resources to deal effectively with development pressures.

Shadows and Portents

I suppose that all occupants of the White House have "played games" at times with the press and the public, but perhaps the Nixon White House played more than most. I had personal experience with only one such situation. That was while I was at CEQ, and it involved a well-known and widely respected national affairs correspondent for CBS, Daniel Schorr, politically liberal in his views and no admirer of Richard Nixon. It was widely reported in the press that the White House had instigated an investigation of Schorr by the Federal Bureau of Investigation (FBI), and this had put the White House very much on the defensive.

In December 1971 I met with Fred Malek, a member of the White House staff, at his request, in John Whitaker's office in the southwest corner of the Executive Office Building. Bob Haldeman, Malek told me, had said that the president was interested in having television material developed about the administration's environmental program. Would CEQ undertake the job? We talked of CEQ hiring a television personality. It sounded great to me, although in retrospect the idea of CEQ putting together its own television program seems pretty nutty. Later, I went to Malek's office to discuss the idea with him further and to get suggestions on possible candidates for the job—Schorr was never mentioned—and to figure out how to deal with the matter within CEQ's budget and personnel ceilings.

Back at CEQ, I talked to several individuals I knew who had national television stature. The conversations went well, although I found no immediate takers. The matter drifted along until the spring of 1972, when a *New York Times* reporter called me at home. Malek had just stated in an interview that Dan Schorr was being considered for the job. That had led to the FBI investigation, which would be normal in such cases, given that the position was as a television consultant to CEQ. Could I confirm that account? At mention of Malek's statement, a great light dawned in my naive brain. To put it simply, I had been had: I had swallowed the bait, hook, line, and sinker. To the reporter, I confirmed that CEQ had been trying to recruit a television news personality, and I went on to describe my efforts but denied any knowledge of Dan Schorr's being considered in that regard. The reporter did not pursue the matter further, and the next day his article reported that I had confirmed the basics of the White House story. That was the end of the matter so far as I was concerned. I certainly did not do any more "recruiting," and I do not recall ever mentioning the matter again to White House staff, nor they to me. The Dan Schorr story pretty much died in the press. Good old naive Train was left feeling like a jerk. In 1998, more than two decades later, Dan Schorr told me that when he talked to Nixon after the latter had left office, Nixon had said to him with a grin, "We tried to hire you once!" With that, I concluded that Nixon had been privy to the entire affair.[58]

As early as March 1972, the White House was beginning to focus on the coming presidential election. I received a memo from Whitaker urging me "to devote substantial portions of [my] calendar to increasing public awareness of what the Administration has accomplished in the environmental area." The White House was interested not so much in individual speeches, he said, as in "utilizing the media, both national and regional, to reach a wider audience. With your name and reputation, you should be able to pick the area where you want to go and build a media-oriented trip around it." He suggested I confine myself to a group of politically important states, which he listed for my benefit. He held up the public efforts of William Ruckelshaus in this regard as an example I should emulate, and then he tried flattery:

> There is no one within the Administration who can take your place as the leading advocate on the environment issue. In terms of background, ability and scope of responsibility you are in the unique situation to present and advocate the President's complete environmental program. Because his time . . . is so limited . . . we must capitalize on your position as his chief environmental advisor to be his public surrogate on the issue.[59]

While I was only too glad to promote to the public the Nixon administration's environmental record, I do not recall that I ever responded to the Whitaker suggestion with a planned and concerted media campaign. The fact was that both I and CEQ got a great deal of press, including national coverage, on a fairly regular basis. Most of that press was positive, and Nixon and his administration benefited politically from it. Given the high level of CEQ activity, those opportunities came often and naturally. Orchestration of a campaign could well have been seen as contrived and counterproductive. Besides, I never was comfortable in taking what seemed overtly political actions. As early as 1970, the White House had urged me to call a press conference to criticize Congress for its inaction on Nixon's environmental agenda.[60] I never did so.

In the summer of 1972, I participated, albeit in a very minor way, in the GOP convention in Miami, during which Nixon was nominated for his second term. Of course, his nomination was a foregone conclusion. Aileen and I flew to Miami with other Nixon administration people on a chartered 727; had accommodations at the Doral Beach Hotel, where Nixon was staying; drove with George H. W. Bush in his limousine to the convention (he was then director of the Central Intelligence Agency); and had excellent seats at the convention on the platform. I spoke at several state caucuses.

Environmental issues did not play an important role in the ensuing campaign. However, I learned later that the television advertisements paid for by the Republican National Committee gave more attention to the environment than to any other subject. Thus, while the environment did not prove controversial in the campaign, the Republican "image people" recognized that Nixon's environmental record was a very positive asset.

Following the election, I believe in late November, there was a Cabinet meeting at which Bob Haldeman announced, after Nixon had left the room, that all Cabinet members and other political appointees were expected to submit their resignations. I was in London at the time, and Aileen called to tell me this cheery news. I went to the U.S. embassy on Grosvenor Square and wrote a one-sentence resignation to the president on official stationery. Following my return to Washington and not having heard a word on my future status (or lack of one), I called John Ehrlichman and said I would like to know where I stood. He called me back the following day to say that I was to stay. It was good to know, but what an odd way to run a railroad!

In mid-December, Aileen and I attended a dinner at the White House for members of the administration. I suppose it was meant as a Christmas celebration of sorts, but the occasion was anything but joyous. I think I was one of the few in the room who knew he or she was staying on. A woman sitting next to me was the wife of a top official at the Department of Justice who had only very recently accepted his appointment. They had sold their home in the San Francisco area and moved their six children to Washington. She said that her husband had no idea whether he would keep his job. (His resignation was accepted.) Aileen sat at a table between Ehrlichman and Secretary of State Bill Rogers. The latter did not know whether he would be retained or not, and he was in fact replaced by Henry Kissinger. Aileen recalls the hatred between Ehrlichman and Rogers as being "palpable."

Meeting with Agnew

In May 1973, shortly after the ending of the Dan Schorr affair and not long before I was nominated by President Nixon as EPA administrator, I had a half-hour private discussion with Vice President Spiro Agnew in his office in the Executive Office Building. I had set up the meeting with a personal telephone call to Agnew at the suggestion of Bryce Harlow, a counselor to the president. The Watergate revelations and the ensuing disarray in the White House had made me anxious to reach out to someone of stature in the administration with whom I could share my concerns. My conversation with the vice president has little, if any, relevance to the matters I have been recounting, but the fact that Agnew resigned in October 1973, pleading nolo contendere to charges that he failed to report for income tax purposes "payoffs" received while governor of Maryland, makes our conversation seem sufficiently bizarre as to deserve reporting in some detail. The conversation also reflects something of the atmosphere within the administration as Watergate unfolded.

I told the vice president that I had been feeling considerable unhappiness over the turn of events in the administration since the eruption of the Watergate crisis and appreciated the opportunity to chat with him about this. Bryce Harlow and I had reminisced together as old hands from Eisenhower days, I remarked, and mentioned that with the exception of about three years, I had been in government service since 1947, and I probably had more experience with Congress than anybody else in the Executive Office—not that this was saying a great deal! I went on to say how necessary I thought it was to maintain the confidence of the American people in their government, and that, in my opinion, no matter how the Watergate situation was resolved, the authority of the president would inevitably undergo some erosion. Agnew agreed.

It seemed to me, I went on, that a couple of courses of action could help preserve the situation. First, I stressed the importance of having individuals of recognized stature in Cabinet and agency head positions, preferably people with their own political bases and some free rein in making decisions. It had become almost an accepted matter of course for a Cabinet officer to be overruled by some junior staff member at the White House or at OMB and I said I found this outrageous.

In my view, the practice of clutching power into the White House made the president very vulnerable and led to great potential instability, which current events had certainly borne out. For some reason, I then embarked on an ecological figure of speech and compared the situation to the instability of a monoculture as compared with the strength and stability of diverse ecosystems. To my surprise, the vice president seemed struck by this metaphor and took it up. He agreed 100 percent, he said, with my analysis and with the objectives I had outlined; the need for diversity extended to political viewpoints and positions.

Agnew expressed concern that things really were not going to change very much, that other "Germans" would simply move into the positions vacated by Haldeman, Ehrlichman, and the like. He mentioned Ron Ziegler, the president's press secretary, as having an enormous ambition for Haldeman's role. Alexander Haig's appointment that day to fill Haldeman's job as chief of staff for the interim period was a bad sign, he thought. He expressed a high regard for Haig but thought that the selection reflected the president's desire to continue to run the operation in a hard, tightly held manner. There was a real struggle going on in this regard, he said. The president had asked him to take over the vice chairmanship of the Domestic Council and to assume some of the president's other functions, but after Agnew left the president's office and started thinking about the matter, he concluded that nothing much had been offered or achieved. He had apparently had Ken Cole over for a talk and got the impression that Ken, who had become director of the Domestic Council, looked upon Agnew's role as somehow to be supportive of Cole's. The vice president laughed in recalling that he had explained to Ken the ludicrousness of having the vice president characterized in the press as Ken Cole's assistant.

Agnew described to me his own difficulties in getting through to the president. He had called Nixon that day in Florida to discuss some of these things, and, instead of getting the president, he got Al Haig, who asked what he wanted. The president was off on a boat trip. Agnew wondered why Haig couldn't have simply taken a message and said that the president would call him back. Apparently, Nixon never did return the call. Agnew then recounted to me that Arthur Burns, counselor to the president and later chairman of the Federal Reserve Board, had tried to reach the president in recent days and had been unable to get through. Certainly, the president ought to have the kind of Cabinet relationships wherein a member of the Cabinet need not hesitate to pick up the telephone and call the president if he really felt the need to do so—and get him.

Was this situation the result of direct instructions from the president or simply the officious acts of ambitious staffers, I asked. Agnew left me with the clear impression that this was really the way the president wanted it. I commented that this policy at the top may be copied on down the line, and I recounted some of my own inabilities to get through to members of the White House staff. I cited my current ten-day effort to reach someone named Jerry Jones, who was ostensibly in charge of personnel, and other examples. I had not gotten a call through to Ehrlichman for about nine months and I had talked with Haldeman only once in four years. The usual response was a call back by a junior staff person who would ask what I wanted.

Agnew described the president as being angry and very hurt and feeling very much besieged. One thing that made the president especially furious at this point was evidence of people trying to move into the power vacuum, although Agnew gave no examples. He did say that he thought that this was a very bad time to try to approach the president.

The president preferred to discuss matters with only a very limited group, Agnew noted, and the fact that Nixon had now lost the two principal members of that group left him feeling bereft. I said that while I was publicly described as the president's environmental policy advisor, I had never had what I would describe as a truly substantive conversation with him in the three years of CEQ's existence. The vice president replied, "Well, I have *never* had a substantive conversation with the president!"

Agnew discussed at some length the problems of a vice president and the lack of a significant role for him, but he said he could well understand Nixon's sensitivity about this. "However," he continued, "I honestly don't think I have ever given him any cause for concern on this score. I have never tried to develop my own power base or my own turf. Certainly," he said, "I never operated to undercut the president in the way that Hubert Humphrey did or Lyndon Johnson. If anyone understands the problems of the vice presidency, it should be the president."

The president was feeling terribly defensive and determined not to permit any weakening of his authority, Agnew repeated. In my opinion, I said, the kind of decentralization of power from the Executive Office of the President that we had discussed would in fact strengthen the president's authority with the country and with Congress. The vice president said he agreed completely.[61] Following the meeting, I never saw Agnew again. He resigned that October.

Some Final Thoughts on CEQ

I served as chairman of CEQ — its first — from February 1970 until September 1973, a period of almost four years. I think that during that time, as a brand-new agency in government, CEQ had an extraordinary record of policy development, both domestic and, as I describe in the next chapter, international. Granted, some of the policy initiatives were the products of other agencies, such as that on strip mining, from Interior. On the other hand, we fostered new legislation for the control of pesticides, which, while having its genesis within the Department of Agriculture, probably would never have surfaced without CEQ's probing and insistence, particularly given the built-in conflicts within Agriculture on such an issue.

The same could be said for our development of a policy promoting integrated pest management, wherein natural controls, rather than chemicals, are used. Noise control legislation was almost entirely a CEQ product. No one picked up the subject of control of toxic substances until CEQ identified the issue as a critical one and began to develop legislation to deal with it. Ocean dumping was a subject that was not clearly within any agency's jurisdiction until CEQ grabbed the ball and ran with it, with strong presidential support. Tax reform to help promote environmental quality was not a subject that interested the Department of the Treasury, and it took CEQ to initiate proposals in the area. Tax changes to remove existing discrimination against historic preservation were espoused by CEQ, as were taxes on sulfur emissions[62] and on lead in gasoline, both proposed by the president. I do not think that Treasury, left to its own instincts, would ever have given these matters the time of day.

This recitation of CEQ's record of success is not intended as implied criticism of other agencies. Rather, it confirms the value of an institution such as CEQ, which possesses an integrative mandate that reaches throughout the executive branch—an institution that itself has but one mission, the promotion of environmental quality, and thus is internally unconflicted.

Likewise, unless CEQ had blown the whistle, it is likely that the IRS would have proceeded with its plans to eliminate or significantly limit the tax-exempt status of public interest law firms. As will become clear in the next chapter, CEQ also provided an ideal vehicle for a wide variety of international initiatives, in part because of its locus within the Executive Office of the President and in part because of the breadth of its jurisdiction.

Then there were broad considerations that were not the business of any particular agency and that would have been ignored were it not for CEQ. The most important of these was land use—an issue that at the same time belonged nowhere and everywhere. CEQ alone had the integrative mandate that allowed it to address the issue. CEQ was able to raise the issue of a national growth policy, even if in a fairly muted way. No other agency would have done so at all. Likewise, CEQ spoke up on the problem of population growth, as I did personally in many public speeches.

In the latter connection, Congress had passed legislation in early 1970 that led to establishment of the Commission on Population Growth and the American Future, chaired by John D. Rockefeller III. Following its passage, I wrote to Pat Moynihan, who was then counselor to the president, urging that the president, when signing the Rockefeller Commission's act, take the occasion to issue a statement making clear the connection between human population numbers and the quality of the environment. It was, I said, "[T]ime for a hard look at not just the effects the predicted 100 million more people by the year 2000 will have on the nation, but whether it is inevitable that this will occur, and what steps might be taken to see that it does not happen."[63] Nixon unfortunately always remained quite guarded on the population issue, and I do not recall receiving any reply to the memo. Similarly, when the Rockefeller Commission report was submitted and made public, there was little, if any, response from the White House.

We did not shy away from controversial issues. We attracted criticism from various sides on occasion and we took on a very wide range of projects.[64] It was thus particularly encouraging that press comments on our performance tended to be quite positive. For example, the *Washington Post* editorialized:

> It should be no surprise that the council has worked quite closely with the White House, or that its output has been occasionally trimmed by the White House staff. To the contrary, the remarkable achievement of the CEQ during the past three years has been the extent to which, despite political pressures, it has managed to impose upon the federal establishment a decent regard for environmental concerns.[65]

CEQ is in many ways a unique institution in government. We were fortunate during my time as chairman to have the considerable support of the White House. Since that time, most presidents have initially tried to abolish CEQ and, when that became politically difficult, have let it continue by sufferance. Several times over the years, at the outset of the administrations of Ronald Reagan, George H. W. Bush, Jimmy Carter, and Bill Clinton, I weighed in with congressional testimony or letters to the new administration, or both, to argue against the elimination of CEQ. So far, the council has survived.

The Clinton administration tried initially to eliminate CEQ and ran into a political buzz saw with both Congress and the environmental community. Presumably, the plan was promoted by Vice President Al Gore, to whom the president had largely delegated environmental responsibility. Gore preferred an environmental office in the White House itself, and this was set up with one of his own senatorial staffers, Katy McGinty, as its head. (Later, she also became chairman of CEQ.) To my mind, the White House is apt to be so driven by the crises of the moment that it is not conducive to any sort of deliberative planning. At the same time, White House interest in CEQ has been almost nonexistent since then, and as a result CEQ often appears quite moribund as an institution. It does not appear that CEQ has any significant role in the policy development processes of the George W. Bush White House.

With strong presidential support, CEQ has an almost limitless potential for creative environmental initiative. It is one of the very few integrative influences available to the president in a government that is mostly characterized by separate bureaucratic fiefdoms, each of which wants to do its own thing. The environment as an issue cuts across the entire fabric of government and has the potential for helping integrate the parts into a cohesive whole. If we truly seek a national energy policy, for example, CEQ could and should play a central role in the formulation of such a policy. I am not aware that it has any such role today.

If, on the other hand, a president has no interest in utilizing CEQ, then I would hope that he or she would have the good sense to at least allow the institution to continue to exist so as to remain available for a later president with different priorities.

Nixon's Ambivalence

By mid-1971, I had already begun to be concerned about the mixed signals that were emanating from the White House on environmental matters. I was convinced that environmental protection as an issue had broad popular support, but I worried about the erosion of presidential leadership. Toward the close of the year, in a lengthy memorandum to John Ehrlichman,[66] I urged that the president develop and maintain a strong, positive environmental position. "Up until about six months ago, the President was well-positioned on this issue," I said, and I went on to recite a list of the administration's initiatives and achievements, both domestic and international, that reflected a position that was positive and balanced and enjoyed public credibility. I then laid out my concerns, which are perhaps worth quoting at length because they reflect how, at the time, I viewed the slippage of Nixon on specifically environmental matters and because they foreshadow similar developments in subsequent administrations.

A substantial erosion in the position [of the president] began to occur about six months ago. This change in position is related to the economic slowdown and the pickup in political activity as the 1972 election approaches. The first of these factors led to a quite natural concern by the Administration over the economic impacts of environmental controls, particularly when those controls are really becoming effective for the first time. The latter has contributed to the tendency in the press, the Congress, and the public generally to treat Administration expressions of concern about the economic impacts of environmental controls as signs of weakness on the issue. I think it can be safely assumed that the politicizing of the issue will accelerate as the election approaches so that it becomes increasingly important to maintain a consistent, positive position and to guard against public utterances and actions that can be exploited politically.

Within this context, I believe that there have been three major and related factors which have contributed to the recent erosion in the Administration's position. First, and most important, the President has himself seemed uncertain about the issue and this apparent ambivalence has been sensed accurately by the press and the public. Second, the President has failed to identify himself with the issue. For example, while he submitted an extraordinarily comprehensive environmental legislative program to the Congress last February, the President has taken little or no occasion since to demonstrate his interest in the specific elements of that program. Likewise, the President has not identified himself with enforcement efforts in the pollution field. Third, and related to the first two points, the Administration has spoken on the environment issue with a number of different voices.

On the latter point, there has been a tendency to try to accommodate both environmental aspirations and business concerns by giving both viewpoints full opportunity for expression from within the Administration. Thus, while EPA has spoken for a strong enforcement program, Commerce has been saying "wait a minute." While the motivation for such a dual posture may have been a highly laudable desire for balance, the approach does not really contribute to an image of balance but rather fosters a picture of uncertainty and ambivalence within the Administration. Given some public and press skepticism about a Republican Administration's firmness in dealing with industrial pollution, the hoped-for "balance" tends to become interpreted as a negative policy. The process may contribute to a favorable public image for EPA but at the expense of the President.[67]

After recommending a comprehensive strategy we could pursue, I declared:

> We have an extraordinary record to point to—in institutional reform, in administrative reform, in legislative innovation, in firm but fair enforcement, in international cooperation, in business response, and, most important of all, in the real beginnings of an improved quality of life. The Administration's environmental program is one of its major assets. We must start treating it as such. We must stop being defensive.[68]

Nixon's ambivalence, as I have described it, carried over to my time at EPA, and it would characterize President Gerald Ford's stance as well. Indeed, later presidents, representing both parties, have reflected to some degree the same difficulty in developing and pursuing a comprehensive and coherent environmental program. Particularly in times of economic downturn or of energy stringency, environmental policies can be seen as a roadblock to improvement. Politicians of all stripes have difficulty in coming to grips with the problem. And bureaucratic divides among the agencies responsible for the different policy areas do not help the situation. While I had a constant interface with energy officials, particularly while at EPA, I do not recall having a single meeting while at CEQ or EPA with a member of the Council of Economic Advisors. There needs to be a serious effort to bring about closer integration of these policy areas. In many ways, they are really only different manifestations of the same problem—how to build a sustainable, high-quality life for humanity.

That Vice President Richard Cheney's energy task force in 2001 heard from only one environmental spokesperson—so far as I am aware—suggests that the problem is getting worse.

Chapter 8

U.S. Environmental Leadership

URING MY YEARS at both the Council on Environmental Quality (CEQ) and the Environmental Protection Agency (EPA), I devoted substantial time and energy to international matters. I believed strongly that international leadership by the United States in environmental affairs is critically important to global environmental quality as well as to America's own national self-interest. Though conviction would have drawn me to international affairs, there was a strong personal interest as well: my introduction to the conservation/environmental world had been through African wildlife and, later, world wildlife. The concerns I developed for conservation on an international scale have stayed with me ever since, evolving over time to include the international dimensions of environmental problems generally.

At CEQ, we developed a wide range of international initiatives, one of which, on regulation of ocean dumping, I described in the preceding chapter. It made a huge difference to the success of these efforts that the White House insisted on looking to us, rather than to the Department of State, to lead in this area.

Having key environmental agencies take the lead in developing international environmental initiatives adds a great deal of credibility to those initiatives, in my opinion. However, having made that point, I must add that my colleagues and I at CEQ always deferred to State on the foreign policy aspects of our initiatives, and we developed a highly effective working partnership with the State Department especially through the indispensable support there of Christian Herter Jr. and his staff.[1] Above all, we were fortunate in having experienced Foreign Service officers Heyward

Isham and, later, W. A. "Ottey" Hayne assigned to CEQ to give us professional expertise on international matters.

My fellow council member Gordon MacDonald was an enthusiastic player in the international environmental field, as was Lee Talbot, CEQ's senior scientist, who played a major role in matters regarding international wildlife and related policy. My own strong interest in international environmental issues and my willingness to involve myself personally in them were also, I believe, significant factors in what we were able to accomplish. With the establishment of EPA at the end of 1970, that agency's first administrator, Bill Ruckelshaus, and I agreed, at his suggestion, that CEQ continue to carry the ball in most international matters. When I moved from CEQ to EPA in 1973, I took the international portfolio with me at the explicit direction of President Nixon.[2] That arrangement was continued by President Ford, so that for the full seven years of 1970–1976, there was a high degree of continuity in our relations with environmental officials around the globe.*

I myself occasionally saw Nixon in the Oval Office before going off to an international meeting. Such sessions were a useful device because, while seldom very substantive, they enabled me to say at the meeting that I had just met with the president, which carried the implication that I had his support for whatever position I was taking. Nixon was widely recognized abroad as an environmental leader—indeed, he was about the only head of government who could be so described. On one occasion, I met with Nixon after some international session and told him, rather apologetically, how I had "used" him at the meeting to influence a decision. He immediately replied that I had done exactly the right thing.

International Initiatives: A Sampling

While, of course, others did most of the work, the extent of my participation in the international arena gives some indication of how active the United States was in those years. In 1972, I headed the U.S. delegations to the landmark United Nations Conference on the Human Environment at Stockholm (Stockholm Conference) and the conference that adopted the Convention on the Prevention of Marine Pollution by Dumping of Wastes and Other Matter (Ocean Dumping Convention). I also represented the president at the 1972 meeting of the International Whaling

*EPA had an Office of International Affairs, whose able director under both Ruckelshaus and me was my longtime friend Fitzhugh Green.

Commission in London, represented the United States in the development with Canada of the Great Lakes Water Quality Agreement of 1972, cochaired two U.S. delegations to conferences that adopted international conventions to control the discharge of wastes from vessels at sea, initiated the U.S. proposal that led to the Convention Concerning the Protection of the World Cultural and Natural Heritage (World Heritage Convention), was the U.S. representative for six years to NATO's Committee on the Challenges of Modern Society (CCMS) in Brussels, headed the U.S. side of the US-USSR Agreement on Cooperation in the Field of Environmental Protection in 1972, and led the U.S. delegation to the 1973 conference in Washington, D.C., that created the Convention on International Trade in Endangered Species of Wild Fauna and Flora (CITES).

Most of those international activities were the result of U.S. initiatives, and several were generated by CEQ. In striking contrast to the situation today, the United States was the clear world leader during the 1970s in terms of both domestic environmental policy and international environmental cooperation. The two went hand in hand. Without a strong domestic program of environmental protection, we would not have had the credibility abroad to provide the environmental leadership we did, not only at international conferences but also in our discussions with environmental policy makers of individual countries. (Of course, prior to 1970, the international community had had little engagement in environmental matters.)

The Great Lakes Water Quality Agreement

Several months before the Stockholm Conference, President Nixon and Prime Minister Pierre Trudeau of Canada signed at Ottawa the landmark Great Lakes Water Quality Agreement, committing our two countries to a rigorous schedule of reduction in the wastes being discharged into the lakes — primarily, of course, from the far more intensively industrialized and populated U.S. side.[3]

The agreement had a considerable history. In early 1970, Nixon had appointed a task force under my chairmanship to make recommendations for addressing Lake Erie's pollution. It was commonly said at the time that "Lake Erie is dead." Pollution of the lakes was becoming a public, even a national, issue. In June 1971, when I addressed a Lions International convention in Las Vegas and declared "We are going to clean up Lake Erie!" I received a standing ovation from the 15,000 delegates.[4]

While Lake Erie suffered in particular from algae blooms, fish kills, and fouled beaches, it was difficult to separate the problems of Lake Erie from those of the Great Lakes as a whole and, with White House agreement, the mandate of our task force was soon expanded to cover all of the Great Lakes.

I took a U.S. delegation to Canada on June 23, 1970, to discuss joint approaches to Great Lakes pollution problems. My opposite number was the secretary of state for external affairs, Mitchell Sharp. I liked and respected Sharp from the beginning. Bright, experienced, practical, and possessed of a wry sense of humor, he was a pleasure to work with. We set up a joint working group, which CEQ's Gordon MacDonald headed for the U.S. side, to explore the feasibility of a joint action program. A sticking point then, as it was throughout the negotiations, was Canada's insistence that both countries be allowed to discharge the same amount of pollutants into the Lakes. Such a fifty-fifty division was required, the Canadians argued, by the Boundary Waters Treaty of 1909. Because of the preponderance of industry and population on the U.S. side, however, the practical effect of such a division would have been to restrict U.S. growth or require extremely high levels of treatment, with just the opposite effect on the Canadian side.[5]

One of the most vexing issues was the problem of phosphates in detergents, which, when discharged into the lakes, acted as nutrients, leading to algae blooms and eventual eutrophication. There was little question that the level of phosphates in the lakes was much too high. The Canadians took an aggressive line on the issue and pushed for a total phase-out of phosphates over several years. A chemical commonly known as NTA was being urged as a substitute, but it was reported to have its own adverse effects.

Secretary of Commerce Maurice Stans, secretary of Interior Walter Hickel, and I had already met with the three principal U.S. producers of detergents — Procter & Gamble, Colgate-Palmolive, and Lever Brothers — and found them completely unwilling to make substantial reductions in phosphates at that time. In reporting on this meeting to the White House, I put forward an alternative method of "inducing reductions in phosphate levels," namely, an incentive tax. I saw such a tax as an incentive to make some reduction in phosphates immediately and to accelerate research toward development of a product with no phosphates, "placing responsibility on the industry to use its 'know-how' creatively."[6] That was the last I ever heard of that particular proposal. A complicating factor in the ongoing phosphate debate was the influence of Bryce Harlow, counselor to the president, who had been close to the industry and later became Procter & Gamble's Washington representative.

On June 10, 1971, at the end of a day-long meeting with Sharp, almost a year after we had first met, the United States and Canada agreed in principle on a program to restore the Great Lakes and to protect them in the future. We called it "an historic first between two countries sharing a common environmental problem."[7] We agreed in principle to set the same water quality standards and to achieve them by 1975, and we set the objectives of building and maintaining a large number of sewage treatment plants, cutting back on the amount of phosphorus entering the lakes, eliminating mercury and other toxic metals, and controlling thermal pollution, radioactive wastes, and pesticides. We said that these objectives would be embodied in a formal agreement that fall. Formalization of the agreement actually took until 1972.

Bill Ruckelshaus and I traveled to Ottawa to be present at the signing by Nixon and Trudeau. The agreement set an example to the world of international cooperation in addressing environmental problems of mutual concern. Canada's minister of the environment, Jack Davis, and I also established a regular consultative mechanism for consideration of environmental issues of mutual interest and by 1976 I found myself able to declare, with little modesty but some conviction, that the cleanup of the Great Lakes represented "one of the greatest success stories in American history."[8]

Of course, the agreement put off until a later day the control of such important but difficult problems as the runoff of agricultural wastes and the pollution of the lakes by airborne pollutants such as PCBs (polychlorinated biphenyls). But it was a good start. More sinister problems have become evident in recent years, such as the discovery that many fish and waterfowl in the lakes have physical deformities and damaged reproductive systems as a result of exposure to certain chemicals that act as endocrine disrupters. World Wildlife Fund researcher Theo Colburn has been a leader in identifying and publicizing these problems.[9]

The 1972 Soviet Agreement

When it became known within our government in the fall of 1971 that President Nixon was planning his historic visit to Moscow that coming

May, it was decided that we would develop a cooperative environmental agreement with the Soviets that Nixon and the Soviet leadership could sign at the time of his visit. The initiative came purely from the U.S. side and originated with CEQ.[10] The State Department assigned an experienced Foreign Service officer, Jack Perry, to CEQ to help coordinate the operation. However, it was clear from the outset that the responsibility for moving the project forward was ours.

We drafted an agreement, which took on the official name of the US-USSR Agreement on Cooperation in the Field of Environmental Protection—an awkward mouthful, admittedly. As the agreement evolved, eleven areas of cooperation were set out: air pollution, water pollution, environmental pollution associated with agricultural production, enhancement of the urban environment, preservation of nature and organization of wildlife preserves, marine pollution, biological and genetic consequences of environmental pollution, influence of environmental changes on climate, earthquake prediction, arctic and subarctic ecological systems, and, finally, legal and administrative measures for protecting environmental quality.

The agreement emphasized the development of new technologies and improvement of existing ones in these areas and for their introduction into everyday use. To accomplish this, the agreement envisaged regular exchanges of scientists and other experts, the exchange of information, and actual joint development and implementation of programs and projects.

I had at least two meetings with the Soviet ambassador to the United States, Anatoly Dobrynin, to discuss the agreement during its development stage and, later, its implementation. The first of these was over lunch at Washington's Metropolitan Club, with Dobrynin as my guest. It was an important discussion because we reached final accord over the terms of the agreement, which, to be honest, had been almost entirely drafted by the American side. Dobrynin, so that it could be said that the terms had been negotiated and the Soviet side had insisted on changes, requested a small change in language, almost totally nonsubstantive, to which I readily agreed. That done, we toasted the success of the agreement.

Dobrynin made clear that Nixon's strong interest in the environment had made a big impression on his government. He volunteered that now perhaps the most important contribution the U.S. side could make was to encourage the USSR to develop a more effective organization for environmental management. The very range and scope of the subjects we introduced for discussion would convey effectively to the bureaucracy an understanding of the need for better central coordination, he suggested. Of course, the very fact that Dobrynin brought up the matter made it quite clear that the Kremlin knew there was a problem in this regard. However, the Soviet bureaucracy proved intractable on the subject and I was to see little or no progress toward Soviet development of an effective mechanism for environmental management over the next four years.

However, the aspect of our luncheon that I remember best had to do with the food. Soft-shell crabs were on the menu, and, when I ordered them, Dobrynin did likewise, even though he had never eaten them before. The picture is indelibly fixed in my mind of the distinguished ambassador with almost an entire crab in his mouth, the legs protruding out to either side and wiggling as he tried to chew and speak. It was one of the great moments of détente.

The agreement was signed by Nixon and Soviet president Nikolai Podgorny, the least known and least powerful of the ruling triumvirate, on May 23, 1972. On the same day, I briefed the press at the White House on the agreement. I said, somewhat expansively, "It's a whole new ball game with the Soviet Union!"[11] I must have been practicing my sound bites.

The following September, I led a U.S. delegation to Moscow to sign an implementing agreement. It was the first of six such trips to the USSR I was to make before leaving government service in 1977; on many of these trips I would be accompanied by Aileen.

There was an entertaining sidelight to the preparations for my first visit to Moscow. Learning that the president had taken one or more gifts to Leonid Brezhnev, including a bullet-proof limousine, I cast around for an appropriate gift for my Soviet hosts. My eventual choice was a breeding pair of Przewalski's horse, an animal that was native to the Siberian steppes but had been extinct throughout its natural range for many years. There were no specimens in the USSR, but a few were scattered in zoos in Europe and the United States. I managed to secure the offer of a breeding pair from two U.S. zoos and then arranged a suitable cargo plane from the U.S. Air Force to transport them to Moscow. I informed the U.S. embassy in Moscow of my plans and in response received a cable from our ambassador, Jacob Beam, stating that he had once seen a Przewalski's horse in the Warsaw Zoo almost bite off the finger of a high official. "It is my personal view," he added, "that the sooner they become extinct the better!" I set out the whole idea in a memorandum to the White House, pointing out the dramatic value of helping restore an endangered Soviet species to its natural habitat.[12] The memo quickly came back with a note on it to the effect that the plan had been rejected as upstaging the president. I still think it was a great idea!

Prior to leaving for Moscow, I met with the president in the Oval Office and briefed him on the purposes of the Moscow meeting.[13] He sat at his desk and, leaning back in his chair, gave me some personal advice on dealing with the Russians. Most Russians, he said, suffer from a strong inferiority complex, so I should go out of my way to praise things Russian. When I mentioned that Senator Gordon Allott had said about my forthcoming trip to the USSR that "there aren't any votes in Moscow," Nixon replied that Allott didn't know what he was talking about; there were plenty of votes. Nixon was convinced that the agreement would bring him real domestic political payout. Moreover, it was plain that Nixon was looking beyond possible short-term political gains from the Soviet agreement; he was also seeking ways to influence attitudes inside the USSR. When I mentioned that Shirley Temple Black was a member of my delegation, he said she should get on Russian television and he urged me to do the same. In discussions with the Soviets, he said, as he had about other meetings I would have, that I should never hesitate to refer to discussions between myself and the president and to make clear his personal interest. And so I did, at our opening session in Moscow a few days later: "Just before leaving Washington, I met with President Nixon and he expressed to me his strong personal interest in our environmental agreement and his sincere desire that our meetings here be productive."[14]

I have said elsewhere that I never had a substantive meeting with Nixon. However, even though this and later meetings on the Soviet agreement may well have been scheduled primarily as photo opportunities for the press, we did manage to cover some interesting ground. Détente was clearly a major objective for Nixon, not only to ease tensions between the two countries but also for its spin-off value to U.S. interests in other parts of the world. Later, when the joint annual meeting of the agreement participants was held in Washington, I took my Soviet counterparts, first E. K. Federov and subsequently Yuri Izrael, into the Oval Office to meet with the president. I had been a guest at a meeting of the Supreme Soviet in Moscow, and now, I said, Federov was accompanying me to a hearing of the Senate Commerce Committee to observe our legislative process. "I hope Academician Federov is more influential with the committee than I usually am," said Nixon. He spoke about détente and how it helped in the Middle East. "We must not allow these great peoples [Russians and Americans] to come into conflict — argue, yes; conflict, no," he said. "We must not collide. This way we can reach the heights together." Nixon expressed strong support for the environmental agreement and concern that it got so little publicity.[15] Actually, I thought it got quite a lot.

Our delegation to Moscow that first fall after the agreement was signed was a large one. Aside from Shirley Temple Black, who drew crowds wherever she went, there were representatives of the agencies that had a programmatic involvement in the agreement. Also along were the heads of two major environmental organizations, Tom Kimball of the National Wildlife Federation and Elvis Stahr of the National Audubon Society.

At the Kremlin, I met with President Podgorny, who had signed the agreement with Nixon in May. He was an affable host and we reviewed the agreement, although not in much detail. I met with Podgorny three times over the years, twice accompanied by U.S. ambassador Walter Stoessel. After the retirement of Federov, his successor, Yuri Izrael, head of the Hydrometeorological Service of the USSR (Hydromet), always attended these meetings. There was usually a certain amount of light banter. I recall briefing Podgorny on the new US-USSR Migratory Bird Convention,[16] which had been negotiated by Buff Bohlen, explaining that U.S. scientists had banded waterfowl in Soviet Siberia that had then migrated to the western coast of North America, where some had been shot in California. Podgorny professed shock at this intelligence and exclaimed, "What? You Americans are shooting Soviet birds?!" On my return to Washington, I gave a personal report to Nixon on my meeting with Podgorny and on the status of the projects.[17]

Some notes from my third and last meeting with Podgorny at the Kremlin, which occurred during the Gerald Ford administration and in the company of Jack Matlock, the U.S. deputy chief of mission, indicate the general setting for these meetings and the extent of ongoing activity generated by the agreement with the Soviets. On this occasion, we waited in an anteroom while Izrael went into Podgorny's suite of offices, presumably to brief him. I opened the blue-gray damask curtains of the one window to see the view — they had always been open before — and looked out on a gray, wintry scene of the Moscow River and the large power plant on its banks. There were snow flurries in the air, and magpies swirled like leaves outside the window.

After Podgorny greeted us affably, we sat at a round table, Podgorny with his back to the window and me to his left, with an interpreter between us. There was a bowl of fruit in the center of the table, a couple of open boxes of chocolates, mineral water, glasses, and ashtrays. The room was as I remembered it from prior visits: light-colored furniture, blue-gray damask-covered walls, curtains the same, and dark blue wall-to-wall carpeting. Podgorny smoked steadily—seven or eight cigarettes during the hour and a half we met. He looked in good health.

After we discussed the status and scope of the agreement (forty projects, 150 activities, 700 individual exchanges during the past year), we turned to more general subjects, such as the election of Jimmy Carter to the presidency and détente. Podgorny remarked that the Soviet Union and the United States would always have problems because of their political and economic differences, but those differences "should not interfere with such matters as the human environment." I replied that I did not believe that environmental cooperation could be separated from the totality of our relations and that U.S. support for such programs as environmental cooperation would depend on how the U.S. administration, Congress, and public perceived the overall trend in our relationship. I was not speaking as a politician, I said, or as a diplomat or a defense expert: I simply believed that what I said was plain common sense.[18]

Nevertheless, overall the relationship was a positive one, as I reported to President Ford on my return to Washington. The Soviet budget showed a significant increase in the environmental area. As evidence of the positive relationship we had developed, I said that, when I told Podgorny that the Soviet bureaucrats had been reluctant to provide us with information on their chlorofluorocarbon (CFC) production, he had assured me that the data would be forthcoming.[19]

Once our first Moscow meetings were complete, in September 1972, our delegation went to Leningrad (which, of course, is again called St. Petersburg). Aileen and I traveled by night train, with our own private compartment in an old paneled car and early morning tea service provided by an aproned attendant from a large samovar. We stayed at the Astoria Hotel, a comfortable relic of pre-Soviet days that produced excellent poached eggs. There were business sessions at an Arctic Institute and a Mathematics Institute. There were visits to the Hermitage and to

Tsarskoye Selo (now Pushkin) and the fabulous palaces there — Pavlovsk, Peterhof, Catherine — which had been meticulously restored after their destruction by Adolf Hitler's forces during World War II. We had a very moving visit to the Piskariovskoye Memorial Cemetery, where 800,000 of the 1.5 million residents of Leningrad who died during the three-year German siege are buried in common graves — large, flat mounds unmarked except by small plaques at the corners. The cemetery was a favorite place for new bridal couples to visit, fresh from their wedding and still in wedding garb, as we saw.

Our delegation was given a gala dinner aboard a large Soviet oceanographic research vessel in the Leningrad harbor. The ship's officers and the enlisted men and women gave us a marvelous choral concert, at which Russian voices excel. At the end of the concert, we Americans were invited to respond in kind. Surprisingly, I had neglected to select our delegation with this sort of challenge in mind. Fortunately, Shirley Temple Black was with us, and, after a hasty consultation, she and I did an impromptu song-and-dance routine to the lyrics of "The Good Ship Lollipop!" I added little to the performance, but it was a smash hit in any event, and once again American honor was upheld.

Aileen and I went on to Irkutsk, on Lake Baikal in Siberia, and then to Yakutsk, north of the Arctic Circle, where I visited the Permafrost Institute, of interest because of the plan to build an oil pipeline across permafrost terrain in Alaska. (I learned nothing about construction in permafrost that we did not already know, however.) Lake Baikal itself was beautiful and interesting, containing about one-fifth of the earth's total supply of fresh water. A two-part New Yorker article by Marshall Schulman had warned that the lake, said to be the earth's largest supply of clear, pure water, was threatened by effluent from two pulp mills on its shores. I visited the pulp mills and inspected their waste treatment facilities. Of course, I did not have the technical capability to judge the quality of treatment. From there, we went to the lake's shore where the effluent was being discharged, and I was invited to drink a glass of the stuff. In the interest of détente I agreed, and I found it relatively clear and tasteless. Subsequently, I learned that the effluent also included the waste from the village where the pulp mill employees lived. Anyway, I survived.

I went to the USSR at least once a year through 1976 and almost always found opportunities for traveling through that fascinating land. In 1975, while I was head of EPA, Aileen and I took our children Bowdy (age nineteen) and Errol (sixteen) with us to Moscow and then to Khabarovsk in the Soviet Far East, on the Amur River border with China. When I pointed out a Soviet power plant belching smoke, my Soviet guide replied, "Yes, but it is blowing into China!" We had the use of an Ilyushin 18 aircraft for the trip — a Hydromet research plane — and visited Samarkand, Bokhara, Dushambe, Tashkent, Irkutsk, Yakutsk, and finally Khabarovsk. Yuri Izrael accompanied us for much of the trip, along with other Soviet staff, including our inseparable KGB agent. While our visits to the cities of the ancient Silk Road were largely sightseeing in nature, there were other stops related to the US-USSR environmental agreement. Thus, near Dushambe we visited the construction site of the huge earthen Nurek Dam, around which a team of American scientists from the California Institute of Technology were working on earthquake prediction problems, one of the areas covered by our agreement.

Other than perhaps the earthquake prediction project, I am hard put to identify any area in which the United States gained anything very concrete from the exchanges under the agreement. The Soviets, on the other hand, had a great deal to learn. They were always on the lookout for new technology, such as advanced computers. Soviet air pollution experts usually wanted to visit our automobile plants; we came to believe they were interested not so much in emission control technology as in automobile assembly line techniques. Their own pollution control efforts were fairly rudimentary, as was usually evident in any industrial area. On our first visit to Moscow, I was a guest at a meeting of the Supreme Soviet that focused on pollution problems. The triumvirate of Brezhnev, Nikita Khrushchev, and Podgorny were all there on the dais before me. There was a lot of denial at work. The principal speaker, V. A. Kirillin, chairman of the State Committee for Science and Technology, started off by declaring that "of course, socialism by definition cannot pollute." My answer to that line whenever I heard it was that, in reality, both socialism and capitalism pollute, but the difference is that, under socialism, the polluter and the regulator are the same person. Of course, there is little basis for being smug about pollution problems under the capitalist system.

It is perhaps worth noting here that because of the success of our environmental initiative with the Soviets, when I learned of Nixon's impending trip to China, I suggested in a memorandum to Kissinger that exploratory contacts with the People's Republic of China (PRC) on environmental matters be made and that CEQ be given the exploratory role.

I referred to the fact that we had met the past November with ten visiting Chinese scientists who had come to the United States under the auspices of the Committee on Scholarly Communication with the People's Republic of China. My impression from that meeting had been that the PRC was increasing its attention to environmental matters and "would quite likely be interested in pursuing a discussion with us." [20] I received no answer.

In the mid-1980s, during the Ronald Reagan administration, when I was with the World Wildlife Fund (WWF), the US-USSR agreement was still on the books but essentially moribund. Relations were far from good. Reagan had made his "evil empire" speech citing alleged violations of arms agreements by the Soviets. Détente was all but dead. My idea — pretty naive in retrospect — was for me to go to the Soviet Union as a private citizen, perhaps wearing my WWF hat, renew old acquaintances, and try to reactivate a dialogue on environmental matters. Such a dialogue would be nonthreatening to both sides yet of mutual concern, and it just might breathe new life into détente.

I tried the idea out on both Jim Schlesinger, then head of the Central Intelligence Agency, and Frank Press, president of the National Academy of Sciences, and they thought it worth exploring. I called Jack Matlock, at that time on the staff of the National Security Council, whom I had met in Moscow when he was chief political officer and later deputy chief of mission at our embassy. He listened to what I had to say and replied that he would talk to others and get back to me. That was the last I ever heard of the matter. I imagine the whole idea had no place in the cold war thinking of the Reagan administration, and I certainly had no interest in pursuing a political objective in the Soviet Union that was not supported by my own government.

Following the demise of the Soviet Union, the environmental agreement was renewed, in 1994, as a U.S.-Russian agreement, "to the credit and benefit of both our countries." [21] However, there is little or no formal activity today under the agreement. Russia's Ministry of Environmental Protection, established just before the collapse of the Soviet Union, was abolished by President Vladimir Putin.

The Stockholm Conference
The June 1972 United Nations Conference on the Human Environment (Stockholm Conference), the world's first international environmental

conference, was a year and a half in the making. Canadian Maurice Strong—brilliant, liberal, ambitious, deeply committed to the environment, and a consummate operator on the world stage—had been selected as secretary-general. He visited CEQ early in 1971 to solicit our support for the conference, our ideas for its agenda, and our participation in the preparatory activities leading up to it. He got all three from us, in conjunction with the State Department, where Chris Herter's office conducted most of the U.S. preparatory sessions.

There was uncertainty for some while as to who would lead the U.S. conference delegation. William Rogers, as secretary of State, had a clear claim to the job if he wanted it. However, the United States was still involved in the Vietnam War; for Rogers to head the U.S. delegation would have made him a lightning rod for anti-American feeling and the conference could have been seriously distracted from its environmental purpose. Actually, Rogers never took much interest in environmental matters, and I doubt he had any desire to go to Stockholm. Secretary of Interior Rogers Morton was another possibility, but Interior had little to do with the issues before the conference. Bill Ruckelshaus at EPA, like Morton a member of the delegation, would have been an appropriate choice, but, consistent with Bill's deferral to CEQ on international matters, he did not seek the role, and the White House gave me the nod.

Aileen and our children Bowdy and Errol accompanied me to Stockholm and they spent two weeks there sightseeing, marching in support of whales, sailing with new friends, accompanying me to various official social events, and visiting the conference. There was a great deal of non-governmental organization (NGO) activity associated with the conference, and this provided a lively forum. For example, there was the large "Whale March," complete with a full-scale mock-up of a whale, which Wally Hickel showed up to lead and in which my family and I took part. Environmental activists of every persuasion held forth at public rallies. The International Institute for Environment and Development (IIED), founded by Barbara Ward, a British economist and a principal advisor to Maurice Strong, convened a meeting in parallel with the conference.[22] Bill Ruckelshaus participated actively in a number of the NGO events and provided a valuable communication link between our delegation and the NGO community. Finally, more than four hundred members of the press were accredited to the conference, a record at that time for such an international meeting. Stockholm was truly an event.

There were a few private citizens on our delegation at the suggestion of the White House, notable among them Shirley Temple Black. Actually, Black had a real interest in environmental matters and had joined the CEQ staff, at least nominally, some weeks earlier as a special assistant to the chairman.[23] John Ehrlichman showed up midway through the conference. He was infuriated that I and one or two other government members of the delegation had cars and drivers while the political members put on at White House request did not. Fortunately, I had nothing to do with the logistical arrangements for the U.S. delegation. Ehrlichman vented his ire on Chris Herter, who was deputy head of the delegation and the senior State Department participant. He did so in a full meeting of the delegation, which was embarrassing for all concerned. So far as I recall, this was Ehrlichman's only input during the two days or so that he was in Stockholm, and he appeared to take absolutely no interest in the proceedings of the conference itself. Whatever the merits or demerits of Ehrlichman's concern over cars and drivers, he managed on this occasion to play the political bully. In his own book about his White House service, the incident provides his only reference to the Stockholm Conference (or to anything remotely related to the environment, for that matter).[24]

The conference opened with a welcoming speech by the Swedish prime minister, Olaf Palme, who, while still in office, was later the victim of an unsolved murder. He devoted a portion of his speech to attacking the United States over the Vietnam War and lambasting us for environmental crimes allegedly committed during the conflict, such as the use of defoliants. He was clearly playing to his domestic political audience, which I thought was a poor show on the part of the conference host. In any event, in my own speech to the conference that followed soon after, I ignored Palme's attack and expressed "our appreciation to the Government of Sweden as the original proposer and generous host" of the conference. Separately, and away from the conference site, I held a press conference at which I fully expressed my opinion of the prime minister's remarks. At a reception that evening, when I met him in the receiving line, I took advantage of the occasion to tell him what I had said at my press conference.

In my own address to the delegates, I set out U.S. objectives for the conference, objectives that had been carefully worked out over the previous eighteen months in Washington and almost all of which would be substantially achieved in the months ahead:

- We called for the establishment of a permanent entity within the United Nations to focus attention on environmental problems and to provide coordination of international environmental activity. The conference endorsed this proposal, and the United Nations established the United Nations Environment Programme (UNEP), headquartered in Nairobi, Kenya. (The choice of Nairobi, which the United States finally supported, was a political sop to the developing countries and unfortunately has helped keep UNEP on the sideline of United Nations affairs.)
- We proposed the creation of a $100 million United Nations environmental fund, to be financed by voluntary contributions from member governments, and this was agreed to.
- We urged regional actions similar to the joint U.S.-Canada Great Lakes Water Quality Agreement signed earlier that spring.
- We supported efforts to strengthen monitoring and assessment of the global environment.
- We urged the creation of a World Heritage Trust, and the conference endorsed the concept, which was embodied in a convention five months later in Paris.
- We urged the adoption of an international agreement to control the ocean dumping of wastes. The conference endorsed the proposal, and the Marine Protection, Research, and Sanctuaries Act of 1972 was drawn up and agreed to at a meeting in London that fall, as described in the preceding chapter.
- We supported cooperative action to protect genetic resources, including wildlife, and specifically asked the conference to support, which it did, our proposals for a moratorium on the commercial killing of whales and for a convention to control the international wildlife trade.
- We urged all nations and international organizations to conduct systematic environmental analyses as a regular part of their planning and decision-making processes. This proposal was akin to asking for the worldwide adoption of the environmental impact analysis mandated by our own National Environmental Policy Act of 1969. I think it is safe to say that most nations and most international organizations still have a long way to go in this regard.

There was a fair amount of tension at the conference between the industrialized, or developed, countries and the developing countries. The latter, led by Brazil, maintained that the developed countries had achieved their advanced status in part because of their freedom to pollute. The developing countries should not now be denied the same right, they argued, inferring that to do so would be to keep much of the world in an undeveloped state.

In my speech to the conference, I tried to address this issue directly. I suggested that the United States had learned that economic development at the expense of the environment imposes heavy costs in health and in the quality of life generally — costs that could be minimized by forethought and planning. It is far less costly and more effective, I said, to build the necessary environmental quality into new plants from the outset than it is to rebuild or modify old facilities. Moreover, the cost of environmental controls is usually quite manageable when included in the initial capital cost of a facility and spread over its useful life.

This was just one aspect of a larger concept that I tried to lay out in my address at the time: the need to bring the economy and the environment together as parts of the same whole. There was a lot of idealism in what I said, but I think there was a lot of truth as well. It is a concept that as a society I think we have yet to learn and to which I would return many times in subsequent years. It thus seems worth quoting at some length:

> Economic progress does not have to be paid for in the degradation of cities, the ruining of the countryside and the exhaustion of resources. And the converse is equally true: Environmental quality and resource conservation for the long future do not have to be paid for in economic stagnation or inequity.
>
> "Environmental quality" cannot be allowed to become the slogan of the privileged. . . . How can a man be said to live in harmony with his environment when that man is desperately poor and his environment is a played-out farm? Or when the man is a slum-dweller and his environment is a garbage-strewn street? I reject any understanding of environmental improvement that does not take into account the circumstances of the hungry and the homeless, the jobless and the illiterate, the sick and the poor. . . .
>
> No longer should there be any qualitative difference between the goals of the economist and those of the ecologist. A vital humanism should inspire them both. Both words derive from the same Greek word meaning "house." Perhaps it is time for the economist and ecologist to move out of the separate, cramped intellectual quarters they still inhabit and take up residence together in a larger house of ideas — whose name might well be the House of Man.

In that larger house, the economist will take full account of what used to be called "external diseconomies" such as pollution and resource depletion, and he will assign meaningful values to the purity of air and water and the simple amenities we once foolishly took for granted. He will develop better measures of true well-being than the conventional Gross National Product. The ecologist, in turn, will extend his attention beyond the balance of nature to include all those activities of man's mind and hand that make civilized life better than that of the cave dwellers. Both will collaborate to advise the planners and decision makers — so that cities and countryside of the future will promote the harmonious interaction of man with man, and/or man with nature; so that resources will remain for future generations; and so that development will lead not just to greater production of goods but also to a higher quality of life.

All things considered, the conference was a success — although it was hard to point to tangible products other than the creation of UNEP in Nairobi. It was the first such global gathering in the name of the environment and it attracted public attention around the world, including heightened awareness of environmental issues on the part of states and their leaders. That awareness may well have been the most important outcome of the conference. At the same time, we succeeded in putting key international objectives of the United States on the conference agenda and these were all endorsed by unanimous or nearly unanimous vote, thereby creating a very positive momentum as we moved from Stockholm to the various international meetings that followed.

When the conference ended, President Nixon issued a statement in Washington not only pointing out that the United States had achieved practically all its objectives but also commenting on the spirit of the conference:

> However, even more than in the specific agreements reached, I believe that the deepest significance of the conference lies in the fact that for the first time in history the nations of the world sat down together to seek better understanding of each other's environmental problems and to explore opportunities for positive action, individually and collectively.[25]

Nixon then cited the Great Lakes agreement, which he had signed with Prime Minister Trudeau in Ottawa in April, and the US-USSR environmental agreement, which he had signed in Moscow in May, as proof of the desire of the United States to work together with other nations on the "common tasks of peace," and he expressed pride that the United

States was taking a leading role in international environmental cooperation. There would be more evidence of the international leadership
Nixon was referring to in the months ahead.*

International Whaling Commission

At the conclusion of the Stockholm Conference, Aileen and our children
flew to Majorca for a week while I returned to the United States to check
up on the home front. I was back in Europe in a week's time, however, this
time to participate as the president's "personal representative" to the
meeting of the International Whaling Commission (IWC) in London.
Robert White, the able administrator of the National Oceanic and
Atmospheric Administration (NOAA) and a good friend, was the U.S.
commissioner. The major issue on the meeting's agenda was our proposal
for a moratorium on the commercial hunting of whales. The Stockholm
Conference had endorsed the proposal, I believe unanimously, with the
USSR not attending the conference and at least two others abstaining,
probably Japan and Norway.

The IWC was a rather odd organization (and still is). Its original members were all whaling nations, making it a sort of self-regulating international whaling club. As the United States and some other member states
gave up whaling, the character of the organization changed; it was now
made up of the few remaining whaling states and their allies plus a number of nonwhaling states such as the United States. With Lee Talbot
providing the staff lead, CEQ had proposed to the White House that the
United States push for a moratorium on whaling. Populations of several
of the principal great whale species had reached alarmingly low levels,
and they clearly needed time and protection in order to recover. Moreover, the protection of whales was now a popular subject with the public,
so the time seemed ripe for a move. NOAA supported the proposal,
Nixon bought it, and I was designated to attend the session as his personal
representative in order to give a clear signal of his interest. Our London
embassy kindly provided me with a car and driver for the several-day conference. The car was a fairly elderly white Jaguar sedan, which inevitably
became known as Moby Dick.

The meetings of the IWC had traditionally been closed to the public.

*The Stockholm Conference was followed up in subsequent years by a 1982 conference
in Nairobi and a 1992 conference in Rio de Janeiro. I was a delegate to both (nominal in
the case of Rio).

Resulting decisions were announced, but the votes of member nations were not. Prior to the vote on the moratorium, I urged that the rules be changed in this regard and that the sessions be opened to the press. These U.S. efforts at transparency were rejected, and we proceeded to a vote on the moratorium, which required a two-thirds majority to carry. A clear majority voted for the moratorium, but we fell short of the required two-thirds. Following the vote, I held a press conference to announce the result and also to disclose how each nation had voted. There was considerable publicity, just as I had hoped, and our efforts triggered an appreciative editorial from the *New York Times:*

> At the United Nations environmental conference in Stockholm and again at the International Whaling Commission, American spokesmen pressed hard for a moratorium on whale-killing.
> Indeed, the spirited efforts of Russell Train, chairman of President Nixon's Council on Environmental Quality, to obtain a moratorium turned the usually moribund sessions of the Whaling Commission into a lively forum of debate between conservationists and industry supporters.[26]

After several more attempts, the moratorium was finally approved in 1982 — ten years after its original proposal. A front-page article in the *New York Times* quoted me as saying that the IWC's moratorium represented "a great victory in the long fight to save these magnificent creatures" and called the vote "a triumph for human decency and compassion."[27]

Another twenty years have gone by. The moratorium is still in effect, but the fight is not over yet. Thanks to the moratorium, most whale stocks have recovered significantly, although several species, such as the northern right whale, remain in dangerously low numbers. Ever since the adoption of the moratorium, however, Japan has taken an exception that has permitted it to continue whaling, ostensibly in the name of scientific research, although substantially all the whale meat is commercially marketed. At the 2002 meeting of the IWC in Japan, the latter made an effort to expand its "scientific" taking to include whale species other than the minke and then to end the moratorium altogether. It lost on both counts but is likely to keep trying.

In 2001, I was interviewed in my WWF Washington office by a Japanese television crew. After the interviewer had established the history of my involvement with the whaling issue, she asked me, "Isn't it true that President Nixon proposed a moratorium on the commercial killing of whales in 1972 in order to distract the public from Vietnam?" The suggestion was preposterous, I replied; Nixon proposed the moratorium because the American people overwhelmingly were opposed to whaling. In fact, I said, pretty much the entire world opposes whaling, and the sooner the Japanese people understand that fact, the better we'll all be. That exchange concluded the interview.

World Heritage Trust

When I first joined The Conservation Foundation, in the fall of 1965, I participated in the White House Conference on International Cooperation and became a member of its Committee on Natural Resources, chaired by Joseph L. Fisher, then president of Resources for the Future (RFF), a private nonprofit organization dedicated to economic analysis of natural resource issues. I was probably the only conservationist on the committee, and Fisher approached me with an idea for "a trust for the world heritage." His thought had its genesis in the fact that our first national park, at Yellowstone, had been established a century before in the belief that the area possessed natural values of such importance that they transcended the interest of any state and, indeed, belonged to the heritage of the entire nation. In the same fashion, reasoned Fisher, there were natural areas around the globe of such value that they should be protected as part of the heritage of all peoples everywhere. I quickly espoused the concept; I believed (as I later expressed it) that the idea could give eloquent expression through cooperative international action to the truth that the earth is indeed man's home and belongs to all of us.[28] We broadened the concept to include "scenic, historic, and natural resources," and, in that form, it was endorsed by the committee and became one of the conference's recommendations to the Lyndon B. Johnson White House. However, no action was taken on the matter by Johnson's administration.

Two years later in Amsterdam, at the 1967 WWF-International Congress on Nature and Man, I gave a speech titled "A World Heritage Trust," outlining the concept and emphasizing its inclusion of great cultural sites such as the Acropolis, Angkor Wat, Machu Picchu, the pyramids of Egypt, and so forth. As part of that speech, I said:

> I believe it to be particularly appropriate at this Congress on "Nature and Man" to urge the launching of an international cooperative effort that brings

together in a unified program a common concern for both man's natural heritage and his cultural heritage. In so doing, we will be recognizing that our civilization, past and present, is inextricably linked to our physical environment. Indeed, the works of man are necessarily founded upon and molded by the natural environment. Can we conceive of a Venice in isolation from the sea?[29]

There the matter lay for several years, although there was some activity on its behalf within the International Union for the Conservation of Nature and Natural Resources (IUCN), which had endorsed the concept in 1966, and in the International Council on Monuments and Sites (ICOMOS). IUCN developed a draft convention in 1970 and agreed to include cultural as well as natural sites in its coverage.

I am sometimes described as the father of the World Heritage,[30] but it was Joe Fisher who really fathered the concept. Unfortunately, Joe died suddenly after serving as a member of Congress from northern Virginia. As chairman of CEQ, I was simply fortuitously placed to make the concept a reality.

The opportunity arose in 1971, when CEQ had responsibility for developing the president's annual message to Congress on the environment. We included the World Heritage Trust proposal in the February 8, 1971, environmental message, with President Nixon describing the concept in these words:

> It would be fitting by 1972 [the centennial of the creation of Yellowstone National Park] for the nations of the world to agree to the principle that there are certain areas of such unique worldwide value that they should be treated as part of the heritage of all mankind and accorded special recognition as part of a World Heritage Trust.

At the June 1972 Stockholm Conference, on the motion of the United States, the delegates unanimously endorsed the World Heritage concept,* and later that year in Paris, again on U.S. initiative, an international conference convened by the United Nations Educational, Scientific, and Cultural Organization (UNESCO) adopted the World Heritage Convention. Today, 176 nations are parties to the convention, and 730 sites around the world are part of the World Heritage, 563 of them cultural sites, such as our own Independence Hall, 144 of them natural sites, such

---

*Assistant secretary of Interior Nat Reed and CEQ senior scientist Lee Talbot played active roles in the United Nations' preparatory work leading up to the conference, ensuring that the World Heritage Trust would be on the conference agenda.

as Yellowstone, and 23 of them "mixed," such as Tikal in Guatemala, which combines Mayan ruins with a large tract of tropical rain forest.[31]

The World Heritage Trust (WHT) has proven a useful tool in upgrading and maintaining the quality of management of the areas in question, and in some cases it has proven critical in preventing the degradation or even destruction of an area. It is not an earthshaking program, but it is one of which, I believe, we can be proud. It takes a very positive American contribution to world culture — namely, the national park concept — and builds on it to create a shared value of common interest to all peoples of the world, a world in which such common interests seem all too rare. The citizen of Venice, for example, not only should take pride in the status of Venice and its lagoon as part of the World Heritage but also should feel a similar pride in the fact that Yellowstone and the Serengeti and the Acropolis *are also part of his or her own heritage.*[32]

There are a number of World Heritage sites in the United States — Redwood, Grand Canyon, Mesa Verde, Olympic, Great Smoky Mountains, Yellowstone, Everglades, and Independence Hall National Parks among them. Americans are generally unaware of the designation, but in many countries World Heritage status is a matter of ongoing pride. Unfortunately, the World Heritage Trust Committee in Paris has few funds and is very limited in its ability to assist poorer countries around the world in their effort to establish and maintain WHT sites.

Sadly, the United States has been extremely weak in its support of the World Heritage program, and that has been true under all presidents. In some years, the budget submitted to Congress has "zeroed" the WHT. On several of those occasions, I contacted the key people on the appropriation committees of Congress and helped get a modest appropriation restored. The $400,000 per year that has often been the U.S. contribution is a piddling amount for this nation to put up in support of what was, after all, a U.S. initiative. While the WHT falls within the budget of the State Department's Bureau of International Organization Affairs, programmatic responsibility lies with the Department of the Interior. Unfortunately, the leadership of the department has generally taken little or no interest in the World Heritage Trust specifically or in international matters generally.

The CITES Convention

Another international environmental milestone of the early 1970s was the negotiation in Washington in January 1973 of the Convention on

International Trade in Endangered Species of Wild Fauna and Flora, known familiarly as CITES. The concept of the convention, designed to control the international trade in endangered species, had been a number of years in the making and had been endorsed by the Stockholm Conference, as I have noted.

CEQ had played a major role in planning for the two-week conference, although, of course, Interior had the principal programmatic responsibility. Buff Bohlen, deputy assistant secretary of Interior for fish and wildlife and parks, was Interior's principal negotiator at the conference. Lee Talbot, CEQ's senior scientist, had been involved in the issue ever since a wildlife conservation conference, which I attended, was held at Arusha, Tanzania, in 1961. There the responsible wildlife and parks officials of the participating countries argued convincingly that they would never be able to control poaching so long as the international market for wildlife and wildlife products remained uncontrolled. The worldwide demand for such products, such as elephant ivory, tortoise shell, rhinoceros horn, and skins of all sorts, as well as the living animals themselves used for the pet trade, such as exotic birds and tropical fish, was having a devastating effect on wildlife populations around the globe. Many rare plants fell into the same category.

The conference, as a result, transmitted a recommendation to IUCN that a convention controlling the international wildlife trade be developed. Two years later, Talbot and Wolfgang Burhenne, head of IUCN's Environmental Law Centre, put together a formal convention proposal, which was circulated and refined over the ensuing years. When I recruited Talbot to join our fledgling CEQ staff in 1970, he and I agreed on an agenda that included the wildlife trade convention as well as the more specific moratorium on commercial whale hunting.

The 1973 Washington conference was chaired by Chris Herter of the State Department, and I had the privilege of heading the U.S. delegation. There was contention over a number of issues, some technical and some wide-ranging. In the latter category was the question of whether to include plants under the convention—as it turned out, they were—and whether to cover whales (which were already covered by the International Whaling Commission, although not always effectively)—and they, too, were. Gratifying to me personally was that Kenya, whose delegation was headed by Perez Olindo, director of the Kenya Wildlife Service and the first university graduate under the African Wildlife Leadership Foundation's education program almost ten years before, became the leading proponent of a strong convention. Kenya's leadership was important because the southern African countries, such as South Africa and Zimbabwe, preferred a weaker approach, particularly regarding the ivory trade.

Agreement was finally reached on the terms of a strong convention, and CITES is today a vital factor in the international protection of endangered species, covering species from the entire spectrum of animal and plant life on the planet (other than humans). WWF's TRAFFIC USA (now TRAFFIC North America) program regularly monitors the movement of wildlife and wildlife products through U.S. ports of entry, blowing a whistle from time to time as necessary.* The elephant ivory trade continues to be a hot issue under CITES. The total ban on the trade imposed in 1989 undoubtedly stemmed the widespread illegal poaching that had destroyed about half of Africa's elephants. Large herds now exist throughout much of southern Africa, and the organized culling of herds by game departments has produced large stockpiles of ivory. The 2002 CITES meeting of parties agreed to lift the ban on ivory sales by South Africa, Namibia, and Botswana, capped by the amount of ivory in their existing stockpiles.[33]

Visits to Japan and China

In addition to the travel required by various international conferences and agreements such as I have described, I undertook from time to time trips abroad designed to open doors and to foster environmental relationships.

Thus, in 1975, following our family trip across Siberia, we flew from Khabarovsk to Japan for a short visit en route to China.[34] (Because of possible sensitivities about the China relationship, I had personally cleared the visit in conversation with Henry Kissinger, who was then secretary of State.) Direct transit from the Soviet Union to China was either impossible or extremely difficult at the time, so we went via Japan, where we spent two days vacationing before flying on to Beijing.

Our visit to China was as the guests of George H. W. and Barbara Bush, some thirteen years before the former would become president.

*For many years, WWF's TRAFFIC-USA program was headed by Ginette Helmley, now WWF's vice president for species conservation.

Since the United States did not have full diplomatic relations with China at the time, George's official position was as U.S. liaison officer. Four of the five Bush children, George W., Neil, Marvin, and Dorothy, were there at the time of our visit, and all were staying at the official residence. We knew all of them quite well because they were friends and contemporaries of our own children, except for George W., who was older than the rest. As a result of there being so many Bushes, we Trains stayed at the Peking Hotel, which turned out to be excellent. George met us at the Beijing airport and over the next several days the Bushes outdid themselves as hosts. Barbara took us to the Forbidden City, the Summer Palace, the Great Wall, and the Ming Tombs. George and Barbara together took us to formal meetings with a Middle School (including an impromptu basketball game with, on the American side, Bowdy; George W., Marvin, and Neil Bush; and John Ballou), the Moon Temple Street Commune (an urban community organization), and the Marco Polo Bridge Commune (a suburban community organization of more than 111,000 households and small farming operations).

Some flavor of our time with the Bushes in Beijing is captured by the following entry from my diary:

> Driving in the ambassadorial limousine is not for the nervous or faint of heart. You proceed at a fast clip, close to the middle of the road, . . . the driver keeping one finger on the horn which he plays like a stop on a trumpet, bicyclists and pedestrians crowding across your path like myriad moths. These seem to be deflected at the last moment, much as a bow wave pushes water and debris away from a speeding ship. George's chauffeur drove with aristocratic disdain for these details. He sat very erect, white gloves on his hands, finger on the horn, dark glasses over his eyes, head hardly turning as near-catastrophe after near-catastrophe swept by to the sides.[35]

Given the state of formal U.S. relations with the People's Republic of China at the time, I could have no official meetings with Chinese officials, but George invited the Chinese government to send environmental officials to lunch with us.[36] The senior Chinese official at the lunch was Wang Chung-chich, apparently the head of the Environmental Office of the State Council, a small coordinating body. He made no bones of the fact that the PRC's environmental program was at a pretty elementary stage. The PRC recognized the importance of environmental protection, he said, but also recognized the need to develop its industries and agriculture. We talked at length about how environmental programs worked (or did not) in the PRC, with special attention to the control of sulfur dioxide (SO_2), a subject of high interest to China because it gets most of its energy from the burning of coal. I described our own organization for dealing with environmental matters. The size, scope, and budget of EPA plainly amazed the group. I explained the organization and scope of our research efforts and could learn of nothing remotely comparable in the PRC.

I described the various bilateral arrangements for environmental cooperation that we had at the time — with Canada, Mexico, Japan, the Federal Republic of Germany, Poland, and the USSR, among others — as well as multilateral activities such as the Stockholm Conference (which representatives of the PRC had attended). Bush commented that he was certain that, if Wang or any other Chinese experts visited the United States, they would receive every cooperation from EPA and other agencies. Wang expressed interest but did not follow up on the idea. Later, Wang said that China should concentrate on putting its own house in order environmentally before engaging in international exchanges and that China should have something to offer before entering into such relationships.

We broke up after about two hours of discussion following lunch. My notes show that the conversation was very friendly and our counterpart was "reasonably outgoing." As was the case with other groups I met in the PRC, little curiosity was expressed about U.S. programs — control of sulfur emissions from coal-fired plants was an exception — and most of the conversational initiatives came from our side. There were many things we did not talk about — migratory birds and other wildlife, parks and other protected areas among them. However, the scope of the PRC's Environmental Office was obviously limited. Moreover, it struck me then, and I suspect it is still quite true, that rules and standards set at the national level may turn out to be meaningless at the local level.

George took us to the airport on our departure. From beginning to end, the Bushes had been fantastic hosts. We had eaten almost every meal except breakfast together. We had visited the principal historic sites of Beijing and the surrounding area. We had been introduced to some of the key educational and community arrangements within the communist structure. And I had engaged in useful talks with environmental officials.

After our time with the Bushes, we flew back to Japan. I spent most of the next morning with the head of the Japanese Environmental Protection Agency, Minister Ozawa, discussing the status of environmental agreements between our two countries. I brought up the subject of the International Whaling Commission's recent meeting and urged him to use his influence to persuade Japan to accept the new quotas. Ozawa was noncommittal and actually had little to do with the issue.

We talked about the U.S environmental impact statement (EIS) process, and Ozawa said that his government would be introducing similar legislation in the next session of the National Diet. He was interested in the role of public participation in the process. Of course, the opportunity for public hearings and comment is central to the entire process in the United States, but the Japanese were obviously very uncomfortable with the concept of public disclosure of what government is planning to do.[37]

This was, of course, not my first official visit to Japan. I have already recounted the first, in 1969, when I traveled there as under secretary of Interior. There had also been a second, which took place soon after the creation of CEQ.

The summer of 1970 was hot and humid in Washington. When we read news of similar conditions in Tokyo combined with heavy air pollution, we seized on the circumstances to launch an environmental exchange with Japan. At CEQ's suggestion, Nixon wrote to Prime Minister Eisaku Sato, calling attention to our similar air pollution problems and suggesting that perhaps we could both benefit from a cooperative effort to solve them. The president received a very positive response from Sato, and, on October 7, the same day he announced the ocean dumping initiative, Nixon announced that I would be going to Japan and would meet with the prime minister.

At the time, Japan had no government structure in place for dealing with environmental matters in any coordinated way. Doubtless prompted by my impending visit, Sadanori Yamanaka, a member of the Diet, was named the prime minister's environmental coordinator. Yamanaka had little real authority, but he provided an opposite number to discuss issues with our mission. I did meet with Sato on one occasion as well, but that seemed more an opportunity for a mass of Japanese press photographers to descend on us than a chance for substantive conversation.

Not long after this trip, Japan created an Environmental Protection Agency, and, of course, that became the U.S. EPA interface in Japan. The rapidly evolving structure in our government for dealing with environmental issues, together with the various international ventures CEQ initiated, seemed to have a strong catalytic effect in promoting more effective government organization for environmental policy and management worldwide.

While in Tokyo, I did a television interview that Aileen watched from our hotel room. She was startled to see me chattering away in Japanese, though she said that the lip sync was not very good. Later, we flew to the northern island of Hokkaido, watched the Japanese black-necked cranes on their home ground doing their beautiful courtship dances in the mist, and visited Akan National Park, at the northern end of the island. There we walked alone out a promontory overlooking a large lake, surrounded by the twisted pines and eroded limestone islets that one usually thinks of as the figment of some Japanese artist's imagination. It was spectacularly beautiful. The only problem was that we had to wade through knee-deep tin cans and other trash to reach our vantage point.

AMONG OTHER countries that I visited on official business was Spain. Prince (now King) Juan Carlos made an official visit to Washington in 1970. When I met with him privately at Blair House, the president's guest house, to discuss environmental matters, he invited me to visit Spain. I did so the following year, meeting again with the prince and also with Generalissimo Francisco Franco, who was then quite infirm, as well as with other members of the Spanish government. I visited the Coto Doñana wildlife reserve, which had been one of the first projects of the World Wildlife Fund. On my return to Washington, I sent a full report to the president on my meeting with Franco, including my observations about his physical condition.[38] Nixon had a voracious appetite for news, including minutiae, about other heads of state.

Nixon always had a fascination with power, particularly as it was exercised by heads of state. Indeed, I always suspected that that fascination helped explain how an otherwise intelligent person got himself into the Watergate fiasco. A somewhat chilling episode in this regard occurred at a Cabinet meeting in 1970 that I attended. The president used the occasion to introduce a new energy "czar"— Bill Simon, who sat on his right. Nixon emphasized the necessity for his energy boss to have broad authority at a time of severe energy shortages and for other agency heads to accept that authority. To illustrate his point, Nixon picked up a copy of Albert Speer's *Inside the Third Reich* and read aloud a passage concerning Hitler's directive to Speer as head of the German procurement effort during the war. It has always struck me as an unfortunate choice of an example.

In many countries where I had an opportunity to discuss environmental problems in the decade of the 1970s, I found an almost intractable bureaucratic structure. It was extremely difficult and often impossible for other governments to develop any central coordinating organization for effective environmental management. The U.S. success in establishing first CEQ and then EPA was highly unusual. Our separation of the executive and legislative branches is an enormous help in giving us greater flexibility in that regard. Of course, on the other side of the coin, congressional committee jurisdictions are often a huge obstacle to effective reorganization in the executive branch. Having said all that, I found that the kind of direct intergovernmental contacts I have described had a considerable influence in focusing attention on specific environmental problems on the part of other governments. Moreover, the prominent attention the United States gave to environmental matters was enormously influential. I always believed that pushing, or at least nudging, other countries to follow our lead is in our own national interest. In addition to its obvious importance in promoting the quality of life on the planet, it is desirable from a competitive standpoint that our trading partners around the world have roughly the same environmental standards as we do in order to ensure a reasonably level playing field for American industry and agriculture.

NATO's Environmental Program

For six years, starting in 1970 while I was chairman of CEQ, I was designated by President Nixon the U.S. representative to the Committee on the Challenges of Modern Society (CCMS) of the North Atlantic Treaty Organization (NATO).[39] The committee was the brainchild of Patrick Moynihan, who was then counselor to the president and a member of his Cabinet. Later, Moynihan became ambassador to the United Nations and senator from New York, after leaving the Nixon administration at the beginning of 1970. CCMS was proposed by Nixon in April 1969, on the twentieth anniversary of the founding of NATO. He called upon NATO to develop a "Third Dimension" to deal with "our concern for the quality of life in this final third of the twentieth century."

There was considerable political ferment in certain of the NATO countries in the late 1960s. Young people in particular were antiwar, anti–United States because of U.S. involvement in Vietnam, and anti-establishment generally. These feelings often translated into being anti-NATO, especially in the Netherlands. Moynihan's idea was simply to provide NATO with a new social and environmental dimension, in addition to the existing political and military dimension, that could help defuse or at least ameliorate some of the anti-NATO feeling.

Soon after the first meeting of CCMS, the responsibility was transferred to CEQ, and I took Moynihan's place as the U.S. representative to the group. A young Foreign Service officer named Harry Blaney, who had been Moynihan's executive assistant for CCMS, came to be my assistant. Harry was bright, imaginative, energetic, and possessed of a certain amount of brass, not a bad attribute on occasion. He brought with him a large supply of White House stationery, which we always used on CCMS business. Thus, when writing to one of the several federal agencies that became involved with CCMS or one of the other national representatives, we were speaking for the White House, or so the letterhead implied.*

CCMS operations were built around individual "pilot projects," each of which a member nation ("pilot country") would lead, with two or three other governments working with it. By early 1974, fourteen pilot projects had been launched and an International Conference on Cities held in Indianapolis. The pilot projects covered air pollution, coastal water pollution, environment and regional planning, advanced wastewater treatment, road safety, and disaster assistance.

The committee met once a year in plenary session at NATO headquarters in Brussels.† Typically, I would make an official call on NATO's secretary-general, Manlio Brosio, who was a friend (and bridge opponent) from the days when he was the Italian ambassador in Washington, or I would call on his successor, Joseph Luns, foreign minister for the Netherlands. I often stayed at the suburban residence of the U.S. ambassador to NATO, either Robert Ellsworth (former congressman from Kansas and later deputy secretary of Defense) or Donald Rumsfeld (later chief of staff to President Ford and currently secretary of Defense). I

---

*Blaney's role was filled later at EPA by F. A. "Tex" Harris and then by Frank Hodsell, both Foreign Service officers. All of them did a great job, despite the fact that we no longer had any White House stationery. Hodsell later became head of the National Endowment for the Arts.

†The vice chairman of the U.S. delegation was at first James Beggs and then John Barnum, both deputy secretaries of the Department of Transportation.

recall arriving at the latter's residence rather late on a Sunday evening. Rummy answered the doorbell himself. He asked whether I had brought any particular news from Washington. I described the "Saturday night massacre" of the previous night and the president's firing of Elliot Richardson and Bill Ruckelshaus, as attorney general and deputy attorney general, respectively, when they refused to dismiss special prosecutor Archibald Cox. Rumsfeld's jaw dropped. He had heard nothing of the event.

The CCMS meetings themselves were interesting although seldom very demanding. They usually were taken up by reports on the progress of various projects that CCMS had undertaken. I found the meetings very useful in providing the United States with an opportunity to raise subjects in which we had an interest, such as ocean dumping, and hopefully mobilize support from our NATO partners. It was also an occasional forum for the discussion of international environmental issues and agreements. Under a resolution (proposed by the United States in CCMS) by NATO's North Atlantic Council, for example, the members of CCMS agreed to proceed within the Intergovernmental Maritime Consultative Organization (IMCO) toward development of a treaty to control oil pollution resulting from the operation of ships—an objective of CEQ, as I have earlier described.

A useful device in the early days of CCMS was a roundtable discussion at which each national representative could bring up topics of concern to him. The discussions were unscheduled and the environmental minister from one country could raise a problem within his own government, such as the control of hazardous wastes, to learn how the other governments were dealing with the same problem. This direct interchange proved to be useful to the policy makers involved and was a major factor in their continuing interest in and support of CCMS. On one such occasion, in 1976, I raised the problem of chlorofluorocarbons (CFCs) in the environment and warned that regulatory systems should be prepared in case the release of CFCs was determined to be damaging the ozone layer and thereby increasing the level of ultraviolet radiation reaching the earth's surface.

In September 1976, the National Academy of Sciences released a report confirming the hypothetical predictions of ozone layer depletion and the resulting increase in ultraviolet radiation to the earth's surface, which in turn increased the incidence of skin cancer, among other consequences. I reported all this to CCMS in October 1976 and suggested an international convention dealing with the problem. Two months later, I was able to announce that I had "scheduled an international meeting of foreign countries to be held in Washington April 26–28, 1977, to explore together the necessity for effective regulatory action by our several governments."[40]

The April meeting, three months after I had left government service, took place, and, given my role in getting the matter underway, Tex Harris, still coordinating CCMS activities at EPA, sent me a personal report and enclosed copies of the meeting documents.[41] Some thirteen CFC-producing countries had participated, although Japan was represented only by a silent observer from its embassy in Washington. A little more than ten years later, the Montreal Protocol on Substances That Deplete the Ozone Layer was signed, committing the producing nations to the elimination of CFCs. The protocol was developed and negotiated under the skilled leadership of Richard E. Benedick, deputy assistant secretary of State and later a senior fellow at the World Wildlife Fund.[42]

Since few, if any, of the CCMS representatives were technical people, we were able to discuss such issues only at a broad policy level. Later, when specific topics for discussion at the roundtable were formally scheduled, the exchanges tended to become dominated by technical staff, leading to a progressive loss of interest on the part of policy people. While CCMS continues and still has an environmental focus, since 1992 the emphasis has been on defense-related matters, such as the cleanup of former military bases.[43]

THAT SEEMS a good point at which to bring to a close this description of my international activities, both as chairman of CEQ and as administrator of EPA.* As I hope I have made clear, I give a high priority to the international dimensions of environmental policy and to the need for vigorous U.S. leadership in the area. To my mind, the United States has largely abdicated such leadership today—to the major detriment of the world and the United States alike.

* Two international involvements while I was CEQ chairman that I have not covered in any detail were conferences in London under the auspices of the Intergovernmental Maritime Consultative Organization (IMCO). At one of these conferences, a convention was drawn up for the control of marine discharge of oil or other wastes, and at the other a convention was drawn up to deal with tanker design. I chaired the U.S. delegation to the first and cochaired that to the second with the commandant of the U.S. Coast Guard. In

Looking back on it, I plainly enjoyed my international involvements and felt at home in them. Moreover, while they were demanding in terms of time and energy, they seldom produced the tensions and stresses that came to typify my responsibilities on the home front, particularly while at EPA.

navigating the highly technical issues involved in both conferences, I had the assistance of a very competent young lawyer, Robert McManus, who later became general counsel of the National Oceanic and Atmospheric Administration (NOAA).

There were several bilateral environmental relationships in addition to those I have covered, including environmental agreements with Poland (1974) and Iran (1976). The latter was concluded during a visit by me, together with Aileen, to Iran as guests of the U.S. ambassador, Richard Helms, and his wife, Cynthia.

Chapter 9

EPA in the Nixon Years

O_N A_{PRIL} 28, 1973, at the request of President Nixon, Bill Ruckelshaus resigned as the first administrator of the Environmental Protection Agency (EPA) and accepted appointment as acting director of the Federal Bureau of Investigation (FBI). Following the death of J. Edgar Hoover, Nixon had nominated L. Patrick Gray as Hoover's successor. However, in the continuing turmoil over Watergate, Gray was reported to have destroyed some relevant documents; his confirmation was thus delayed and his nomination eventually withdrawn.

It did not take me long, once Ruckelshaus had resigned, to decide that I wanted the EPA job. I had been at the Council on Environmental Quality (CEQ) more than three years, and I believed we had accomplished a great deal in that time. Indeed, it is my belief that the environmental initiatives, both domestic and international, taken or proposed by President Nixon during those years of 1970–1973, put together largely under the leadership of CEQ and often developed by it, represented the most comprehensive set of policy initiatives in a single broad policy area ever undertaken by any administration in United States history.

Nevertheless, it was clear by mid-1973 that the action had shifted to EPA. There was a substantial backlog of legislation that the president had proposed and on which the United States Congress had still to act. What was needed was not more policy development but implementation of existing legislation and pressure on Congress to act on the president's legislative agenda. In addition, with Nixon's interest in the environment waning, there were obvious advantages in moving from the White

House–dependent CEQ to the more independent EPA. What I did not see clearly at the time, however, was the extent to which the environmental honeymoon had come to an end and how much the conflict between environmental and energy objectives would characterize the years immediately ahead at EPA, with the agency constantly put on the defensive within the administration. Nor did I see that, farther down the road, energy concerns would not be EPA's only problem. As the economy soured during the Gerald Ford administration, environmental programs also became the whipping boy for inflation and job losses.

H. R. (Bob) Haldeman and John Ehrlichman had departed the White House in the Watergate firestorm by this time, and Major General Alexander Haig had replaced the former as the president's chief of staff. (John Whitaker had also left the White House earlier that year to become under secretary of the Department of the Interior, the job he later told me he had really wanted when the Nixon administration first came to Washington. His assistant at the White House, Richard Fairbanks, had replaced him there.) I let Haig know of my interest in the EPA job, and in due course he asked me to come and see him. When we met at his office in the West Wing of the White House, Haig said the president was ready to name me but wanted to make sure that I would avoid extreme positions and would maintain a balanced approach. I got the impression that Nixon was anxious not so much about me personally as about anyone moving into the EPA position. We talked about this, and Haig seemed satisfied with my responses.

Nomination and Confirmation

The president sent my name to the Senate on July 26. I held a press conference following the announcement and used the occasion to distance myself a bit from the White House. "EPA is an independent regulatory agency with a strong independent character," I pronounced. "I made that clear to the President and he agrees with me. The independence of EPA is of paramount importance."[1] I believed that this point was particularly important for me to emphasize, given the close White House association of my job at CEQ.

Public reaction to the appointment was generally favorable.[2] Senator Edmund Muskie was quoted as saying I had "the background and experience to vigorously pursue" the job with "independence and objectivity."[3] The one discordant note I recall came from Ralph Nader, who was quoted in the same article as saying that I was not "temperamentally suited for the job. I don't think he has the cutting edge." In the EPA job, you're damned if you do and damned if you don't, *Time* magazine suggested, and "as of last week, there is a new damned man . . . Russell E. Train."[4]

The confirmation hearing the following week conducted by the Senate Committee on Public Works went smoothly, with essentially friendly statements from both sides. The one exception was Senator William Scott, Republican from Virginia. He picked up my *Who's Who* biography and called attention to the fact that I had described myself as a "conservationist." He asked why I had identified myself in that fashion when I had been a federal judge. "Are you ashamed to have been a judge?" he inquired. I assured him I was not, but he continued to go around and around on the matter. It was plain that I could not satisfy him no matter what I said. (At some point, unrelated to my confirmation hearing, the Senate press gallery had voted Scott the dumbest man in the Senate. He had responded by calling a press conference to deny the charge.)

The committee voted out my nomination favorably, but Scott put a hold on Senate floor action, as did Senator Clifford Hansen, Republican from Wyoming. The rules of senatorial courtesy require that such holds be respected for a reasonable period. Hansen never explained his action to me, but I understood it was done at the behest of the coal-mining industry, a strong factor in Wyoming. The industry presumably looked upon me with a jaundiced eye, given my support of coal mine health and safety legislation as under secretary of Interior and CEQ's sponsorship of legislation requiring the reclamation of strip-mined sites. As for Scott, I called on him in his Senate office once or twice, but he remained adamant in his opposition. I concluded that it was almost entirely ideological.

Scott finally removed his hold on the nomination,[5] as did Hansen, and the Senate confirmed me 85–0 on September 10.[6] After the vote, I visited Nixon in the Oval Office. The meeting was brief and we remained standing the entire time. I asked whether he would swear me in at EPA. He replied, "That's probably the very worst thing I could do for you!" And, of course, he was right.[7] Elliot Richardson swore me in at an outdoor ceremony at EPA headquarters with Bill Ruckelshaus standing by—lending me legitimacy, I hoped, in the eyes of the EPA troops.* Many EPA staff members, as well as a number of my family, were present. Aileen and I drove to our farm on the Eastern Shore of Maryland that evening, and on the way I suffered an attack of kidney stones — a harbinger of tough times ahead.

Grace Creek Farm

We had bought Grace Creek Farm in 1967. Situated near the village of Bozman, a community of watermen, in Talbot County on the Eastern Shore of Maryland, the farm encompasses 170 acres "more or less," according to the deed — mostly less, I was apt to say, at high tide. The property of mixed fields and forest lies on relatively low land with almost two miles of shoreline along tidal creeks leading to the Chesapeake Bay. It was not a grand estate but had probably once been a subsistence farm. The old frame house dates to the early eighteenth century. We've made some modifications to it over the years, but the scale remains modest. We have placed conservation easements on the property so that it can never be subdivided or otherwise developed.

There is a dock where we keep a small catboat, which Aileen and I sail around the neighboring creeks. For a number of years before buying the farm, we had owned a forty-foot ketch. On this we spent weekends cruising the waters of Chesapeake Bay, which is one of the largest and most productive estuaries in the world, though continually threatened today by development.†

The small cove directly in front of the house is filled with Canada geese in late fall and winter. There are ducks, too, but far fewer in number. Our beautiful native tundra swans (formerly called whistling swans) are only occasional visitors today. Ospreys nest in the spring on an old wood piling and wild turkeys have returned to the area. About thirty deer move in and out of our woods and fields.

*Ruckelshaus had served only about three months as acting director of the FBI before Nixon nominated him as deputy attorney general on July 26, 1973, the same date on which he nominated me as EPA administrator. Both Attorney General Richardson and Ruckelshaus were soon to lose their jobs in the so-called Saturday night massacre, triggered by Richardson's refusal, followed by Ruckelshaus's, to fire Archibald Cox, the Watergate special prosecutor.
†Aileen is a longtime trustee of the Chesapeake Bay Foundation, which seeks to restore and protect the bay.

Aileen produces quantities of flowers and vegetables from the garden, including raspberries in season; we have fruit from the orchard and eggs from the chicken house. Her kitchen produces jellies and jams, chutney, tomato juice, and other wonders that not only grace our own table but also go to friends and family.

The farm was part of our children's lives as they grew up and it is still the place where we all gather for Thanksgiving. Aileen and I spend every weekend there when we are not traveling away from Washington, D.C. It has for years been a cherished haven of peace and tranquility. During my most stressful government years, escape to the farm for at least part of a weekend was what helped preserve my sanity.

My Introduction to EPA

Ruckelshaus had done an outstanding job at EPA. He had put together in a single operating organization the diverse parts that had previously functioned in different agencies, always a difficult task and particularly so in government. He established a strong environmental enforcement policy. He was popular within EPA and well liked by the environmental community. He was respected in Congress, yet he displayed enough independence to please the public and keep the White House a bit nervous. It was a tough act to follow.

The EPA job was a highly visible one, an element I admit to liking. The agency had overall responsibility for carrying out the nation's laws dealing with air and water pollution, toxic wastes, solid waste disposal, radiation, pesticides and agricultural chemicals, noise pollution, and so forth. It was an enormous challenge. The country was just beginning to feel its way in the area. The science necessary for understanding pollution problems and the technologies for dealing with them were in their infancy. Economic effects were poorly understood. The White House was becoming increasingly ambivalent toward environmental goals and was giving a higher priority to meeting energy needs. With all this, the public demanded aggressive action to address environmental problems, particularly those with perceived adverse health effects. The road ahead would not be an easy one, and I had no doubt that my new EPA colleagues would be withholding judgment on my performance for the time being.

I was able to move into the EPA job with minimal transition problems. John Quarles, who had been on my staff at Interior and was assistant administrator for enforcement at EPA, was named deputy administrator, and, of course, he already knew the agency well. Alvin Alm was assistant administrator for planning and budget, a key position, and he had been at EPA for some months. Roger Strelow came from CEQ as my executive assistant and Marian O'Connell, who by now had been with me at the Departments of the Treasury and Interior and at CEQ, came as my executive secretary.* I made no effort to change the organization or the senior staff in place when I took over, although the staff changed over time.†

In addition to our Washington staff, EPA had ten regional headquarters. The regional administrators were on the front line with respect to much of EPA's interface with state and local governments, businesses, farmers, the press, and the general public. I met with them as a group once or twice a year but was in frequent contact with them individually. Finally, there were a number of research facilities around the country. EPA was situated in a converted apartment building on a shopping mall in southwest Washington, well away from most other government agencies.

---

*I had three outstanding executive assistants at EPA, all of whom had worked with me at CEQ: Strelow, William J. Dircks, and Steffan Plehn. After a tour at the Nuclear Regulatory Commission, Dircks went on to become executive director of the International Atomic Energy Agency in Vienna. Plehn became EPA deputy assistant administrator for solid waste and emergency response. After retirement and after a long bout with cancer, he died in March 2002. Not only was Steff an extremely intelligent and able public servant, but he was also one of the kindest, most decent human beings I have ever known.

†The air and water programs had originally been combined under one assistant administrator, Robert L. Sansom, who left shortly after I took office. Strelow became assistant administrator for air and waste disposal and James L. Agee became assistant administrator for water programs. Alan G. Kirk II, who had been Quarles' assistant in the office of enforcement and general counsel, succeeded him as assistant administrator. Later, Stanley Legro replaced Robert Zener as general counsel, and Wilson Talley replaced Stanley M. Greenfield as assistant administrator for research and development.

Among those at the associate administrator level were Ann L. Dore, director of public affairs, and Fitzhugh Green, director of international affairs. Others were Robert G. Ryan, director of legislative affairs, and Sheldon Meyers, director of the office of federal activities. Randolph (Randy) Arndt was my special assistant for press relations.

Ann (Dore) McLaughlin went on from EPA to be an assistant secretary of Treasury, under secretary of Interior, and secretary of Labor. When she left EPA, she was succeeded by Marlin Fitzwater, who would later be press secretary for President George H. W. Bush.

Energy-Environment Conflicts

Any honeymoon for me at EPA was nonexistent. The so-called energy crisis brought about by the Arab oil embargo, led by Saudi Arabia, occupied much of the president's time not already taken up by Watergate. The embargo was designed to push up oil prices, which the Saudis considered unfairly low. (Out of this effort came the Organization of Petroleum Exporting Countries, or OPEC.) The first of several energy "czars," former Colorado governor John Love, was in place. In June, in a widely publicized speech, I had attacked the tendency to make the environment the whipping boy for U.S. energy problems and cited an energy executive who had charged environmentalists with blocking the creation of new power plants and refineries. "Such statements obscure the facts, confuse the issues and can only serve to delay effective solution of our energy problems," I said.[8]

One of the major difficulties EPA faced was that compliance dates for meeting environmental standards mandated by statute, particularly the Clean Air Act, began to hit just as the nation was feeling the pinch of the energy crisis, was in the midst of inflation, and was on the edge of an economic downturn. We prepared our defenses as best we could against the opponents of environmental regulation, who typically argued either that the cost of compliance with a given regulation far exceeded the benefits to be achieved or that the risks addressed by a regulation were overstated and did not justify the cost of compliance. EPA contracted for nationwide studies of six industries—electric power, steel, nonferrous metals, oil refineries, chemicals, and paper and pulp. The purpose was to get up-to-date data on the costs of pollution control equipment and the effects of those costs on gross national product, inflation, the balance of payments, and employment. A separate study was undertaken on availability of capital for industries having to invest in control technologies.

The economic model we constructed was also designed to report the economic benefits that would flow from environmental legislation and regulation, including the profits of and employment by companies making control equipment. Al Alm was largely responsible for getting this crucial economic analysis under way, and, as I record from time to time, the possession of such analytic capability gave EPA a distinct advantage in its constant battle with energy- and economics-oriented critics of environmental policy. With knowledge came strength. So armed, I spent a great deal of time disputing claims that cleaning up the environment was unacceptably costly. I asserted, for example, that air pollution was causing about $16 billion worth of damage annually in the United States in damage to health, crops, and so on, an amount far in excess of cleanup costs.

Cabinet Sessions on Clean Air

I had been barely sworn in when, on September 8, I was asked to attend a Cabinet meeting on energy problems, particularly that winter's potential shortage of heating oil. At the meeting's outset, the president said he had asked me to be present because difficult decisions had to be made with regard to the environment, he knew I was a team player, and he wanted me to participate in the discussions. It sounded ominous.

John Love described the winter heating situation: the need to burn more coal because of the shortage of oil, and the resulting increase in sulfur oxide emissions (because coal contains considerably more sulfur than heating oil). He then posed the question of whether we would have to institute mandatory controls on the allocation of fuels. When the president asked Love to explain the sulfur oxide variance problem, I chimed in and explained the relevant aspects of the Clean Air Act and the procedure for approving variances — temporary departures from permitted limits on sulfur oxide emissions.

The president made quite clear his conclusion that it was going to be necessary to "lower the emission standards." He directed Love to call the governors and tell them this. My memorandum of the meeting says, "I don't think — even after my explanation — that the President understands that variances must be initiated by the States."[9] I had made the point that the standards we were discussing were *health* standards and pointed out their relevance to such issues as emphysema, bronchial disorders, respiratory disease generally, cardiac conditions, and lung cancer. We needed to be clear that these adverse health effects would increase as the emission standards were lowered. The president commented that when he was young there were more cases of tuberculosis from cold houses than from most other causes.

From time to time during the meeting, Nixon suggested that "environmentalists" would oppose the steps he was talking about. I tried to counter this line of thought by saying that, while I could not speak for the environmental community, EPA itself did not in principle oppose variances. In fact, I pointed out, EPA had approved a number of variances the previous winter without problem or controversy.

Near the close of the meeting, Secretary of Commerce Frederick Dent said to the president that he thought it important to emphasize the ethic of energy conservation, which the president had called for in his April energy message. Nixon's response was, "What's that?"

Since I would have to bear the brunt of explaining the administration's policy on air standards, I said I would like to clarify what it was that Love would announce to the press following the meeting. Would he be urging the governors to adopt procedures that would permit the expeditious handling of applications for variances on a case-by-case basis if the need arose that winter? Was this what we were talking about? "Yes," said the president, "and, Russ, stress that we are only talking about temporary action this winter."

Straight from the meeting but unbeknownst to me at the time, the president went before the press, along with Love, and called for a relaxation of air pollution standards.[10] That evening, I had a call from a reporter who had been at the press conference and who told me that Nixon, when asked whether I had agreed to what he was announcing, had said that I had. I told the reporter I had not.

To be fair to Nixon, the provisions of the Clean Air Act were complicated, and his presidency was collapsing around him. He was to leave office less than a year later. Moreover, the country did have an energy problem. If the motivation for his pro-environment initiatives prior to 1973 had been largely political — with an eye on Muskie and on the 1972 election — as it probably had been, that motivation had now evaporated. In his weakened condition, Nixon doubtless wanted to sound decisive. Merely to encourage governors to seek variances at the state level would hardly fill the bill.

The fact is that there never was any significant easing of clean air standards. In the winter of 1973–1974, I approved a few temporary state variance plans (as had been done the previous winter), but that was about it. I was careful to explain that we were not relaxing the standards themselves but making temporary adjustments.[11] However, for the rest of my time at EPA, meeting energy needs was paramount for both Nixon and Ford, and the issue was always with us.

On November 6, I attended another meeting on the energy situation with the president and selected Cabinet members.[12] Gerald Ford was there, now vice president, following Spiro Agnew's resignation. John Love briefed the group on the growing energy crisis resulting from the Arab embargo and the petroleum shortfall, which he described as going "beyond cold homes and gasoline rationing. It could seriously affect the economy." The current authority to deal with the problem was limited, he claimed, and current environmental laws had insufficient flexibility. He recommended legislation that would authorize the president, "acting through the EPA administrator," to exempt energy facilities from the Clean Air Act and the Federal Water Pollution Control Act. The effects of the latter would have been primarily through its restrictions on the "thermal discharge" by power plants of water used in cooling their generating facilities. According to my notes, no one, including me, commented on this extreme proposal. In any event, there was never any follow-up on it. John Love was eventually removed as energy czar by Nixon for not being strong enough.

Sometimes such meetings took surprising turns. For example, my notes on a later Cabinet meeting on energy and the Middle East show no discussion of energy or environmental matters but report the following dialogue between Nixon and Henry Kissinger:

> *Kissinger:* The Syrians are the most bizarre people I have ever negotiated with — and that is saying something!
> *Nixon:* More bizarre than the Sunset Strip?
> *Kissinger [after a pause]:* That is more negotiable.
> *Nixon:* At a price!

At the same meeting, there was a discussion of Aleksandr Solzhenitsyn in comparison with Leo Tolstoy, with Nixon commenting that *Anna Karenina* is a "great love story that ends as all great love stories should, with the girl throwing herself under a streetcar." Then, on a more serious note, "Always remember that great nations consult their own interests — not those of friends and relatives."[13]

Regulating Pesticides

During his tenure at EPA, Bill Ruckelshaus had outlawed all except emergency uses of DDT, following extensive research into the pesticide's harmful effects. He had announced his decision just prior to attending the June 1972 United Nations Conference on the Human Environment at Stockholm and had alerted the White House shortly beforehand. Nixon was angry about the proposed decision, Ehrlichman told him, and was considering ordering Ruckelshaus not to make it. Ruckelshaus contacted John Mitchell, attorney general and the manager of Nixon's re-election campaign. The two met in Lafayette Square and discussed the problem on one of the park benches. Ruckelshaus outlined the merits of his proposed decision and urged that Nixon not inject himself into such a regulatory decision. To do so would create an "awful" precedent, Ruckelshaus continued, and would potentially expose the president in such situations to political fallout that he could otherwise keep at arm's length.[14] Ruckelshaus went forward with his announcement and never heard anything further from the White House on the matter. (I report this episode because of its relevance to the growing tendency of the White House to become involved in regulatory issues.)

DDT was probably the most widely used of the group of highly effective pesticides known as chlorinated hydrocarbons, which were extremely long-lived in the environment and tended to accumulate in the food chain with deleterious effects. One of the most difficult and contentious issues that I inherited when I moved to EPA involved the banning—which I did—of most uses of several of the other widely used chlorinated hydrocarbons, namely, aldrin, dieldrin, heptachlor, and chlordane. In each case, the decision-making process involved a quasi-judicial procedure with findings of fact and a final decision by the administrator (me). Inevitably, these decisions brought me under attack from the House and Senate agriculture committees and also from EPA's appropriations committee in the House and its powerful chairman, Jamie Whitten of Mississippi. Whitten invariably attacked the decisions in public, but I discovered that giving him a few hours' advance notice did much to reduce his rancor. It was Whitten who said on some occasion that "Train has more power than a bad man should have or a good man would want!"

Aldrin and dieldrin were manufactured and marketed by the Velsicol Chemical Corporation of Chicago, which bitterly fought the deregistration of its products. Velsicol fought the decision[15] not only legally—as was its right—but also by such means as trying to disrupt my press conferences, whatever the subject. On one such occasion in Houston, whenever I opened my mouth, a voice in the back of the room would call out, "Liar!" This went on for a while until the press discovered who the heckler represented and made him leave the room. Earlier, the chairman of Velsicol had made a speech in Houston in which, according to a local reporter, he called me dishonest as well as a liar.[16]

Later in 1974, after dealing with the chlorinated hydrocarbon issues, I also ordered an immediate ban on, and recall of, all aerosol sprays using vinyl chloride, which had been judged to be a significant carcinogen.

Another highly charged issue I inherited was whether to permit the use of DDT on an emergency basis to control the tussock moth, which, in one of its cyclical population explosions, was devastating the forests of the Northwest, primarily in Washington, Idaho, and Oregon. These three states' governors (led by Tom McCall of Oregon), all six of their senators, and their entire delegations to the U.S. House of Representatives petitioned me to permit the emergency use of DDT. It was a tough issue. On the one hand, I could do nothing and pray that the tussock moth had come to the end of its growth cycle and would disappear naturally. If that did not happen, there could be adverse economic effects throughout the region. On the other hand, if I permitted the use of DDT, there could be adverse ecological effects.

It was a classic EPA issue, complete with inadequate scientific data on which to base a decision. Moreover, it was not a case in which I could "wait and see" because doing so would amount to a decision in itself. The upshot was that with great reluctance I permitted the use of DDT, imposing such restrictions as we could in order to limit ecological damage. I chose to make the announcement in Seattle, at the heart of the region and of the controversy, rather than in Washington, D.C. It was an emotional occasion, and I remember how some members of the audience wept as they heard the decision. As it turned out, the threat of the tussock moth soon ended — but was it the DDT or was it the end of the moths' natural cycle?

Catalytic Converter Debate

By the time I went to EPA, the Clean Air Act Amendments of 1970 had been law for about three years and implementation of their provisions was proceeding on schedule. Automobile emission standards had been set by Congress, mandating a 90 percent reduction in hydrocarbons and carbon monoxide from allowable 1970 levels by 1975 and a 90 percent reduction in nitrogen oxide emissions by 1976 over actual 1970 cars. The levels Congress mandated were those that Delbert Barth of the National Air Pollution Control Administration (then in HEW, the Department of Health, Education, and Welfare) had suggested as being desirable for meeting air quality goals.[17] Given the state of relevant technology, he had spoken of meeting those goals by 1980 rather than 1975 and 1976, as Congress had required. Thus, Congress, spearheaded by Muskie and the Senate Committee on Public Works, had mandated a timetable that was arbitrary and had little reference to the likely availability of appropriate control technology. As Whitaker put it, "In effect, Congress had 'legislated technology.'"[18] The auto industry appealed for a one-year extension of the timetable; however, Ruckelshaus denied the appeal in May 1972, on the ground that the applicants had not established the unavailability of control technology adequate to meet the 1975 requirements. One effect of that decision was to ensure that the automakers had to stick with the catalytic converter as the only technology that gave them a chance of meeting, on a mass production basis, the 1975 and 1976 deadlines. While the auto industry resisted the catalytic converter on the basis of cost, a less tangible but nonetheless real factor was that the industry had almost no familiarity with the chemical and electronic engineering required by the catalyst.

When I moved to EPA in September 1973, evidence was beginning to emerge that catalytic converters themselves produced small amounts of sulfuric acid vapor, which could result in lung damage under certain conditions. This evidence had first been reported by the Ford Motor Company and then had been confirmed by EPA's own tests. Opinions and feelings about the problem ran strong within the agency, and there were heated meetings in my office in which our health experts warned of the potential health risks of catalytic converters, while the "mobile sources" pollution office of the air quality program, led by Eric Stork, warned of the adverse health effects that would follow if catalytic converters were abandoned and auto emissions returned to 1970 levels. In November, I testified before the Senate Public Works Committee on the problem and the conflicting considerations.[19] It was my conclusion that the risks from sulfuric acid emissions were sufficiently uncertain that they would not justify at that time the abandonment of the catalytic converter and the resulting rollback of controls on hydrocarbon, carbon monoxide, and nitrogen oxide emissions.

In recognition of the practical difficulties the auto industry faced in putting catalytic converters into production, the Energy Supply and Environmental Coordination Act of 1974 provided an extension until 1977 of the 1975 auto emission standards and also gave the auto industry the right to petition for a one-year suspension of the 1977 hydrocarbon and carbon monoxide standards. The industry promptly petitioned for such an extension in January 1975, during the Ford administration.

EPA conducted extensive public hearings on the matter in early 1975, many of which I attended as an observer. The issues centered on the sulfate emission problem caused by the catalytic converter. On the afternoon of Monday, March 3, at my request, I met with President Ford in the Oval Office to brief him on the decision I expected to announce publicly two days later.[20] Also present were Jim Lynn (director, Office of Management and Budget), Alan Greenspan (chairman, Council of Economic Advisors), Jim Cannon (director, Domestic Council), Frank Zarb (administrator, Federal Energy Administration), and Mike Duval (Domestic Council staff).* During the hour-long meeting, the president and I sat in chairs in front of the fireplace; the others sat on two sofas flanking us.

The president said he had called the meeting to hear how I was coming out on the auto emission question, but he emphasized that the decision was entirely mine and that no effort would be made to influence my decision. I believe that Ford sincerely meant that statement, and, so far as I was concerned, his White House stuck to that principle — a far cry from what appears to be current practice.

I explained the nature of the decision to the group and the various numbers involved. The decision was being driven, I said, by the sulfate issue, which I described in detail. I explained that EPA's own scientific analysis of the sulfate issue had been completed only in January, just as the hearings began. The conclusive tests had been made on General Motors Corporation's proving grounds; the tests had involved vehicles from the industry as a whole, and EPA scientists had participated along with industry scientists. The results made clear that the catalytic converter did not pose a health threat. I indicated that the 0.9 grams per mile (gpm) hydrocarbon level and 9.0 gpm carbon monoxide level for 1980 and 1981 mandated by the 1974 act were important in that they signaled a commitment to continued progress in reducing auto emissions. I explained that I was

---

*Duval had been assistant to Richard Fairbanks toward the end of the Nixon administration and had taken his place in the Ford administration.

recommending a 2.0 gpm nitrogen oxide standard (the president having publicly recommended 3.1) because the shift did not involve a significant fuel penalty and because testimony at our hearings indicated that nitrogen oxide was potentially a more significant health problem than we had assumed earlier. There was only a brief discussion. As we broke up, I told the president how much I appreciated his attitude toward the decision-making process.

Two days later, on March 5, I announced a one-year suspension of the 1977 auto emission standards and recommended a program for reducing hydrocarbon, carbon monoxide, and sulfate emissions for the 1977–1982 model years. That is a very broad characterization of the decision. The actual decision document ran sixty-two pages. I made clear that, had it not been for the sulfuric acid emission problem, I would not have granted the one-year suspension. I also made clear that, despite the one-year suspension, emission levels would continue to go down. The decision was a classic case of risk balancing. The public reaction was generally favorable.[21]

The debate over the catalytic converter was highly contentious. In one incident, Republican senator Barry Goldwater blasted me and EPA in his Arizona newspaper column, charging that EPA had forced the catalytic converter on the auto industry: "Only now, as this is written, have the EPA bureaucrats admitted that they bought 'a lemon' when they began promoting the converter as a prime anti-pollution device. . . . Russell Train, director of the EPA, didn't say it that way (bureaucrats never admit costly errors); rather, he announced that EPA was relaxing and revising its emission standards, so the converters won't be needed on 1976 model cars. Not a word about sulfuric acid emissions."[22]

Disturbed by the misconceptions reflected in his column, I replied to Goldwater at some length. The auto emission standards were not EPA's "self-made standards," as he had stated. Congress had established these standards and written specific emission numbers and deadline dates into the Clean Air Act Amendments of 1970, before EPA had even come into existence. The sole role of EPA was to carry out the specific standards and deadlines Congress had mandated in 1970 "despite the Administration's strong plea that there be more administrative flexibility. Indeed, Congress rejected the Administration's position overwhelmingly."[23]

I rejected the suggestion that EPA had forced the industry to use catalysts. Under the Clean Air Act, no particular technology was specified to meet auto emission standards. The standards were set by statute and it was left to the industry to develop the technologies and the systems for meeting them.

About this time, Goldwater and I happened to share close quarters aboard a small commuter plane from Washington, D.C., to Easton, Maryland. While he continued to be unhappy about catalytic converters and bureaucrats, his animosity toward me had abated. He wrote to me afterward to tell me that he was giving up his column.[24]

I have laid out this correspondence at some length because it highlights some of the misconceptions and problems inherent in the congressional decision to mandate technology-forcing standards in addressing auto emission problems. Nevertheless, despite the difficulties involved, I believe the approach was the right one under the circumstances, given the auto industry's resistance to change. At the same time, such flexibility as I had, limited as it was, was essential to making the system work.

At a full Cabinet meeting on March 12, President Ford asked me to describe my suspension decision, in particular the catalyst problem. I stood and talked for twenty minutes, setting out the ramifications of the decision, including the congressional and public reaction. Coincidentally, the meeting was reported on at length by John Hersey in an article titled "Week in the Life of the President." After quoting me at some length, he quoted Vice President Nelson Rockefeller to this effect: "Garages catching on fire and people burning to death; cars catching on fire, gas stations exploding — all because of the catalytic converter." Apparently, I replied that EPA had little or no information regarding this sort of occurrence and that if "we do pull the catalyst off the automobile at this time, we will have an increase of three times in the level of pollutants."[25] Rockefeller's rather lurid picture provides an indication of the heat the issue engendered. HEW secretary Cap Weinberger remarked at the meeting that the health scientists in his department strongly supported my action. Overall, I found considerable interest on the part of the Cabinet and no particularly adverse reaction.[26]

Catalytic converters were, of course, rendered ineffective if used with leaded gasoline. That fact, together with the well-recognized adverse health effects of lead itself, led to the elimination over time of lead in gasoline by EPA regulation authorized by the Clean Air Act Amendments of 1970. EPA also issued a regulation mandating a fuel tank design for vehicles equipped with catalytic converters that made it impossible to insert the nozzle from a leaded-fuel gas pump. These actions led to a telephone call that woke me one winter night at home. The conversation went something like this:

"Is this Mr. Train?"

"Yes, it is."

"The Russell Train who heads the Environmental Protection Agency?"

"Yes, it is."

"Well, Mr. Train, I have something to tell you."

"You know, it is almost 3:00 A.M. here in Washington. Could you call back later?"

"No, Mr. Train, this is something I want you to know about right now."

"Okay, go ahead."

"Mr. Train, it's a very cold, snowy night out here in Minnesota. A few hours ago, my wife and I were driving home and our car ran out of gas out in the middle of nowhere. I walked about two miles through the snow-drifts to a filling station, where I was able to get a tank of gas. I carried it the two miles back through the snow, took off the cap of my gas tank — and you know what, Mr. Train?" His voice was deceptively soft. "The nozzle wouldn't fit the gas tank," and here his voice rose to a crescendo, "all because of your goddamned stupid EPA regulations!"

I mumbled something to the effect that I didn't blame him for being mad.

"I just thought you ought to know about it, Mr. Train," he said, no longer yelling, and hung up.

While many public officials have unlisted home telephone numbers, I never did. So far as I remember, this particular call was the only one of this nature I ever received.

Assault on the Clean Air Act

In early 1974, while Nixon was still in office, the Federal Energy Office,[27] the Office of Management and Budget (OMB), and the White House put together a package of thirteen amendments to the Clean Air Act, all without consultation with EPA. Among these was a two-year extension, until 1977, of the automobile emission standards deadline. Other recommendations included (l) permitting tall smokestacks not as an interim device but as a permanent way of meeting standards — by dispersing the pollution (what I described as "pollution dilution") rather than by controlling it at the source by technology such as "scrubbers"; (2) requiring EPA to take economic and social effects into account in setting standards rather than just health effects, as required by existing law; (3) providing federal preemption if individual states set more rigorous standards than those set by the federal government; and (4) exempting all energy-related activities, such as power plant siting, strip-mining under federal permit, oil shale development, and nuclear power plant development from the environmental impact statement (EIS) process mandated by the National Environmental Policy Act of 1969 (NEPA). It was an outrageous set of proposals.

While EPA may have provided technical information on request, we were otherwise not engaged in putting together this anti–Clean Air Act legislative package. Personally, I was thoroughly disgusted by this blatant violation of proper process and I could only ascribe its occurrence to growing disorganization in the White House. I made my position clear to the press. I was quoted by the *New York Times*, for example, as saying: "I want it known that I am strongly opposed to most of these proposals, and I am going to fight against them to the last wire, because I don't think they are necessary and I do think they'd do substantial harm." [28] The same article said that I described the NEPA exemption as "designed emasculation." The *Wall Street Journal* reported that I said I could not support many of the amendments and that "I have made that pretty damn clear." [29]

A firm believer in flexibility of administration, I was also quoted at the time as stating that I preferred to work out schedules for the installation of scrubbers for coal-fired power plants on a plant-by-plant basis. [30] However, such a policy was not permitted by the Clean Air Act, and neither Congress nor the special interests involved, specifically environmentalists and industry, have been willing historically to trust any administration with such flexibility.

The aforementioned *New York Times* article carried the headline "White House Challenged by Environmental Chief." Other press coverage at the time was equally dramatic: "EPA Chief Fights Easing Clean Air Laws," [31] "White House Clash with EPA," [32] and "EPA Defends Clean Air Act." [33] In an editorial titled "Mortal Threat to NEPA," the *New York Times* lent support to the clean air cause, calling my stand "indisputably right and admirably bold." [34] Well before going public in this fashion, I had sent the president a memorandum setting out my views. I had voiced particular concern over two of the amendments: "I am strongly opposed to the proposal to allow permanent use of so-called 'intermittent control systems' [i.e., tall stacks] and the proposal to include an economic and social test throughout the Clean Air Act."[35]

What finally went to Congress represented a compromise between Bill Simon, who at the time was head of the Federal Energy Office, the White House, and me. A number of the worst amendments were dropped, including those exempting energy projects from the environmental impact analysis requirements of NEPA and the proposal that EPA be required to take into account economic and social costs (rather than just health effects) in setting standards. With respect to those amendments on which Simon and I disagreed, the White House simply told us to take our conflicting positions to Congress while the White House itself remained neutral. Given the point at which this whole legislative exercise had started, this arrangement represented a major victory for EPA. The *New York Times* described the revised legislative package as a considerable retreat from the drastic revision originally proposed, and "a limited victory" for Train.[36] The Clean Air Coalition denounced the proposed amendments: "With minor reservations, the EPA today joined the rest of the industry-oriented Nixon Administration in proposing unnecessary weakening of the Clean Air Act." (To this day, I fail to understand the coalition's criticism of EPA in this situation.) The same article reported that Senator Muskie "credited Train with blocking some planned anti-pollution rollbacks."[37] In any event, whatever the comments at the time, the amendments were essentially "dead on arrival" at Congress.

It was a tense and fairly unhappy time. While I was confident of the correctness of our EPA positions, I got no pleasure from fighting the White House, OMB, and the energy people. By nature, I prefer to be a team player. Our differences were on matters of policy, not personality. John Quarles, EPA deputy administrator, has said that I threatened to resign rather than concede.[38] I do not recall ever saying so explicitly, but perhaps such a threat was implicit in my position. Very possibly, I would have been fired had the president not been badly weakened by the Watergate scandal. One former EPA official wrote that Train survived only "because Richard Nixon did not."[39] However, it should be said that no one ever threatened me with firing. One commentator has said, "with Watergate weakening Nixon, the EPA administrators openly allied themselves with Muskie rather than with the president."[40] This is a mischaracterization. By necessity, we worked with Muskie and his staff for the simple reason that they represented the committee majority. However, I kept in constant touch with the Republican minority and the latter was always supportive. I do not recall ever opposing a Nixon White House proposal unless the Republican members of the committee agreed with me. Nor do I ever recall supporting a Muskie proposal unless the Republicans agreed.

Of course, my press notices were not all positive. The *Wall Street Journal*, for example, charged me with simply being opposed to any amendments to the Clean Air Act. On March 19, the *Journal* carried my reply, in which I laid out for the record that I believed in flexible administration of the Clean Air Act and had supported a number of amendments, giving the details.[41] Three days later, the *Journal* published a front-page article headlined "Train's Troubles / Energy Crisis Widens / Gap between Nixon, / Environmental Aide — EPA Head Compromises, / But Doesn't Yield Easily, / He Insists He Won't Quit."[42]

The article reported: "Some people in the agency [EPA] describe the 55-year-old Mr. Train as 'bordering on being dull' to work for, and many continually speak of Mr. Ruckelshaus as the man who gave the agency identity, spirit and a good name. But the disputes with the White House are improving Mr. Train's standing with his troops." Since taking the EPA job the previous September, the article went on to say, I had never met with the president, and, in contrast, Bill Simon saw him constantly. "The three-year-old agency's first chief, William Ruckelshaus, waged anti-pollution offensives with strong public support. Mr. Train, on the other hand, finds himself defending the environmental movement and his agency against attack. . . . But Mr. Train is not giving ground easily." While I had barely been in the job six months at the time of the article's appearance, its characterization of my performance was reasonably accurate. Ruckelshaus was, as I have said, a hard act to follow, and, most important, the game had changed radically from the pro-environment focus while I was at CEQ to a strong pro-energy bias in the White House when I went to EPA. Moreover, the pro-energy forces now had an organizational champion in the FEA.

On March 31, a nationally syndicated column by Rowland Evans and Robert Novak picked up the issue. Their column, titled "Russell Train Remains on Track," described a luncheon session in the White House mess that included Bill Simon, Senator Bill Scott of Virginia, and me. We were thrashing out our dispute over the Clean Air Act amendments. Suddenly, Scott stood up and declared: "Anyone who will not support the administration on this ought to quit, and I mean you!" Then, recalled one witness, he added, "They can find some ambassadorship for you, maybe Russia or China." According to the column, I replied quietly, "Bill, you're way out of line."[43] (The quotations were quite accurate, and I probably had been the source.) The same column speculated, "If President Nixon were stronger politically, he might well have fired Train outright." In retrospect, I think one could also speculate, had the White House not been so disorganized, we very likely would not have gotten into such a mess in the first place.

Transportation Control Plans

Another very contentious issue that came my way at EPA involved transportation control plans mandated by the Clean Air Act. For urban areas that were not otherwise able to meet air quality standards by 1977, the states concerned were required to include transportation controls in their plans for achieving national air quality standards. Los Angeles was a case in point. It had perhaps the worst automobile-related smog in the country, and, given its vast sprawl and almost total absence of any meaningful mass transit system, it appeared to have no viable options for solving the problem. A transportation plan imposed by the state of California was totally inadequate to the problem, and a federal court ordered EPA to propose a transportation plan for the city by January 15, 1973, that would reduce vehicular pollution.[44] Ruckelshaus did so, announcing the plan at a press conference in Los Angeles. It would have essentially shut down the city.

An EPA study showed that thirty-eight cities would require transportation control plans if they were to meet Clean Air Act mandates. To develop such plans, each tailored to the different circumstances of these cities, was a stupendously complicated task and a time-consuming one. Nevertheless, the Natural Resources Defense Council secured a federal court order requiring EPA to proceed with issuing the necessary rules. The plans EPA came up with contained a variety of control techniques. They required gasoline stations to install sealing devices on their tanks to prevent fuel evaporation and owners to get periodic inspection of their vehicles to determine whether they met emission standards. Many plans required changes in traffic patterns, such as designation of one-way streets to reduce emissions by achieving a smoother flow of traffic. Other requirements called for exclusive lanes to encourage car pools and use of public transportation. Most controversial of all were requirements that discouraged car use by restricting opportunities for parking or by imposing parking surcharges.

Taken individually, these various elements were not all that unreasonable. What aroused public and congressional outrage was that such local requirements should be imposed by the federal government. I inherited an uproar when I moved into the EPA administrator's office in September 1973. Soon after I arrived, and again under court order, EPA proposed regulations that would require developers of new shopping centers, convention centers, and large parking areas to seek Clean Air Act approval from the federal government. In response to all the controversy that swirled around the federal role in these issues, Congress inserted language in EPA's appropriation bill requiring, in effect, that none of the funds appropriated be used to enforce transportation plans. That essentially was the end of a no-win effort.

The experience carried some important lessons. The most important was that EPA could possess undoubted statutory authority, backed up by federal court orders, but such authority availed us very little when we were confronted by broad-scale public opposition. It was not a lesson that came easily to some of the young environmental crusaders in the clean air program. At the EPA awards ceremony held early that December on the anniversary of the agency's creation, I referred to this bit of experience and quoted from an interview I had just read that had been conducted with President Harry Truman after he left office:

> Mr. President, it has been said that the Presidency is the most powerful office in the world. Do you think that's true?
>
> Truman: Oh, no, Oh my, no! About the biggest power the President has, and I've said this before, is the power to persuade people to do what they ought to do without having to be persuaded. There are a lot of other powers written in the Constitution and given to the President, but it's that power to persuade people to do what they ought to do anyway that's the biggest. And if the man who is President doesn't understand that, if he thinks he is too big to do the necessary persuading, then he's in for big trouble, and so is the country.[45]

It was a lesson that all of us could take to heart. In a democratic system, ultimate power resides in the people. The exercise of authority, whether derived from statute or from judicial decision, unless accompanied by persuasion and the agreement of the public, will never achieve a given goal.

One could excuse the young Turks of the clean air program for their failure to appreciate such a principle because of their inexperience. But it was a principle that Nixon himself, in his focus on the exercise of executive power, would seem never to have truly appreciated or ultimately understood.

Balancing Acts

Energy needs, real or perceived, and their interface with the environment defined my tenure at EPA more than any other set of issues. EPA's consistently independent line during this period, and the fact that we generally got away with taking it, was highly unusual, to say the least. However, times were not normal. Nixon was deep in the Watergate morass, and, at the time of my fight over the effort to gut the Clean Air Act for energy reasons in March 1974, his resignation was a scant five months away. He was fighting for his political life. Impeachment loomed as a very real threat, incredible as it doubtless seemed to a man who had been overwhelmingly reelected only a short time before. Nixon looked for allies wherever he could find them, particularly among the traditionally conservative business constituency. The environmental community had never been more than lukewarm in its support for Nixon, even during the heyday of his pro-environment initiatives. Thus, Watergate encouraged whatever pro-energy bias Nixon might naturally have felt.

On the other side of the coin, the preoccupation with Watergate on the part of the White House and its principal incumbent created an unusual opportunity for independence among the executive agencies, especially so in the case of EPA, which, after all, had been created in the first place to be an "independent" agency within the executive branch. I recall being interviewed at the time for an article intended to depict administrative nightmares, even chaos, within the executive agencies resulting from the White House disarray over Watergate. When the reporter asked me to describe the effects on EPA, I replied, "It's the best thing that ever happened to us!" While that was said somewhat facetiously, there was more than a bit of truth in the remark.

I certainly never thought of myself as being disloyal to Nixon; I was simply doing the job I had been given. Probably it was a case, as Whitaker is reported to have once said, of my being "for the environment first, Nixon second."[46]

I took every occasion that presented itself to address the energy-environment nexus. For example, in July 1974, I argued in a speech that the energy crisis was in fact an opportunity to reduce waste and inefficiency and to cut the annual energy growth rate from 5 percent to 2.5 percent or lower by 1985. I maintained that average vehicle weight could be cut from 3,500 to 2,900 pounds, with corresponding reductions in fuel use, and I spoke in favor of standards for space heating, restrictions on commercial lighting, and development of more mass transit, recycling, and energy conversion from wastes. I declared that there were opportunities for significant energy savings in agriculture: "We should seize upon the energy crisis as a good excuse and a great opportunity for making some very fundamental changes that we ought to be making anyway for other reasons."[47] What we as a nation were actually doing, however, was trying to cut the control of pollution in order to achieve short-term cost savings in energy. How familiar all this sounds today, more than a quarter century later, as the George W. Bush administration continues to emphasize finding more energy rather than encouraging a reduction in demand.

It was not an easy time. I seldom went to a meeting on energy and the environment without feeling like the proverbial bastard at a family reunion. Nevertheless, while I doubtless felt somewhat isolated at such times, I was fortunate in having many friends in the administration and in Congress. Several members of the Cabinet, such as secretary of Interior Rogers Morton and secretary of Commerce Fred Dent, were personal friends. Even Bill Simon, head of the Federal Energy Office and its successor, the Federal Energy Administration, and my principal adversary at the time, was a friend on the Washington scene. Many of those I had known as fellow under secretaries or deputy secretaries were still in high positions. With all these people, I was able to maintain a spirit of collegiality in our associations. There was never any "ganging up" on me.

Throughout this period, I paid close attention to my congressional relationships. With the exception of Senator Scott, I had unfailing support from the Republican minority on the key Senate Committee on Public Works (now the Senate Committee on Environment and Public Works). The ranking Republican on that committee, Howard Baker, was a good friend and ally, as was Jim Buckley of New York. Other Republicans on the committee, such as Pete Domenici of New Mexico, Jim McClure of Idaho, and Bob Stafford of Vermont, were always friendly and helpful.

I assume that the Democratic majority under the leadership of Chairman Jennings Randolph and Ed Muskie were delighted with the whole affair. Muskie, of course, had been the key figure in the development of both the air and water pollution laws in the Senate. He and his assistant, Leon Billings, kept a close eye on EPA and its implementation of the laws, and we were in frequent touch. Muskie had a quick temper, but incidents usually blew over rapidly and we developed a mutual respect. Some twenty years later, in testimony before this same committee, I said—and I meant every word—that "during my tenure at EPA, it would have been impossible to have had a more supportive relationship than I had with this committee on a bipartisan basis. I shall always be grateful for that support." [48]

In the House, Paul Rogers, Democrat from Florida and chairman of the Committee on Interstate and Foreign Commerce, which had jurisdiction over the Clean Air Act, was always helpful. I have to confess that I did not hesitate to stoop to a bit of friendly persuasion on occasion as Aileen delivered the odd basket of ripe figs and tomatoes or other produce from our farm to key legislative friends or executive branch officials. Jamie Whitten, chairman of EPA's appropriations subcommittee, and George Mahon, chairman of the House Rules Committee, loved her tomatoes. An entry in my diary records that (while Aileen was away) "I sent two beautiful boxes of tomatoes to Senators Randolph and Baker (to be bipartisan!). Distributed squash, tomatoes, figs, and zucchini to staff." [49]

In 1976, during a conversation while waiting for a Ford Cabinet meeting to get under way, Vice President Nelson Rockefeller said to me:

> Russ, you are generally accepted as *the* master politician in this town! I was talking to a group of people about it last night. You have had about the toughest job in government where you could have been chewed up by everyone, but you have stayed in there. Everyone likes you, and I think it is because you are always willing to listen. [50]

Several days later, I stopped in at the office of Bob Jones, chairman of the House Public Works Committee (which had jurisdiction over water quality programs), who had announced plans to retire. We were joined by

Congressman Jim Wright of Texas, who would be taking Jones' place as chairman. It became apparent that Jones was one of those with whom Rockefeller had talked, giving rise to the above story. Jones said to me, "You listen but you don't hear!" He meant, I assume, that I listened to other points of view and then went ahead and made the decision I was going to make anyway.[51]

Having said all that, I have no question that the most important element of strength in the situation was the unfailing support of the highly competent EPA staff. From deputy administrator John Quarles on down, I could always count on the loyalty, integrity, and sheer ability of the EPA people. As head of EPA's Office of Planning and Management, Al Alm had put together a topflight economic analysis staff, and the analytic data on costs, both to business and to the public health, that we were able to present were outstanding. In fact, we won many an argument simply because of the quality of our data. John Whitaker has commented, "Because EPA is obviously an advocate of environmental improvement, other agencies are often suspicious that EPA's cost estimates are too low, but few other agencies have any real capability to challenge EPA's assumptions."[52]

Best of all, I think that the EPA troops came to like and respect me. I even heard that Ralph Nader admitted having been mistaken in questioning whether I had the requisite toughness for the job.

Chapter 10

EPA under Ford

T HE CLIMATE established by the Gerald Ford administration, in which I spent two-thirds of my time as head of the Environmental Protection Agency (EPA), was remarkably different from that of its predecessor, if for no other reason than it encouraged a far more open process of government. Ford's willingness to engage in discussion of EPA issues contrasted starkly with Richard Nixon's consistent refusal to do so. In large part, the change reflected the different natures of Nixon and Ford.

In August 1974, Aileen and I were vacationing at the Ausable Club, in the heart of the high peak region of the Adirondack Mountains, a part of New York where I had spent several summers as a boy. We had a small cottage but went for meals to the rambling old frame clubhouse. There, at 9:00 P.M. on August 8, we and other guests watched Nixon's televised resignation address to the American people. It was a sad talk, disappointing in its defensiveness, but we shared the relief of most Americans at the outcome.

I flew the next morning to Washington, D.C., and went straight to EPA on my arrival. I had called Bryce Harlow for advice on whether to come back to Washington immediately; there was probably no need, he said, but if I were not there and were wanted for some reason, I would always regret my absence. It was good advice, although, as it turned out, I found everything proceeding as usual. There were no calls from the White House, none from Congress, none from the press.[1] All was quiet. And only members of the Cabinet were invited to the day's activities; together with colleagues, I watched Vice President Ford sworn in to the presidency on my office television set. I called a meeting of top staff, primarily to signal the change in authority, and then returned to Aileen and the Adirondacks. Looking back on it all, I realize that the very calmness of the events was an extraordinary testimonial to the strength and stability of our American democracy.

The Ford Transition

The transition committee Ford appointed was chaired by Donald Rumsfeld and made up additionally of Rogers Morton; William Scranton, former governor of Pennsylvania; and Jack Marsh, former congressman from Virginia and at that time counselor to the president. I called Morton from the Ausable Club to discuss my concerns about management and decision making, in hopes of stimulating from the beginning a better working relationship than we had had under Nixon. With Morton's encouragement, I finally developed a short memorandum on the subject, which I sent to him, with copies to the other members of the transition team as well as Bryce Harlow and John Sawhill.[2] I talked with Rumsfeld on the same subject at the time and again several weeks later. As an aside, Rummy insisted that he "wouldn't touch the top White House staff job with a ten-foot pole." When I talked to him later, after he had taken over from Alexander Haig as chief of staff, he said, "I still wouldn't!"

The recommendations I made to the transition team went along these lines:

1. In the development of presidential policy, there should be open and direct communication on a regular basis between the president and agency heads.
2. There should be full advance consultation with Congress, on as bipartisan a basis as possible.
3. Agency heads should be given maximum freedom in decision making consonant with overall presidential policy. Neither Office of Management and Budget (OMB) nor White House staff should become a barrier between the president and agency heads. In particular, OMB should avoid making decisions with major policy implications, as it had done from time to time in the Nixon administration, usually in the guise of a regulatory review process. The key decisions must instead be made by the president.

4. The heads of EPA and the Federal Energy Administration (FEA) should attend all Cabinet meetings. In EPA's case, environmental concerns tend to cut across the entire fabric of government, having a central relevance to such issues as energy, economic, agricultural, transportation, housing, and public lands policy.

5. The traditional practice of budget appeals by agency heads made directly to the president should be restored.

I returned to Washington once more during that "vacation" when President Ford met with what was called the Little Cabinet—the officials in his administration of less than Cabinet rank. The East Room of the White House was crowded, mostly with people I did not know—an indication of the changes in top personnel that had taken place in recent months. The president's remarks were brief—in fact, so brief that we were left wondering why we had been invited—and then we queued up to shake hands with him in the Blue Room. After I congratulated him, I stood to one side and introduced each of the other EPA officials in attendance. A photographer asked us to pose; the president said he would be glad to and asked where he should stand. I said. "Right in the middle, Mr. President!" He said, "That's where I am used to being!"

I had known Ford slightly for a number of years as a member of Congress. However, he had never been a member of any committee with which I had a close association and I did not know him at all well. To my good fortune, I was able to arrange an appointment with him for September 4, soon after our vacation was over.

Ken Cole, who was acting as chief of staff (and soon would be deputy to Rumsfeld in that capacity), accompanied me into the Oval Office.[3] The president came across the room to shake hands, and we then sat on chairs in front of the fireplace, with Cole at the far end of one of the sofas flanking us. Ford opened the meeting by saying something to the effect of "Well, how's EPA?" I told him that we had a lively agency with lots of very dedicated people; we tended to be controversial and doubtless would continue to be. I said that the country had been making good progress in dealing with environmental matters and commented that it would be hard to find any other area of domestic problems in which comparable progress had been made. As a case in point, I mentioned the Great Lakes. This reference immediately caught the president's attention, just as I had hoped—since his hometown was Grand Rapids, Michigan. He asked how Lake Michigan was doing and then how the municipal waste treatment construction grant program was progressing.

We then turned to the subject of automobile catalytic converters, and Ford expressed the opinion that Congress had acted in some environmental areas with insufficient information, referring specifically to automobile emission requirements. I made no effort to force any issue of this sort; it seemed more important at this first meeting to establish a rapport. I was certain that the president was conservative on environmental issues, particularly those with immediate economic implications and I believed it important at this stage in our association to assure him that I was not an emotional crusader and had a good sense of balance. I injected a bit of my own history to reinforce this, particularly my time with the Ways and Means Committee and as a judge of the United States Tax Court. Ford interrupted me to say, "Russ, I know all that!"

The president brought up the adverse reaction of environmentalists and the *New York Times* to a speech Rogers Morton had just delivered on his behalf at Expo '74 in Spokane, Washington. Ford said he had read the speech "over again carefully" and was puzzled by the reaction. Though it had also stressed the need for balance, the speech had mentioned very positive things about the need for environmental protection. I pointed out that the speech had attacked those who support no-growth policies, yet in fact few environmentalists fell into this category and thus the reference had been seen as a straw man. "Mr. President," I continued, "you might as well accept the fact that whenever a Republican president speaks of the need for balance, that is going to be read as a code for 'tilt for industry.' I suggest that, when you are addressing environmental matters, you take a straight pro-environment line and have me do the balancing!" He clearly heard me but showed little reaction except to puff on his pipe.

Ford indicated his wish for me to continue dealing with international activities. We also spoke about my hope that there would be a closer relationship between the executive branch and Congress in developing legislative policy. Before the administration developed a position, I suggested, we should actively solicit congressional viewpoints. I pointed out that failure to do so on critical legislation, such as the Federal Water Pollution Control Act Amendments of 1972, had led to the administration's loss of any real negotiating position on the issue. Could he, I asked, direct agency heads, such as myself, to consult directly on a bipartisan basis with key committee members to elicit their views and then to report back to

As judge of U.S.
Tax Court, 1958

As president of
WWF-US, with live
bat in hand, 1979
(WWF photo)

Author, age eleven, 1931

My father, Charles Russell Train, 1918

My mother, Errol Cuthbert Train, and my brothers, Middy and Cuth, ca. 1916

Aileen and I on our honeymoon, 1954

On safari, Kenya, 1956

Richard Nixon introduces the new Council on Environmental Quality
to the press, January 1970 (UPI/Corbis)

Nixon and Prime Minister Pierre Trudeau at signing of the
Great Lakes Water Quality Agreement, 1972

Reporting to Nixon on my return from Moscow, 1972

A contemporary comment on the Teton Dam disaster — see page 215

With Gerald Ford on Air Force One

Interior, CEQ, and EPA staff reunion at Train home (photo by Marjory Train)

On the trail of the giant panda with George Schaller, Wolong Nature Reserve, western China, 1982 (WWF photo)

Receiving the Presidential Medal of Freedom from George H. W. Bush, with an assist from Barbara

With Education for Nature scholars (WWF photo)

Back to Africa: along the Zambesi River, Zimbabwe, 1998

the president? His response to this seemed very positive. He told Ken Cole to remind him to raise it at a Cabinet meeting.

This exchange led me to suggest that I should attend Cabinet meetings on a regular basis. I said that in the case of both EPA and the FEA, our responsibilities tended to cut across the entire fabric of government. Somewhat to my surprise, the president's reaction seemed favorable, and, as it turned out, I attended the next Cabinet meeting and most such meetings thereafter.

The high point for me of that meeting with the president came when I said I had a lot more to cover and did not know when I would get to see him again. He immediately responded that that would be no problem. Turning to Cole, he said, "I want to see Russ on a regularly scheduled basis such as once a month or at least every two months," and, turning to me, "If you ever have any issue you should discuss with me, all you have to do is call up and say so."

At the end of our meeting, I mentioned that I would be on the same program as he at a mass transit conference in Pittsburgh the following Monday. (Obviously, I was hoping for an invitation to travel aboard Air Force One and the invitation came later in the week.)

All of this signaled a refreshing change of atmosphere in the White House. Aside from three energy meetings with Nixon and members of his Cabinet, I had had no meeting with Nixon after I became EPA administrator, a fact duly noted by the press.[4] Ford seemed thoroughly relaxed in his role and willing to listen. In an interview published the previous day, I had said that being now part of the Ford administration was "like coming in from the cold."[5]

A Clean Air Flap

An incident occurred in the first weeks of the new administration that at least initially gave me pause about how easy our relations might actually be. On October 7, Roger Strelow, then EPA's assistant administrator for air programs, called to alert me to a story in that morning's *Wall Street Journal*. The article claimed that the economic message Ford was scheduled to submit to Congress the next day was expected to include a "warmed over version" of the Nixon proposals of the previous March to amend the Clean Air Act, including permission for the use of so-called intermittent controls (tall stacks). I was stunned. I had received no call from the White House or anyone else about the message. This was the very proposal I had refused to support earlier in the year and had transmitted without endorsement to Congress.[6]

I immediately got on the phone. Frank Zarb at OMB said he recalled nothing about tall stacks in the message and Bill Simon said he very much doubted that there was anything in it on tall stacks. When I said I thought I should see a copy of the message, Simon became evasive. I next called Rumsfeld (already now chief of staff). He said he had no knowledge of the matter, so I confined myself to commenting that it was a "helluva note" for a major presidential policy statement, directly involving EPA's specific responsibilities, to be prepared without any consultation with EPA whatsoever. Rummy said he would look right into it. Jack Carlson, an assistant secretary of Interior, called on behalf of Morton. He, too, doubted there was any reference in the message to tall stacks. I said, "Jack, why don't you just read the language of the message itself?" Al Alm, Bill Dircks (who had come to CEQ to replace Roger Strelow as my administrative assistant), and several others were with me in my office at the time. Now quite certain that the draft contained the objectionable language, I turned to the others and said, "I am going to scream like hell in a few moments!" As Carlson hit the tall stacks language, I hit the roof and responded with a high-pitched yell: "Wh-a-a-a-t? I can't believe it!"

Bill Seidman, Ford's assistant for economic policy, called, and we agreed on a 7:00 P.M. meeting at the White House to resolve the matter. When I walked into the Roosevelt Room at the appointed hour, the whole economic team was already there: Bill Simon (presiding), Paul McCracken, Alan Greenspan, Bill Seidman, Roger Porter (Seidman's assistant), Bill Eberle (trade negotiator), Arthur Burns, and Jerry Parsky of the Treasury. I raised the tall stacks issue and suggested they read me the language. Simon said, "Russ, why don't you just look at the Fact Sheet, because that is what the press will be focusing on." I wanted to see the words the president himself would be saying, I replied; I would look at the Fact Sheet later. Seidman began to leaf through the draft in front of him and finally found the critical passage, which he began to read— after saying he had no recollection of any tall stacks language. Suddenly, as he read "and amend the Clean Air Act," he said, "I'll be darned, it does talk about tall stacks," and went on to read the language I had heard about. "I wonder where that came from," he said, half to himself. Then, to Simon, "Bill, I think that must have been in the language which you sent over." I carefully did not look at Simon at that point.

As a result of this meeting, the language on tall stacks was removed and a relatively innocuous reference to the amendments to the Clean Air Act submitted in March was left in. Of course, the main point of the whole matter was not so much substantive as procedural. I think I succeeded in conveying the point that EPA should be consulted. In the absence of tall stacks, scrubbers, which removed a large percentage of the sulfur from coal, were the only available technology for meeting emission standards. EPA had won on scrubbers, the *Wall Street Journal* reported, and the Ford administration was supporting their use.[7]

The following Saturday, Rowland Evans and Robert Novak's column in the *Washington Post* reported that neither Simon nor Ash had been able to make any last-minute changes in the message to weaken the pro-environment aspects of the coal conversion program. Apparently, Bob Hartmann, counselor to the president and speechwriter, had been the keeper of the official text, and he would not let them through the door.[8]

I did not conclude that all this signaled a new pro-environment posture in the administration, but perhaps it did mean that I had their attention. *Time* magazine indicated that the president himself had apparently been concerned about whether I had been consulted.[9]

The press continued to give positive coverage to these events. For example, William K. Wyant Jr., Washington correspondent for the *St. Louis Post-Dispatch*, wrote at the time:

> Train as EPA chief has yielded some ground on the coal issue but has insisted on something more than a cosmetic approach to the problem of dangerous stack emissions. He has not hesitated to speak out or to strike back. He has immense prestige, and a heavy responsibility.[10]

Ford's First Cabinet Meeting

Several days later, on October 11, I attended my first Cabinet meeting in many months and the first called by President Ford.[11] I sat along the wall behind the empty vice president's chair and next to Bill Seidman. There were far fewer staff members than in Nixon's time. Rumsfeld sat in Haig's (previously Bob Haldeman's) seat near the door to the president's office. I was the only agency head, as distinguished from department head, present. The fact that John Sawhill, head of the FEA, evidently had not been invited seemed an indication of his and his agency's declining fortunes, as compared with Rog Morton and Interior, Morton having been designated by the president as energy coordinator in his economic message earlier that week.*

There was nothing at the meeting of direct relevance to EPA, but Roy Ash announced that an executive order was in preparation that would affect us—on the president's request for federal agencies to develop "inflation impact" analyses of their projects. Those who opposed environmental and other regulatory programs saw the new requirement as a way of rolling back such programs on the assumption that they added to costs and were thus inherently inflationary. While I believed we could usually counter such an attack—primarily because of the large external costs of environmental damage incurred when controls were not in place—I also suspected that we could use inflation impact analysis to our advantage as a useful additional weapon against projects, such as highways and dams, that had the potential for seriously adverse environmental effects. In other words, if this was a weapon, it could be a two-edged one.

Economics and the Environment

While the interface of energy and the environment provided the most obvious source of friction during my time at EPA, an ongoing and broader debate was taking place over the effects of environmental standards on the economy in general. Environmental programs were constantly being charged with costing jobs and causing inflation.[12]

The subject was addressed head-on at the White House Conference on Domestic and Economic Affairs at Portland, Oregon, in November 1974, one of a series of town hall meetings organized by Bill Baroody at which President Ford and selected members of his administration gave talks and answered questions from the audience. I took part in several of these events and thought them a first-rate idea.[13]

Ford himself attacked the economy-versus-environment view in his prepared remarks in Portland with these words:

*John Sawhill got into political hot water by stating on a Sunday morning talk show that an increase in the federal gasoline tax was an option that should be considered. His independence on this and other energy issues led to his early resignation.

I assure the people of the Northwest that I do not accept the dismal proposition that pollution is the inevitable price of prosperity nor that we must compromise the environment to gain economic growth. We cannot enrich our lives by impoverishing our land. We can raise both standard of living and the quality of life.[14]

In my own remarks, I underscored the fact that environmental expenditures were a relatively small factor in the current inflation and capital "squeeze" and that their effect would remain small for the foreseeable future. Environmental expenditures were no more inherently inflationary or nonproductive than expenditures for national defense, law enforcement, health, or education. Their purpose was to protect the public health and welfare from very real hazards.

Like any other outlay, environmental expenditures could not be justified simply because their goals were important, I agreed. It had to be demonstrated both that we got what we paid for and that what we got was worth the cost. "All the available evidence," I said, indicated that our pollution control expenditures were worth their cost and I cited examples of EPA's careful analytical work. I went on in words that seem just as apt today, almost thirty years later:

The fundamental economic aim of the environmental effort is to improve the quality of growth in this country by encouraging the reduction or recovery of the enormous waste of energy and other resources within our economy — wastes that, in large measure, represent economic as well as environmental costs. To the degree that clean air and water, and indeed land itself, have become increasingly scarce and costly goods — and that energy and other materials, whose extraction, production and consumption generate the pollution we are trying to clean up, have themselves become increasingly scarce and costly — it makes both environmental and economic sense to make the conservation of energy and the reduction or recovery of waste a matter of the highest priority.

Our environmental, energy and economic interests converge to put a premium upon greater and greater efficiency in the industrial process — a new efficiency which can, at one and the same time, cut costs, conserve energy and curb pollution — a new efficiency which can thus help reduce inflation as well as pollution.

We don't really have the option of *not* paying pollution costs at all, I pointed out. The only question is in what form we pay them — in higher electricity bills or in higher doctor bills and higher rates of mortality and morbidity. Capital requirements for environmental protection were very small in relation to the total flow of capital within our economy. Over the next ten years, the pollution-related investment by industry would equal only about 2–3 percent of gross private investment, I projected, and on average only about 6 percent of private investment in plant and equipment. Although I have not tried to develop comparable numbers for, say, 2003, I have no reason to think the situation has changed appreciably. To be fair, averages are not always an accurate yardstick for particular industries. When a mom-and-pop filling station, for example, learns the cost of replacing a leaking underground gasoline tank, the owners may well decide to go out of business. Then as now, plants that shut down because of new environmental costs tend to be small, old, and marginal. Their demise may have been hastened by environmental requirements, but they probably would have closed down soon anyway for straightforward economic reasons. There was simply no evidence, I pointed out, that environmental requirements had had or would have any marked adverse effect on jobs or existing productive capacity, especially since investments in environmental protection, such as new technologies, created new markets, new jobs, and new profit opportunities.[15]

It was occasionally claimed that U.S. environmental standards made it difficult for U.S. producers to compete with foreign producers (who supposedly had no such standards to meet). Clearly, a disparity in pollution control costs would contribute to an uneven playing field in world markets, just as would be the case with a difference in labor costs. However, the only acceptable way to address that problem, I argued, was for the United States to take a strong leadership role in international environmental affairs, helping raise the awareness of environmental problems abroad, encouraging the growth of political institutions in other countries capable of initiating and managing environmental programs, and creating pressures for the raising of standards.

The Second Meeting with Ford

Later that November, I asked for another meeting with President Ford, and that meeting turned out to be even more wide-ranging than the first. Its content seems worth reporting in some detail, to give a sense of some of the issues of these first Ford years and to illustrate several of its extraordinary features. No meeting I had with Nixon was remotely comparable in range or depth. I was given an opportunity to bring up anything I wanted and the president responded to every issue I raised.

I was up at 5:00 A.M. that November 27 to organize my thoughts for the meeting. Since I had a press conference scheduled for 10:30 A.M. to announce our final regulations on the "no significant deterioration" requirement of the Clean Air Act (discussed in more detail in the next chapter) and also our plans for a hearing on the automobile emission issue, I went from home to EPA to get briefed for the press conference before heading to the White House.

Ken Cole and Mike Duval were with the president when I was ushered into the Oval Office. Duval took notes, and he and Cole offered comments from time to time. A golden retriever named Liberty was also part of the group, and the meeting's first minutes were taken up by the president trying to get her to sit down next to him for a photo opportunity.

Ford was just back from his meeting with Leonid Brezhnev in Vladivostock and he emphasized that he and Brezhnev had established "a strong personal relationship." I told him of my imminent visit to Moscow in connection with the US-USSR Agreement on Cooperation in the Field of Environmental Protection. In my travels around our country, I said, I had found a continuing high level of interest in the environment: people were obviously concerned about economic and energy matters, but they wanted these dealt with in conjunction with environmental needs. I said it was not so much a matter of maintaining a *balance* among these concerns as of recognizing their essential interrelationship—that they were all part of the same overall problem. I went on to suggest that the interrelationship of economic, energy, environmental, agricultural, population, and related issues could provide a theme for his State of the Union Address. Ford didn't really respond.

As an example of domestic public attitudes, I reminded him of the positive response he had received to his strongly pro-environment remarks at the Portland, Oregon, town hall meeting. He agreed that he should maintain a positive image regarding environmental matters. Looking ahead to 1976 and beyond, I went on, I could see only growing public concern over environmental problems. Increasing technology was creating new cancer problems, such as with vinyl chloride, asbestos in Lake Superior, carcinogens in New Orleans's drinking water, and measurable levels of dieldrin in humans, and advances in measurement technology and further research would doubtless reveal other, similar problems.

The president believed we should not set standards unless we were really sure of our data. I agreed but pointed out that it is seldom practical to delay decisions until one is 100 percent sure. We normally have to proceed on the basis of the best evidence available — which, I said, I was certain was the way he himself made decisions. I added that EPA had a pretty good track record: our standards had, almost without exception, been validated by the National Academy of Sciences and other scientific groups. Furthermore, we constantly reviewed our standards, and when a correction was needed, I didn't hesitate to say so.

When we turned to current legislative matters, I mentioned that the Senate had voted, with unanimous consent and by voice vote, to accept the safe drinking water bill, which had passed in the House by a vote of about 295–80. He might, I said, get a recommendation for a veto, and I wanted him to know that I considered it important that he not veto the bill. The president asked how much money was involved. About $150 million in authorization over three years, I replied. I was convinced that his staff was biased against the bill, so several days later I sent a memorandum again urging his approval of the legislation.[16] (Ford did not veto the bill and it became law.)

The Scrubber Settlement

I also reported on the gist of a two-hour talk the previous week, particularly on the Clean Air Act and more specifically on the scrubber issue, that I had had with the leadership of EPA's principal committee in the Senate, the Senate Committee on Public Works — particularly Senators Jennings Randolph, Howard Baker, and Ed Muskie. Without exception, they had confirmed my conviction that Congress would never approve permanent intermittent controls (i.e., tall stacks). Baker, who was not an enthusiast of scrubbers, was in full agreement with this assessment, and Senator Randolph, who could hardly be described as a wild-eyed environmentalist, strongly supported EPA's scrubber policy.

The scrubber issue had finally been resolved by the Energy Resources Council (ERC) and I described the agreement to the president in general terms — a commitment to permanent control technology, with 1985 as the outside date for company compliance. I considered the agreement within ERC to be a tremendous breakthrough and the basis for moving an effective new Clean Air Act package through Congress. The president expressed himself as pleased with the result. I doubt that he was well informed on the issue, but he was aware of its being a tough problem. This discussion of developments with the president may have helped nail the decision down. Duval pretty much confirmed the correctness of my report on the matter, although I knew he was very much against the decision.*

I also briefed the president on the progress of discussions with the automakers on achieving his goal of a 40 percent improvement in fuel economy by 1980. As he already knew, all the companies were insisting on a five-year extension of emission standards. The Clean Air Act allowed a one-year extension (at the EPA administrator's discretion) after an application was filed and after full EPA public hearings. I realized he wanted a decision on an extension as early as possible. I believed, though, that a full public record was essential to the credibility of any legislative proposal; it would be impossible for EPA to join in supporting extension legislation without that kind of public airing of the facts. The president agreed and said, "Let the facts speak for themselves." Duval mentioned Morton's desire to preserve an option for the president to make a recommendation in his State of the Union Address. I thought it would serve the purpose, I said, if in the message the president could simply refer to his concern and the fact of the EPA hearings. Ford seemed perfectly agreeable to this approach, which made me feel a lot more comfortable at my press conference later in the morning.

Since the subject of the State of the Union Address had already been broached, I took the bull by the horns and suggested the president use the message to propose combining EPA and the National Oceanic and Atmospheric Administration (NOAA), and perhaps some other units, such as the U.S. Fish and Wildlife Service, into a Department of the Environment. The idea had been triggered, I said, by the talk of establishing a Department of Energy and Natural Resources and by his own announced desire to maintain balance. I had discussed the idea with Roy Ash over lunch the previous Friday, I reported, and Ash had not been at all

*The so-called tall stacks issue gradually went away as scrubbers came more and more into use. On January 4, 1976, the *New York Times* editorialized that I had reason to feel vindicated by the growing success of scrubbers. The number of scrubbers built, under construction, or planned had increased over the past two years from 44 to 118.

negative—mention of which brought an expression of amusement from the president, who apparently found Ash seldom anything but negative. The president seemed open-minded on the department idea and agreed on its being explored, but neither he nor his immediate staff seemed to have any interest in pursuing the matter themselves.

Finally, I raised another issue, to which the president listened but showed no interest in following up: how to make the best use of the federal share of leasing of Outer Continental Shelf (OCS) oil and gas development rights. I recommended that proceeds of such leasing activity (either bonus or royalty payments) be used for the acquisition of parklands, recreation areas, wildlife refuges, and the like. OCS oil and gas are nonrenewable resources and represent assets belonging to the public. When removed, I argued, the proceeds should not simply go into the government's operating budget but should be reinvested in new permanent assets for all the people. The president said Ash and OMB were all against the idea. I said, "That's why presidents have to overrule budget directors occasionally!" He laughed, but that was pretty much the end of the matter—a great pity. It was obvious that the president would not embrace some of my suggestions, but still, I thought as I left the meeting, he was clearly living up to his earlier assurance to me that I would have access to him for full discussion.

Struggle over Strip-Mining

In President Nixon's 1971 environmental message to Congress, he had proposed a "Mined Area Protection Act" to establish federal requirements and guidelines for state programs to regulate the environmental consequences of surface and underground mining, including the reclamation of mined lands. Under the proposed act, such lands would be restored to the original topography and vegetation and soil and water condition would be stabilized. Poorly regulated coal mining frequently led to badly scarred landscapes, streams blocked by mine spoils, acid runoff into waterways, surface subsidence, and other problems. Though my own concern for the issues remained strong, the legislation languished and was never finally acted on. White House interest evaporated.

The issue remained alive, however, and I kept stirring the pot. In March 1974, for example, the *Washington Post* editorialized:

It is not the use of coal at issue but the use of the land to get it; in the past, government figures have estimated that only a small portion of the nation's total coal supply is in strippable land, with the rest overwhelmingly in deep mines. With that in mind, Russell E. Train of the Environmental Protection Agency offered excellent counsel when he said recently that "the sooner we make underground (mining) more economically attractive, more technologically feasible and more socially acceptable as a way of life, the better off we are going to be." [17]

In July of that year, in the waning days of Nixon's presidency, during a swing around strip-mining areas of North Dakota, I announced my support of a strip-mining bill sponsored by Morris (Mo) Udall, chairman of the House Interior Committee. Titled the Surface Mining Control and Reclamation Act, it would impose strict reclamation requirements on mine operators. [18] In what the *New York Times* called "a complete break with the administration," I said that surface-mined coal—about half the country's production at that time, 600 million tons per year—should be "under very strong Federal control." [19]

Looking back on the matter, I think my announcement seems a bit gratuitous: Interior had principal jurisdiction over the subject matter of the legislation. However, strip-mining had a significant adverse effect on water quality, which was definitely an EPA concern—a clear example of the fact that such issues cannot be compartmentalized but have ramifications reaching into other program areas. In any event, my announcement did signal another sharp split with the White House. I also found myself in opposition to my friends, secretary of Interior Morton, who was responsible for mineral policy, and John Sawhill, administrator of the FEA.* Sawhill cited huge coal losses he believed would result if the legislation were enacted and a substantial reduction in strip-mining occurred. On the basis of EPA data, I estimated the losses as much lower. (Sawhill later substantially reduced his estimates to a level much nearer EPA's.)

I argued that the eastern coal industry should be emphasizing the extraction of deep coal and developing the technology to do so, which

*Sawhill had replaced Simon as head of the Federal Energy Administration. He had previously been deputy director of the Office of Management and Budget. Later, he went on to become president of New York University and then president of The Nature Conservancy. In all these capacities, he performed in outstanding fashion. When he died suddenly in 2000, the nation lost a splendid public servant.

would cause far less environmental damage than did strip-mining. Once again, my willingness to stake out an independent position received, if not White House enthusiasm, favorable press coverage. The *Washington Star* published an editorial titled "Battle over Stripping," which declared, "A recent courageous endorsement of the legislation by Russell E. Train, head of the Environmental Protection Agency, has done much to offset mining-industry favoritism in the White House."[20] A *Washington Post* editorial called attention to my remarks on strip mine devastation in the West and went on to say: "It is unfortunate that Secretary of the Interior Rogers C. B. Morton is offering no leadership on this issue. . . . Mr. Train, however, offsets the timidity of Mr. Morton."[21] Such invidious comparisons were neither helpful nor welcome to me.

The strip-mining issue remained very much alive in the Ford administration. The Interior Department continued to oppose the legislation, as did the administration generally, except for EPA. The Ford White House did not come out publicly against the legislation but did so behind the scenes. In March 1975, for example, Congressman John Anderson of the House Rules Committee told me that the White House had lobbied him to help kill the strip-mining bill then working its way through the House. On March 22, President Ford met with the House Republican leaders regarding the legislation. I was invited but could not attend the meeting, and John Quarles went in my place. Congressman John Melcher, a sponsor of the House bill, had indicated willingness to accept some of the changes the administration wanted, and I met with him several times to try to work toward an acceptable bill, but we were never able to get Tom Kleppe, the new secretary of Interior, to meet with us. Quarles now reported that the president was committed to killing the bill. It was a tricky situation for me as I continued to work to develop a bill that would be acceptable. The strip-mining bill did finally pass the House by a vote of 291–81, but it was backed only by me in the administration.

While it may seem that I was simply opposing my own administration on the strip-mining issue, the fact was that the last official executive branch policy on the matter had been the Nixon administration's proposal of strong strip-mining legislation. The Ford administration had never officially departed from that policy, nor did the president or his White House ever instruct me to the contrary.

In May 1975, I took part in a meeting with Ford to discuss the strip-mining legislation and whether the president should veto it.[22] Jim Cannon, staff director of the Domestic Council, reported that Ford had asked for eight major changes in the legislation and Congress had accepted six of these in part. Three new problems had been created, he said: a requirement that strip-mining on federal lands conform to state requirements, the regulation of mine spoils dumped into alluvial valleys (which was really not new), and a requirement that miners provide replacement water to farmers. Cannon estimated that the legislation would result in the loss of 40–160 million tons of coal production and about 40,000 jobs.

The president then called on me. I took issue with the cost estimates. I cited the experience of Pennsylvania, which had enacted legislation similar to the bill about three years before. The record showed production up, employment up, and the number of operations up. The president asked whether it was really possible to have effective reclamation, and I gave a strong affirmative response, citing again the Pennsylvania example and also referring to the Tennessee Valley Authority's support of the bill. I urged the president to sign the bill; the time had come, I said, for the country to get this issue behind it.[23]

Frank Zarb spoke next and cited a series of negatives: the states had undertaken more and more effective regulation without federal legislation; the bill was coming at a time when Congress had failed to act on any other energy matters; the bill would impede our coal conversion program; it would create uncertainties and litigation "just like the Clean Air Act."

A number of others also spoke — all in favor of a veto. I spoke again and addressed a question that had been raised about investment. The biggest impediment to capital investment in new coal mine capacity was continuing uncertainty as to the rules; I believed that clear and certain regulation would do more for investment than anything else. Simon disagreed. John Hill (of OMB) said the bill would improve the investment climate for deep mining in the East and hurt it for strip-mining in the West. This was really the guts of the issue: East versus West.

President Ford vetoed the legislation and sent a revised proposal to Congress. A modified bill again passed and again was vetoed. The veto was sustained.

Land-Use Plans: A Second Attempt

Even though the national land-use policy initiative put forward by the Nixon administration had died in Congress, the issue stayed alive. I remained very much interested in it—not so much because of my earlier role in putting together the land-use proposals at the Council on Environmental Quality (CEQ) as because of my later EPA involvement in problems, such as auto emissions in urban areas and the construction of municipal sewage treatment plants, that had a major effect on land use.

Somewhat surprisingly, President Ford called a Cabinet-level meeting on land use at the end of November 1974. Rogers Morton, whose Interior Department was to have had the lead in carrying out the earlier legislation, probably had suggested the session. It was not a particularly productive meeting.[24]

Morton and I urged that the administration initiate and support land-use legislation, describing the history of the issue and pointing out the various ways in which federal agencies influenced land use, all in a totally uncoordinated fashion. EPA had set up a land use office earlier that year to help meet the need for coordination within the agency. The states needed a multipurpose, comprehensive planning capability that was process oriented, I maintained. No one was talking about actual national land-use planning but rather a national effort to stimulate states to establish and coordinate a process that would be carried out largely at the local level.

There was unexpected support for land-use legislation from secretary of Agriculture Earl Butz, who cited the unplanned loss of farmland to highway construction. The meeting ended with the president asking that an option paper be prepared by Christmas, but I never heard anything further about the land-use issue, and it essentially faded away. I imagine it was too radical an issue for the conservative Ford.

Meeting at Vail

The president and the First Lady took a break for skiing at Vail, Colorado, and while there Ford called a meeting on energy and economic issues for the waning days of 1974, December 28–29.[25] The flight to Grand Junction, Colorado, took slightly more than four hours; once there, we transferred to three helicopters for the flight to Avon, near Vail.

It was a brilliant, clear day, and we had a gorgeous flight through the snow-covered mountains. After landing, we drove straight to the house the president had rented. A large number of reporters and photographers were on hand as we went in. We went directly to a ground-floor living room, where the president was talking with Roy Ash and Don Rumsfeld. The president greeted and shook hands with each of us as we came in. A fire was blazing in the large stone fireplace, around which chairs and sofas were arranged. The president took a large chair flanked by Morton and Simon, and the rest of us found seats. Rumsfeld was out of the room for a good part of the time and took little part in the meeting.

The president was dressed informally, as were the rest of us, and wore a striped pullover and checked trousers. He thanked all of us for having traveled what he referred to as "several hundred miles." He said: "The skiing has been great. I have really enjoyed it. Rummy and I have put in about three hours of work a day together, and we have skied every day except today."

An energy issue book was distributed, Rog Morton opened the discussion with some general remarks, and then Frank Zarb led us through the book. Although this had not been described as a decision meeting, the president indicated his clear choice in almost every case. Presumably, all of this was to be reflected in either the State of the Union Address or an energy message. Several Clean Air Act issues were raised that called for my participation. Of those, the only one on which I lost was a fairly technical question of whether EPA could make a determination of the public health risk associated with sulfate emissions without holding formal public hearings on the matter. On preemption of state plans, the president sided with me and turned down the FEA's effort to get federal preemption authority over state implementation plans where these imposed stricter limitations than required by federal standards. It was plain that the president was strongly opposed to federal intervention in state affairs as a matter of general principle. (There was also a lengthy discussion of automobile emission requirements, but the matter was rendered moot by the EPA hearings and my regulatory decision a few weeks later, as described in the previous chapter.) On most matters not of direct concern to EPA, I had little or nothing to say, although I supported some energy conservation proposals.

We broke up at 1:15 and went up to the next floor for lunch — another large, high-ceilinged living room, another big fire, a bar-buffet, and a twenty-three-foot Christmas tree. We stood around and talked, had a drink, soup, and sandwiches, and returned to our meeting.

I was tremendously impressed with the process by which the president directed and guided the discussion. Strong differences of opinion were expressed on a variety of issues but there was a fair amount of good humor as well and the president laughed easily. He encouraged each of us to give full expression to our views, and there seemed not the slightest inhibition on anyone's part to do so. Even after the president had indicated where he would be coming out on an issue, there was no hesitancy in stating an opposing view. Nothing was rushed. At the same time, there was very little wandering from the point. The discussion remained remarkably focused the entire day. The president himself both asked questions and expressed opinions. He seemed both to be seeking full understanding of an issue and to be feeling his way to a decision. When he stated an opinion, he did so in a rather tentative fashion, as if he were putting it forward primarily to elicit reactions and a further sharpening of the issue. When he did make up his mind, he did not hesitate to say so clearly—a far cry from the practice of Nixon.

After a late afternoon break, we joined the president in his downstairs living room before dinner. Somehow, I missed securing a chair, so I sat on the floor by the fire, directly facing the president. He talked about Camp David and Ash described Camp Hoover. This led me to say that my father had been President Herbert Hoover's naval aide and that he and my mother had often stayed with the Hoovers at what was then called Rapidan Camp. Jim Lynn said something about the trout fishing in the Rapidan River, and the president commented that he was a poor fisherman and doubted that he would catch any. Lynn said he was sure that whenever the president fished there, he would be certain to catch something. The president said he had once caught a sailfish off Puerto Vallarta, on the Pacific coast of Mexico. I asked him whether he had enjoyed the experience, and he said, "Really, not very much." Roy Ash then remarked that he had never fished in his life. Neither one of the men was a hunter. Hunting and fishing aside, it always seemed both surprising and unfortunate to me that so many people in leadership positions had so little exposure to the outdoors.

I did not attend the economic talks the next day but joined the others for lunch and then I left for the return east.

The Maturing of EPA

In 1975, an environmental reporter, Linda Ba Thung (formerly Linda Durkee), who had observed EPA from its beginning, said in a speech that EPA was "becoming an institution and learning the art of exercising power." She went on: "Gone are the banner, slogan days, and much of the glamour that surrounded a new agency born of a popular cause. Gone too is the relatively quick and highly visible environmental offensive that produced the early wave of regulation."[26]

The new approach came from harsh realities, she said. EPA too frequently found itself in a position wherein its economic database was vulnerable and support was lacking. It could ill afford for long to spend the chips of public credibility on programs that drained agency and national resources and that had questionable effect on cleaning up the environment. The controversy over transportation plans, parking management, and similar indirect controls on pollution became symbolic of the problem. These federally mandated programs had little political or scientific support, according to Linda. They raised the risk of an environmental backlash, and EPA found its flanks unguarded and weak.

At the same time, EPA found itself in the middle of the economic and energy crisis that had begun in the last years of the Nixon administration and continued during Ford's. "No longer was environment the golden child, the exclusive and favorite national concern," she said. Although public support for the environment had continued, environmental goals had become subject to the administration's push to balance national objectives such as economic recovery and EPA had begun to evolve as an institution and to draw from its bureaucratic form the tools to ensure the survival of its position and the furtherance of its objectives.

EPA's Office of Planning and Management reflected this evolution. We developed an in-house capacity for analysis, especially economic, that stood us in good stead in dealing with proposals from other agencies and in enabling us better to order our own in-house priorities.

Ba Thung drew some comparisons of Ruckelshaus's tenure and my own early days at EPA:

> The days of highly vocal, stormy leadership are over. . . . Some say the easier battles are over, and the more difficult cleanup jobs remain. In any event, EPA's Administrator is a man for the times. . . . He brings to the job a strong environmental reputation and longstanding commitment to conservation.

He brings also experience in the Washington bureaucracy. Train is agile at the Congressional witness table, at home in cabinet-level circles, and able in behind-the-scene Administration battles.

As with any top figure, there are those who criticize. Some say Train travels too frequently, leaving the store seemingly untended. Others say he relies too heavily on his assistant administrators to run agency programs.

Nevertheless, one development is clear and growing. With Russell Train, the Environmental Protection Agency is becoming a national institution, interested in long-term environmental objectives. . . . The honeymoon is over, and EPA is digging in for the long pull. It is here, and it intends to stay.[27]

A Cincinnati Trip with Ford

On July 3, I flew on Air Force One with the president to Cincinnati, where we were to dedicate EPA's new $28 million National Center for Environmental Research, helping to emphasize our continuing commitment to a strong scientific research base for our actions. Russell Peterson, my successor as chairman of CEQ, was with us.

I had just returned from my extensive trip across the USSR, visit to Beijing, and brief stop in Tokyo in between,[28] and on the flight to Cincinnati I briefed the president on the US-USSR environmental agreement. I went on to describe our time in Beijing as guests of the Bushes, and the president said that he thought George was in a good spot for the present time and he would expect him to come back in about a year. "Of course," said Ford, "I don't know what his plans are." I mentioned my interest in a possible environmental exchange program with the Chinese. He told me to feed the idea into the National Security Council mill. (I did, but nothing came of it.)

On the drive to the laboratory, the president asked how the municipal sewage treatment construction grant program (90 percent federally funded) was going. When I reported that we had succeeded in reaching our target of $3.5 billion in obligations in the fiscal year just ended, he seemed pleased and emphasized the economic (jobs) benefit of the program. I agreed; the program was special in its dual benefit—both environmental and economic. I then seized the opportunity and mentioned that we needed five hundred more positions to make the program go forward strongly. If it would help move the funds faster, Ford indicated, he would be very sympathetic to the request.

There was a good crowd at the lab, including Senator Robert Taft and Congressman William Gradison. The EPA lab director, Andrew Breiden-bach, acted as master of ceremonies. The president and I unveiled the cornerstone together. I then spoke briefly and introduced the president, whose statement that he would not tolerate the symbol of America as "an empty beer can in a river of garbage" got a good response from those attending.

Following the ceremony, there was a meeting for the president with environmental leaders — the first during his ten months in office. In addition to organization representatives, there was the Citizens' Advisory Committee on Environmental Quality, chaired by Henry Diamond. Its former chairman, Laurance S. Rockefeller, was also on hand. The president made it clear that he wanted to hear their concerns and they raised the subjects of land use, predator control, wilderness preservation, and whale protection. On the predator issue, the group made plain its view that the president had heard only one side of the issue — that of the wool growers and the cattlemen. That was a general theme of the discussion: concern that the president was getting most of his advice from industrialists and not from environmentalists.

At one point, the president brought up the matter of our construction grant program and laughingly said that Russ Train had made a pitch in the car for two hundred more staff members. "Five hundred, Mr. President," I interjected, correcting him. This brought good-natured laughter.

Downtown, a White House Conference on Economic and Domestic Policy was in progress at the convention center. Frank Zarb and I each spoke briefly and then answered questions for an hour, mainly on the interrelationship of energy and environmental policy. The president gave a strong speech lambasting Congress for inaction. His delivery had certainly improved rapidly in strength and self-assurance since he had taken office.

I was reasonably pleased with the whole Cincinnati affair, but not everyone felt the same way. Bill Shannon blasted the president in a *New York Times* op-ed piece: "Although a pollution alert was in effect, Mr. Ford delivered a speech that thickened the air with additional noxious materials." [29] Ford delivered a fairly strong pro-environment speech, but he also said: "I pursue the goal of clean air and pure water but I must also pursue the objective of maximum jobs and continued economic progress. Unemployment is as real and as sickening a blight as any pollutant that threatens this nation."[30] Given the rest of his talk, it did not seem unreasonable that Ford also expressed his concern for the economy.

At a Cabinet meeting in August,[31] I pursued this environment-economy issue. One very positive program that we should be talking about, I asserted, was EPA's construction grant program for municipal sewage treatment. Of the $5.6 billion obligation level we estimated for the current fiscal year, each billion in construction activity represented about 45,000 jobs. The program was, in my opinion, a good example of a project that helped both the environment and the economy, and I said that the president had been very supportive of the program — referring to the recent addition of three hundred new personnel.

During the meeting, the president noted that he was going to Rhode Island and Maine that weekend and asked me to provide him with specific information about waste treatment construction in those areas. Though we did provide the information, we never heard whether or not he had used it. Reluctantly, I concluded — and, of course, not just on the basis of this particular exchange — that there was little interest in the White House in trying to cast environmental programs in a positive light. Conservative Republicans seemed simply not interested in that sort of message.

Governors, Mayors, and EPA Politics

I do not want to leave the impression that my time at EPA was largely taken up by sessions with the president or the Cabinet. These meetings just happened to be the ones I took the greatest care to record and they indicate some of the underlying issues in the government's policies.

Mayors I saw relatively infrequently except in large groups, such as at meetings of the U.S. Conference of Mayors. Richard Daley of Chicago was an exception. He, of course, represented the old-fashioned "boss" approach to city management. I remember sitting with him in his office at city hall, discussing various EPA issues. He was behind his desk and I sat to his right. To his left sat a row of about five subordinates facing him. If Daley agreed to a suggestion I made (as in the case of improved movement of automobile traffic in the interest of better air quality), he would turn toward one of his henchmen and say, "Joe, take care of that!" That would be the end of that particular item. Of course, if he disagreed, that was also the end of it for all practical purposes.

On an earlier occasion, while Nixon was still president, my wife found herself sitting next to the president at a White House dinner. Nixon brought up the subject of large city management, saying that there were two contrasting modes: the no-nonsense, dictatorial mode epitomized by Daley and the more open, conciliatory mode practiced by our friend John Lindsay in New York. Nixon made clear that he strongly favored the Daley approach, which perhaps provides a bit of insight into his thoughts about governing.

There is a sequel to that story. Some months later, Aileen and I were going through the receiving line at some White House affair. When she reached Nixon, he said: "You know, I have been thinking a lot about that conversation we had at dinner about Daley and Lindsay. I have changed my mind a bit about Lindsay because he seems to be doing a pretty good job." Aileen was dumbfounded by Nixon's memory.

I also made official calls on Governors Ronald Reagan and Jerry Brown in Sacramento. Reagan was affable, but the meeting was mostly non-substantive. I recall his asking me to shift seats with him so that he would present his preferred profile to the photographers. Brown met with me for more than an hour, so long, in fact, that I missed my plane back to San Francisco. On his part, he ignored the fact that he was supposed to be meeting with his own cabinet. He asked a lot of questions—did I worry about irreversible effects on the environment? What did I think about the need for a national energy policy? What were the economic costs (in terms of percentage of gross national product) of pollution control programs? He expressed concern about potential adverse public reaction in the event that high costs of pollution control were combined with little discernible improvement. I stressed that we really were making progress. This discussion led Brown to one of his favorite themes—the necessity for people to lower their expectations. He worried about the effect of ever-increasing regulation on business and personal freedom. I commented that I thought he and President Ford had a good deal in common in this respect. My notes state, "Brown doesn't agree or disagree with statements of this sort but just keeps looking at you."[32] He indicated that although he worried about the matter, it was probably inevitable. We then had a considerable philosophical discussion of the problem of personal freedom in a large, complex society.

Also in 1975, I attended a meeting in Mobile, Alabama, of the Southern Governors' Conference. The governors met around a horseshoe-shaped table and several members of the Ford administration, including me, appeared before them individually. I spent at least an hour sitting at a small table in the open end of the horseshoe, mostly responding to quite vituperative attacks on EPA by conservative governors of both parties. What one needed most was patience and a thick skin. Of course, not all the criticisms were unfounded and it was not all bad for a bureaucrat like me to have to experience some of the reactions our policies generated in some quarters.

That was the occasion on which I first met Jimmy Carter. Then governor of Georgia, he was not present during my grilling. Instead, I met him as he was arriving and I was leaving the room. We stopped and shook hands and he suggested we sit down and talk just outside the meeting room. We spent at least half an hour talking about environmental issues, about which he displayed a strong interest. When I suggested that perhaps he should join the governors, he brushed off the comment and said that our conversation was more important. How could I fail to like Jimmy Carter after that?!

Republican governor Bill Milliken of Michigan was always particularly helpful and supportive, as, indeed, were most of the governors with whom I came into contact. Then there was Meldrim Thomson Jr., arch-conservative Republican governor of New Hampshire. In early 1974, I had sent out to all governors a legislative package of Clean Air Act amendments that EPA planned to propose and asked for the governors' comments and suggestions and, I hoped, their support. I received appreciative acknowledgments from most, substantive comments from some, and no reply from a few. From Thomson I received a letter declaring, "In all frankness, I must tell you that I am very much opposed to a number of your proposals, and in general, to your leadership which, in my judgement, set America back decades in terms of its progress and security." [33]

On another occasion, in 1975, during the Ford administration, I was invited to attend a meeting at the White House of representatives of the coal and railroad industries, mostly the former, who filled the East Room. I did not have a speaking role, nor was I asked to respond. I simply sat and listened and made occasional notes while one speaker after another vilified EPA and the entire environmental movement. Arch Moore Jr., Republican governor of West Virginia, with whom I had met several times on his home ground, was present. He finally rose to his feet and very decently called attention to the fact that I had sat there listening to all the attacks on EPA; he thought the audience should express its gratitude for my patience and courtesy in listening to their complaints. Thereupon I got a round of polite applause. (Moore later went to jail for misconduct in office.) I apparently did make a few remarks at some point because a news article describing the occasion reported: "But it took Russell E. Train, head of the Environmental Protection Agency and regarded by most coal men as something of a villain, to rouse the gathering with an amiable assertion that the Clean Air Act's air pollution standards are the law and must eventually be implemented." The same article noted that one coal executive was overheard saying to another during the coffee break, "That Train gets away with murder."[34]

The "Squeaky" Fromme Threat

One of the oddest experiences I had in government came during the Ford administration, when I received a life-threatening letter from Lynette "Squeaky" Fromme, a twenty-seven-year-old follower of convicted mass murderer Charles Manson. She was in federal prison in California, serving a life term for trying to assassinate President Ford.

The letter (with one omission of incoherent phrasing) read as follows:

> You weak mealy mouth Don't you understand we are dying of the poisons you <u>are</u> aware of and you're so afraid of your reputation that no one is even hearing about [omission] You are warned <u>now</u> There are <u>Fake Breakers</u> from the International People's Court who can be as mean as you are weak and that is beyond mutilation As head of the Environmental Protection Agency for the entire country you are <u>warned</u> and will have your own life and face shoved in the pollution which you allow to go on & on & on — The state of the country is clearly an example of your uselessness Shout. Lynette A. Fromme. I.P.C.R. [International People's Court of Retribution][35]

While I was accustomed to receiving fan mail of all sorts, I took this one a bit seriously. The Manson gang's record was a bloody one and they supposedly still had cohorts around the country. EPA had a security detail, and for a period I had an armed agent at the house and accompanying me in my car. Finally, I ended the security watch and I never heard anything further about the matter. It has always struck me as strange that Fromme had the use of government stationery and the privilege of free postage for her letter to me posted from federal prison.

TOSCA and the Chemical Industry

As I have reported previously, President Nixon had included in his 1971 environmental message to Congress a detailed proposal for the regulation of toxic chemicals. The legislation, which was introduced as the Toxic Substances Control Act and came to be known as TOSCA, was very much the brainchild of our early CEQ days. Particular credit is due to J. Clarence "Terry" Davies, the responsible CEQ staff member and principal author of the legislation as submitted. TOSCA had subsequently had a frustrating career in Congress, having twice passed both the House and the Senate only to twice die in conference. Early in 1976, it was again working its way through Congress, its fate once again in doubt.

The chemical industry, led by the Dow Chemical Company, generally opposed the legislation, claiming that the cost to the industry of compliance, including testing of new chemicals, would be about $2 billion per year. (EPA's comparable cost estimates were far, far lower, between $79 million and $142.5 million.) The DuPont company was an exception to the industry's outright opposition to the legislation. DuPont's chairman and chief executive officer, Dick Heckert, gave strong personal leadership to the effort to secure a legislative solution that effectively addressed the need to regulate the introduction of toxic chemicals yet did not unreasonably burden industry.

The most divisive issue was whether or not to require pre-testing before new chemical substances were introduced into the environment. Both the House and Senate bills provided for pre-testing. The chemical industry opposed the requirement, and the Ford administration, while supporting legislative control of toxic substances, had doubts about pre-testing. EPA strongly favored pre-testing as the best way to avoid disasters before they happened. Now, in early 1976, I decided that we had to make a push for final enactment of the legislation out of concern that, if it died once again, that would be the end of it.

On February 26, 1976, I made a major speech on the subject before the National Press Club in Washington. The timing was propitious. Not long before, the public had been shocked by the disclosures of workers having been poisoned by a pesticide called Kepone (chlordecone) in the Hopewell, Virginia, plant of the Life Science Products Company, which made the pesticide under contract with the Allied Chemical Corporation. Twenty-eight employees and the wife of one of them had been hospitalized for what doctors said were Kepone-related illnesses. (Later, it was discovered that the bottom sediments of a major stretch of the James River were also contaminated by Kepone.) On the day of my speech, EPA announced the finding of minute traces of Kepone in mothers' milk from nine women living in the southeastern United States.

At about the same time the Kepone poisoning episode hit the media, the discharge of PCBs (polychlorinated biphenyls) into the Hudson River by a General Electric Company plant had become publicly known. The finding of significant levels of PCB—a carcinogen—in Hudson River fish had led to the closing of the river to fishing.*

It was also a time when there was pressure from within EPA for more aggressive use of existing air and water pollution authorities to deal with toxic discharge problems. Likewise, the National Water Quality Commission was about to recommend that EPA set limits on the discharge of toxic pollutants under the Federal Water Pollution Control Act Amendments of 1972. In my mind, none of these approaches really presented an effective solution to the problem. They put the burden on EPA to police toxic discharges throughout the country, an impossible burden because most of the chemicals involved had never been tested for their risks to human health. Moreover, such approaches represented an effort to regulate "after the fact" rather than before the chemicals were introduced into the environment, as would be required by TOSCA.

My speech to the National Press Club received media coverage throughout the country.[36] It was the only time that I recall engaging in a certain amount of emotional rhetoric. The statements I made were factually correct, but they were delivered in a manner designed to excite public reaction. Thus, I declared:

> We can no longer afford to wait for the basic authority to deal effectively with the problems of chemical pollution. It is time we gave the people of this country some reason to believe that, every time they take a breath or eat or touch, they are not taking their lives into their hands.[37]

Charging that untested chemicals were increasingly responsible for fatal or crippling diseases, I said:

> These diseases are going to take an increasingly heavy toll upon our lives and well-being unless and until we stop trying to deal with them by treating them

*The widespread presence of PCBs in Hudson River bottom sediments remains a major problem. EPA administrator Christine Whitman announced in August 2001 that EPA would require General Electric to dredge the river sediments.

after they occur, and start taking serious steps to prevent them from occurring in the first place.[38]

And in response to claims that the legislation would cripple the chemical industry and give the EPA administrator nearly dictatorial authority over the introduction of new chemical products, I said:

> Nor has it been on the "near dictatorial authority" of the EPA administrator that so many such agents are introduced into the environment without any effort to find out what their health effects are, much less let the public have a say about whether or not, or in what circumstances, it is willing to be exposed to them.[39]

That afternoon, I was interviewed on National Public Radio's *All Things Considered.* I was really wound up: "It is time we started putting chemicals to the test, not people." An hour later, I was being interviewed on WRC-TV, and then I was reported on by the ABC evening news. The following day, I met with representatives of the Manufacturing Chemists' Association to discuss TOSCA.[40]

In due course, TOSCA passed in Congress and was signed by the president. It had taken almost seven years from the genesis of the idea to its fruition into law. There is no question in my mind that our ability to keep the issue of toxic chemical contamination constantly before the public was a key ingredient in building the political support that finally resulted in the legislation's enactment.[41] It is my understanding as I write this that the George W. Bush White House has put a lid on the freedom of administration officials to make public appearances and statements of the kind I have described without advance clearance. I can appreciate that no president wants his administration to appear disorganized and undisciplined. However, I believe that, in the usual case, the public interest is better served by leaving such matters to the discretion and judgment of the officials involved. The president can always get rid of an agency head whose views are consistently discordant with those of his administration.

I might note that, at the time of this writing, TOSCA has been law for about twenty-five years and would not seem to have destroyed either the chemical industry or the American economy. Moreover, the constant exposure of the public to news of chemical contaminants was not something concocted by EPA or by me but was the direct result of real-life events such as Kepone and PCB spills and other contamination.

Chapter 11

The Last Ford Years

B Y MARCH 1976, as another presidential election loomed on the horizon, the environment as an issue had begun to receive less attention from the Ford administration and my relations with the White House were becoming increasingly difficult.

Debate over a major environmental issue at the time, centered on the Clean Air Act concept of "significant deterioration," was an indicator of the changing relationships. In states where air quality was already better than the Clean Air Act required, new developments, such as the introduction of a coal-fired power plant, that could lead to a significant deterioration of air quality—even if the state's overall air quality was still better than required—were not allowed. This rule was not written into the Clean Air Act itself but had been enunciated by a federal district court in a suit brought by the Sierra Club and ultimately based on one of the stated purposes of the Clean Air Act: "to protect and enhance the quality of the nation's air resources." The lower court's decision was affirmed in a 4–4 vote (without opinion) by the United States Supreme Court.[1]

While the decision may seem in some respects a highly technical one, it raised basic questions about trade-offs between economic growth and environmental protection. Western states in particular considered the rule to be an unfair deterrent to their future growth and by early 1976 the issue had become a political hot potato. EPA developed regulations to implement the Court's decision, only to have Senator Frank Moss of Utah introduce an amendment to the Clean Air Act designed to postpone promulgation of the EPA regulations pending further study. Meanwhile, the Senate Public Works Committee had drafted its own amendment, essentially writing the Court's decision into law but with modifications designed to soften its effect. Thus, the battle lines were drawn.

On March 29, Bill Gorog, a member of Bill Seidman's staff at the White House, came to see me. EPA's support of the Public Works Committee's amendment was undercutting the president on the Clean Air Act, he claimed. "That's a lot of bullshit," I told him, according to my diary. The White House was taking a completely negative view toward the significant deterioration amendment, I asserted. They would do much better by trying to get further modifications included than by trying to kill the provision. "The latter [approach] guarantees no credibility and no negotiating position."[2]

No one at the White House had ever discussed with me the significant deterioration issue before Gorog began to actively lobby members of the Senate to support the Moss amendment. I had repeatedly sent word to Jim Cannon, head of the Domestic Council staff, and to Dick Cheney, by then Ford's chief of staff, that I wanted an opportunity to meet with the president before he made any decisions on the Clean Air Act. Silence.

On May 3, Gorog called again, this time to report unhappiness on Capitol Hill over EPA's report to the Public Works Committee on the economic effects of the significant deterioration policy. The report was purely technical; the problem was that our analysis did not support the White House's negative position. I commented in my diary that evening, "I have a distinct feeling that there is a fair amount of effort to poison the atmosphere as to EPA (and probably me)."[3] The next day, after an Energy Resources Council meeting at the White House, I told Jim Cannon that I had been through one period of paranoia "in this house" and did not want to go through that again.

Cannon responded that President Ford had given lots of leeway to his agencies when he first came into office, but now there was considerable feeling that agencies (not necessarily EPA) had taken advantage of him, and it was time to correct the public perception that he was not really in charge. Since the president had gotten "whitewashed" by Ronald Reagan in the Texas primary three days earlier, I wondered what all this portended.[4]

Then, on June 1, a Tuesday, I received a copy of a letter the president had sent the previous Friday to Senator Jennings Randolph, chairman of the Senate Public Works Committee, opposing any legislative treatment of significant deterioration unless it legislated away the basis for our regulations. In other words, the president himself was thus, in effect, supporting the Moss amendment, although he did not expressly say so. His letter asserted that there was insufficient evidence on which to base action on the significant deterioration issue at that time and suggested that the EPA analysis was not persuasive. Gorog's accompanying note said he had tried to reach me the previous Saturday—the day after transmittal of the president's letter.

I was outraged by this whole matter—not so much because of the president's position on significant deterioration, which I considered wrong on the merits, unnecessary, and politically faulty, as because of the procedure followed.[5] It seemed likely that Dick Cheney was responsible for the way the White House dealt with the matter. However, I could not be sure of this because I so seldom had any direct contact with him.

Some of the tensions of the time come through in other events of the same day. At 11:00 A.M., I was informed of a 4:00 P.M. meeting with the president in the Cabinet Room on H.R. 9500, the House water pollution bill, and particularly on an amendment to section 404, a perennially controversial section covering the dredging and filling of wetlands. Jim Tozzi of the Office of Management and Budget (OMB) told me that OMB's director, Jim Lynn, had sent a memo to the president on the entire House bill, with various options on section 404. He could not send me a copy of the memo (which EPA had had no part in preparing or even knew of), he went on, but I could send someone to his office to read it! I decided not to go to the meeting with the president and asked John Quarles to go for me. (The meeting turned out all right: the president decided on an approach to section 404 that I had already endorsed in meetings with members of the House Public Works Committee.)

I called Dick Cheney and told him that I had been put into an impossible position and I had been trying to meet with the president since April. Cheney said he was unaware of the situation and asked for a memo setting out what I wanted to discuss with the president. I had the memo delivered to him the following morning.

It was a troublesome situation, to say the least, but the press of day-to-day business at EPA left little time for worry. The day after my talk with Cheney, for example, I flew to Chicago to deliver a speech to the National Solid Wastes Management Association. On arrival in Chicago, I went to the new EPA regional headquarters building, where I met with about fifty senior staff members, briefed them on recent developments at EPA headquarters, and answered questions. Then I did a walk-through of two floors of the building, stopping to shake hands and chat as I went, and did a CBS radio interview and a telephone interview with Casey Bukro, environmental reporter for the *Chicago Tribune*. Then it was off to the McCormick Place Convention Center for lunch and my speech, and afterward a television interview. I even made it back to Washington, D.C., by 6:30 P.M., in time to join Aileen for a party given by Nat Reed, assistant secretary of Interior for fish and wildlife and parks, and his wife, Alita.

Sometime during that day, I also managed to talk to Howard Baker, who expressed astonishment at the president's letter on significant deterioration. He had met with Ford the day before the letter was sent to the committee and had been given no inkling that it was in the works. "I certainly bombed out!" said Baker. He advised me not to get further embroiled in the issue and suggested that I leave matters to him and his Republican colleagues on the Public Works Committee. Senator Jim Buckley, I also learned that day, would issue a statement the next day on behalf of the committee Republicans rejecting the president's letter as having been based on a misunderstanding of the facts.

The following Monday, while at a board of trustees' meeting at Princeton University,* I was called to the phone and learned that there would be a meeting at the White House the following afternoon with the president and the Republicans on the Senate Public Works Committee. "About time!" I later commented in my diary, having pushed for such a meeting several months earlier.[6]

It was a fair-sized group that convened in the Cabinet Room the next afternoon.[7] I thought that the president was noticeably cool when he greeted me, but that could well have been my imagination. All five Republican members of the Public Works Committee were present and sitting on either side of the president: Senators Howard Baker (Tennessee), Jim Buckley (New York), Pete Domenici (New Mexico), Jim McClure (Idaho), and Bob Stafford (Vermont). Secretary of Commerce Elliot

*When I reentered government service as under secretary of Interior in 1969, I resigned from all my various board involvements. These organizations had included the World Wildlife Fund, the African Wildlife Leadership Foundation, The Conservation Foundation, the American Conservation Association, the Metropolitan Club, and the vestry of St. John's Church on Lafayette Square in Washington, where I was senior warden. However, in 1975 I accepted election as an alumni trustee of Princeton University and I served in that capacity until 1979.

Richardson, Frank Zarb, Jim Lynn, and Jim Cannon sat at the table with me, facing the president. Most of the White House brass were also there: Bill Seidman, Phil Buchen (the president's legal counsel), Max Friedersdorf (director of the Office of Legislative Affairs), and Jack Marsh among them.

The president opened the meeting by mentioning the Teton Dam disaster to McClure—the dam had given way, causing disastrous damage downstream—and promising all possible federal aid. (I couldn't help but recall that CEQ, when I was chairman, had opposed constructing the Teton Dam on environmental grounds in the first place. However, uncharacteristically, I managed to keep my mouth shut.)

Each of the senators spoke in turn on the significant deterioration issue. They all opposed the Moss amendment. The Public Works Committee amendment, however, was endorsed by all of them; it had been carefully developed and would not interfere unduly with economic development. That this position was supported by such western senators as Domenici and McClure was a telling one.

Frank Zarb argued that the committee's significant deterioration amendment would lead to unacceptable use of oil, given that oil produced lower sulfur oxide emissions than coal. EPA disagreed with this analysis. Referring to attacks by the U.S. Chamber of Commerce on the policy for prevention of significant deterioration, Domenici interjected, "The Chamber is flat-assed wrong!" Buckley emphasized that the committee amendment provided more certain criteria for assessing economic effects, flexibility, and a strong state role: "On its inherent merits, we believe our amendment should be supported."

When the president finally called on me, I spoke at some length. I supported the high quality of EPA's economic analysis (to which Domenici expressed his agreement). I gave a strong pitch for protecting air quality in relatively clean areas and said that the prevention of significant deterioration would help provide growth options for the future.

However, when all was said and done, the president said he was sticking with the position he had taken in his letter, that the best way to achieve improvements was to stand firm. "Where does this leave us?" asked Baker as we left the room. The other senators reflected the same thought.

I found it difficult at first to understand the rationale or the motivation for the president's position. It made little sense to me from the standpoint of policy and even less sense as a matter of legislative process. In the latter connection, the White House staff had clearly been going around the Republicans on the Public Works Committee to try to build support for the Moss amendment. In so doing, they had failed to consult with the very senators whose committee had jurisdiction over the issue — an inexcusable breach of accepted process — and, of course, they had never consulted with EPA. Later, I came to understand better the pressure on the president to appeal to the conservative wing of the GOP — the Republican National Convention was only two months away and Ronald Reagan was a strong contestant for the nomination.

As I was about to leave the White House after the meeting, I was told that the president wanted to see me. I went into the Oval Office along with Lynn, Cannon, and Mike Duval. The president was behind his desk, and I took the armchair at its right-hand corner, facing him. "Russ, I understand you have a problem!" he said. I replied that I had not thought of it exactly that way, but I guessed that when he took a position on an issue on which I was committed to the contrary, it was a problem — especially, as I had indicated, when I had not had a chance to discuss the matter with him.

After some discussion, I suggested that, rather than my simply appearing to be in opposition to the president, I could oppose the Moss amendment but at the same time push for amendments to improve the committee bill. This approach would have the advantage of pushing Congress in the direction the president wanted it to go. Ford said that seemed all right to him and asked me simply to let Cannon know what amendments I was pushing. Duval then interrupted and referred to a recent "Dear Colleague" letter supporting the Moss amendment sent out by a group of conservative Republican senators, including John Tower, Dewey Bartlett, Jesse Helms, and Roman Hruska. Duval said he thought a check should be made with Max Friedersdorf to see "whether any commitments had been made." The comment made it pretty clear that the White House had been deeply involved in promoting the writing of the letter.

In any event, I came out of the meeting with a reasonably free hand insofar as the significant deterioration issue was concerned. On August 3, the Moss amendment to defer action pending further study was defeated in the Senate by a vote of 63–31. Jim Buckley was of great help. However, in the final analysis, the Clean Air Act amendments never became law. When the conference committee report reconciling House and Senate differences reached the Senate floor, Senator Jake Garn of Utah filibustered the bill, and the public utility and automobile industry lobbies succeeded in killing it. Water pollution legislation dealing with the section 404 wetland issue, as well as EPA's construction grant funding for sewage treatment plants, also died in the closing days of Congress.

The whole significant deterioration flap highlighted the energy-environment trade-off issue, which colored so much of EPA's (and my) relations with the White House during the latter months of the Ford administration. And, of course, the Court ruling on significant deterioration and EPA's regulations on the issue remained in effect.

Strains over Emission Testing

When I finally met with President Ford on the significant deterioration matter, I also raised with him the issue of the so-called selective enforcement audit (SEA), which would allow EPA to test emission controls on the automobile assembly line. Without such testing, EPA was limited to accepting the test results of only the design prototypes for various automotive models. We needed, in addition, real-world testing of the actual production vehicles on the assembly line. Without the latter, we could have no assurance that a particular fleet of automobiles was actually meeting emission standards.

EPA had developed and then officially proposed SEA regulations in December 1974. Following comments from the public, including the automakers, and from other government agencies, the regulations were submitted to OMB for interagency review in January 1976, almost six months before my meeting with the president. The Senate Public Works Committee had written an amendment to the Clean Air Act actually mandating EPA assembly line testing (rather than leaving such regulations and their scope to the discretion of EPA). The amendment, which appeared to have the support of the entire committee irrespective of party, had been developed purely because of the failure of EPA to issue final SEA regulations. If it became law, the amendment would require EPA to develop a far more stringent assembly line testing procedure than that provided in EPA's proposed regulations. It was presumably for this reason that at least one automaker (the Ford Motor Company) had urged promulgation of the original regulation as soon as possible.

I laid out this history to the president and then told him I had been informed by OMB that he had directed (1) that I was not to issue the EPA regulations and (2) that I was to oppose the Senate amendment. The president looked surprised and said he did not recall any such decision. Jim Cannon reminded him that he had checked an option paper indicating his choice on various issues, including SEA. (EPA had never seen the final option paper, but my understanding was that it contained nothing with regard to our regulations.)

I had caught them out, I thought. The upshot was that the president told Jim Lynn to take a another look at the matter. I said to the president that this was the first time, so far as I was aware, in the six-year history of EPA that the president or the White House had purported to tell EPA how to make a regulatory decision. He seemed quite taken aback. The meeting lasted for a little more than half an hour. All in all, I thought it had been a good afternoon!

However, six weeks later, EPA still had not received a go-ahead from OMB. The whole episode represented one of the most egregious examples of bureaucratic foot-dragging I can recall. There is clearly a place for interagency review of proposed regulations and for the White House to be kept aware of what is transpiring at the regulatory level. However, if such objectives are not accomplished quickly, representatives of special interest groups, who presumably have already had a full opportunity to present their views in public to the regulatory agency, have a golden opportunity for another crack at the regulations behind closed doors.

On July 19, I sent a letter to the president reviewing the history of the SEA regulations and pointing out that the Senate would be acting on the Clean Air Act amendments the following Monday. If I were to have any credibility in opposing the assembly line testing requirement then in the bill, it was imperative that EPA issue its regulations immediately. Accordingly, I informed the president that I would promulgate the regulations by noon the following day (July 20) "unless I have direct instructions from you not to do so."[8]

I never heard a word from the White House and the regulations were issued in final form the next day. The Senate amendment was dropped as a consequence and SEA as developed by EPA went into effect. Jim Lynn said I had held a pistol to the president's head. I replied that, rather, it had been Lynn who was holding the pistol! At a Cabinet meeting the next day, I felt some trepidation at first. But Bill Seidman, who was sitting next to me, said I had done exactly the right thing. Even Jim Lynn seemed perfectly good-humored about the matter. So it was over.

Run-in with John Tower

Sometime in the spring of 1976, as the next presidential election approached and the political climate grew more heated, the deputy regional administrator in EPA's Region 6 (Dallas) headquarters resigned, and I chose a highly qualified professional to succeed him. I then received a call from President Ford's chief of staff, Don Rumsfeld, who said that Senator John Tower of Texas had notified the White House that he wanted me to appoint someone else, namely, Paul Commola, a junior member of the Dallas regional office. Commola was a very congenial person who had acted as a kind of informal liaison for the regional headquarters to Tower and other political figures and who had done them a lot of favors. In my opinion, he did not have the professional qualifications for the number two position.

Tower was very important to the president and was to be his floor manager at the Republican National Convention that August, Rumsfeld told me. I certainly did not want to hurt the president in any way, I said, but supporting Tower's choice would be an embarrassment to me, to EPA, and to the president. When Rumsfeld pushed a bit more, I said that if the president really wanted Tower's guy appointed, I would do so, but then I would resign. The president could not have both of us. Rummy quickly replied, "Russ, forget it, but make your peace with Tower."

I duly went to see Tower in his Senate "hideaway" office in the Capitol. A member of his staff sat in the background, taking notes. Tower came straight to the point. He wanted me to appoint Commola and he made it clear that he (Tower) was in a position to make life difficult for the president at the convention. In return, I made it clear that I was not going to appoint his man because he was unqualified. The meeting ended in a standoff, with Tower angry and unpleasant. A few days later, I called and said I was ready to appoint a third individual—neither his choice nor mine—and Tower accepted that. Thus, we both saved face. My fallback was eminently qualified, so I was quite happy with the result. The blatant political pressure applied by Tower was one of the few incidents of that kind—perhaps the only one—that I had in all my years in government.

Commola later came to see me and said he thought I had been unfair to him. I told him that I believed he was so "wired in" to the power structure of the Dallas region that I simply did not want him in a top position in a regulatory agency.[9]

Presidential Politics and the Environment

President Ford had his sights set on the Republican National Convention, which was scheduled for mid-August and clearly hoped to be the party's nominee for a full term in office. Ronald Reagan was opposing him for the nomination. Ford brought up the subject of the convention at several Cabinet meetings at which I was present. Nothing was said about any participation on my part. On August 11, however, I received a "Dear Russell" letter from Dick Cheney asking me to make myself available to the press the following week at the convention for two hours a day. I called Frank Zarb, told him of the letter, and said it was the first word I had received about the convention. He replied: "That's hard to believe. There must be a mistake. You could be very positive there." Frank was planning to be at the convention the entire time and was scheduled to talk to several state caucuses. He suggested I call Stan Anderson of the White House staff, who was in charge of convention arrangements.

I reached Anderson in Kansas City, Missouri, and told him I would be delighted to come out if I could help the president. Anderson came right to the point: Cheney's letter to me was a mistake, he replied, and he went on to say, "You are not expected," adding that Cheney himself did not expect me to go. So that was the end of the matter. The way my non-invitation was handled hardly added to my enthusiasm for my party. In 1972, I had taken full part in the GOP convention that nominated Richard Nixon for his second term as president. Now my comment to myself was, "It is quite apparent that the 'environment' is an issue the GOP wishes was not around and that my identification with the administration is not particularly considered an asset." [10] Perhaps the hard-liners in the White House planned to get rid of me in the event Ford won reelection. As I watched the convention proceedings on television with Aileen and saw so many familiar faces—Simon, Rumsfeld, Lynn, and so on—I felt oddly out of it all, and saddened.

Not long afterward, I talked to Bill Ruckelshaus about his part in the convention. He had been a principal candidate for the vice presidential nomination and, I believe, Ford's first choice. Indeed, Bill told me that at one point he understood that he had gotten the nod. His friend Bob Teeter, the GOP pollster, had been one of a small group, including John Tower and Bryce Harlow, giving counsel to Ford on the matter. When the group broke up late on the afternoon of August 19, the choice was definitely Ruckelshaus, and Teeter had so informed him. Several hours later, the choice shifted to Robert Dole. Evidently, during the interim the chairmen from the southern and western states had gotten in their "licks" and insisted on a conservative candidate for the vice presidency. Bill did not believe that they were opposed to him personally; they just wanted their own man. Ford had simply not been in a position to risk a possible floor fight on the vice presidential nomination. In other words, Bill did not get the nomination because Ford did not really control the convention. I wrote in my diary, "However the election turns out, this is a decision that will have a long-term impact on the future of the Republican Party."[11]

More than twenty years later, in January 1998, I called on former president Ford at his home in Rancho Mirage, a community next to Palm Springs, where I was attending a meeting. Ford and his wife, Betty, had lived there since leaving government in 1977, spending five months each year at a home in Vail. He was approaching eighty-five at the time of my visit, but he looked little changed from when he left Washington.[12]

Ford asked what I had been doing since I left government, and I responded that I had worked with the World Wildlife Fund for substantially the whole time. He did not respond and simply went on to other subjects. I took the occasion to raise the matter of the vice presidential nomination at the 1976 convention. It had been my understanding, I said, that Ruckelshaus had been his choice but that Bryce Harlow, representing the conservative forces, had told Ford the night before the vote that the nomination of Ruckelshaus would precipitate a floor fight and that, as a result, Ford had accepted Dole. That was not entirely right, Ford replied. The Democrats were expected to carry the South, so it was essential that he carry the farm states between the Mississippi River and the Rocky Mountains. The choice fell to Dole because he was believed to provide the best chance of carrying those states.

"And we did," he said, "with the exception of Minnesota, which went with Mondale [Jimmy Carter's running mate], and Texas, which we lost by just a few votes." The election had been extremely close, I replied, but I had always thought that Ford would have won with Ruckelshaus, who would have been an extremely attractive candidate across the country. "Perhaps," said Ford. He went on to say that he had no criticism of Dole's performance, that he had done a fine job. Later, when I recounted this discussion to Ruckelshaus, he confirmed my original understanding and pointed out that Bob Teeter had been present at all the discussions of the vice presidential nomination.

The environment played only a small part in the 1976 presidential campaign. On one occasion, at a Miami meeting of the American Public Health Association that I attended, Jimmy Carter attacked the administration's environmental record, specifically its record in enforcing anti-pollution laws. The specific charge got my ire up and I rebutted it the next day at a press conference. It would be one thing to attack the Ford administration on environmental policy matters — although, of course, I did not say so — but on enforcement, I asserted, I believed we had an outstanding record, such as our recent $13.2 million fine against Allied Chemical. I also volunteered that I had never had the slightest interference from the White House in any enforcement matter during my entire time at EPA.[13]

As the Ford administration wound down, it was plain that the environment remained of little interest to the president and those around him. I continued to attend Cabinet meetings and at one of these Jack Marsh gave a rundown on the legislative agenda. The first three on the "don't want" list were the Clean Air Act amendments, the water pollution bill, and the toxic substances bill. When he listed the latter, the president looked around the table and said, "We don't want that, do we?" It was a purely rhetorical question. George H. W. Bush, then director of the Central Intelligence Agency, was sitting next to me along the wall. I leaned over and said, "Did you notice that the first three bills on the administration's 'don't want' list are all EPA's?" "Yes," said George, "You are about as popular as the CIA!" "How about merging?" I said. I invited him to fly to the Eastern Shore to join Aileen and me for the weekend, but he was heading for Kennebunkport and Barbara.[14]

The Debate over Nuclear Reprocessing

While environmental issues were not of much interest to Ford in these waning days of his administration, such issues continued to force themselves on his attention from time to time. Thus, in September 1976, following a regular Cabinet meeting, Ford convened a special meeting on nuclear reprocessing as part of his effort to move toward a general nuclear power policy. (The usual nuclear reactor in operation in the United States was the light water reactor, which operated on a once-through fuel cycle.

The enriched uranium fuel could not be used to make nuclear weapons, and the spent fuel was then disposed of. The "breeder" reactor, on the other hand, would rely in its final cycle on the recycling, or reprocessing, of plutonium, which could be used in weapons.) Bob Fri, formerly EPA deputy administrator and at that time with the Energy Research and Development Administration (ERDA), had prepared a report on the issues, which had been distributed to agency heads. The options presented were (1) to go ahead with reprocessing, (2) to move forward with reprocessing if it was environmentally safe and economically cost-effective, or (3) not to go ahead. Almost all present spoke strongly in favor of the second option. The president turned to me and asked, "What does the Environmental Protection Agency think?"

I said that I found myself, as occasionally happened, in disagreement with almost everyone who had spoken. To maximize my credibility, I prefaced my remarks by saying I was not an opponent of nuclear power as such, and I pointed out that I had publicly opposed the nuclear moratorium in California and, more recently, a moratorium in Oregon. There was no way to resolve the environmental and economic questions concerning reprocessing, I believed, except by going ahead with a plan (which Bob Seamans, head of ERDA, made clear was the administration's intention). But once we embarked on a commercial reprocessing program, we would lose our credibility in the international arena to deter reprocessing by others and, thus, nuclear proliferation, since reprocessing of nuclear power wastes produces reactor grade plutonium, which can be used in the production of nuclear weapons. I suggested that the president need not make a permanent decision at the time but could say that the United States would not go ahead with reprocessing plans until after a summit meeting of nuclear powers convened by him early the next year to consider the entire issue.

John Busterud (CEQ) and Fred Ikle (head of the disarmament agency) both spoke on my side, but no one else did. I left the meeting profoundly depressed. I told Bob Seamans that I thought a fundamental mistake was being made.[15]

My divergent views on the breeder reactor should have come as no surprise. The previous year, in May 1975, I had been called before the Joint Committee on Atomic Energy to explain why EPA differed from ERDA on the timing for commercializing fast breeder reactors. I was reported to have left the meeting after a ninety-minute grilling, apparently remarking as I left that I was thankful I had "the toughest hide in Washington." The same source reported, "The debate was as entertaining, the pace as lively and the witnesses as uncomfortable as they ever were before the JCAE. . . . How effective the lashing will prove is another question. To [Congressman Mike] McCormick's accusation that EPA was making things difficult, Train replied, in effect, that's tough. More precisely, 'that's hard for me to avoid,' he said." [16]

Daily Life at EPA

Aside from the specific incidents and issues I've chosen to highlight, the grist for EPA administration was extensive. The daily pace was usually frenetic in the Ford years, just as it had been under Nixon. EPA had ten regional headquarters plus a half dozen or so research laboratories, such as those at Cincinnati, Ohio; Corvallis, Oregon; and Research Triangle Park, North Carolina. All of these had to be visited. I also tried to make and maintain contacts with members of the agricultural community around the country, as in a July 1975 tour I made of hog-feeding facilities and livestock lots in Iowa. [17] I had appointed an agricultural advisor in my office, Nat Chandler, who did a superb job of developing such contacts. [18] There were constant press interviews, including radio talks and television appearances. There were contacts with members of Congress that had to be maintained. In one year alone, I counted fifty-four appearances on the part of EPA representatives before committees and subcommittees of the Senate and House. I personally did a substantial number of these. In addition, there were all the internal staff meetings, meetings of our Science Advisory Board, meetings on cancer policy and numerous others.

The regulatory treatment of carcinogens was a continuing issue throughout these years. I appointed a Carcinogen Assessment Group, under the chairmanship of Roy Albert of the Nelson Institute of Environmental Medicine at New York University, to examine methods for assessing cancer risk. The most difficult problem EPA had in this regard was not in determining whether or not a substance was a carcinogen but, if it was, in determining what to do about it. It seemed plain that the mere fact that a chemical posed a cancer risk should not automatically require it to be banned, given that some risks were quite small. After all, we do not ban automobiles just because they may pose certain health risks. However, the issue was highly controversial. In the regulation of pesticides, we moved in the direction of risk assessments the results of which could be weighed against a chemical's benefits, and this was the approach that Congress would embody in the 1976 toxic substances control legislation.

There were meetings with various interest groups—industrial, labor, agricultural, environmental, and others. There were constant calls to and meetings with my energy counterparts. There were speeches to be given all over the country—literally hundreds during my time at EPA—made possible by the outstanding work John A. Burns Jr. did as my special assistant with responsibility for drafting speeches and other public statements. There were calls to be made on governors and mayors. And, of course, there was a fair amount of foreign travel to sandwich in to all these engagements.

Typically, any issue that came to me for a decision tended to be a political hot potato. One such issue, in 1976, was whether to deny a permit for the construction of a sewage treatment plant—known as the Dickerson plant—in Montgomery County, Maryland, bordering on the District of Columbia. Lack of sewage capacity had resulted in a building moratorium in the area, furiously fought by the developers. There were tough issues involved—a cost for the proposed plant of $200 million more than needed, according to EPA estimates; excessive use of energy; and a risk to the area's water supply.

I met with Governor Marvin Mandell on the issue in Annapolis, Maryland, as well as with officials of Montgomery and Prince Georges Counties in my office. The chairman of the EPA appropriations subcommittee, Congressman Ed Boland of Massachusetts, commented that I was "getting more publicity than Kissinger." On August 20, after first calling Mandell, I held a press conference announcing my decision not to grant the Dickerson permit. Mandell said of my decision, "Mr. Train's latest demonstration of indecision is nothing short of capriciousness, arbitrary, and politically motivated."[19]

There were enforcement actions against U.S. Steel and EPA finally closed down an old open hearth furnace at the company's Ensley Works in Birmingham, Alabama. Steel's chairman, Ed Speer, came to see me about the issue. He talked about the job implications for Birmingham, which were significant, but the company had been dragging its feet on modernizing the plant for years. The open hearth furnace was shut down on June 30, when we refused any further extensions. By the end of 1976, we had reached a major settlement with regard to U.S. Steel's coke works at Clairton, near Pittsburgh, Pennsylvania. The company committed to spending some $600 million at Clairton to build three new coke batteries and replace all the old, dirty ones.[20] It was a reasonable settlement, and it put an end to legal proceedings that could have dragged on for years.

Wool growers and other interests in the West pressured the White House to revoke the executive order prohibiting the use of chemical toxicants on public lands to control predators (principally coyotes). The prohibition had been put into effect by President Nixon on our recommendation when I was at CEQ. I kept in touch with Nat Reed at Interior on the issue, as well as with Lee Talbot at CEQ, and finally wrote a memorandum to the White House urging that the executive order be left intact.[21] I told our press office to release copies of the memo to the press if there was interest. In fact, the story was widely covered, and on Christmas Eve the president announced from Vail, Colorado, that he had decided not to revoke the executive order.[22]

And then there were the major oil spills. In mid-December 1976, for example, a Liberian-flag vessel, the 30,000-ton oil tanker *Argo Merchant*, went aground on the shoals southeast of Nantucket. The ship had been ten miles off course en route from Venezuela to Salem, Massachusetts. There was a hole in her bow, and she was leaking oil badly. Along with Admiral Owen Siler of the U.S. Coast Guard, EPA's Ken Biglane and I flew to Otis Air Force Base on Cape Cod and thence by helicopter to the site of the wreck, about an hour's flight. My diary describes the scene: "The tanker lay deep on the shoal, her stern down, bow up, about a 30-degree list to starboard so that waves washed up the deck, carrying oil to sea as they receded. . . . The tanker was a pretty sickening sight, a heavy pool of black oil along her side (#6 fuel oil), patches of oil tailing away from her. You could see the great sand ridges beneath the surface."[23]

We helicoptered back to Boston, where Governor Mike Dukakis joined Admiral Siler and me in a crowded press conference. I suggested that, with the sophisticated satellite technology then available, we should set up a system for surveillance of offshore traffic — even in international waters — so that we could warn ships that were off course. The Coast Guard was pretty negative about the suggestion.

We returned to Washington that night, and the next morning the *Argo Merchant* broke in half. I held a press conference on the problem, mainly to give journalists a chance to ask questions.[24]

The next morning, I appeared on the *Today Show* and then flew back to Boston on short notice to testify at a public hearing called by Senator Ted

Kennedy. The hearing was jammed, with Kennedy presiding, and he was joined by Senators Ed Brooke and Claiborne Pell, senator-elect John Chafee, Congressman Gerry Studds from Cape Cod, and Congresswoman Margaret Heckler. The governor, the lieutenant governor, and representatives of the Coast Guard all testified. I confined my testimony to what could be done in the future to reduce the risk of tanker spills. I called for much more stringent controls on ships coming to U.S. ports and increased surveillance of their courses such as I had already recommended. It was also time, I said, to take unilateral action to improve safety standards on foreign ships.

My statement [25] seemed to be well received. Kennedy was particularly complimentary about my having made two trips to the area and spoke well of EPA's role in the whole matter.

Hardly a week later, another Liberian-flag tanker, the 63,000-ton *Olympic Games*, lost power in the Delaware River and drifted into a rock, which tore a hole in her bottom. I chartered a single-engine plane to fly me up the Delaware to Philadelphia. Above the Camden bridge, the river was a mess. In Philadelphia, I was joined by the EPA regional administrator, Dan Snyder, and other officials for a helicopter tour down the river and bay. The oil stretched for about twenty-five miles, mostly along the Pennsylvania side. We saw some diving ducks in the mess.

Back in my office that afternoon, I sent a memo to the president on the oil spills and formally proposed a presidential task force to consider the problem and make recommendations. (Nothing came of the suggestion.) There was constant press attention on the issue, and I had become the principal government spokesman on the problem.

There may have been a bit of grandstanding on my part in all this. EPA had little direct responsibility for the spills or their cleanup. At the same time, these were events that tended to excite a high level of public interest and concern. In my mind, it was important for members of the public to know that their government *cared* about the problem and one way to demonstrate that was to take the trouble to visit the scene. A number of years later, when the *Exxon Valdez* hit a rock in Prince William Sound, Alaska, spilling tons of oil into those pristine waters, I called Marlin Fitzwater,* President George H. W. Bush's press secretary, to urge that Bush

---

*Fitzwater had joined EPA as a junior press officer in 1970; he became press director and then left EPA in 1980 to go to the Department of the Treasury. After two years at Treasury, Fitzwater went to the White House, where he remained for ten years with Presidents Ronald Reagan and George H. W. Bush.

fly to the scene immediately. Marlin said that he had already made that recommendation, but the president had decided not to go—a missed opportunity for Bush.

Last Days at EPA

I had a last budget appeal meeting with Ford in the Cabinet Room early in December. I sat facing the president, with OMB director Jim Lynn on my left and his deputy, Paul O'Neill, on my right. The president was cordial. I had worried a bit about how he would respond to environmental issues at that time, given that the environmental community had, almost in its entirety, been in the Jimmy Carter camp during the election. Both the *New York Times* and the *Washington Post* had run lead editorials comparing the environmental records of Ford and Carter, the comparison being highly unfavorable to Ford. I wrote in my diary after the meeting: "He seemed tired and depressed—'down' is the word. He was responsive, courteous, and paid attention to the issues but one sensed that his heart was not in it." [26]

I was the first agency head to be scheduled for a budget appeal, perhaps because EPA had submitted its written appeal before any others. In any event, Ford asked what I and other agency heads like me—as well as other presidential appointees—planned to do about resigning at the end of his term. As to my own resignation plans—and those of my associates at EPA—I responded with a laugh and said, "I was hoping we would get some guidance." It quickly became evident that Ford had not thought about the transition at all. I described the process of transition from the Lyndon Johnson administration to the Nixon administration. Of course, when Ford took office on Nixon's resignation, he had inherited a full administration and had filled vacancies only as they occurred.

My budget appeal was extensive, in terms of both money and positions. In the past, I had always tried to accommodate EPA's budget to the overall budget situation, which had always been tight. But now, I said, we had "reprogrammed and reprogrammed," and "we have finally reached the end of our rope." I pointed out that our municipal waste treatment construction grant program had grown very large, that we had reached or were approaching the statutory attainment dates under the air and water pollution programs, and that EPA had major new programs to support, such as those mandated by the toxic chemicals and solid waste legislations, both of which he had signed. The meeting, scheduled to last half an hour, finally broke up after an hour and a quarter. We agreed to have one more meeting before January 20.

The transition to the new administration occupied a good deal of our time at EPA in the last weeks of 1976 and early 1977. It went smoothly, and we carried out our responsibilities as if we were continuing in office. I had emphasized to the agency that there should be "no marking time" during the transition.[27] Barbara Blum, who in due course became the agency's new deputy administrator, later congratulated us on our transition efforts, saying we had left "no booby traps."

On December 13, I attended the annual EPA awards ceremony, scheduled roughly on the anniversary of the agency's creation. I saw it as an opportunity to suggest future priorities. I emphasized the importance of (1) involving the public in our decision making; (2) maintaining the decentralization of our functions; (3) conducting research to establish and maintain the scientific integrity of our programs; (4) using economic (market) approaches, such as effluent and emission charges, where feasible as a supplement to regulation; (5) establishing energy conservation programs; and (6) engaging in international cooperation and action. Looking back on those priorities, I do not see much that I would change. They were priorities that I had stressed throughout my time at EPA and they remain equally important today.

A few days later, I was interviewed by Gladwin Hill of the *New York Times* and had the opportunity to reemphasize some of these themes. In reviewing my three and one-half years at EPA, I said: "With the passage in this last session of Congress of toxic substances control and an expanded solid waste act, we have completed the statutory framework for pollution control. But there are still a lot of problems to be solved in implementing the laws. . . . The hardest job still lies ahead."[28]

There was a critical shortage of money and personnel for EPA to carry out its statutory functions. The agency then had 9,500 employees and needed 1,000 to 1,500 more. EPA needed about a 50 percent increase in its $773 million operating budget. We had used all the $18 billion in sewage treatment plant funds. We needed to address storm water runoff, agricultural runoff, urban runoff, and forest erosion.

Despite "wrenching" experiences, I said, EPA had demonstrated its effectiveness, and the basic strength of the laws remained unimpaired. Finally, I said to Hill that the failure to make energy conservation a prime aspect of energy policy had represented "a disastrous failure of the national will."[29] One could say the same today, more than a quarter century later. Frankly, I believe the American people have the good sense to attack the problem, given some real leadership at the top. It is the politicians who lack the will.

In another interview toward the close of 1976, I gave an upbeat assessment of what the nation had accomplished in its battle against pollution.[30] Of the approximately twenty thousand major point sources of pollution (such as at the end of a pipe), about 80 percent were either in full compliance or on schedule to be in compliance. Industry was substantially meeting the goal of "best practical treatment" by 1977. Sulfur oxide emissions were down by about 25 percent, and "Chicago [had] traced a significant drop in respiratory disease and deaths to reduction of sulfur oxide in the air." The 1975 auto models were achieving an 83 percent reduction in carbon monoxide emissions and a 60 percent reduction in nitrogen oxides compared with pre-1968 models. Construction was under way by the summer of 1975 on more than seven thousand municipal waste treatment facilities, and EPA was operating the nation's largest public works program. There was also marked improvement in water quality in the country's lakes, rivers, and shorelines.[31]

Gladwin Hill had again asked me what I would do in the event Carter asked me to stay on at EPA. I did not answer the question at the time because I really did not know the answer. Actually, I had no interest as such in serving in a Carter administration.[32] My problem was that I hated the thought of leaving EPA. Despite all the anxieties and frustrations — and there had been plenty — I had thoroughly enjoyed the job. It was an opportunity to work on the cutting edge of one of the great issues facing humanity. It was a job in which what one did clearly made a difference. Moreover, the work itself was never a matter of just doing the same old thing. Every day seemed to bring a new challenge. I also unquestionably enjoyed the prominence of the position and the constant attention of the media. I was generally blessed with positive press reviews and strong public support. And continuing pressure on the part of the environmental community was an important factor in building support on Capitol Hill. My own relations with key members of Congress on both sides of the aisle were generally excellent, and I worked hard at maintaining those relationships. Likewise, I tried to keep on good working terms with key people in the administration. The men and women I worked with at EPA, both at our Washington headquarters and in the field, were great — dedicated and highly competent. In the best sense of the word, the job had been fun.

I was proud of what the agency had become. EPA needed more resources in both money and people, but it was basically in fine shape, doing a tough job with competence and integrity. Moreover, morale was high despite the perceived lack of support from the White House. I believed I had made my own mark and I felt totally comfortable with my role in the agency. An unsolicited letter I received early in 1976 from an intern as he was leaving the agency, which I have kept all these years, said, in part: "Nearly everyone I met spoke highly of your dedication to the environment balanced by political savvy, and of your faith in the EPA employees in the freedom you give them on all levels. That this respect has lasted over two years in such difficult times, in such a large agency, is a great tribute."[33]

I have been asked from time to time what I consider to have been EPA's principal accomplishment while I was at the agency. The Toxic Substances Control Act (TOSCA), dealing with toxic chemicals, and the Resource Conservation and Recovery Act of 1976 (RCRA), dealing with hazardous and other solid wastes, were landmark achievements. I felt personally very much identified with the former, whereas the latter had been primarily a congressional initiative. Both were adopted by Congress despite a lack of interest on the part of the White House. However, in both cases, EPA kept very much involved in the legislative process.

Some of the unsung accomplishments were extremely important. EPA did a superb job in getting effluent discharge permits (commonly known as NPDES permits, for the National Pollutant Discharge Elimination System) issued under the Clean Water Act in a remarkably short period of time. The agency also carried out the $20 billion municipal sewage treatment facility construction grant program, a huge public works program, and did so without a breath of scandal. In a 1994 interview, Al Alm succinctly put this era in context: "Train had the good fortune of being at EPA during the years when most was accomplished. During the first three and a half years, EPA was mainly getting its act together and getting the programs started to implement the Clean Air Act and the Clean Water Act of 1972. During the '74 through '77 period, very measurable improvements in air and water pollution occurred from EPA implementation of this legislation."[34]

In retrospect, perhaps the greatest achievement over the three-plus years that I was administrator was simply that, despite the White House attitude toward the environment, ranging from seeming disinterest to outright opposition to specific environmental initiatives, EPA and its programs kept on track. Throughout that period, from the first day I went to EPA, the agency and its programs were under constant assault because of the nation's energy needs, real and perceived, during both the Nixon and Ford administrations. We fought every inch of the way, at every level. That is not to say that we refused to recognize that environmental requirements sometimes gave rise to or exacerbated real energy problems. On our own initiative, we approved temporary variances under the Clean Air Act to permit the burning of high-sulfur fuels. However, overall, the remarkable fact was that the basic standards and the basic structure of our environmental laws remained intact. In that sense, I really believe we won the war — or at least our phase of it.

I also was proud of my role in keeping environmental issues constantly before the public, not only through the national media but through trips around the country. Frequent give-and-take with local media, environmental and other groups, and individual citizens helped build public awareness and acceptance and prevent polarization of the issues. Just as important, we continued to exert U.S. leadership in international environmental matters and I remained actively engaged in the US-USSR environmental agreement and NATO's Committee on the Challenges of Modern Society during the Ford years.

Thanks to EPA's congressional, press, and public support, we established that we were a tough critter with which to tangle. Toward the end of the Nixon administration, as I have previously mentioned, it was also White House disarray over Watergate that allowed EPA to stake out and pursue a fairly independent line. Some might say I got away with murder! (On one occasion, at a White House bill-signing ceremony, Senator Jesse Helms introduced me to his wife as the "Grand High Lama.")[35]

During the Ford administration, it was the president himself who permitted and actually encouraged a fair amount of independence among the executive agencies. Some complained that the White House itself was not tightly enough organized, but I think that is the way Ford really wanted it. John Osborne, Washington editor of the *New Republic*, commented as follows in his book about the period and Gerald Ford:

But he was reflecting the true Gerald Ford when he said in answer to a question about balancing economic against environmental needs that the way to do it is to get FEA Administrator Frank Zarb and EPA Administrator Russell Train together and let them work it out.[36]

Ford was a thoroughly decent man. At the same time, he had little or no interest in the environment. In his autobiography, Ford makes no mention of environmental matters during his administration.[37]

Important elements in the Ford administration, however, did try to make end runs around EPA, such as on the tall stacks (intermittent controls) issue under the Clean Air Act, the significant deterioration issue under the same act, and the effort of OMB to kill EPA's regulations on assembly line testing of auto emissions. How to explain such tactics?

A good part—perhaps all—of the explanation lies in the fact that, as 1976 progressed, the Ford White House more and more had its eyes fixed on the upcoming primary election fight with Ronald Reagan. Environmental issues came to be seen as nothing but a political handicap. The fact that no part of me was wanted at the GOP convention was a case in point and once Ford had nailed down the Republican nomination and entered the campaign, I was never asked to participate in any way whatsoever. The political operators had taken over. Moreover, it was not just the contest with Reagan. When Dick Cheney took on the job of Ford's chief of staff, he brought a tougher, more authoritarian, hard-core conservatism to the White House.

I have to admit that, even though exclusion from campaign politics annoyed me, it suited me just fine. It always struck me as a tricky business for the head of a regulatory agency, such as EPA, to play a very active political role. However, it puzzled me then and puzzles me now that the GOP in a national campaign saw no centrist appeal in environmental programs.

Early in 1977, I had another meeting with Ford, my last before he left office. I talked a bit about the oil spill problem and once again made my pitch for a more active regulatory policy with respect to foreign ships off our shores. I had just finished reading an interesting book about supertankers and I gave him a copy.[38] I told the president how much I appreciated the honor of heading EPA and he replied that I had done "a really fine job." It was a rather sad time, this last meeting. The president did not volunteer his plans and I had no idea what I was going to do.[39]

The day following Carter's inauguration (and my departure from EPA), I was cheered up by an editorial in the *New York Times* titled "Mr. Train and Other Departures." The editorial said, in part:

> Among these departing officials, we should like to speak a special word for Russell Train, who led the Environmental Protection Agency with devotion and imagination. His was surely among the most sensitive and politically dangerous positions. Yet he demonstrated that fairness and the general welfare could both be served in actions that a decade ago would have been deemed unthinkable impositions on our private economy. He stood up to industrial giants and won a degree of compliance however modified by delaying tactics.[40]

There was no question but that this and other generous comments eased my regret at leaving EPA. At the same time, they gave me little help in deciding what I would do next.

It was not until January 27 that I learned who my successor would be at EPA. Douglas Costle called that day to say that he was getting the job. He was a fine choice, I told him, and I would be glad to say so publicly. We set a time to get together. I had had a fairly long association with Doug, starting when he was on the staff of the President's Advisory Council on Executive Organization (Ash Council) and worked on the reorganization act creating EPA. My diary says, "He is quiet, balanced, and has good judgement."[41] He would need it!

Chapter 12

World Wildlife Fund: Transition Years

A s MUCH AS I regretted leaving the Environmental Protection Agency, my departure at the beginning of 1977 was probably none too soon. I was pretty stressed out after eight years of intense engagement at the Department of the Interior, the Council on Environmental Quality, and EPA, and my lower back would go into painful spasms at the drop of a hat. I had no clear idea of what I was going to do, however, and it would take me more than a year to settle on an involvement that, as it turned out, would engage me to the present time and broaden the scope of my environmental activities.

I spent the year after my departure from EPA largely just catching my breath and exploring various possibilities for the future. In order to bring in a bit of income, I joined the lecture circuit and gave a number of unmemorable talks around the country for fees reaching $5,000 at the most. I joined the boards of the Natural Resources Defense Council (NRDC), one of the most prominent public interest law firms, and the Union Carbide Corporation, a major chemical manufacturer with a worldwide business.[1] My only other involvement that became business-related was membership on the advisory council of Roger Sant's Energy Productivity Center at Carnegie Mellon University. The center evolved into the AES Corporation, an environmentally sensitive global power company on whose board I served for a number of years.*

*Sant came to Washington at the beginning of the Ford administration and served as assistant administrator for energy conservation of the Federal Energy Administration (FEA), the principal focus of energy policy in the federal government until the creation of the Department of Energy. At the frequent interagency meetings on energy and environ-

I served for only one term on NRDC's board. I had (and continue to have) a high regard for the organization and for its longtime president, John Adams, as a highly effective proponent of environmental values, but on the board I tended to be "more of the same." On the Union Carbide board, on the other hand, I believed I could make a difference, and for a number of years following the tragic accident at the company's agricultural chemical plant at Bhopal, India, I served as chairman of its Health, Safety, and Environmental Affairs Committee. There I enjoyed my first exposure to the business world (other than as a regulator) and I respected and liked my fellow board members as well as Union Carbide's senior management. The fact that board membership carried with it a fee was doubtless not an inconsiderable factor, given my impecunious state.

At the invitation of Denis Hayes, who, together with Wisconsin senator Gaylord Nelson, was the initiator of Earth Day, I joined a small group traveling to Saudi Arabia to provide environmental advice to the government there, particularly with respect to some rapidly developing industrial areas. Aileen and I visited Riyadh, Jeddah, and the Asir region in the southwest and met with various ministers, themselves mostly princes of the realm. At the conclusion of the visit, our group submitted a detailed set of environmental recommendations to the Saudi government.[2]

The Conservation Foundation

Finally, Bill Reilly offered me a senior fellowship at my old stand, The Conservation Foundation (CF), which he then headed. I accepted quickly. CF gave me a place to hang my hat for the next year while I pursued a variety of activities, several of them centered on the nation's energy policy.

Among these was participation in early 1978 on a government task force called the Liquid Metal Fast Breeder Reactor (LMFBR) Review Steering Committee, charged by the White House (specifically by President Jimmy Carter's assistant for energy affairs, James Schlesinger) with a review of federal policy toward a fast breeder reactor program. With me as one of the few dissenters, as mentioned in the preceding chapter, the Ford administration had looked favorably upon such a program but had

---

mental issues, at which I usually felt beleaguered, Roger Sant was a friendly and sympathetic voice. He and his wife, Vicki, became close friends of Aileen and me. They are leading citizens of Washington, D.C., and active in a number of public-spirited endeavors. Roger succeeded me in 1994 as chairman of the World Wildlife Fund.

taken no steps in its development. When the Carter task force filed its majority report,[3] four of us filed a separate review strongly opposing the development of the fast breeder reactor, primarily because of the risks of nuclear proliferation. I also filed my own additional views in opposition.[4] The program never went forward.[5]

I also became a member of the World Commission on Coal Policy, sponsored by the National Academy of Sciences and chaired by Professor Carroll Wilson of the Massachusetts Institute of Technology. My role was to ensure that the commission paid appropriate attention to environmental factors. Coal was the world's cheapest and most abundant energy source and I became satisfied that the technology existed at the time to permit, in most cases, the use of coal in environmentally responsible ways. The relatively high levels of carbon dioxide emissions associated with the combustion of coal were not an important issue then, although Wilson expressed concern about their effect on global climate change and the need for the international community to address that issue. In a letter to me, he said, "It does seem to me that the overarching environmental issue in a large and continuing increase in fossil fuel combustion is the climate effect of CO_2."[6]

When Wilson was due to present the commission's report[7] to President Carter in the Oval Office, he asked me to accompany him. Wilson handed a copy of the report to the president and gave a brief summary of its findings. I was somewhat startled when Carter turned to me and said, more or less, "Russ, is this report all right?" I replied that it was, whereupon he said, "Then it's OK by me!"

In early 1982, I testified on the commission's findings before the Joint Committee on the Economic Report, chaired by Congressman Henry Reuss. In thinking about my testimony a few days in advance, I jotted down some thoughts, which I find of interest today: the validity of the premise of the World Coal Study (WOCOL) that the use of coal could be significantly increased while meeting environmental, health, and safety standards at acceptable cost depended on whether in practice we *maintained and enforced* high environmental standards. On the basis of what was happening at EPA during the early years of the Ronald Reagan administration and how little the United States was doing to control acid rain, I was pessimistic that we had the necessary will to do so. Also, in my mind, the validity of the premise depended on a continued research effort — and I saw no evidence of this, either.[8]

While still at CF, I also became chairman of RESOLVE, a newly formed nonprofit organization designed to promote mediation and other alternative mechanisms to settle disputes between environmentalists and other interests, usually business, over natural resource use. The RESOLVE involvement reflected my ongoing interest in trying to develop nonadversarial approaches to problem solving and in building bridges of communication between conflicting points of view. I suspect I came by this interest both by natural temperament and by my earlier judicial experience.[9]

Even after I became president of the World Wildlife Fund, I continued to undertake some tasks that were not strictly WWF-related. Some of this activity was probably inevitable, given my recent role at EPA. As it was, I succeeded in turning down a good many opportunities, such as a request that I chair a National Academy of Sciences panel to review federal regulation of the airline industry,[10] and a solicitation in 1982 from Murray Gell-Mann, on behalf of the John D. and Catherine T. MacArthur Foundation, to take on chairmanship of the board of the World Resources Institute (WRI).*

Return to the World Wildlife Fund

While all of my involvements in those months after leaving EPA engaged my attention, none of them pretended to hold out any vision of the future for me. Finally, early in 1978, I was approached by a good friend, S. Dillon Ripley, secretary of the Smithsonian Institution and chairman of the board of WWF-US, together with John Hanes and Joseph F. Cullman III, both members of WWF's board. They asked whether I would be interested in becoming president and chief executive of WWF-US. It was as if a curtain over the future had been lifted.

I had had little contact with the organization since I resigned from the board when I entered government as under secretary of Interior in 1969. During its seventeen years of existence, WWF had remained a relatively

---

*I had worked with James Gustave (Gus) Speth, CEQ chairman during the Carter administration, to develop the concept of the World Resources Institute as an organization designed to focus on global resource policy issues. I had written to the MacArthur Foundation to endorse the concept and the foundation was planning to provide substantial funding for three years.

minor player among U.S. environmental organizations, even though, aside from the African Wildlife Leadership Foundation and the New York Zoological Society, it was the principal U.S. organization involved in international conservation and the only one with a truly global outreach. The income of WWF-US as of 1977 was less than $2 million per year, its membership was about 30,000, and it had about twelve employees. WWF-International and other national WWF organizations were highly critical of this less than robust U.S. performance. To be fair to WWF-US, several of the other national WWF organizations were either the principal environmental organization in their countries, as was the case with WWF-Netherlands and WWF-Switzerland, or one of the principal such organizations, as in the case of WWF-UK, whereas in the United States, many major conservation groups predated WWF-US.

It did not take long for me to make up my mind. The year since I left government had convinced me that my life was too fragmented. Individual activities had been interesting and worthwhile, but they lacked focus. The WWF presidency promised to provide that focus. WWF was international in scope, which I liked, and was headquartered in Washington, D.C., my home. Moreover, I felt comfortable with its emphasis on wildlife and habitat. In some measure, it would be taking me back to my environmental roots. I accepted with enthusiasm.

Early in March 1978, the WWF board met in Washington, and, while Aileen and I waited together in an adjoining room, I was elected as their first paid president. I had insisted that they not push Aileen off the board, a position she had thoroughly enjoyed, but she decided to resign anyway. That evening at home, I wrote in my diary: "Aileen and I both feel we have passed a new milestone today. I hope we have fun together in WWF." [11] And we surely have. It was the beginning of an involvement that started with a period as president and chief executive officer and continued with service as board chairman and now, since 1994, chairman emeritus. Aileen has been involved every step of the way.

I had anticipated a fair amount of press interest in my new assignment and scheduled a press conference after the board meeting, replete with a buffet luncheon. Several inches of snow fell that morning, and the only member of the press to show up was John Fogarty, who had been my press assistant at EPA and was at that time Washington bureau chief for the *San Francisco Chronicle*. Snow or no snow, press interest in my new involvement and in the change at WWF was just about nil. It was a new experience for me and probably a useful one: it helped put both me and my new job in perspective. Anyway, Fogarty and I had a good lunch together.

Just after joining WWF, I had another piece of good fortune: I was honored to receive the Tyler Prize for Environmental Achievement. This international prize, established by John and Alice Tyler of Los Angeles and awarded by an independent panel, carried with it an enormously welcome check for $150,000. There were, no doubt, some who expected I would contribute all or part of the award to a suitable charity, but I decided that I was my own most important charitable cause at the time.[12]

The award ceremony was held in Beverly Hills, California, and I gave a talk at the Tyler Ecology Symposium in which I tried to indicate the continuity between EPA work and the work of WWF. I noted that some people had expressed surprise at my accepting the position as head of WWF after my time at EPA dealing with what they obviously considered more serious stuff, such as air pollution and toxic chemicals. In response, I said that, when you added up all the anti-pollution responsibilities of EPA, the bottom line was support for life — life in all its wonder, complexity, and diversity. *That*, I said, was what WWF was all about. Some of the activities were different, but the overall goal was the same.[13]

WWF Changes

Today, WWF-US is an organization with some 1.2 million members and an annual budget of more than $100 million. As part of the international WWF network of organizations, the largest private group working to save species and habitats worldwide, WWF-US has a global access and outreach that is unequaled. Worldwide, the WWF family of organizations now operates in about 100 countries and counts more than 5 million members.

In 1978, when I rejoined WWF-US, the institution was far different and far smaller. The organization was mainly a grant-making agency then, with few projects of its own and focused on species-by-species conservation. Today, while continuing its traditional concern for endangered species of both animals and plants, WWF-US has pioneered a strategic ecoregional approach to conservation, emphasizing community-based conservation with benefits accruing to local peoples. Moreover, the organization carries out a strongly proactive program.

WWF-US builds that program on a strong scientific base. It carries out by far the largest science-based marine conservation program of any organization today, working to protect coral reefs around the world and to promote sustainable international fisheries. It operates and funds the largest education program for training conservation professionals in the developing world, emphasizing the role of women in this regard. And, since 1978, WWF-US has assumed primary responsibility in the private sector, first through its TRAFFIC USA program and now through TRAFFIC North America, for monitoring the movement of wildlife and wildlife products through U.S. ports of entry.

WWF-US has been a leader in introducing new financing mechanisms for international conservation, such as debt-for-nature swaps, environmental trust funds, and environmental foundations, to help provide access to new sources of capital for conservation purposes. It promotes the use of market mechanisms to support conservation objectives, such as through the Forest Stewardship Council and the Marine Stewardship Council, and it has fostered working partnerships with international organizations such as the World Bank, governments of such countries as Brazil, and other conservation organizations.

In the mid-1980s, WWF developed along another dimension as well. This came about through a fateful discussion I had in early 1985 with Bill Reilly, then president of The Conservation Foundation (CF).* We were lunching together in Washington, as we did periodically. The National Audubon Society had approached Bill to become its new president, but, he had made clear, he did not want to move to New York and was troubled by the lack of a significant international dimension to the Audubon job. As he spoke, I had a flash of inspiration and suggested that CF be merged into WWF, with Reilly taking my job as president and chief executive of the combined organization. I could then become a full-time, active chairman of the board. And that is essentially what we did after we secured the full approval of our respective boards, the affiliation taking place in October 1985. The combination of the two organizations gave us

*William K. Reilly had been on the staff of the Council on Environmental Quality during my chairmanship and was the principal architect of the National Land Use Policy Act, which President Richard Nixon twice submitted to Congress but which was never enacted. Reilly left CEQ in July 1972 to head the Rockefeller Brothers Fund Task Force on Land Use and Urban Growth, chaired by Laurance S. Rockefeller. In 1975, he became president of CF, succeeding Sid Howe, who had in turn followed me.

the capability of joining biological and social science expertise in address-ing key conservation issues.

CF brought a new public policy capability to WWF, a strength that has stood the organization in good stead in the years that have followed. Issues such as the North American Free Trade Agreement (NAFTA), sus-tainable forest management, international fisheries, toxic contamination of air and water, and global climate change have increasingly engaged WWF and the expertise of CF in the policy arena has added significant credibility and scope to WWF's work on such matters.

My first year with WWF, 1978, proved to be a year of transition for the organization.[14] WWF evolved rapidly from its early emphasis on species conservation to the broader ecological approach that came to character-ize our conservation strategy. In our annual report for that year, after referring to WWF's traditional concern for species, I said:

> The programs of WWF today increasingly reflect the fact that long-range protection of plant and animal species can only be effective if developed in the context of other urgent human needs, such as agriculture, that conservation plans must often be developed on a regional basis, and that the thrust of our efforts must be toward the protection of whole ecosystems rather than their component parts.[15]

The staff was small but excellent. Tom Lovejoy was senior scientist and ran the conservation program. A strong personal interest of his was a multi-year project near Manaus, in Brazil, called the Minimum Critical Size of Ecosystems project, designed to demonstrate the relationship between the size of a protected area and the diversity of species it would support—a vital consideration in establishing parks and other conserva-tion areas. All too often, protected areas have been established at such a small size that they inevitably suffer a serious erosion of species, both plant and animal.* Tom has been an articulate and influential spokesman for the conservation of biological diversity and, in particular, of tropical forests. Among other senior staff members were E. U. Curtis "Buff" Boh-len, who came from Interior to be senior vice president, continuing, in addition, pursuit of his longtime interest in Alaskan conservation issues;

---

*Lovejoy left WWF some years later to be an assistant secretary for environmental and external affairs at the Smithsonian Institution. Subsequently, Lovejoy became science advisor to the executive director of the United Nations Environment Programme and biodiversity advisor for the World Bank. In 2002, he became president of the H. John Heinz III Center for Science, Economics and the Environment.

Kathryn Fuller, lawyer and marine biologist, who worked first with our wildlife trade monitoring program and then on our legal structure; and Michael Wright, who joined us from The Nature Conservancy to head our Central American program.[16]

The WWF-US board of directors met three times a year, usually in Washington but occasionally in different cities around the country. Not having state chapters or other affiliates within the country, it was important for us to reach out in this fashion as much as possible. Our board members' collective experience, wisdom, generosity, and enthusiasm for our program made them an invaluable asset and a joy to work with. After I assumed the WWF presidency in 1978, Aileen and I made a practice of having regular board dinners at our house whenever possible and spouses of the members frequently joined these occasions. About once a year, the board traveled together to visit project sites elsewhere in the United States, in the Caribbean region, or in Latin America. In 1981, we established the WWF National Council, an advisory group that met twice a year, normally in conjunction with a regular board meeting. All of us developed warm friendships within the extended group and an atmosphere of collegiality has been a consistent earmark of the relationships among WWF board, council, and management. Aileen, with her natural warmth and sociability, has made a major contribution in this regard. As others have moved in over time to fill our roles, this collegial aspect of WWF continues to be a major strength of the organization.

Closely related to my WWF-US responsibilities were my regular meetings in Switzerland with the bureau (executive committee) of the International Union for the Conservation of Nature and Natural Resources (IUCN, now known more simply as the World Conservation Union), of which I became vice president for North America and the Caribbean region in 1978, and with the board of WWF-International, which met twice a year. Initially I attended the latter in my role as WWF-US president, but later I attended as an elected member of the WWF-International board and of its executive committee (EXCO), on which I served as one of two vice presidents until my retirement in 1994. Since Prince Philip, the Duke of Edinburgh, was president (chairman in U.S. terms) of WWF-International's board, as well as of EXCO, at least one board meeting each year was apt to be at Buckingham Palace, and several of the semiannual EXCO meetings were held at Windsor Castle. Other WWF-International board meetings over the years were held in such far-flung places as Washington, Hong Kong, Vienna, Buenos Aires, and Assisi, Italy.

When the World Wildlife Fund was created in 1961, its primary purpose was perceived to be raising the funds needed to finance the growing needs of international conservation. The WWF-US corporate charter reflected this mission and referred specifically to funding IUCN and the International Committee for Bird Protection (ICBP). When I took over the presidency, much of the program budget represented grants to other organizations as well. Thus, in addition to the IUCN and ICBP support grants, there were annual $50,000 grants to The Nature Conservancy (to help it develop an international program), to the Environmental Defense Fund (to help support its wildlife legal work under Michael Bean), and to the New York Zoological Society (to fund the work of primatologist Russell Mittermeier). Likewise, we provided funds to NRDC to fight the establishment of a major oil port in the Palau Islands of the western Pacific region—home of magnificent coral reefs and associated marine life.

These were substantial grants, given the fact of WWF's modest income at the time and the relative value of the dollar then. As far as I could determine, WWF received little or no public credit for this support of other organizations. Had we been a fully capitalized foundation, lack of public credit would have made little difference. But we were not. We depended for our income on the same sources as did our grantees, and thus we were, in a very real sense, competing for the same dollars.

None of this meant that our grants were ill spent. On the contrary, we could point to concrete results, such as creation of the great Corcovado National Park in Costa Rica. Nevertheless, the route we were on, while laudable in many ways, held little or no promise for "growing" WWF for the future. From a personal standpoint, I had no interest in simply presiding over a small, static WWF, and I was determined to see our program grow in terms of money, geographic scope, and, above all, in conservation effectiveness.

WWF's predicament was brought home one day during lunch with a foundation executive whom I was trying to persuade to support WWF. After I had given what I hoped was a very positive report on our program, he replied, in effect: "But, Russ, your program largely consists of grants to other organizations. That's what we do at the foundation. Why should we give you money which you then simply pass on to other organizations?" That comment marked a turning point in my thinking about

WWF. From then on, I insisted that our emphasis be on staffing and running our own programs, first in the Western Hemisphere and then globally. We continued to make grants to organizations when those made sense in light of our own objectives, but such grants became progressively a smaller part of our program.

As a first step in refashioning our organization, we terminated the annual grant to The Nature Conservancy and persuaded Michael Wright to leave his job as head of its international program and join WWF. Subsequently, Russ Mittermeier moved from the New York Zoological Society to WWF, establishing a global primate program as well as undertaking major conservation initiatives in Madagascar and in the Atlantic coastal forests of Brazil.* The new focus on our own conservation programs was accompanied by a sharply increased fund-raising effort. That effort paid off in a dramatic improvement in WWF's finances. As I had hoped, our strengthened program and fund-raising became mutually reinforcing objectives.

Trade in Endangered Species

Early in 1979, in the city of San José in Costa Rica, the third meeting of the parties to the Convention on International Trade in Endangered Species of Wild Fauna and Flora (CITES) took place that came to have special significance for our new direction at WWF. I had headed the U.S. delegation at the 1973 Washington conference that adopted the convention. Both Aileen and I were accredited as official observers at the San José meeting, and I was the unofficial head of a large nongovernmental organization (NGO) delegation. The U.S. government had proposed weakening the criteria for delisting species as endangered, but effective lobbying on the part of our NGOs resulted in defeat of the U.S. proposal.

It was at that meeting that I succeeded in persuading the newly organized TRAFFIC program (then operating out of the New York Zoological Society) to become an integral part of WWF. This established WWF as the key U.S. organization monitoring and reporting (to government, the media, and environmental groups) on the international trade in wildlife through U.S. ports of entry, and the organization thereby became a prin-

*Mittermeier became program director of WWF when Lovejoy went to the Smithsonian Institution. Later, he left to become president of the newly formed Conservation International.

cipal link in the worldwide TRAFFIC network, headquartered in England. TRAFFIC USA, under the highly capable leadership of Ginette Hemley, became the main U.S. NGO link to the international secretariat responsible for the implementation of CITES.

WWF-US had provided funding to bring selected journalists, particularly from Latin America, to the CITES meeting. I saw this as an important opportunity to expose these influential writers to conservation issues and, through them, to help educate the general public. During the course of an all-day session with the journalists, I emphasized that I considered the single most critical issue facing wildlife and other natural resources worldwide to be the need to control human population growth. In my introduction to WWF's 1978 annual report, I picked up on this theme:

> Flying over Costa Rica, . . . I was dismayed to see the steady encroachment of 'slash and burn' cultivation on critical forest areas and the destruction of forest cover on steep slopes throughout the country, contributing to widespread erosion. Here and elsewhere around the globe, one cannot avoid the stark reality of the impact of the pressure of human numbers on critical habitats as farmers are forced onto marginal lands.[17]

As a side benefit, the CITES meeting gave Aileen and me our first of several visits to Costa Rica. I met privately with President Rodrigo Carazo and then Aileen and I visited Corcovado National Park on the Pacific coast (where my notes indicate I identified fifty-six species of birds). We went on to visit the cloud forest of Monteverde, an area WWF had been helping to protect, and there we had a glimpse of the spectacular quetzal. WWF has remained an active supporter of the CITES program, but, only a few years later, the Reagan administration would eliminate funding for CITES in its budget, an action symptomatic of the constant uphill struggle in recent decades to have the United States play a leadership role in international environmental affairs or even meet its existing commitments.

Travel was a frequent part of my life at WWF. Some of this was simply to attend meetings, such as those of WWF-International in Europe or of CITES in Costa Rica, as I have just described. Some of the travel was designed to explore opportunities for new WWF involvements, as in, for example, Nepal, Botswana, Namibia, Thailand, and the Philippines. Some travel was done to visit and inspect ongoing WWF projects in the field, as in Brazil or Bhutan. Many of the trips were basically personal excursions, undertaken during vacations at our own expense but often having important WWF implications, as in the Galápagos Islands.

Galápagos Interlude

In August 1978, Aileen and I made the first of three visits to the Galápagos Islands of Ecuador, surely among the most fascinating and moving wildlife experiences to be had on the earth and the site of numerous WWF conservation initiatives over the years. On this occasion, we were accompanied by two of our children, Bowdy and Errol, and we joined up with our old friends Elliot and Ann Richardson and their son, Henry. (These "children" were all roughly in the age range of eighteen to twenty-two.) We chartered a small motor vessel named the *Beagle IV* and spent nearly ten days cruising the archipelago, that astounding showplace of evolution. Elliot, taking a brief break from his work as chief U.S. negotiator of the 1982 United Nations Convention on the Law of the Sea (which sought to develop rules for use of the oceans), was an avid birder and full of enthusiasm for our activities.*

We saw essentially no other tourists on that trip, except on the main island of Santa Cruz, and those were few. We were told at the time that about 6,000 tourists per year visited the Galápagos, and the government was determined to hold tourism at that level. Today, annual visitation numbers 100,000 or more. With Ecuador in difficult economic straits, the current prognosis for preservation is not good. Tourism is one of the world's great growth industries, moving irresistibly toward greater mass markets. The nonresident tourist fee in the Galápagos, currently $100 per head, is the principal source of revenue for Ecuador's national park system, which includes magnificent but little-visited areas on the mainland. Add to these pressures another: the desire of many of those among a rapidly growing and increasingly impoverished population on the coast of Ecuador to migrate to the islands in search of a fishing livelihood.

*At a dinner at our home later that year, Roger Tory Peterson said that "Elliot Richardson was the best student he ever had — at the age of sixteen a fine artist, a top student, excellent naturalist, and fine athlete." Apparently, as a bit of a needle to Elliot, who was at the dinner, I rejoined, "It's a wonder he has turned out as well as he has!" RET, Diary, November 13, 1978. Elliot later served a term on WWF's board.

Other pressures continue to multiply as well. In 2000, an international tanker went aground and spilled thousands of gallons of oil into the fragile ecosystem. (WWF responded with an immediate $100,000 in emergency help.) Japanese boats fish illegally for sharks, taking only their fins for soup, and sea cucumbers are harvested illegally for Asian markets. In 2001, a number of sea lion carcasses were discovered with their teeth and genitals removed, presumably for the Asian "traditional medicine" trade. In 2002, fishing trawlers dragged their nets for tuna through the islands, with all the usual bycatch, such as sea turtles, killed in the process. The government did little to enforce its laws against these violators.

All in all, it is almost a miracle that Ecuador has done as good a job as it has. The presence of the Charles Darwin Foundation has been an important factor and both WWF and The Nature Conservancy have provided vital support. Roque Sevilla, a member of WWF's board, and the Ecuadorian conservation organization he founded, Fundación Natura, an important associate of WWF, have been critically important in helping to bolster protection of the area. WWF also has recently fostered a partnership with Ecuador's government and the Toyota Motor Corporation to promote the use of non–fossil fuel energy, such as solar power, in the islands.

The Galápagos Islands are a World Heritage site and no other natural area in the world has a better claim to that status. However, the economic and population pressures that Ecuador faces in protection of the islands contribute to political pressures that are difficult to deal with in a volatile society. These pressures will doubtless grow in intensity in the years ahead. Unfortunately, one can make the same generalizations about many — perhaps most — conservation areas around the globe.

Conervation in Ireland

In December 1978, I made a fruitful visit to Ireland on my way to a WWF-International meeting in Switzerland. The primary purpose of the visit, made at the invitation of William Finlay, governor of the Bank of Ireland and a keen wildlife enthusiast, was to meet with the new statutory Wildlife Advisory Council, which he chaired, and with an ad hoc group of environmental officials, industrialists, and environmentalists to discuss the interrelationship of industrial development and environmental protection in Ireland.

I spent half an hour with the minister for fisheries and forestry. His plans for acquiring private land and establishing wildlife preserves were ambitious, but it was plain that the government's limited resources would make their realization difficult. The minister was intrigued by my description of U.S. tax law and its provision of deductions for charitable contributions, including gifts of land, with which he apparently was unfamiliar. I emphasized the need to find ways to promote conservation through incentives and otherwise to enlist the private sector in the effort. He seemed quite enthusiastic about such approaches.

In meetings with the Wildlife Advisory Council, the potential consequences of a major wetland drainage scheme in the west of Ireland, funded by the European Economic Community, surfaced as a major concern. I described in some detail our environmental impact analysis process, including public hearings. The most interesting part of the discussion involved the question of dissent and how to deal with it. I said that effective advance disclosure of government and industry plans, combined with an open process of public discussion and comment, was the best way I knew to minimize confrontation and obstruction.

Numerous comments from the forty or so participants around the room followed. It soon became apparent that a policy of full and open advance disclosure of government plans was not customary. And Irish business itself apparently made a practice of not disclosing anything of its plans in advance. This tradition of secrecy had to change, it was agreed. Indeed, it was the sense of the group that there should be follow-up meetings to discuss how such changes could be brought about.[18]

The fact that such a diverse group was willing to meet with me to discuss such sensitive matters said a lot about the credibility of the United States and recognition of its leadership at that time in international environmental matters. It made little difference in that regard that I was no longer in government and was speaking in a private capacity.

As THE EXECUTIVE head of WWF, I found most of my time taken up by fund-raising, program management, board relations, personnel and other management issues, speeches, letter writing, meetings, and the like. However, as in the Galápagos, there were from time to time opportunities in the field for deeply moving personal experiences with wildlife. These gave both meaning and reality to what WWF was all about and allowed me to see some of our efforts worldwide.

Monarch Migrations

One of the most spectacular wildlife phenomena I have ever observed was the annual migration of the monarch butterfly *(Danaus plexippus)* from Canada and the United States east of the Rocky Mountains to a few small wintering sites in the pine-clad mountains of the Mexican state of Michoacán, southwest of Mexico City. I visited several of those sites on trips beginning in 1980. A young Mexican businessman, Rodolfo Ogarrio, had taken up the cause of the butterflies and formed a nonprofit environmental group called Monarca dedicated to their protection. Aileen and I became good friends of Rodolfo and his wife, Norma, and they introduced us to the monarchs and their wintering sites.

There is apparently a special combination of altitude, temperature, air currents, climate, and Lord knows what else that makes these mountain wintering sites essential to the monarchs. As many as 100 million of them arrive in late November to cluster on the pine boughs, and they have been doing so for thousands of years. There they remain, conserving their energy, until late February or early March, when they start their migration north. On each visit, we trekked into a site along a narrow footpath through the forest. At first, we would see a few monarchs fluttering by, but most striking as we neared the heart of the site was the increasing litter of dead or expiring butterflies on the ground. When we finally reached the center, we stood awed by the sight of millions of monarchs clustered on trees that bordered large, open glades. When the sun broke through, many of the monarchs would leave their quiescent positions on the branches and rise in great swirls to absorb the radiant energy, only to return to the tree branches as the clouds again covered the sun. "We lay on our backs in a grassy clearing and gazed at the countless butterflies silhouetted against the sky overhead," I wrote in a report to the WWF board. "The constant beating of their wings sounded like the movement of wind through tree branches or the fall of raindrops on leaves."[19]

Seeing the monarchs at their wintering sites is a breathtaking experience. But that is only a part of their extraordinary life cycle. When the monarchs leave the sites in late winter, they move north, following the blooming of the milkweed, with which they have evolved a symbiotic relationship. The butterflies feed on the blooms and act as essential fertilizing agents for the plants. The monarchs mate soon after leaving the wintering site. The male then dies, and the female lays her eggs on the underside of the milkweed leaves, after which she, too, dies. When the eggs hatch, they produce larvae (caterpillars), which feed on the milkweed until they pupate and eventually emerge as a new generation of monarchs. While feeding on the milkweed, the larvae absorb ill-tasting and poisonous toxins from their host, which persist in the body of the adult butterfly and protect it from most potential bird predators, in both its larval and adult stages. The familiar bright colors of the butterfly help predators identify and avoid it. The slow, strong flight of the monarch, which helps sustain its migration over thousands of miles, would not be possible if it were the constant aerial target of predatory birds.

Successive generations of monarchs continue the migration north until the fourth- or fifth-generation descendants of those that left the wintering site reach their summer range in the northern United States and Canada. Finally, in September the southern migration begins and the butterflies head south for their wintering sites in the mountains of Michoacán. Unlike the group that migrates north, the generation that goes south makes the entire journey.

The monarch is evidently a tropical butterfly that has developed the ability to exploit the northern milkweed but has not become able to tolerate cold weather. No other butterfly — indeed, no other insect of which I am aware — does anything like the migration of the monarch. In fact, no other living organism follows a migratory pattern with a gap between generations. Unlike the case with other migrants, none of the monarchs that make the trip to Mexico in a given winter have ever made the trip before, a trip evidently made possible by a genetically transmitted guidance system.

All of this runs through my mind one day much later while I watch a lone monarch fluttering south across a Canadian marsh beside Lake Erie, as the late September sunshine begins to turn the marsh grasses to gold. What vast distances and unknown landscapes lie before it! That tiny bit of life and the phenomena of which it is a part fill me with wonder. And our world is a single, interconnected, infinitely complex web of such phenomena.

Today, the monarchs' wintering sites in Mexico are gravely threatened as loggers move in to take down the forests. For some time, WWF has been trying to protect those areas, but it is a difficult problem involving not only money but also complex rules of land tenure (*ejido*) and the livelihood of local people. The latter's lives have long been intertwined with those of the monarchs, and the monarchs will be protected only within that context. Generous support from the David and Lucile Packard Foundation has recently enabled WWF to establish a trust fund in Mexico that will protect the wintering sites from timbering and, at the same time, provide economic opportunity for the local people. A severe freeze in January 2002 resulted in a massive die-off of the monarchs at the wintering sites, but the population is reported to be recovering.

The fate of the monarch is today in our hands. But given the interdependence of all nature, as I watch that little bit of life fluttering over the Canadian marsh, I wonder to what extent our own fate is clasped in those fragile monarch wings.

The Fate of Marine Turtles

In November 1979, WWF-US conceived and coordinated the first World Conference on Sea Turtle Conservation. Essentially every species or subspecies of sea turtle worldwide was—and is—endangered or threatened as the result of overexploitation. Convened at the State Department in Washington, the conference brought together more than three hundred scientists, conservationists, government officials, and representatives of turtle industries to discuss the issues. I headed the steering committee and gave the opening remarks.[20]

The conference adopted a strategy for sea turtle protection and management that identified 140 specific project needs for international action to protect habitats—beach nesting sites, migratory routes, and feeding and hibernation areas. The strategy also urged that enforcement of CITES, which bans all trade in sea turtles and their products, be strengthened. It has always rankled me that, in signing CITES, Japan took an exception regarding sea turtles. However, it would be only two years later, in 1981, that the Reagan administration knocked out of its budget all funds for the administration of CITES, which struck me as even more outrageous. Just six years before, I had headed the U.S. delegation to the CITES convention, which had been adopted in the same conference room at the State Department.

WWF-US had, on its own, undertaken a number of initiatives to help protect sea turtle populations. In late 1981, I visited the site of one of these projects on the Pacific coast of Michoacán—the same Mexican state that holds the wintering grounds of the monarch butterfly. Along a stretch of beach there, both green sea turtles and olive ridley turtles came ashore to lay their eggs. Both species were in danger of extinction. At this beach, for example, about 150,000 egg-laying turtles once came ashore annually, but only about 1 percent of that number were returning there at the time of my visit.

The turtles breed at sea, and then the females return to the beaches of their birth to lay their eggs at night. They deposit large clutches of eggs, which look a bit like ping-pong balls, in holes they have dug, which they then cover with sand before returning to the sea. The nests are often dis-covered by local dogs and pigs as well as a variety of wild animals, which dig up and devour the eggs. Worst of all are the human predators, who dig up the eggs and sell them to markets in Mexico City and other urban areas, where they are much prized for their supposed aphrodisiac proper-ties. Our WWF project team was harassed from time to time by these poachers.

Kim Cliffton, an American from the Arizona-Sonora Desert Museum in Tucson, ran the WWF project that tried to protect turtle nests from predation along one principal beach, Maruata, which had the highest concentration of turtle usage. Our project paid local children the going market price to dig up the eggs, which were then relocated to new nests, all carefully marked, within a fenced enclosure near the project head-quarters, a large thatched hut on the edge of the beach. It was a remote area close to a fishing village and I traveled there by small plane and pickup truck with Archie Carr, a scientist with the University of Florida and a renowned expert on marine turtles who had chaired the World Conference on Sea Turtle Conservation held in Washington, D.C., two years earlier.

The WWF headquarters hut had a cooking area at one end, a working area in the center, and a sleeping area at the other end, where hammocks were strung. It was all pretty crude and very congenial. To make certain of the latter, Archie and I had brought a bottle of rum. We napped a bit in our hammocks after dinner, until Kim roused us about midnight, when the moon was right.

Several of the relocated nests were expected to hatch out that night, so we went straight to the fenced enclosure. The baby turtles are genetically programmed to hatch at night, which enables them to avoid gulls and other aerial predators that are active during the day. I swung open the gate and put a lantern at the entrance. Almost immediately, the turtle hatchlings, whose shells were about an inch long, started crawling toward the light. Marine turtle hatchlings instinctively head toward the brightest light. Under natural conditions, without artificial light associated with human activity, this means they will head for the sea, which is lit by the moon and stars, as if drawn by a magnet. It was not long before the turtles were piled up several inches deep against the board blocking the entrance. I began picking them up—one by one, so that they could be counted and their species recorded—and placing them in a metal washtub. When a reasonable load had accumulated, I carried the tub down the darkened beach toward the edge of the sea. There, I knelt down and slowly tipped the turtles out onto the wet sand. After a moment or so of hesitation, they headed toward the sea. It was a windless night without surf, and the tiny creatures crawled out into the little waves running up the shore. There they quickly disappeared, heading for whatever fate was in store for them.[21]

Michoacán beaches and Mexico's Pacific coast remain major breeding and nesting grounds for olive ridley, leatherback, and green sea turtles. All marine turtles have been legally protected from harvest, use, and trade by the Mexican government since 1990. Nevertheless, stubborn problems remain with illegal harvest and trade, primarily domestic, for eggs, leather, and meat. In that regard, I have recently learned that sea turtle meat is consumed during Lent because it is considered the same as fish. Only about 500 sea turtles are reported to have nested on Michoacán beaches in 2001, compared with the 150,000 of a few years earlier. Such stark statistics may speak for themselves, but they should be crying out to us.

Connectedness on the Amazon

The old Brazilian city of Manaus stands on the bank of the Río Negro just before it joins the Amazon River. On a 1978 WWF trip, our party was joined there by Michael Goulding, an American scientist with the National Institute for Amazonian Research (INPA) of Brazil. Michael's work, funded by WWF, involved studying the feeding habits of fish species of the Amazon basin. He had discovered that more than sixty species of fish inhabiting the Amazon basin depend on the annual flooding of riverine forests for food because they feed on fruit, seeds, and insects falling from living, standing trees during times of high water.

Together with Goulding and Tom Lovejoy, WWF's senior scientist and program director, we took two small, open boats up the Río Negro for several hours. The river was a mile or more wide, clothed at its banks with dense forest. We eventually reached our camp—three one-story frame buildings built on huge floating logs secured together and lying in a strong current between a small island and the mainland. Several piraña had been caught for the pot. Their vicious teeth were obviously designed for tearing flesh, but when the fish were opened up, their stomachs were shown to be filled with fruit and other vegetable matter.

The river was in flood stage at the time and twenty or more feet above its normal level. The water reached up into the forest canopy and flowed miles inland from its normal banks. The next morning, Aileen and I took a small boat and paddled off into the forest. It was an eerie sensation to be up among the branches, within touching distance of an occasional orchid. Silvery freshwater dolphins cavorted close to our bow. From time to time, there was an audible plop nearby as a nut or other fruit dropped into the water. Almost instantaneously, a swirl would occur at the spot as some fish gulped down the morsel. Most of these fish, we were informed, not only feed almost exclusively on such products of the forest but also do not feed during the remainder of the year, when the river is at its normal level, between its banks. Moreover, in feeding on the fruits of the forest, these fish act as primary agents for the dispersal of seeds.

The fish of the Amazon and its tributaries are a major source of protein for the growing human population of the Amazon basin, and it was made plain to us that a large proportion of those fish depend for their existence on the continued health of the forests bordering the rivers of the region. Thus, we were privileged to observe, in this case at first hand, the direct and complex interrelationship of wild species, ecosystems, and humans.

EQUALLY EXTRAORDINARY experiences from around the world and over many years crowd my memory: humpback whales gathering off Maui in the Hawaiian Islands and singing their seasonal songs, tense meetings with elephants in the African bush, camping in the midst of the vast Serengeti migration, the incredible wildflower spectacle of South Africa, emperor penguins on their Antarctic breeding grounds, dawn in the Himalayas, black-necked cranes from the Tibetan plateau arriving through mist and falling snow at their wintering grounds in remote eastern Bhutan,[22] close encounters with chimpanzees in Tanzania, snorkeling over coral reefs and their incredible marine life in tropical seas around the world, and, in the Wolong Nature Reserve of western China's Szechuan Province, tracking the giant panda, the subject of WWF's eye-catching logo and the living symbol of endangered species throughout the world.*

Most of the experiences I have mentioned — and they are but the tip of the iceberg — have involved WWF projects. Many of them helped teach the close connection between the health of a particular ecosystem and the well-being of local people. All of them demonstrated the amazing diversity of life with which we share this planet, and its interconnectedness. And their geographic scope reflects vividly the dramatic expansion of the WWF-US program worldwide — with the advice and support of our board of directors, carried out by a great staff, and made possible by the fantastic generosity of our members and other donors, all within a strong working partnership with the WWF family as a whole.

*The giant panda logo was conceived and sketched by Sir Peter Scott, the eminent British artist and conservationist, while he was attending the first board meeting of WWF-International in 1961. Scott was the son of Robert Falcon Scott, the Antarctic explorer who died tragically in 1912 on his return from the South Pole.

Chapter 13

Encounters with Three Presidents

DURING THE YEARS that followed my becoming president of WWF-US, I had a variety of contacts, both professional and personal, with the succession of administrations in Washington.

While the Jimmy Carter administration may not have established a dramatic environmental record, it was definitely not anti-environment. Douglas Costle did a solid job at the Environmental Protection Agency; Cecil Andrus was a first-rate secretary of the Department of the Interior; Cyrus Vance at the Department of State was usually sympathetic to the environmental cause; James Gustave (Gus) Speth, as chairman of the Council on Environmental Quality (CEQ), was a forceful advocate of environmental policy within the administration. Moreover, important new legislation, such as the Superfund law, dealing with cleanup of toxic waste dumps, was enacted during Carter's term.

That environmental initiatives did not loom large in the Carter administration can best be explained by and understood within the context of the times. First of all, environmental concerns did not have the same urgency for the public as they had in the late 1960s and early 1970s, probably because laws enacted in those decades had begun to address the most pressing environmental issues and an institutional structure had been put in place, principally at EPA, to carry out those laws. Second, because many environmental issues had already been put on the public agenda in the previous decades, progress toward their solution did not seem particularly newsworthy to the media. Some of the uncompleted tasks, such as development of a national land-use policy, were probably too hot to handle for either party. Finally, whereas Richard Nixon had had a formidable political opponent in Edmund Muskie, who was the Democratic leader in Congress on pollution issues, Carter had no such Republican counterpart to confront. He could afford to deal with environmental issues in a much more relaxed way.

Hudson River Mediation

I had little direct contact with the Carter administration, but in 1979 I was asked to mediate a complex set of Hudson River environmental issues involving EPA, Consolidated Edison of New York, known as ConEd (as well as a number of other utilities), the New York State Power Commission, and a group of environmental organizations, including the Natural Resources Defense Council (NRDC), Scenic Hudson, and the Hudson River Fishermen's Association.

One of the key issues involved scenic Storm King Mountain, which rises on the west bank of the Hudson near Cornwall, New York. ConEd had been planning for some time to dig out the top of Storm King and install a "pumped storage" facility there. The concept was that, during off-peak energy periods, water from the river would be pumped into the reservoir thus created; then, during periods of peak electricity demand, the stored water would be released back into the river through power-generating turbines. The proposal was highly controversial and had been locked in litigation for several years.

An equally controversial proposal—this one originating with government agencies, notably EPA—was to require power plants along the Hudson, particularly the nuclear plant at Indian Point, to install cooling towers in lieu of simply pumping water out of the river and then returning the warmer water to the river, a process known as "once-through cooling." The towers would be hugely expensive and were considered by many to be a potential blight on the outstanding scenic values of the river valley. However, the existing once-through cooling system had been very destructive of the Hudson's fish life because of the warm-water discharges and a lack of effective screening devices at the point of intake.

After months of negotiation and many heated meetings, we hammered out an agreement canceling the Storm King pumped storage project, setting up systems to minimize fish kill at the water intake facilities of the power plants along the river, and establishing and funding the Hudson

River Foundation to research and monitor the environmental health of the river on a continuing basis. The agreement was signed at a public meeting in New York City on December 10, 1980.

The *New York Times*, in a lead editorial, called the agreement the "Hudson River Peace Treaty."[1] I received a lot of credit for the agreement, but I consider my most valuable contribution to have been simply keeping the parties meeting on the issues and keeping the negotiations alive. I did also help bring EPA's Washington, D.C., headquarters into the dialogue, which facilitated the cooling tower agreement.*

Toward the Reagan-Bush Administration

George H. W. Bush's presidential ambitions became pretty generally recognized in the late 1970s. In 1978, when Aileen and I spent Christmas on Jupiter Island, Florida (where we maintained a winter home, which we seldom saw), those ambitions were made quite explicit by the future president himself. George Bush's mother was a longtime resident of the island and many members of the Bush family had gathered there for the Christmas holidays. Aileen and I joined them at her home one afternoon. Young George W. was there with his new wife, Laura. Barbara Bush said to me, apropos of George H. W. ever becoming president, "When I stop and think, it terrifies me!" I could not understand anyone wanting the job, but she said George really did and she did for him, too. George took me aside to ask whether I would be willing to advise and assist him on environmental issues. I assured him that I would, but I said I did not believe, in view of my job at the World Wildlife Fund, that I should become publicly associated with an individual candidacy. He thought Ronald Reagan would get the 1980 Republican nomination if he wanted it, but he believed Reagan would ultimately decide that he was too old for the job.[2] Later during that visit to Jupiter Island, I spent a private hour with Bush, at his request, to discuss environmental issues. He was a good listener, and my sense at the time was that, while Bush had little knowledge of these issues, he recognized their importance.

*Charles Luce, my predecessor as under secretary of Interior and, at the time of which I am writing, chairman and chief executive officer of ConEd, played a particularly important role in making the mediation a success. Ross Sandler, attorney for NRDC, and Albert Butzel, attorney for Scenic Hudson, the principal environmental protagonists, also deserve much credit.

Three months later, Bush called from Houston to ask if I would be his finance chairman for the District of Columbia in his bid for the Republican presidential nomination. I was enormously flattered but decided that the job would create a conflict with my presidency of WWF. More important, I thought I would be a poor choice because I had practically no contact with the D.C. business community. Later, I did serve as an alternative delegate for Bush at the Republican National Convention in Detroit,[3] where Reagan won nomination as presidential candidate, with Bush as his running mate. And following Reagan's election, I served as a member of a task force to advise the incoming administration on environmental issues. That William Ruckelshaus and I both served in that group some interpreted — incorrectly, as it turned out — as a sign that the Reagan administration would not be "the disaster environmentalists feared."[4]

The transition from the Carter to the Reagan administration was a lively time socially for Aileen and me. On January 6, 1981, we attended a dinner given by Time Inc. for the president-elect at the Renwick Gallery (where William Corcoran first displayed his art collection), at the corner of Fifteenth Street NW and Pennsylvania Avenue, next door to Blair House and a block west of the White House. The co-hosts were Henry Grunwald, editor in chief of *Time* magazine, and Ralph Davidson, chairman of Time Inc.'s board and vice chairman of WWF's board, which may have accounted for our invitation.

At dinner, Aileen was seated between Reagan and Grunwald. There were plenty of luminaries at the dinner who far outranked us, so this arrangement must simply have been a tribute to Aileen's beauty, charm, and intelligence. We heard from Time Inc. staff that Reagan hoped to meet "local people" — perhaps we were considered at least highly qualified for that. From where I sat, at the next table, I had a good view of Aileen and the president-elect. "Every time I looked up," I wrote in my diary, "they seemed to be deep in conversation or laughing."[5] Aileen found Reagan very agreeable company, with a good sense of humor, taller than she expected, and much younger-looking than his age. Did it worry him at all that he was about to be president, Grunwald apparently asked him. Reagan seemed genuinely surprised by the suggestion, Aileen reported, as if the thought had never crossed his mind. Grunwald went on to predict that Reagan was going to be far more self-confident and at ease in the presidency than Carter had been. Reagan agreed and commented that

Mexican president José López Portillo had said much the same about him during their recent meeting.

On the way out after dinner, Aileen was besieged by fellow guests asking, "What did you talk about?" I pretended to be her press secretary and repeatedly said she had "no comment!"

Several days before the dinner for Reagan, we had given a much more modest dinner at our home for vice president–elect George Bush and his wife, Barbara. The thirty guests were mostly old friends of the Bushes and ours, including some who would assume important positions in the new administration, such as Mac Baldrige (to be secretary of Commerce) and Frank Carlucci (to be secretary of Defense) and their wives.

In my after-dinner remarks, I recalled our visit to Beijing as the Bushes' guests in 1976 and how they had entertained us royally at meal after meal. We had insisted on taking the Bush family out to dinner as our guests on our last evening in Beijing. They agreed, and Barbara made the arrangements at a small restaurant near the U.S. Liaison Office. The sixteen of us ate course after course of delicious Chinese food, washed down by quarts of beer. At the end, with a flourish, I called for the bill, which, as I recall, came to $10.84, including tip. I said at the time: "We feel that you have another meal coming from the Trains!" This was it. As I wrote later in my diary, the occasion had the atmosphere of a cheerful family wedding.[6]

At the inauguration itself, which soon followed, we were among Bush family and friends in three buses going to and from the Capitol. We were assigned seats for the actual ceremony—fairly distant, but not bad with binoculars. The president was sworn in by Chief Justice Warren Burger; the vice president, by Justice Potter Stewart. When the latter finished administering the oath to Bush, we distinctly heard him say, "God bless you, George!" It suddenly struck me that I had been sworn into office by both of these justices: as under secretary of Interior by Potter Stewart in 1969 and as chairman of CEQ by Warren Burger in 1970.

The Time of Watt

The era of the Reagan administration was not the best of times for a Republican environmentalist. James Watt, who I had first met in 1969, was Reagan's secretary of Interior and became a lightning rod for environmentalists across the country. In June 1981, I talked with Watt at a

White House reception and found him very tense. It was our first meeting since the inauguration. Environmentalists' attacks on him, he said, were motivated by their desire to attract new members to their organizations. As I wrote in my diary, "he let his tension pour out."[7]

I generally left it to others to attack the Reagan administration's environmental record. On a WWF trip to Jackson Hole, Wyoming, I was quoted as saying in a press interview: "Some are trying to get Watt's scalp. That is outside the traditional way the World Wildlife Fund operates. We tend not to be militant political activists." Our goal was instead to develop a dialogue, I said. "In this current situation involving the administration and particularly James Watt, it is important, more than ever, [that] some organization or some person maintain a bridge of communication. I spent an hour privately with him last Monday. I welcome that and don't want to abuse that."[8]

I had not been keeping completely silent, however. In a United Press International interview, for example, I expressed concern that the Reagan administration's neglect of environmental needs might trigger a worldwide pullback by other nations.[9] When Watt finally tried to become more conciliatory in response to the opposition to his policies, it was really too late. He had antagonized not only the environmental community but also a number of influential lawmakers. Many Republican politicians "definitely [felt] they have been burned" by Watt's unyielding stance, I was quoted as saying in June 1982. "It's one thing to have a lot of rhetoric about shaking things up, but it's quite a different matter to achieve effective legislative and regulatory reforms."[10]

Regulatory Reform

Vice President Bush had been designated by the president to head the Task Force on Regulatory Reform. C. Boyden Gray, counselor to Bush and later his counsel in the White House, had the day-to-day responsibility, working closely with staff of the Office of Management and Budget (OMB). I was always nervous about such White House incursions into regulatory functions.

In my own experiences at EPA when OMB held up issuance of a regulation, the underlying reason, more often than not, was that OMB disagreed with the substance of the proposed regulation. What was originally intended to be "oversight" could thus become an effort by the White House, OMB, or both to substitute their judgment for that of the agency whose head was charged by statute with responsibility for making the decision. At its worst, such a review provided an opportunity for interested parties to circumvent the regulatory process and press their views behind closed doors, before a more sympathetic audience, without a public record, and without equal opportunity for others to express a contrary viewpoint. It is an open invitation to abuse of the system, abuse that can lead to loss of credibility on the part of government and distrust on the part of the public.

My general feeling was, and is, that the White House and OMB should keep their distance from substance in the regulatory process. OMB can appropriately keep an eye on process — whether proper procedures are being followed, whether other agencies have had an opportunity to comment, and whether these comments have been considered. Beyond that, the president should appoint agency heads in whom he has confidence and then leave them alone to do the job. If the president does not like the way they do their job, he can always get rid of them.[11]

In early 1981, Vice President Bush held a meeting with the heads of about six environmental organizations in his office in the Executive Office Building (EOB), across from the White House. He described the regulatory review process that he and his task force were proposing. I thought it sounded like an intolerable interference in the business of an agency head. As a result, when Bush turned to me and said, "Russ, what do you think of that?" my reply was, "Mr. Vice President, if that process was applied to me as an agency head, I would resign."[12]

In addition to the Reagan administration's attempts to influence the regulatory process, there were attempts to undermine the Clean Air Act. I joined Bill Ruckelshaus and Doug Costle in testimony before the Senate Committee on Public Works urging that the Clean Air Act be retained essentially unchanged except for adding provisions to deal with acid rain and toxic air pollutants. Evidently some members of industry and even EPA were calling into question the validity of clean air standards and questioning whether their costs outweighed their benefits. But in the long run, it is pollution and not its control that will represent the real constraint to economic growth and development.[13]

Defending EPA

As his presidency got under way, Reagan named Anne Gorsuch administrator of EPA. A protégé of Jim Watt, Gorsuch proceeded to undo much of what EPA had accomplished in its first ten years of existence. I watched this process with growing alarm as 1981 ended and 1982 began.

I lunched with Vice President Bush in his office early in 1982. In the course of our discussion of WWF's Year 2000 Committee work, he asked what I thought about developments at EPA. I said, "It's a disaster!" I warned of serious adverse political reaction. Boyden Gray had joined us. They both agreed and both were also critical of Watt.[14]

About the same time, I spoke with Dick Darman, White House deputy chief of staff, about EPA. He said that Gorsuch was "almost paranoid" about any criticism and had become impossible to talk to. Things were so bad at EPA that they were going to have all EPA policy decisions made in Bush's office, with Boyden Gray "carrying the laboring oar." I told Dick that I probably would have to say something publicly about Gorsuch, and he said he would not blame me if I did.[15]

Finally, in early February 1982, after Reagan submitted his first budget, I wrote an op-ed piece on EPA for the *Washington Post*, which I quote here in its entirety because it expressed so much of my philosophy of government as it relates to the environment.

The Destruction of EPA

The Environmental Protection Agency is rapidly being destroyed as an effective institution in the federal government. Current and planned budget and personnel cuts, if continued, will inevitably reduce the agency to a state of ineffectualness and demoralization from which it is unlikely to recover for at least 10 years, if ever. While some may greet this situation with enthusiasm, I am convinced that the business community, among others, has very little to gain and a great deal to lose.

I see EPA's mission as a critically important one. I am convinced that, in the long run, our free enterprise system can only prosper and grow within the context of adequately protected public health and environment. I am also convinced that responsible business leadership knows this and asks only that regulatory requirements be reasonable, cost-effective, have an adequate scientific basis, and be fairly and uniformly enforced.

Corrected for inflation since 1981, President Reagan's expected 1983 budget request for EPA will represent a reduction of approximately 45 percent. Administrator Anne Gorsuch has reportedly been working on 1984 numbers of $700 million, or a cut of 61 percent. EPA's research branch would be cut by two-thirds, far more than any other basic research program.

In the personnel area, the cuts are equally drastic. If Gorsuch is allowed to carry out plans that have been circulating within the agency for some time, by this coming June — one year and four months after the Reagan administration took office — 80 percent of EPA's headquarters staff will have quit or been fired, demoted or downgraded.

It is hard to imagine any business manager consciously undertaking such a personnel policy unless its purpose was to destroy the enterprise. Predictably, the result at EPA has been and will continue to be demoralization and institutional paralysis. Attrition within the agency is running at an extraordinary 2.7 percent per month or 32 percent a year.

From an administration that quite rightly emphasizes the need for good management, what we are seeing at EPA is its very antithesis. Permits that businesses need do not get issued. Required rules and regulations do not get promulgated. Enforcement has ground practically to a halt. The most competent, technically proficient, professional staff have either already left or are looking for jobs. If one is not necessarily an environmentalist but believes that our environmental programs need to be managed efficiently, scientifically and less burdensomely, the current situation is equally disastrous.

Congress and the courts will effectively impede the ability of the administrator to bring about substantial change by administrative action alone. But they will provoke an upsurge in lawsuits and more decision-making by confrontation. While adversarial approaches to conflict resolution seem to be deeply ingrained in American society, there have been encouraging signs lately of growing appreciation of economic realities within the environmental community and a greater environmental sensitivity on the part of the business community. A return to the early days of polarization benefits no one.

Many of EPA's difficulties over the years can be traced to the fact that Congress loaded the agency with far more statutory responsibilities within a brief period of time than perhaps any agency could effectively perform. Surely, those problems can only be compounded by drastically reducing its resources while its responsibilities remain the same or grow. When EPA came into being in 1970, it took over the air pollution, water pollution, solid waste, pesticide and radiation programs scattered around the federal government. Since then those programs have been broadened and improved, and Congress has added major new responsibilities — including the Toxic Substances Act, the Safe Drinking Water Act, the Noise Control Act, the hazardous waste control program, and Superfund. These are not hangovers from the concerns of prior generations. EPA has been on the frontier of today's concerns, and there is every indication in the polls that environmental protection remains high on the public agenda.

Environmental protection needs are not going to lessen if EPA becomes ineffectual. The kepone problems and the Love Canals will continue to crop up from time to time. Unless the public has reasonable confidence in the public institutions charged with responsibility for handling such problems, there is real danger of a backlash developing against business. The pendulum will swing once more and in even more violent oscillations. EPA will be forced to react and will do so without adequate staffing and with a reduced research base. Business needs greater stability and predictability of policy, and for that it needs a credible EPA. The tendency of our political system to ignore the need for reasonable continuity in institutions and policies is one of its most serious failings.

As one who served two Republican administrations from 1969 to 1977 and who voted for President Reagan, I must record my profound concern over what is happening at EPA today. The budget and personnel cuts, unless reversed, will destroy the agency as an effective institution for many years to come. Environmental protection statutes may remain in full force on the books, but the agency charged with their implementation will be a paper tiger.[16]

The immediate effect of the article was a call from Anne Gorsuch and an invitation to come and see her at EPA. It was my first contact with her of any sort. She said that my analysis was unfair and that perhaps she should have gotten together with me earlier. We did meet in due course, in my old office. Nothing much had changed there physically. Robin Hill's paintings of endangered birds still hung on the wall. Gorsuch and I met alone. She described and defended what she was doing at EPA. None of her explanations altered my perception that the ability of EPA to carry out its statutory mission was being significantly prejudiced. It was my understanding, I said, that she was keeping the senior career staff at EPA at arm's length and was relying primarily on a small coterie of advisors whom she had brought in. I said I thought she was making a serious mistake in that regard. (Shortly after my op-ed piece appeared, the press reported that Gorsuch had announced there would be no more forced departures that year.)[17] Finally, as evidence that I was not trying to politicize the matter, I mentioned to Gorsuch that I had declined the invitations of five congressional committees to testify on the EPA situation.[18]

The point I had made in my op-ed piece about business needing a credible EPA was confirmed in my mind about a year later when I was attending a board meeting of the Union Carbide Corporation. Union Carbide was having a difficult time over regulation of a particular pesticide it produced, and, at the meeting, top management complained that the lack of a credible EPA was compounding its problems.[19]

Fortunately, the White House came to realize that the administration's anti-environment image was hurting the president politically, and Gorsuch resigned in March 1983. There was considerable speculation as to who would be her successor, with Bill Ruckelshaus, John Quarles, Henry Diamond, former senator James Buckley, and me among those mentioned. When I discussed the matter with John Chafee, the ranking Republican on the Senate Public Works Committee, he said I was apparently out of the running because of my criticism of the administration's handling of EPA. That suited me just fine.[20]

Ruckelshaus called soon thereafter from Seattle to say that he had been offered the job. I urged him to accept and said I thought he was by far the best person for the job. I suggested he should insist on reporting directly to the president and should not be part of the Cabinet Council on Natural Resources, chaired by Watt. He should insist on having a free hand on personnel and should also insist on being able to review his entire budget, I added. It would be a high-risk enterprise because the administration had already dug itself into a deep hole and the task of rebuilding EPA's credibility would not be easy. Moreover, the Democrats, particularly in the House, saw the debacle at EPA as providing one of their best political issues against Reagan, and they could be expected to do what they could to keep the issue alive. Bill recognized all these pitfalls, but he agreed that the need was so great that it would be difficult not to try.[21] And, of course, he did take the job, along with Al Alm, whom he chose as deputy administrator.

Bush Hospitality to WWF

Despite the generally poor environmental record of the Reagan administration (and perhaps because of it), George and Barbara Bush went out of their way to be hospitable to WWF during the former's vice presidential years. I think Bush genuinely wanted to reach out to the environmental community and he felt comfortable with the international character of WWF. On the occasion of a regular WWF board meeting, he and Barbara invited the board and senior staff to the vice presidential mansion on the U.S. Naval Observatory grounds for cocktails before we went off to our board dinner. And, when WWF-International and the various WWF national organizations held their biannual meeting in Washington, the Bushes had all of us—numbering in the hundreds—as guests for a barbecue feast under a tent at the same location. They personally received each and every guest at their residence as they arrived. It was a most hospitable and gracious occasion, and their guests loved every moment.

Meetings with Reagan

I knew Ronald Reagan only slightly in the years before his presidency. I had first met him when, as head of EPA, I had called on him at his gubernatorial office in Sacramento. I had also sat next to him at a GOP dinner in Seattle and exchanged pleasantries on a few other occasions.

Such contacts as I had with Reagan as president were largely ceremonial. In July 1983, we succeeded in having the president personally present the J. Paul Getty Wildlife Conservation Prize to the awardees at a ceremony in the Rose Garden at the White House.[22] When the president walked out of his office and stepped up to the microphone, he opened the proceedings by saying to the large assemblage: "Well, first let me welcome you all to the White House. I don't need to welcome Russell Train of the World Wildlife Fund. Russell's more at home here than I am. (Laughter.) He served in two administrations, and this is my first. (Laughter.) . . ."[23]

Reagan went on to describe the Getty Prize as the Nobel Prize for conservation and praised the democratic government of Costa Rica. When he was through, I pinned a panda button on his lapel and told him he was now a member of WWF.

I didn't see the president again until a year later, in July 1984, when the White House scheduled a luncheon meeting for him and the heads of a few selected environmental organizations.[24] There was no particular agenda other than to enable the White House to say that the president had met with a group of environmental leaders. For reasons best known to the administration, the White House had announced that morning the appointment of Anne Gorsuch, late of EPA, as chairman of an air quality advisory commission at the Department of Commerce. It was pretty much a nonjob, but the environmental community took it as a kick in the teeth.

At the luncheon, Reagan was his usual affable self and launched into several stories. I saw the opportunity for the environmentalists to address their concerns slipping away, and, at what seemed an appropriate point, I broke in on the president. I thanked him for inviting us to meet with him and then said: "Mr. President, I am sure you have a very busy schedule this afternoon, and I know that several of your guests have matters they would like to bring to your attention." He seemed somewhat startled and looked at me as if to say, "What do you know about my schedule that I don't?" In any event, everyone had a chance to say their bit and the meeting ended with little response from the president. It was pretty much a nonevent, unfortunately, but not unexpectedly.

The 1988 Bush Presidential Campaign

In early 1988, as Reagan entered his last year in office, Bush geared up his own presidential campaign. I had been chairman of WWF for three years and felt comfortable agreeing to co-chair an Environmentalists for Bush Committee with Bill Ruckelshaus. He and I met with Bush in his EOB office, along with former governor of New Jersey Tom Kean, pollster Bob Teeter, and other close supporters to discuss strategy.[25] I subsequently drafted a proposed speech for Bush designed to put him out front on environmental issues.[26] The draft committed him to White House submission of Clean Air Act legislation, to the objective of no net loss of wetlands, and to strengthening of the Superfund law to clean up toxic waste dumps. Later, I flew with Bush to Michigan and heard him deliver an edited but quite acceptable version of the speech I had drafted. On the plane on the way out, he had asked me to explain the "ozone layer" problem, which I did fairly inexpertly but followed up with a more informed letter on the subject. Bush gave a somewhat similar speech before a business audience in Seattle.[27] The response was positive, if somewhat muted.[28]

As co-chair of the Environmentalists for Bush Committee, I made one "surrogate" appearance in Ohio,[29] but otherwise I had no role in the campaign beyond what I have described. Our committee was pretty much pro forma, as most such groups tend to be.

In his acceptance speech at the Republican National Convention, Bush highlighted education and the environment as two areas in which he was going to put a lot more emphasis than had Reagan. Shortly before the election, I sent Bush a lengthy letter "setting down a few thoughts concerning the planning for a Bush Administration."[30] I urged him to make the environment a major theme of his presidency. There was a fresh wave of environmental concern both in the United States and abroad. Mikhail

Gorbachev and even Margaret Thatcher had now begun to address environmental problems. If environmental protection were "established as a priority element of U.S. foreign policy," I maintained, "it would assert strong U.S. international leadership of a very positive kind in addressing critical global environmental issues."[31]

Reilly and the First Bush Presidency

Although Bill Ruckelshaus rescued EPA from the worst excesses of the Anne Gorsuch period, the Reagan administration's environmental record, both domestically and internationally (with the major exception of the Montreal Protocol to limit the use of chlorofluorocarbons, or CFCs, which deplete the ozone layer), had been steadfastly negative. Bush, on the other hand, was eager to chart a new environmental course.

Following his election, Bush asked Bill Reilly, then WWF's president, to become EPA administrator. He did not know Reilly but acted on Bill Ruckelshaus's recommendation, which I fully supported. It was hard to lose him at WWF, though. Bill had done a brilliant job at WWF — building our revenues and membership, growing the program, and blending it with the public policy strengths that came from The Conservation Foundation.

As I recall, I gave Bill three bits of advice as he went to EPA. First, I urged that he get himself well and favorably known to the public early on so that opponents would have a tough time trying to undercut him; second, to exercise regularly; and third, to keep a diary. He failed on the last count and I think did reasonably well on the second. But on the first, he was a real star. He did so well in that regard in his first few months at EPA that, when his photographic portrait appeared on the cover of the *New York Times Magazine*, I called to congratulate him but also suggested he might want to cool it a bit because he was risking resentment from other members of the administration. He did a great job at EPA, not only on the domestic front but also in his efforts to reestablish U.S. leadership in the international environmental arena. Michael Deland became CEQ's chairman, and I had the honor and pleasure of administering the oath of office to him in the Oval Office as President Bush stood by.

As Reilly left WWF, Kathryn Fuller quickly became the overwhelming choice to succeed him. An environmental lawyer and marine biologist, as I have mentioned, Kathryn had already been on WWF's staff for some years. She, too, has done a superb job and she remains leader of WWF today.

Together with Bill Reilly, I had a dramatic opportunity to be with Bush at the outset of the first Gulf War. It came about in this way. Early in January 1990, Reilly called me in Florida to invite Aileen and me to dinner with him and his wife, Libbie, at their home outside Washington a few nights later. That would not really be possible, I said, because we would not be returning to Washington until two days after the date in question. Bill then said that a "very important person" was coming for dinner. I understood immediately that this meant the president, and, after a quick consultation with Aileen, I said we would be there. On the evening before the Reillys' party, we happened to be giving a dinner of our own in Florida. The 6:00 P.M. news announced the beginning of the Persian Gulf War, and the next morning we took off for Washington, not knowing whether or not the dinner would be canceled. What we discovered on arrival was that the Bushes could not come to dinner that evening but had invited us for drinks beforehand at the White House.

And so the Trains and Reillys, along with Bob Grady (presidential speechwriter and advisor) and a young woman accompanying him, joined the Bushes at the west end of the gallery that runs the entire length of the second floor of the White House. That particular area is furnished with sofas, comfortable chairs, and tables so that it makes a sort of adjunct living room. I remember it having been similarly used by Lyndon B. and Lady Bird Johnson.

Barbara and I sat on the sofa that backed against the Palladian window at the west end of the hall. Aileen sat with Bill Reilly on the sofa facing mine; the president was seated in a wing chair next to her. A butler brought us drinks and we talked, as might be imagined, about the war, which was then about twenty-four hours old.

A telephone sat on a small table at my elbow at the end of the sofa. Suddenly the phone rang. Conversation was instantly frozen. I remember having a mad thought: suppose it's Saddam Hussein? A butler immediately answered the phone and then proffered it to the president, saying, "It's General Scowcroft." The president took the phone and walked a few feet away, where he listened briefly with his back toward us. Then he brought the phone back and hung it up next to me. "That was Brent," he said. "The Iraqis have just fired a Scud missile at Israel. He'll call back as soon as we know where it lands."

He was perfectly calm and his tone was almost conversational. However, he went on to express his anxiety about Israel's reaction and his hope that Israel would not try to retaliate. If it did, that could radically change the entire character of the limited war we and our allies had undertaken. Minutes later, the phone rang again. This time, the president picked it up, and there was another brief conversation. When he was through, the president told us that the missile had landed in Tel Aviv.

We left soon after, having spent at least forty-five minutes with the Bushes. It was extremely kind and generous of them to entertain us at such a time. They were relaxed and hospitable, although the president was clearly in a very serious frame of mind. We were privileged to have had a glimpse of history in the making and from a vantage point that could hardly be equaled. Any thought of Bush as being "disengaged" at that time would have been ludicrous.

In the spring of 1992, in George Bush's last year in office, I was greatly honored by being awarded the Presidential Medal of Freedom in a ceremony at the White House, which was attended by most of my family.

Chapter 14

Of Ostriches and Dinosaurs

D URING MY LAST year at the Environmental Protection Agency, I was invited to testify on the foreign policy aspects of environmental programs before the Senate Committee on Foreign Relations. In that testimony I emphasized that the growing imbalance between increasing human numbers and available resources, combined with rising expectations in all segments of human society and all parts of the world, would inevitably lead to greater stress and conflict. Whatever the prospects for the future, one central fact of crucial significance to U.S. policy had emerged: our nation would not remain immune to the stresses that afflict the rest of the world. We could not maintain our well-being at home if the world abroad was in disarray. We were, like it or not, part of an increasingly interdependent and inter-related world:

> There can be no thought of a retreat into isolationism. Even if it were pos-sible, which it is not, isolationism in today's interdependent world is the road to disaster. The United States has an overriding self-interest in helping find acceptable solutions to the world's problems. Failure to find those solutions will exact an enormous price, not just from others, but in terms of the ultimate security and well-being of our own country. . . . Never in history has the opportunity and the need for U.S. leadership in world affairs been more critical.[1]

These words ring even more true today, twenty-five years later. Indeed, they have an almost eerie resonance in the aftermath of the tragedy of September 11, 2001.

Planning for an Environmental Future

Blueprints abound for dealing with growing national and international environmental problems. The year 1980, for example, saw publication of the World Conservation Strategy, prepared by the International Union for the Conservation of Nature and Natural Resources (IUCN) with the advice, cooperation, and financial assistance of the United Nations Environment Programme (UNEP) and the World Wildlife Fund. The document was released simultaneously at several national capitals around the world. In addition to my duties at WWF, I was the North American vice president of IUCN at the time and I chaired the launching ceremony in Washington.

The strategy focused on conservation of living resources rather than control of pollution, and it had three principal objectives: (1) maintaining essential ecological processes and life support systems, (2) preserving genetic diversity, and (3) ensuring the sustainable utilization of species and ecosystems. Although the strategy made detailed recommendations, its major effect was to give international currency to the concept of sustainability as an important touchstone of environmental policy.

The Brundtland Commission

In 1984, the United Nations General Assembly created the World Commission on Environment and Development, usually referred to as the Brundtland Commission in honor of its chair, Gro Harlem Brundtland, former prime minister of Norway. The General Assembly's action was taken in response to a Japanese resolution adopted at the 1982 Nairobi conference marking the tenth anniversary of the United Nations Conference on the Human Environment in Stockholm.[2] At an early morning meeting of the U.S. delegation to the conference, held at the U.S. embassy in Nairobi, EPA administrator Anne Gorsuch, as head of the delegation, had stated her plan for the United States to oppose the Japanese proposal, apparently on the urging of her mentor, Secretary of Interior James Watt. As a member of the delegation, I spoke up to point out that, ever since World War II, the United States had been encouraging Japan to play a more active role in international affairs. For us now to oppose the Japanese initiative would be inconsistent with that long-term policy. The U.S. ambassador to Kenya, who was sitting in on the delegation meeting, expressed his agreement, and the United States ended up not opposing the Nairobi resolution.

Bill Ruckelshaus was appointed by Reagan as the U.S. member of the Brundtland Commission. Nevertheless, despite the U.S. participation, Reagan and his administration ignored the commission's report, *Our Common Future*. If the commission's recommendations had little or no influence on U.S. policy, they did have considerable effect around the world and they provided the principal blueprint for the United Nations Conference on Environment and Development that would take place in 1992 at Rio de Janeiro. The commission defined sustainable development as development that allows people "to meet the needs of the present without compromising the ability of future generations to meet their own needs."[3]

That definition would also be adopted by the President's Council on Sustainable Development, established by President Bill Clinton in 1993 and co-chaired by Bill Ruckelshaus and Jonathan Lash.[4] The council's report urged that the concept of sustainability be incorporated into government policy and decision making, but it was, in my view, short on mechanisms for instituting, monitoring, and enforcing such a policy. I suggested that the Council on Environmental Quality (CEQ) be given that role — CEQ was a natural for it — but nothing came of it. In fact, the council's report as a whole suffered the fate of most such commissions: little public attention and little, if any, follow-up.

CEQ's Global 2000 Report

In 1980, the same year the World Conservation Strategy was published, CEQ submitted its *Global 2000 Report* to President Jimmy Carter. The report represented the results of a three-year study, conducted by CEQ and the State Department, of "the probable changes in the world population, natural resources, and environment through the end of the century."[5] The report declared that environmental, resource, and population stresses were intensifying and would increasingly determine the quality of human life on the planet. These stresses were already severe enough to deny many millions of people basic food, shelter, health care, and jobs, or any hope for betterment. At the same time, the report continued, the earth's carrying capacity — the ability of biological systems to provide resources for human needs — was eroding. To begin to meet these challenges, the report concluded, the federal government would need a much stronger capability to project and analyze long-term trends.

While the *Global 2000 Report* was reasonably well received, it was not without its detractors. Julian Simon and Herman Kahn collaborated on a book disparaging the study. One of their opening sentences summed up their reaction quite succinctly: "But it is dead wrong."[6]

It was sometime during the summer of 1980 that Gus Speth called me at the cottage Aileen and I rented on Martha's Vineyard to ask whether I would chair a citizens' committee on the *Global 2000 Report*. I was sympathetic with the report and recognized the need for building public support for it. At the same time, I felt cautious about taking on the job just as the 1980 presidential campaign was approaching its peak and I finally declined.

WWF's Year 2000 Committee

Be that as it may, in the spring of 1981, with the Reagan-Bush election behind us, I initiated under WWF auspices the Year 2000 Committee, which addressed many of the same global issues but, we hoped, with greater focus on solutions. Robert Anderson, chairman of the Atlantic Richfield Company and an environmentally sensitive business leader, co-chaired the committee with me. Joel Horn, fresh from the Stanford Graduate School of Business, became our executive director and was a real spark plug. Our participants were a stellar group of experienced leaders drawn from business, government, diplomacy, science, law, environment, and communications media.[7] They came from across the political spectrum, but I must admit, with considerable chagrin, from the vantage point of twenty years' hindsight, that the group included only one woman and no minority representation.

The committee as a whole strongly supported the concerns raised by the *Global 2000 Report*. There was, for example, nearly unanimous agreement on the threat posed by human population growth. (It is nothing less than extraordinary that one hears so little of the population issue today.) It was clear, though, that we would dissipate our potential effectiveness if we tried to promote the *Global 2000 Report* as a whole. What should we do? Cyrus Vance, a member of the committee, argued strongly that we should deal with the problems of nuclear arms, including nuclear proliferation, and he brought in MacGeorge Bundy to support his view. We

finally agreed to avoid specific resource issues such as population, deforestation, water supply, climate change, and loss of biological diversity,
recognizing the limitations of our small group and the fact that those
issues had been addressed in detail by others. We did not want to promote
yet one more grab bag of critical resource problems. Instead, we put our
emphasis on process and the need for the United States to develop a systematic and comprehensive capability for gathering and analyzing information on global resource trends. We believed, somewhat naively, as it
has turned out, that such an approach was one that both conservatives
and liberals could agree on. Thus, in essence, we embraced the conclud-
ing recommendation of the *Global 2000 Report*—that our government
should develop "the capability to project and analyze long-term trends"
on which long-term planning could then be based.

It was pretty much left to me and the WWF staff, specifically Joel
Horn, to implement the recommendation in some fashion. I called on
various officials and was urged by Secretary of Commerce Mac Baldrige
to meet with Jim Watt, which, I suspect, I had been somewhat hesitant to
do. However, I telephoned him about 5:00 one afternoon, and he suggested I come over right then. I jumped in a cab and soon found myself in
the Interior secretary's offices for the first time since the days of Rogers
Morton. Jim used the big office primarily for ceremonial purposes; otherwise, he worked out of an adjacent room normally used by the under secretary or staff.

The two of us sat and talked alone. I made it clear that I was not there
to pursue what I called another installment in the "Watt versus the Environmentalists" drama. I told him about the Year 2000 Committee and my
conversation with Baldrige. "Yes," said Watt, "Mac called me and told me
about the discussion." Watt then said, "when Mac said I should get into
the Global 2000 issues, I said, 'Mac, that's what we are all against!'"

There was no question in my mind that Watt had a deep bias against
the *Global 2000 Report* and believed that the pessimistic projections about
global resources, population, and environmental trends were all so much
doomsaying. I tried to use this bias to our advantage by telling Watt that
our concern was with process and that, if the analysis behind the report
was faulty, it underlined the need for the federal government to improve
greatly its data gathering and analysis in this area. He agreed and said he
would welcome an effort by our group to develop recommendations on
the matter.[8]

At the beginning of January 1982, I lunched with Vice President Bush in his office in the Executive Office Building, along with his counsel, C. Boyden Gray. The vice president's office had been considerably spruced up since my last visit there with Nelson Rockefeller. The water and heating pipes had disappeared. The beautiful parquet floor had been uncovered and polished. There was handsome furniture. I explained our Year 2000 Committee and our emphasis on improving data gathering and analysis within the government with respect to global resource issues. Bush expressed interest and commented that the Central Intelligence Agency had considerable capability in several of the resource areas. Getting people viscerally excited about data gathering and analysis is not easy, as we found out time and again, and the vice president was no exception.

Soon thereafter, Joel Horn and I had a breakfast meeting with Congressman Newt Gingrich at the Hay-Adams Hotel. Gingrich was a fairly junior member of Congress at the time but was already known for both his conservative views and his intellect. The following year, Gingrich and Tennessee congressman Albert Gore cosponsored, at our instigation, a bill titled the Critical Trends Assessment bill. It had several innovative qualities. It called for a report on critical trends every two years, prepared alternately by the executive branch and Congress. Each report was to address both the trends themselves and the process by which those trends were assessed. Thus, one principal purpose of the bill was to spark a continuing debate over global resource trends. The bill died in the House Interior Committee and our effort to find a sponsor for a similar bill in the Senate was to no avail.

No small number, I have found, oppose in principle the idea of developing and analyzing information because they fear that such an effort will lead to a new government program or—worse—a new program that the individual concerned does not want. During the Clinton administration, for example, Congress prohibited the use of appropriated funds for any research on global climate change—a true head-in-the-sand approach to policy making. Our proposal died, as had the proposal for an environmental policy institute when I was at CEQ. Political leaders would appear to have little interest in an independent analytic institution. Moreover, there is legitimate concern that such an institution might pursue its own agenda.

Chapter 15

WWF around the World

WHILE THE VARIOUS environmental task forces and international commissions I have described made important contributions to our understanding of environmental needs both at home and abroad, it was my own direct, hands-on involvement in actual WWF projects around the world that provided excitement and a personal sense of fulfillment.

WWF's international conservation program was at the beginning largely carried out by WWF-International from Switzerland, where it shared its headquarters with the International Union for the Conservation of Nature and Natural Resources (IUCN) in a large house on the outskirts of the ancient town of Morges, on the shores of Lake Geneva. When WWF-International brought into being a new national WWF organization, it usually chartered the organization as essentially a franchise operation. The normal arrangement was for the national organization to do its own fund-raising. The national organization would then apply one-third of its revenue to its own internal operation, apply one-third to conservation projects within its own national borders, and transmit one-third to WWF-International for the latter to expend as it saw fit.

From the outset, WWF-US did not operate in this fashion. We did provide financial support to WWF-International and to IUCN for specified purposes, but never as unrestricted funds and always at the discretion of our own board. To do otherwise would have been inconsistent with the tax status of WWF-US as a U.S. charitable organization. In our early days, this difference in the way WWF-US operated was not too important, given the modesty of our finances. Moreover, initially, WWF-

US concentrated its international efforts in Latin America and the Caribbean region, where WWF-International was relatively inactive. As time went on, however, our finances improved and our energy grew, and we began to expand our conservation activities elsewhere around the globe. Today, WWF has a major programmatic commitment not only in the United States, Latin America, and the Caribbean but also in Africa, Asia, and the Pacific region as well. Such an expansion inevitably led to frictions between WWF-US and WWF-International, frictions that today have largely dissipated under the leadership of Claude Martin as director-general of WWF-International and Kathryn Fuller as president and Roger Sant and now Bill Reilly as chairs of WWF-US.

It would be impractical to describe here all of the programmatic initiatives of WWF-US outside the Western Hemisphere, and I had direct involvement in only a few of these. Moreover, our programmatic reach has not simply been geographic in scope but involves such problems as global climate change, international fisheries policy (including the fishing subsidies of the European Union), toxic chemicals, and population growth. Having said that, I shall endeavor to set out some highlights of my involvement in the expansion of the WWF-US program on one continent, Asia, starting in the early 1980s. I have selected Asia because I had a considerable and ongoing personal involvement in our Asian program development and also because the countries there were largely new in my experience.

WWF's expansion into Asia was probably more opportunistic than the result of some grand strategic thrust. If a country had a rich and diverse biota and at the same time was receiving little or no international conservation help, we explored the opportunity for WWF-US to be proactively engaged there. On the following pages, I describe early efforts of this kind in China (briefly), Nepal, Bhutan, Thailand, and the Philippines.* In the typical case, I used such visits to build a working relationship with local conservationists and also to open communications at a high level of government. Moreover, firsthand exposure to this and other similar projects was vital to my leadership of WWF-US, including my ability as a fund-raiser. The organization's income was growing, so there were usually some uncommitted funds that could be devoted to these purposes.

---

*Early on, there were WWF national organizations in India, Pakistan, Japan, Malaysia, and Indonesia, where WWF-Netherlands was particularly active. I visited all of these countries but did so primarily as a base-touching exercise.

Then, as specific commitments were entered into, we raised the money to fund them. We never had available a large pot of money on which large strategic plans could be built. Ours was much more of a bootstrap operation. However, both project development and fund-raising assumed a growing and mutually supportive momentum at the time.

China: Giant Pandas

My first visit to Asia under WWF auspices came in 1982, following the biannual congress of IUCN, held in Christchurch, New Zealand. Aileen and I, together with Charles de Haes, then director-general of WWF-International, flew from New Zealand to Chengdu, the capital of Szechuan Province, in western China. From there, we drove to the remote Wolong Nature Reserve, close to the Tibetan border. Wolong was the site of George Schaller's research on the giant panda. One of the world's leading wildlife biologists, Schaller was on the staff of the New York Zoological Society (NYZS, now the Wildlife Conservation Society), and his work on the giant panda was being jointly funded by NYZS and WWF-US.

The giant panda, one of the best-known and most beloved members of the animal kingdom, epitomizes the plight of endangered species throughout the world. And the image of the giant panda, in a stylized version, has provided the organizational logo of WWF, as described earlier. Thus, our visit to the panda project had a special significance for both de Haes and me.

In our treks along the mountain trails with Schaller, we never managed to see a panda, although we found relatively fresh droppings. The problem was that the radio collar on the most likely panda had broken down. We were fortunate, however, in having a splendid view of a troop of very rare golden monkeys.

Schaller's research was designed to provide knowledge of the needs of pandas in the wild—their food requirements, their range, their movements within that range, their breeding behavior—so that conservation efforts could be properly designed. Sadly, there are only five to six hundred giant pandas left in the wilds of China and the principal reason is loss of habitat. The animals, which once were able to range over large areas of bamboo-clad mountains, have seen the valleys steadily fill with human settlements and cultivation. Because of this pressure, the giant panda population has been increasingly split into small, isolated groups confined to the higher slopes. WWF's effort today is to work with China to develop protected corridors between these populations. The enormous and continuing human population pressure in that country makes this a daunting challenge. In many ways, the giant panda epitomizes the plight of endangered creatures throughout the world and the challenges they—and we —face in ensuring their survival.

Nepal: Elephants, Tigers, and Rhinos

One of WWF's first major involvements outside the Western Hemisphere was in Nepal. Since the early 1970s, WWF-US had worked in partnership with the Smithsonian Institution to conserve tigers and their habitat in that beautiful Himalayan country lying along India's northern frontier. It was a natural association: the Smithsonian, like WWF-US, was headquartered in Washington, D.C., and its head, S. Dillon Ripley, was chair of our WWF-US board. Under our arrangement, the Smithsonian performed the essential scientific studies and we provided much of the funding for the project, as much as $100,000 per year. The project paralleled what was termed Project Tiger in India, where WWF and the Indian government cooperated in setting aside and protecting critical tiger habitat. Project Tiger enabled the Bengal tiger to maintain reasonably healthy populations on the subcontinent until quite recently, when rising demand created by traditional Chinese medicine for tiger bones and other animal parts triggered a tremendous increase in tiger poaching in India and elsewhere in Asia.*

Our tiger project in Nepal focused on Royal Chitwan National Park, a former royal hunting preserve situated in the thickly forested Terai region along the Indian border. The fact that the forest was in such good condition was largely a result of the high incidence of malaria in the area, which had discouraged human settlement. With the eradication of malaria-bearing mosquitos within recent times, the Terai was rapidly being settled. Chitwan was becoming a large island of forest surrounded by small farms

---

*As I write this, the pioneering work of vice president Ginette Hemley and others at WWF-US with practitioners of traditional Chinese medicine both in the United States and China is proving remarkably successful in helping curb this development. The Chinese government has cooperated in this effort, which has as its goal the exclusion of endangered species and their products from use in traditional medicine.

and villages. It did contain, however, Nepal's only remaining viable population of tigers.

The WWF-Smithsonian project sought to determine both the size of the existing tiger population and the process of tiger dispersal as their numbers increased. Each tiger needs an exclusive hunting territory. As tigers bred and the offspring matured, where did the offspring go? How many breeding tigers were needed to maintain a viable breeding stock? What was the health of the tigers' prey populations? Answers to such questions were critical to the development and implementation of national park policy and tiger reserve management.

By 1981, the Smithsonian had monitored closely about three generations of tigers in Chitwan and decided that it had essentially completed its research. Accordingly, the Smithsonian decided to withdraw and urged WWF-US to take on the job of working with the Nepalese government not only on tiger conservation but also on wildlife conservation more generally in that country. In addition, David Challinor, who had led the Smithsonian on the project, suggested to the Nepalese that they create their own organization to undertake conservation projects. Such an organization would need assistance, both financially and professionally, from WWF or other organizations outside the country.

With this background in mind, I went to Nepal in early 1981, accompanied by Aileen. In Kathmandu, we stayed with the U.S. ambassador, Philip Trimble, a Jimmy Carter appointee and an enthusiastic mountaineer who loved Nepal. He was most hospitable and helped me make important contacts in the Nepalese government. I am glad to say that just about everywhere around the world that I recall visiting on WWF-US business, the official U.S. representation in the particular country was uniformly helpful to me and our staff.

One of my most memorable meetings in Kathmandu was with Mother Teresa at a reception in her honor at the British ambassador's residence. She was in Nepal as a visitor and was not tied directly to our conservation work there. A diminutive but charismatic presence, she addressed the crowd of guests for a few minutes about her remarkable ministry to the poor of Calcutta. Afterward, as she received the guests, I told her how much I admired her and how honored I felt in meeting her. At the same time, I could not help but tell her that I disagreed with her views on family planning, particularly her opposition to the use of contraceptives. In a very low voice, she replied that she approved the "temperature" method of birth control. I learned later that this involved a woman taking her temperature regularly over a period of time, recording the information, and then avoiding intercourse during those times when her temperature was elevated, indicating that she was ovulating. Such an approach struck me as totally impractical, particularly among the teeming poor of Calcutta.

The manager of the WWF-Smithsonian project on the ground in Nepal was Hemanta Mishra, whom we met on our arrival at Kathmandu and who over the years, with his wife, Sushma, became close friends of Aileen and me. Hemanta is an energetic and highly motivated conservationist — a leading Nepalese in that regard.

After several days in Kathmandu and the surrounding countryside, with its ancient towns and temples, we flew with Hemanta to Royal Chitwan National Park. We landed on a grass strip outside the park, steps were rolled over to the plane, and we disembarked. The steps were then rolled to a group of Asian elephants standing nearby. Aileen and I climbed aboard one of these and Hemanta boarded another. Meanwhile, our gear disappeared into a Land Rover, to reappear, we hoped, at our camp.

We had about an hour's ride, a wonderful introduction to travel by elephant. Our driver (called a mahout in India, a term I use here for want of the correct Nepali name) sat astride the animal's head, heels dug in behind its ears. He steered by pressure with his knees or kicks of his heels. We sat on a thin quilted pad on the elephant's back secured by a rope girth. One of us rode astride the neck and the other sat sideways on the back. It was reasonably comfortable — certainly a good deal more so than riding in a wooden howdah — and I liked the feel of the elephant's back muscles moving beneath the pad.

We followed a trail — through fields, across a river, and into the forest — finally coming to a halt at Saurha, the headquarters of our tiger project. The site was a large, relatively flat clearing with accommodations for scientists and staff, guest quarters, a kitchen, and elephant ranks — all arranged in vaguely military fashion around the sides of a somewhat uneven parade ground. One of the scientists-in-residence I met there was Eric Dinerstein, who was doing research for the Smithsonian on the greater one-horned rhinoceros, the largest of its genus. Now WWF's vice president for science, Eric has been responsible for mapping the global ecoregions, a cornerstone of contemporary conservation strategy. Hemanta's wife, Sushma, the couple's two children, and Sushma's brother were on hand to greet us as well, making the occasion a sort of family out-ing. Sushma cooked a delicious lamb curry that evening and, indeed, pre-pared all our meals for the next several days.

Aileen and I spent those days exploring adjacent areas of the park with Hemanta — almost always on elephant back. We participated in a game drive with about six elephants and managed to corner a rhino. Hemanta fired a dart to anesthetize it, and when the rhino had sunk unconscious to the ground, he installed a radio collar around its neck. Aileen and I dis-mounted from our elephant — after it had knelt at our mahout's soft com-mand — to gather around the supine rhino and watch the whole process, which was carried out with great care and professionalism. A wet cloth was spread over its face and forehead to help keep the animal's tempera-ture from rising. Hemanta said the rhino would be named Russell in honor of the occasion, but that went unacknowledged by the animal in question.

Sometime later, we took part in a large elephant drive — large, at least, by today's standards. Some twenty-five elephants were gathered from near and far for the purpose. The goal was to dart and radio-collar a large and rather ill-natured male tiger. Hemanta had installed a *machan*, or hunting platform, in a tree over a game trail, down which it was hoped the tiger would come to escape the advancing elephants. Along with Hemanta and his dart gun, Aileen and I took our places on the cramped platform, which we reached from elephant back. Supposedly, the *machan* was high enough above the trail to be safe from the leap of an infuriated tiger, but, to the two of us, it seemed awfully close to the ground. Hundreds of feet of white cloth fencing, funneling toward the game trail above which we waited, had been erected on either side of the drive area, although we could see none of it through the dense forest around us.

For a time, we heard little but the occasional sound of a bird. Finally, we began to make out the faint sounds of voices and pot-banging from the elephant line, advancing unseen in the distance. The racket grew louder and louder, and then it suddenly stopped. Later we learned that the elephant line had in fact flushed the tiger, but he had turned and man-aged to run back through the line. The elephants regrouped and again flushed out the tiger. The action was closer now. Suddenly we heard tiger roars and a crescendo of elephant trumpeting — then again relative silence. The tiger had again turned toward the elephant line, but this time, instead of slipping quietly through, he had charged the center elephant, which happened to be carrying David Challinor. The tiger leapt halfway up one side of the elephant, raking it with its claws, before disappearing into the high grass behind the line, this time for good. Thus ended our effort to dart a tiger.

There were other less dramatic but also memorable experiences. One afternoon on our first visit, Aileen and I rode out into the forest on our elephant. We were alone except for the mahout. There were birds all around, and we initially tried to identify them through our binoculars, with the help of Robert L. Fleming's *Birds of Nepal*, but that was next to impossible to do from the swaying back of a moving elephant. We relaxed and enjoyed the sights and sounds of the forest, including the occasional crashing sound of some unseen animal—perhaps a rhino—making its escape through the dense undergrowth. We were entranced when our mahout spotted a small piece of trash, most likely an empty cigarette pack, on the trail, and stopped his elephant—which then, at a softly spoken command, picked up the offending article with the tip of its trunk and passed it over its head to the mahout. As the sun began to set, we turned back toward camp and when we reached the bank of a small river our elephant paused for a moment before heading across. Flights of white egrets flew down the river, heading for their roost for the night. Then, as we started across, three peacocks flew overhead, calling raucously. It was a magic moment—one of many such, I am afraid, that are fast disappearing from the face of the earth and thus from our human experience.

Back in Kathmandu, Hemanta Mishra and I went to the royal palace for a meeting with H.R.H. Prince Gyanendra Bir Bikram Shah Dev, King Birendra's eldest brother. We sat in a small, rather formal parlor. The prince was in traditional Nepalese attire, including a cap called a topi, which reminded me of the "overseas" cap I wore as an officer during World War II. He asked politely about our visit to Chitwan and about WWF, but we quickly got down to business: the establishment of a conservation trust in honor of the prince's father. Conceptually, the King Mahendra Trust for Nature Conservation (KMTNC) would be a nongovernmental conservation organization, to be chartered by the parliament but with close ties to the monarchy. King Birendra would be royal patron, Prince Gyanendra would be board chairman, and Hemanta would be chief executive officer. The board of directors would be overwhelmingly Nepalese in makeup but with two outside directors, one of these to be me, initially at least, and the other to be Sir Arthur "Jerry" Norman, chairman of WWF-UK at the time. Implicit, if not explicit, in the arrangement was a "special relationship" between KMTNC and WWF-US. While KMTNC would be free to seek funds anywhere it could, it was expected that WWF-US would do most of its Nepal program development and implementation in partnership with the new organization and would provide major funding.[1]

In time, KMTNC's charter received the formal assent of the king and was approved by the parliament and we were in business. KMTNC usually met twice each year in Kathmandu and I tried to attend at least one of those meetings. These arrangements in Nepal were by no means a model that we would necessarily follow elsewhere. Each country in which we worked had different circumstances and we adapted our organizational approach to the circumstances and opportunities we found.

In the years that followed, WWF-US had many programmatic involvements in Nepal, principally at the beginning through KMTNC. One major project undertaken by WWF-US in Nepal through KMTNC was the translocation of rhinos and then tigers from Chitwan to other areas in western Nepal, particularly to Royal Bardia National Park. With WWF's help, sixty-two rhinos, one individual at a time, were translocated to Bardia between 1986 and 2001, a huge task. Today, there are about eighty-six rhinos in Bardia, a good breeding population, and at least six hundred in the country as a whole, about five times the 1960 total.[2]

Nepal: The Annapurna Conservation Area Project

The most significant of our Nepalese involvements, however, was establishment of the Annapurna Conservation Area, covering more than 2,700 square miles of Himalayan foothills and high peaks and containing many villages and farms as well as one of the most popular trekking routes in Nepal. The concept was not to establish a fully protected area such as a national park—which would have been impossible in any event, given the extent of human settlement and usage—but to create what was to be the world's first "integrated conservation and development" area.

From the beginning, a major effort was made to involve the local people and their communities. Our first step was to put together a small group, consisting of Chandra Prasad Gurung, Mingma Norbu Sherpa, and Brot Coburn to develop community relationships. Chandra was a native of the Annapurna region, Mingma was a native of the Mount Everest area, and

Brot was a young American anthropologist who had worked for several years in Nepal. Mingma had firsthand experience with the establishment of Sagarmatha National Park in the Everest region and the tragic mistakes made in that case. Sagarmatha had been established essentially by Kathmandu fiat, with little or no consultation with those most directly affected, the local Sherpa people. The latter were simply given several weeks' notice of the park's formation and the resulting strictures on cutting trees for firewood, among other rules. The Sherpas, in response, went into a frenzy of tree cutting in order to stockpile firewood. The whole process ensured antagonism for many years between the park authorities and Sherpa people. We were determined that the Annapurna Conservation Area not be a repeat of that experience.*

The three-person committee, funded by WWF-US, spent six months in the Annapurna region. Starting in June 1985, the committee traveled from village to village and held extensive community meetings in each one. All attendees had a chance to have their say, to ask questions, to raise objections, to make suggestions. It was a case of bringing conservation to the community and community involvement was ongoing once the project was approved. Committees were set up to represent farmers and other interests in the area. Even a mothers' group was established. The project also set up and financed a centrally located health clinic, which, I was glad to learn, offered free contraceptives in addition to regular health services.

In addition, we organized a training course for managers of the numerous private lodges in the area catering to the thousands of trekkers who came to the Annapurna region. A standard rate schedule was set up that ensured a reasonable return and the quality of the facilities was improved across the board. Sanitary facilities had been essentially nil and waste disposal a mess, but communitywide efforts resulted in cleanup of the trail and establishment of latrines, which were serviced regularly.

One of the most serious conservation problems in the area (as in most of Nepal) was the destruction of hillside forests for household firewood, for grazing, and for planting as human numbers continued to grow. Trekkers exacerbated the problem by collecting firewood for cooking and heating in their overnight camps. This aspect of the problem was addressed, in part, by requiring trekkers to use kerosene instead of wood

*Mingma Norbu Sherpa became the first Sherpa to be warden of Sagarmatha National Park. He is currently director of WWF's Eastern Himalayas Program, which focuses on the eastern Himalayas and Tibet.

for their fires and by establishing kerosene dumps at strategic locations along the trail. More important, the project fostered the development of forest plantations as a renewable source of fuelwood. The kerosene fuel dumps thus became a bridging technique, pending the maturing of the forests.

From the outset, the Annapurna Conservation Area Project was intended to be self-supporting and it essentially was. A fee system, approved by the government, was established for trekking the trail, and it yielded gross receipts in the neighborhood of $1 million annually. Mingma Norbu Sherpa managed the project in the beginning, followed by Chandra Gurung. The project was in many ways a conservation flagship and was featured in *National Geographic* magazine in an article by famed photographer Galen Rowell.[3] Over time, as management of KMTNC became less effective, the Annapurna project ran into difficulties. Some of the trekking fees were diverted to other purposes. While KMTNC's royal patronage and connections gave it important influence in the country, the association also brought with it a considerable measure of "palace politics," to its detriment. More recently, the so-called Maoist insurgency in Nepal has disrupted tourism and resulted in considerable armed violence in many rural areas, including the Annapurna region. All of this reminds us that conservation is a continuing battle. Nevertheless, the Annapurna Conservation Area Project was the first example, and a highly influential one, of what came to be called integrated conservation and development projects (ICDPs), pursued by the international conservation community over the ensuing years.

I had an opportunity to visit the Annapurna project in 1985 after it was under way when, together with Bruce Bunting, at that time WWF's director for Asia, and Michael Wright, WWF's vice president, I flew to Jomsom, a village in the Kali Gandaki River valley. From there we would trek to Muktinath, at 12,800 feet, a site sacred to both Buddhists and Hindus. Having been on the seacoast only the day before at Karachi, Pakistan, I had had no chance to acclimate to the new altitude.

The Kali Gandaki valley separates Dhaulagiri mountain and the Annapurna range, both of which rise more than 26,000 feet above sea level. The Kali Gandaki flows down from the Tibetan plateau and slices right through these stupendous mountains. This river valley is easily the deepest in the world, with the riverbed some 20,000 feet below the peaks on either side.[4] When Aileen and I made a short trek in Nepal in 1981, we were in farming hill country, walking among terraced fields and old farm-houses. Trees were common. Now we were trekking with three Sherpas and four porters on the north side of the Annapurna range, in the rain shadow of the mountains. Stark, treeless heights rose on every side. A gale-force wind howled up the valley, fortunately from behind us, as I am not certain we could have walked into it.

The Kali Gandaki is one of the oldest of human trade routes, leading from India up onto the Tibetan plateau. On the far side of the valley, several pony trains passed, loaded with goods, the lead horses with bright red pom-poms nodding above their heads and each animal carrying a brass bell around its neck. The sound of those distant bells in the wilderness around us, the horses and humans alike dwarfed by the vastness of space and heights, had not changed, I felt sure, for a thousand years or more.

We left the riverbed and started climbing into the hills. At one point, the trail passed through a narrow cleft with sheer walls on either side. Just after I entered the cleft, a herd of yaks (actually a cross between the wild yak and domestic stock) thundered through the passage in single file, their long horns practically spanning the space between the walls. I managed to flatten myself against the left-hand wall, held my breath, and somehow remained unscathed.

We walked for six hours that day, finally making camp on the edge of a little village called Khingar at about 11,000 feet. We had passed no other settlement since Jomsom. Here water and some flat land combined to make a bit of cultivation possible and, thus, the village. That evening we huddled around our cheerless kerosene stove for supper and then crawled into our small tents and sleeping bags.

We were up at 5:30 the next morning and continued our walk along the side of a broad, barren valley across which I could see caves in the cliffs, where, we were told, Tibetans fleeing from the Chinese takeover of their country had taken refuge. We passed through Jarkot and finally reached Muktinath, one of the holiest places in Nepal and a major goal of pilgrimage. Here springs flow through 108 bronze fountains, and, inside a low, dark temple in a cleft in the rock, one could see a small flame dancing on water and another flickering on a rock. The flames are considered manifestations of the Buddha. There were no pilgrims other than us, and no one else around. It was easy to understand the mystical appeal of the place.

From Muktinath, we retraced our steps to Jomsom. It was a ten-hour walk, the last two of which were in an icy, drenching rain for which we were totally unprepared. It was a tough two days for the old man (I was then sixty-five), and I do not think I would have made it except that I was goaded along by a porter's query on the first day as to whether I was my WWF colleague Mike Wright's father.

We were scheduled the next evening to attend the annual dinner and ball of the Nepal Heritage Society at our hotel in Kathmandu. Most of local high society was expected to attend—black tie, no less. Given the fact that I could barely hobble around after our little trek, I looked forward to the dance floor with less than my usual enthusiasm. Sir Edmund Hillary was to be the guest speaker, and I, minus my voice, which had vanished from fatigue and exposure on the trail, was to introduce him. Hillary came to my room before the dinner for a drink and a talk. We discussed the draft plan for the Annapurna Conservation Area Project in detail—particularly its emphasis on involving and benefiting the local people of the area—and he became an enthusiastic supporter. He gave me a strongly worded written endorsement that would be extremely helpful in fund-raising. Hillary had recently been named New Zealand's high commissioner to India and was accredited as ambassador to Nepal. The conqueror of Mount Everest, Hillary was a heroic figure in Nepal, particularly to the Sherpa people, for whom he has done so much by way of education, health care, and community development. I have met Hillary several times in both Nepal and the United States. He is an extremely likeable individual—quiet, modest, and friendly while strongly committed to helping the Himalayan region and its people.[5]

The following evening, Prabhakar Rana and his wife gave a small dinner in honor of Prince Gyanendra and Princess (now Queen) Komal. The discussion was surprisingly open on a variety of subjects. Nepal had an official birthrate of 2.9 percent, and Jerry Norman and I never missed an opportunity to raise the issue before any audience we could. When I was in Karachi, Pakistan, just a few days before, I had been interviewed by a reporter for the English-language newspaper *Dawn*. The headline for the resulting article read "Population Growth Foremost Threat to Wildlife."[6]

At the meeting—my first—of the KMTNC board the following evening, the principal subject of discussion was the plan for the Annapurna Conservation Area. There was unanimous agreement on the concept, and the only real question raised was how much of the project to bite off at the start. The concept itself—combining protection of a magnificent natural area with provision of new economic opportunities for the local people—was a fairly radical departure from the more traditional national park concept. We came away from the meeting with definite authorization to proceed with the project.

On our last day in Nepal, the king inaugurated a workshop (funded in part by WWF-US) on the management of national parks and protected areas in the Hindu Kush–Himalaya region. The king launched the enterprise at a formal outdoor ceremony north of Kathmandu in the presence of the diplomatic corps and workshop participants. Prince Gyanendra was the opening speaker. I followed, once again outlining the Annapurna project plans. That evening, the prince gave a reception at his home, where I met the king and queen. I also talked with the crown prince, who was then in school. Tragically, in 2001 the crown prince killed his parents and much of the rest of the royal family before committing suicide.

At the time of this writing, for ten years WWF has maintained an office in Kathmandu, with a staff of over thirty, including field staff, all of them Nepalese, which serves as headquarters for our Nepal program. Our relationship with KMTNC, however, has become increasingly tenuous. Hemanta Mishra left Nepal several years ago to join the World Bank and then the Asian Development Bank in Manila. After the murder of King Birendra and much of the Nepalese royal family in 2001, Prince Gyanendra succeeded to the throne, and his son, now Crown Prince Paras, has become chairman of KMTNC. Kathryn Fuller, who took my place on the KMTNC board several years ago, left the board in 2002. Thus, the picture has changed, though WWF is an increasingly strong presence on its own in the area.

We have continued to work on rhinoceros translocation and improvement of national park management. In both cases, WWF's working relationship is directly with the national park service of Nepal. One innovative program is called the Successful Communities project, involving five villages in the Sherpa area of Nepal and in Bhutan. The concept is that, for a community to be successful in environmental matters, it must first of all be a successful community as demonstrated in key areas such as leadership, health, education, and the role of women. All of this strikes a responsive chord with me. Environmental quality is not an abstract concept but one that is integral to the entire fabric of society. One could easily pick additional factors to emphasize, but the project needs to have a manageable focus. I find it particularly heartening that it is the Nepalese and Bhutanese staffs that conceived and are implementing the program—an inspiration for all of us.

India and Nepal: Terai Arc Landscape

Another ambitious project involving the same region, called the Terai Arc Landscape (TAL) project and directed by Mingma Norbu Sherpa, seeks to link all eleven national parks and other protected areas of the Terai region of Nepal and India, which stretches from Royal Chitwan National Park in Nepal to Jim Corbett National Park in India—a distance that ranges well west of Nepal and spans an area of about 12.3 million acres. The linkage would comprise natural corridors of protected land so that wildlife could migrate with reasonable freedom and safety among these areas, a concept known as connectivity. The project not only involves cooperation among park managers and local conservation groups but also requires the support of the intervening agricultural communities. Certain crops, for example, are better than others in providing cover and protection for a migrating tiger or elephant. Fortunately, some crops, such as sugar cane, provide economic benefits for farmers as well as cover for wildlife. WWF also provides economic incentives, such as for the construction by local communities of biogas facilities for cooking and heating. Funding for TAL is provided not just by WWF but also by other partners in the project: the U.S. Agency for International Development (USAID), the Save the Tiger Fund, and the U.S. Fish and Wildlife Service. However, the Maoist rebellion in some of the rural areas of Nepal has caused some cutback in fieldwork for this project.

Bhutan: A Rare Opportunity

To the east of Nepal and separated from it by the once-independent kingdom of Sikkim—now part of India—lies the kingdom of Bhutan, the site of a major countrywide WWF commitment. It is a beautiful country that draws much of its spiritual tradition from Tibet. It is extremely mountainous, with a section of the forested Terai region along its southern border with India. The people are very bright, cheerful, and energetic. To some, Bhutan is reminiscent of the Nepal of fifty years ago.

Bruce Bunting went to Bhutan in the mid-1980s and immediately recognized the need and the potential for an effective conservation program. WWF could have a central role in that regard because no other international environmental organization had a presence there. Bhutan's response was enthusiastic, and we quickly developed program plans. I visited Bhutan three times over the ensuing years, twice accompanied by Aileen, to help build WWF's relationship with the country and also to gain firsthand knowledge of the country's conservation needs and opportunities.

On one occasion, Paljor "Benjie" Dorji, head of the Royal Bhutan Wildlife Society and a former chief justice of Bhutan, took us by road from the capital, Thimphu, to the remote Phobjika Valley in eastern Bhutan to see the black-necked cranes on their wintering ground. They were just arriving in small groups from Tibet and there was a light snow on the ground. With their predominantly whitish color, the gray sky, and the snow and mist, the cranes seemed every bit as mysterious as they in fact are. When they arrive from Tibet, as Peter Matthiessen has written, they circle the local monastery three times before settling on the ground, and when they leave in February, each bird, whether singly or in a large flock, again flies three times around the same monastery before departing.[7]

Under Bunting's leadership, WWF put together a remarkable conservation program in Bhutan, the centerpiece of which was the creation and funding of the Bhutan Trust Fund for Environmental Conservation. The time was ripe for such an effort. The country was still in a relatively pristine state, but the pressures for development would inevitably bring major changes in their wake. We thus had an unusual window of opportunity to help Bhutan address those pressures in advance rather than after the fact, as is all too often the case.

The Bhutan Trust Fund for Environmental Conservation was the first of its kind in the world, a truly innovative accomplishment. WWF-US kick-started the operation with an initial grant of $1 million. Substantial help was secured from economic development assistance agencies in Europe and Japan, and by the year 2000 the trust had assets of $36 million. (There are now forty somewhat comparable national trust funds for environmental purposes around the world; of those, WWF-US has been responsible both for pioneering the concept and for launching seventeen of the funds.)

When I first visited Bhutan, the annual budget of the conservation office in the Ministry of Forests was about $100,000, but it is now substantially augmented by the trust fund. The latter provided the resources for managing Bhutan's system of national parks and reserves, as well as for funding research into the country's biological diversity in order to establish a sound scientific basis for that system. It also funded the costs of training conservation staff at all levels. One of WWF's principal objectives was to build Bhutan's *own* capacity to manage its *own* resources. Some seventeen Bhutanese people have received advanced degrees in natural resources management, all from the Yale School of Forestry and Environmental Studies, and all five members of the Bhutan Trust Fund are Bhutanese. Bhutan's national park system has been redesigned, on the basis of surveys done by the Bhutanese themselves, to better represent the country's most important habitats. The parks are now connected by biologically appropriate corridors—announced by Queen Ashi Dorji Wangmo Wangchuck as a "gift to the earth" during WWF's Living Planet Campaign. Recently, Bhutan signed the World Heritage Convention, designed to protect outstanding sites, both natural and cultural, around the world as part of the heritage of all humanity. Some years earlier, Bhutan had also cooperated with India to cancel a hydroelectric project that threatened the Manas River valley in India, a World Heritage site.

WWF has had an office in Thimphu for several years, which was run for a time, along with the office in Kathmandu, by Mingma Norbu Sherpa. Both offices report to him.

Thailand: WWF Initiatives

I also made several trips to Thailand in the mid-1980s on behalf of WWF-US, after Bruce Bunting made the necessary initial contacts. WWF-US developed a close working relationship with Wildlife Fund Thailand and its dedicated director, Pisit Na Patalung. The latter had been IBM's representative in Thailand but had become increasingly involved in conservation issues and now enjoyed the patronage of Queen Sirikit, a fact that guaranteed his organization considerable stature in the country.

WWF helped substantially with development of the Huai Kha Khaeng–Thungyai Wildlife Sanctuaries along the border with Burma (Myanmar) in Uthai Thani Province. These two reserves covered an area of about some 1.2 million acres and represented "the largest single piece of relatively untouched forest in Thailand," according to an interview I gave at the time.[8] I also announced WWF's financial support for a two-year, $300,000 ecological survey of the area. Two days before, I had presented the forestry department with nine sets of radio transceivers, valued at $20,000, to help fight poachers. We also supported a community development project in partnership with Mechai Viravaidya on the border of Khao Yai National Park.

Mechai was, and is, a remarkable individual. A connection of the royal family and a communications expert, he had become convinced that Thailand urgently needed to reduce its population growth rate and he led a one-man crusade in that cause. He publicized the use of contraceptives, particularly condoms, and succeeded in bringing the whole subject "out of the closet" in the country. Over time, there was a dramatic decline in Thailand's birthrate and I firmly believe that Mechai had a good deal to do with that result.

There is a story involving Mechai that was first told to me by Charlie Whitehouse,* the U.S. ambassador to Thailand in the late 1970s. When Charlie first arrived in Thailand, Mechai invited him for an interview on a weekly television program that he hosted. When Charlie appeared at the studio at the appointed hour, Mechai handed him a T-shirt and asked him to put it on in the interest of informality. Being a good guest, Charlie took off his jacket and slipped on the T-shirt. An hour later, when the program ended, Charlie said to Mechai, "By the way, what does this Thai writing on the front of the T-shirt say?" "Oh, that," said Mechai. "It says, 'I have had a vasectomy!'" Mechai has recently been reported in the press as having opened restaurants in Bangkok and in Bucharest, Romania, called Cabbages and Condoms.[9]

On my last visit to Thailand, in late 1986, I was accompanied by Aileen and our good friends Constantine (Connie) and Anne Sidamon-Eristoff.†

---

*Charles S. Whitehouse had a distinguished career in the Foreign Service, including ambassadorships in Thailand and Laos. Following retirement from the Foreign Service, he served as assistant secretary of Defense for special forces during the Ronald Reagan administration. On his retirement from government service, he became a leader in the fight to preserve the landscape of northern Virginia. He died in 2001.

†Anne Sidamon-Eristoff has been for many years a member of the board of directors of WWF-US and was previously director of The Conservation Foundation, which merged with WWF-US in 1985. She was chairman of the board of the American Museum of Natural History in New York City and retired from that position in 2001. Constantine Sidamon-Eristoff served with distinction as regional administrator of the Environmental Protection Agency (Region 2, headquartered in New York) during the George H. W. Bush administration.

We were the guests of U.S. Ambassador William Brown at the U.S. embassy residence in Bangkok. He had been my special assistant at EPA, under assignment from the State Department, to coordinate the U.S. side of the US-USSR Joint Committee on Cooperation in the Field of Environmental Protection.

Bill was highly regarded by the Thai people and made many helpful contacts for me and WWF. The culmination of these was a private audience with King Phumiphon. Bill had given us a bit of protocol instruction beforehand, including the admonition never to show the soles of our feet or shoes to the king, a near-mortal offense. When I asked Aileen recently what she recalled of the meeting, she said that she had been so preoccupied with keeping both feet planted firmly on the ground she could remember little else. Of course, I went into the audience with a considerable agenda of matters that I wanted to raise with the king, and I left with my agenda pretty much intact. Kings, like presidents, are difficult to interrupt, and King Phumiphon did most of the talking. Aileen and I were astonished when servants dropped to their knees at the doorway and remained in that position while they passed tea and sandwiches to all of us, regaining their feet only as they exited through the door.

As the audience ended, the king showed us a single black elephant tusk displayed on a stand at one side of the room. Such tusks are very rare, the result of a disease condition, I believe, and their rarity has endowed them with mystical qualities. In the next room, the royal family and other dignitaries gathered and I presented Queen Sirikit with a WWF award of honor for her conservation leadership and her support of Wildlife Fund Thailand. The ceremony and my remarks concerning the queen were nationally televised—a good note on which to end our visit. WWF still has a program office in Bangkok, but WWF-US has little direct involvement.

Philippines: Debt-for-Nature Swaps

In the fall of 1984, while attending the biannual congress of IUCN in Madrid, I took the opportunity to breakfast with Celso Roque, president of the Haribon Foundation in Manila. It was the beginning of a long and fruitful relationship.[10]

Until shortly before I met him, Roque had been under secretary of the Philippines' Department of the Interior and of Natural Resources. He had also been head of what would have corresponded to the Council on Environmental Quality in the United States. The Philippine version proved relatively powerless, according to Roque, and he had left government service after an argument with President Ferdinand Marcos. Since then, he had joined the Haribon Foundation, a nonprofit nongovernmental organization (NGO) dedicated primarily to the interests of bird-watchers. Roque himself was not a bird-watcher, but he was determined to broaden the scope of the organization and enlarge its membership.

WWF's involvement in the Philippines went back to the organization's earliest days, when Charles Lindbergh, then a WWF-US director, had persuaded our board to support protection of the rare and endangered monkey-eating eagle. Since then, WWF had had little involvement in the Philippines, a situation I wished to change.

Roque believed that a major need was to put the Philippine national park system on a firmer footing. At that time, he said, there were sixty-eight national parks, but many of them existed largely on paper. They had been established not by statute but by presidential decree (or, earlier, by order of the U.S. governor-general). Of course, what can be created by decree can also be undone by decree, and there had been a constant whittling away of these areas for hotel sites, for logging, and for other purposes. There were apparently few, if any, trained park staff members, and thus the parks that did exist were hardly managed at all.

I sent the WWF staff in Washington a memo on my meeting with Roque, which closed with, "I must admit to an interest in building a linkage there and in getting a modest foot in the door."[11]

The "modest foot" became quite a major presence, but from the beginning our efforts were directed toward building the capacity of the Filipinos to manage their own environmental affairs. In this, I think WWF was very successful. We opened a small office in Manila, staffed almost entirely by Filipinos. Then, in 1987, Bruce Bunting engineered a small debt-for-nature swap, which was expanded over time and which ensured a permanent source of funding for environmental efforts on the islands.

The idea of debt-for-nature swaps had first been put forward by Tom Lovejoy, then vice president for science of WWF-US, in a *New York Times* op-ed piece in 1984.[12] The concept was relatively simple: take advantage of the debt crisis among many of the world's poorer nations by purchasing their dollar-denominated debt at the current market price (usually a heavily discounted debt—for example, 50 cents on the dollar); canceling the face amount of that debt; and then transferring funds equal to the face amount of the debt (or a negotiated percentage of that amount) in local currency to a nongovernmental conservation organization there (either preexisting or created for the purpose) as an endowment. Of course, the actual execution of each swap was usually a complicated matter.*

WWF's involvement in the largest commercial debt-for-nature swap to date illustrates the leverage capacity of such deals when they are structured successfully. In a series of four swaps involving the Philippine government, USAID, the Bank of Tokyo, the John D. and Catherine T. MacArthur Foundation, and WWF, $30.1 million (face value) of debt was purchased for $18.6 million, resulting in $27.2 million for conservation. Most of the proceeds from the swap were used to endow the newly created Foundation for the Philippine Environment (FPE), and today the foundation has an endowment of about $22 million.[13] For the first two years of FPE's existence, I served as a member of the board and in each of those years I attended at least one meeting in Manila.

The pioneering initiatives of WWF with respect to both debt-for-nature swaps and conservation trust funds, going back about fifteen years as of this writing, have generated a considerable number of these and related financing mechanisms worldwide. These initiatives have raised more than $1 billion over the past ten years, and in many of them WWF has been the initiator.[14]

Our office in Manila ultimately evolved into a full-fledged WWF national organization, which has been quite successful in generating funding from Philippine sources. Today, WWF-Philippines is an active and effective member of the WWF family.

During my visits to the Philippines, I met with the NGO community and government officials concerned with environmental matters; developed contacts with the Asian Development Bank and also with private banks in Manila, such as J.P. Morgan; met with our own diplomatic and development assistance missions; and visited projects in the field. Aileen

---

*What happened might go something like this: say Philippine $1,000 (U.S.) bonds were selling at $500 (U.S. dollars). We would buy them at that price and then contribute them to the Central Bank of the Philippines; the bank would then cancel the bonds and give the *face value* in *Philippine currency* to the local environmental group. The bank would thereby get rid of its debt and it would not have to use scarce U.S. dollars to do so.

and I met with President Corazon Aquino, who I found to be most cordial and responsive until I mentioned how important it was for her government to promote family planning to help curb the burgeoning population of the Philippines.

When the United States closed its military bases in the Philippines in the 1990s, the U.S. Navy gave up its base at Subic Bay, north of Manila. Frank Wisner, who had been U.S. ambassador to the Philippines and then deputy secretary of defense, came to see me to urge WWF's involvement in protecting Subic Bay, which was being developed as a large duty-free port. The area includes a large bay surrounded by extensive forests, including the last major growth of lowland diptocarp in the Philippines. I visited the area and met with the people involved in the port development and WWF made the project a major priority. To this day, the forests are largely protected.

THE FOREGOING covers the principal areas in Asia of my own direct involvement in program development as head of WWF-US. Later came other opportunities to visit Asian countries, such as Papua New Guinea, where WWF-US has had major projects, and Vietnam, where WWF maintained a program office in Hanoi. In 1998, in Ho Chi Minh City (formerly Saigon), I keynoted a conference cosponsored by WWF and the United Nations and designed to highlight the importance for businesses investing in Vietnam to take environmental factors into account in their planning and operations. Everywhere I have been, the need and opportunity for positive engagement by those of us from the developed countries was manifest.

Overall, WWF now has eight program offices in Asia and the Pacific region: in China, Tibet (reporting to the Beijing office), Nepal, Bhutan, Thailand, Cambodia, Vietnam and Laos, and the South Pacific (headquartered at Suva, in Fiji). In addition, there are eight WWF national organizations in the same area: in Pakistan, India, Malaysia, Japan, the Philippines, Indonesia, Australia, and New Zealand. While some of these centers are, of course, more effective than others, the WWF network has a remarkable scope and outreach in the conservation field in Asia and the South Pacific.

Chapter 16

Education and Nature:
A Global Vision

I N THE PRECEDING chapter, I described a few of WWF's expanding
programs in Asia, with emphasis on those areas where I had a personal hand in program development. Of course, WWF-US has been
active on other continents as well. In Latin America and the Caribbean, WWF-US has spearheaded the program of the WWF international network from the beginning, and I visited those areas on numerous
occasions to promote conservation and WWF involvement. As might be
expected, since Africa played such a formative role in my own development as a conservationist, I seldom missed an opportunity to promote
WWF-US involvement there as well. Three extensive visits to Namibia
and the contacts made in the course of them helped pave the way for a
long-term program under contract with the U.S. Agency for International
Development (USAID) that fostered community involvement in conservation. In addition, we undertook a number of projects in East Africa and
central Africa as well as Madagascar.

However, a simple listing of program developments around the world
not only would be tedious to read but also would risk missing the point of
the extraordinary evolution of the WWF program over the years. At the
outset, most projects were defined in terms of saving particular species —
rhinos, marine turtles, mountain gorillas, red colobus monkeys, whales,
peregrine falcons, Siberian cranes, and so forth. While conservation projects of that sort still continue, particularly in the face of an urgent threat,
such as to the few remaining Javan rhinos, the emphasis at WWF soon

evolved into protection of habitats such as wetlands, coral reefs, and tropical forests. The health and survival of a species is usually tied to the health of the particular habitat or ecosystem in relation to which it has evolved. Increased emphasis on habitats necessarily led to our addressing the needs and activities of indigenous peoples in these areas, which in turn led to a major emphasis on community-based conservation. The CAMPFIRE[1] project in Zimbabwe, our USAID-supported efforts in Namibia, the Annapurna Conservation Area Project in Nepal, our work with the Kuna Indians of Panama, and with Sherpa villagers in Nepal and Bhutan — these are but a few examples of what is really a programwide emphasis. Closely related to WWF's focus on the role of communities in the management of natural resources is its Education for Nature program (EFN), designed to provide members of those communities with the capability to manage their own natural resources (and described in detail later in this chapter).

From Species to Ecoregion

As habitat became more and more a focus of WWF's conservation efforts, the concept constantly broadened to embrace whole ecosystems. The simple truth is that, in most cases, the biological realities force one to look beyond a specific site. Effective action to remedy a particular problem at a particular location on the reef that lies off the coast of Belize in the Caribbean, for example, will probably require consideration of the conditions and pressures, both natural and man-made, that occur throughout the nearly 450-mile length of the Mesoamerican Barrier Reef of which it is a part, a barrier reef second in extent only to the Great Barrier Reef of Australia. Associated with the reef are extensive areas of relatively pristine coastal wetlands, lagoons, sea grass beds, and mangrove forests, which provide critical habitat for threatened species such as sea turtles and manatees. Other, ecosystem-level pressures undermining the health of the reef include coastal development, tourism, intensified land use for agriculture (resulting in siltation from soil erosion, pollution from herbicides and fertilizers, and sedimentation from deforestation), and commercial and recreational overfishing. Conservation is indeed a highly complex process today, involving consideration of many environmental factors.

In the mid-1990s, David Olson, then director of WWF's conservation science program, and Eric Dinerstein, WWF's chief scientist, collaborated to develop an ecoregional approach to conservation. They defined an ecoregion as "a relatively large unit of land or water containing a characteristic set of natural communities that share a large majority of their species, dynamics, and environmental conditions. Ecoregions function effectively as conservation units at regional scales because they encompass similar biological communities and because their boundaries roughly coincide with the area over which key ecological processes most strongly interact."[2]

While the ecoregional approach is grounded in science, the logic behind this concept is undeniable even to a nonscientist. The ecoregion concept was not in itself exactly revolutionary, but no one before Olson and Dinerstein had attempted to analyze the entire earth's surface in ecoregional terms and had then made use of such analysis as a strategic basis for thinking about conservation on a planetary scale.

In their seminal article on the concept, Olson and Dinerstein agreed with the emphasis conservationists had placed on tropical moist forests because these contain about 50 percent of all the species, plant and animal, on the earth. At the same time, they argued, a truly comprehensive strategy for conserving global biological diversity must seek to save the other 50 percent of species and the distinctive ecosystems that support them. Tropical dry forests, tundra, temperate grasslands, lakes, polar seas, and mangroves, they point out, all contain unique expressions of biological diversity with characteristic species, biological communities, and distinctive ecological and evolutionary phenomena.[3] Indeed, some of these habitat types are more threatened than are the tropical moist forests and require our immediate action to protect them.

In order to better incorporate these distinctive ecosystems into conservation strategies, Dinerstein and Olson led an analysis of ecoregions representing the earth's nineteen terrestrial, freshwater, and marine biomes (large areas with similar climate and vegetation types and characteristic species). They identified 238 ecoregions — which we at WWF came to call the Global 200 — as priority targets for conservation action, on the basis of a comparative analysis of species richness, species endemism (species found nowhere else), unusual ecological or evolutionary phenomena, and global rarity of major biomes and habitat types, among other factors.

With that said, it is necessary to recognize that, with finite resources and time, we cannot save everything. Conservation groups, as well as governments and donors, must be strategic and earmark the greatest amount of resources for those areas richest in biological diversity while at the same time ensuring that all ecosystems and habitat types are at least *represented* within regional conservation strategies.*

Although conservation action is usually carried out at the national level, work such as Dinerstein and Olson's brings home the fact that patterns of biological diversity and ecological processes, such as migration, do not conform to political boundaries. Strategic conservation planning and the setting of priorities thus need to be done instead at the ecoregional level.

Moreover, effective conservation action at the ecoregional level requires much more than the application of conservation biology. The ecoregional scale forces us to take into account such factors as demographics, land-use patterns, community development, natural resource use, economic activity, and development pressures. Effective conservation thus requires a variety of social science skills as well as biological skills—a combination that represents one of WWF's greatest strengths. To recognize and deal effectively with the inherent complexity of conservation problems requires far more sophistication than seen in the relatively simplistic approaches that were the norm when WWF was in its early days.

While the WWF network operates in many other areas, there are, as I write this, twenty-three ecoregions in which WWF-US has assumed a conservation leadership responsibility under its overall Endangered Spaces Program, led by the program's vice president, Bill Eichbaum.[4] That number will probably contract somewhat, given the tightness of funding in the current economic climate.

A good example of successful application of the ecoregional approach, as Jim Leape has pointed out to me, is work in the Western Congo Basin Moist Forests.[†] This vast expanse of tropical wilderness is second in size only to the Amazon basin forest. "To protect that forest," said Jim, "we had to pull together all the six governments involved. To do it piecemeal

---

*Dinerstein has pointed out to me that earlier efforts to identify global conservation priorities, such as the hotspots, and the megadiversity country approaches largely overlook marine and freshwater diversity and distinctive ecological or evolutionary phenomena.

[†]James P. Leape was a member of the WWF-US staff from 1989 to 2001 and was executive vice president for program when he left to join the David and Lucile Packard Foundation as director of the foundation's conservation and science program.

just wouldn't work. We needed a shared vision." In December 2000, representatives of those six central African nations met under WWF auspices at Yaoundé, in Cameroon, and committed their governments to protecting more than 10 percent of the forest, using WWF's biological vision as a blueprint.

That same meeting also produced a groundbreaking agreement by the governments of Cameroon, the Republic of the Congo, and the Central African Republic to manage jointly the newly created Sangha River Tri-National Protected Area, as the result of an ongoing WWF project led by Richard Carroll. The three nations agreed to work together to manage forests, control logging, fight poaching, and develop tourism in an area covering more than 6.9 million acres—roughly the size of Vermont. These are enormously ambitious undertakings, and, if they are to be successful over the long term, continuous monitoring of performance under the agreements will be essential. Cameroon has already canceled timber concessions in the areas under its control.

Conservation needs tend to be enormously complex. In the Western Congo Basin Moist Forests ecoregion (the Republic of the Congo, Cameroon, the Central African Republic, the Democratic Republic of the Congo, Equatorial Guinea, and Gabon) the highest-priority conservation problem today is the killing of animals in the forests—anything from rodents and small antelopes to chimpanzees—to provide "bushmeat." So long as this poaching was done for local subsistence, its adverse effects were manageable. However, in many areas it has now become a large, commercialized operation supplying markets in major urban areas distant from the forests. As such, it poses a continuous, growing, and potentially ruinous threat to the area's wildlife.

Two developments have helped accelerate this threat. The first is logging, which opens roads in what was once relatively inaccessible forest. WWF is working with the several governments on improving forest concession rules and also offering options for sustainable forest management, including independent monitoring and certification of that management.

The second development is the result of even more complicated factors and involves the heavily subsidized fishing trawlers from Europe, particularly Spain, that suck the coastal lagoons clean of fish, thereby destroying the livelihood of whole coastal communities that historically have relied on fishing. Many of these people have now turned inland to illegal hunting for bushmeat as an alternative. Exacerbating the problem is the fact that European Union countries provide development aid to this area that is sometimes conditioned on access to fisheries for the European countries' boats. This sort of deal—using aid as bargaining leverage—is not uncommon. Japan, for example, was reported to have conditioned aid to Gabon on the latter's favorable vote within the International Whaling Commission.

WWF has been actively engaged in trying to improve fishery prospects for the Gulf of Guinea countries to help relieve the pressure to hunt for bushmeat. In Gabon, for example, WWF is providing funds for the Gamba Protected Area Complex to develop a fisheries cooperative, which will enable local people to support sustainable fishing in the lagoons, and a marketing system for their catch.* WWF's president, Kathryn Fuller, has said of these issues, "In today's world, policy and advocacy efforts with trade organizations in Brussels and Geneva to reduce trade-distorting and environmentally damaging fish subsidies are a conservation tool that connects to the fate of chimpanzees in the Congo."[5]

Globalization of the marketplace is with us, like it or not, and at times with somewhat bizarre consequences. For instance, Richard Carroll, African program director at WWF-US, has described to me the effect of such markets on one of the world's highest-priority conservation areas, the "spiny forest" of Madagascar, with its high degree of endemic species—those not found anywhere else. The European Union—in response to pressure from environmentalists—has required the use of biodegradable floor coverings and packaging materials. Sisal is the product of choice, and the spiny forest region of Madagascar has turned out to be the site of choice for growing it. So, to borrow a bit of anti-environment rhetoric, one could say that the ecologically unique spiny forest of Madagascar is being destroyed so that European "greenies" can feel good about their floor matting and packaging.

To make matters worse for the spiny forest, its soils and climate turn out to be ideal for corn cultivation. Since Madagascans are hungry for corn, one might understand conversion of a portion of the spiny forest for corn production to meet local food needs. But that is not what is happening. The corn being grown in the spiny forest is instead going to the neighboring French island of Réunion—where it is being fed to ducks in order to produce duck liver pâté, in demand by gourmets the world over.

*Scott Burns is director of WWF's Endangered Seas Campaign, including these fishery initiatives.

The effects of the global marketplace on the natural world can also be seen to the east across the Indian Ocean, on the island of Sumatra. There WWF is actively trying to protect the remaining Tesso Nilo lowland forest, the earth's richest forest in vascular plants and also home to seriously threatened elephants, tigers, and orangutans. Commercial exploitation has already wiped out wide areas of Sumatran forest and converted them to fast-growing tree and oil palm plantations. Time is running out for saving the remainder of the Tesso trees.

An Indonesian company, APRIL, logs and pulps the forest. A Finnish company, the UPM-Kymmene Corporation, turns it into paper in China. America's International Paper Company sells that paper to the Hewlett-Packard Company, which in turn sells it to consumers across the United States for home and office printing. Along the way, the governments of Germany, the United States, Austria, and Japan provide export credit to their machine manufacturers to install pulping and papermaking machinery in the various mills that handle the Tesso tree. As Kathryn Fuller has commented,[6] a Tesso tree travels widely.

Protecting Tesso Nilo will require not only stepping up antipoaching patrols and granting the area park status but also identifying the chain of investors, creditors, financial advisors, processors, merchants, and customers who handle the tree. It means engaging them one by one, telling the story of Tesso Nilo, and asking them to use their influence with Indonesian business partners and companies to help protect the remaining forest and to operate in the most environmentally sensitive way possible.

Thus, just as WWF's strategic emphasis in dealing with conservation problems around the world has grown and matured to the ecoregional approach, so, too — particularly with ever-increasing globalization — have those problems grown in complexity and scope. To be able to analyze and deal effectively with those problems requires organizations with broad disciplinary capabilities such as WWF possesses and, wherever possible, partnerships among environmental organizations. The job is far too great for any one of us. It also requires local participation and something in which I have remained interested throughout my environmental career, even after retirement from WWF — conservation education throughout the developing world.

Education for Nature

I retired as chairman of WWF-US in 1994, having completed the nine-year term permitted under our bylaws. Roger Sant was elected chairman to succeed me and also took my place on the WWF-International board. Roger is a longtime friend, going back to our days together in the Ford administration, when he was assistant administrator of the Federal Energy Administration (forerunner of the Department of Energy). In my battles within the administration when energy and environmental goals often seemed to be at loggerheads, Roger was a sympathetic and helpful ally.[7]

At the retirement dinner held in my honor, Kathryn Fuller announced the establishment of the Russell E. Train Education for Nature program (EFN) to provide scholarships, fellowships, and institutional grants for environmental education around the world, particularly in those developing countries where most of WWF's programs are concentrated. The initial target for the fund was $10 million, of which more than $6 million had already been raised.

It was the WWF staff, particularly Diane Wood, then WWF-US vice president for the Latin America and Caribbean program, who came up with the idea of an environmental education fund as an appropriate way to honor me, and they really hit the nail on the head. As I have set out earlier, my first major conservation involvement was the founding of the African Wildlife Leadership Foundation, and at that time my colleagues and I made our highest priority the training of Africans to manage their own wildlife resources. I firmly believe that conservation efforts everywhere will succeed over the long term only if local people have the commitment and technical training to carry out the job. The effectiveness of community-based conservation, as pioneered by WWF, receives widespread acceptance today.[8]

The first grants under the program were made in 1995, and as of June 2003 EFN had provided support for nearly 350 individuals in forty countries. Forty-one percent of EFN grantees have been women, whose motivation, hard work, and intellectual capacity have proven truly outstanding.

In addition to direct aid to individuals, EFN has supported training activities that have benefited hundreds of people through institutional grants to forty-four conservation nongovernmental organizations (NGOs), wildlife colleges, and other training organizations. EFN grants have been remarkably evenly distributed geographically among Africa,

Asia, and Latin America. From its inception, EFN has awarded approximately $4 million to aspiring leaders and forward-thinking institutions in thirty-four countries. One of the most heartening facts about this overall WWF program is that practically all grantees who received EFN support for studies outside their home countries have, on completion of their studies, returned home to work. The WWF experience in this regard is quite unusual.

EFN's flagship initiative is the Russell E. Train Scholarship and Fellowship Program. This program supports current and future leaders in conservation for as long as two years of academic study anywhere in the world and at any level of study, from a two-year diploma course to doctoral research. Under its program director, Shaun Martin, EFN has also developed several new initiatives. For example, the Russell E. Train Conservation Leadership Awards recognize and reward EFN's top graduate fellows with a networking visit to the United States and $3,000 for professional development on completion of their academic programs. The first cohort of Conservation Leaders visited Washington, D.C., and New York City in January 2002 and collectively met with more than fifty individuals at fourteen conservation organizations, government agencies, foundations, and corporations. During the visit, the Conservation Leaders not only learned from their peers in the United States but also had many opportunities to educate Americans about conservation issues in their home countries.

The work of one of the 2002 Conservation Leaders, Nicole Auil from Belize, helps illustrate the nature of the program. Prior to beginning her master's degree program, Nicole served as a researcher at the Coastal Zone Management Institute. She was, and remains, Belize's only researcher studying countrywide manatee issues. In 1998, at the age of twenty-four, Nicole helped establish the Belize Marine Mammal Stranding Network, a nonprofit organization that rescues stranded manatees and nurses them back to health. In that same year, she authored the Belize Manatee Recovery Plan under the UNDP/GEF Coastal Zone Management Project. With her Train Fellowship, Nicole pursued a master's degree in wildlife management at Texas A&M University. And in May 2002 Nicole served as a consultant at a nature reserve in Niger. Manatees are suspected to be present in the river system there and she is helping that reserve establish an ecotourism program based on the model used in Belize.

Instead of long-term academic training, sometimes all that is needed is a short workshop or seminar to update and upgrade the knowledge and skills of professional conservationists. In that regard, another new EFN initiative is the Russell E. Train Professional Development program, which provides support to mid-career professionals seeking short-term, nondegree training in disciplines important to conservation as well as to institutions that provide such training. The program has proven extremely popular and cost-effective: with just $150,000, in its first year more than one hundred individuals received training under this program. In June 2001, for example, three Indonesian environmental educators attended a two-week course on learning children's perceptions and attitudes about the environment, particularly as these are revealed through children's drawings. The course, conducted by Laura Barazza at the Institute of Ecology at the National Autonomous University of Mexico (UNAM), provided participants with new ways of planning and evaluating educational activities in their work with children on sea turtles back home, and it also provided a forum for rich cross-cultural interaction between the Indonesian EFN grantees and their Mexican colleagues. EFN has also established an alumni program that provides former Train Scholars and Fellows with free WWF publications and ongoing financial support for their professional development and research.

EFN's commitment to institutional capacity building is illustrated by a new five-year project to develop a course on the issue of bushmeat, considered by many to be the most significant threat to conservation of wildlife and to biological diversity in Africa today, especially in central and West Africa. The growing illegal trade in bushmeat particularly threatens the mammals of central African forests, yet few in the region are trained to tackle this huge problem. To address the issue head-on, EFN developed a partnership with the Bushmeat Crisis Task Force to create a multidisciplinary course on the bushmeat crisis to be taught to francophone Africans at the École de Faune de Garoua in Cameroon. With the generous support of James R. and Barbara R. Palmer, EFN will invest $300,000 over a five-year period not only to develop a curriculum for this course but also to train faculty, produce instructional materials, and provide scholarships to enable park rangers and wardens, civil servants, and NGO leaders to attend the program.

The individuals EFN has supported since 1995 are a varied group, and I will mention a few to give some idea of their range of interests and work.

In Colombia, Zoraida Calle discovered as a Train Fellow how local rural communities can play a key role in forest restoration if given the chance to participate in the research and implementation phases of a project. Today, she works at a small organization dedicated to research and promotion of sustainable agriculture in Colombia, training rural youth to participate as coresearchers in various scientific studies. Dechen Tsering, who was a Train Fellow in 1997, is now chief of planning for the National Environmental Council of Bhutan. Lilian Munyyar Nfor of Cameroon is now a legal officer for her country's Ministry of Environment and Forestry, helping draft Cameroon's biological diversity legislation. Jaqueline Maximillian from Tanzania became the first female faculty member at Sokoine University of Agriculture's School of Forestry and Nature Conservation. Shakil Visram, a Train Fellow and Conservation Leader from Kenya, will soon return to Kenya to become one of his country's handful of coral reef biologists. The coral reefs are a vital resource, given the richness of the East African marine ecoregion and the threats to its coral reef system.

The future of world conservation is in the hands of these exemplary individuals and institutions and others like them. The need for capacity building for conservation in the developing world is immense. Without education and training, the full potential of promising leaders will never be achieved and the earth will suffer as a consequence. With programs such as EFN, the conservation community is beginning to make a difference to ensure that dedicated people have the ability to manage the resources of their own countries.

Whenever I get discouraged about the world we live in, some news from EFN gives me fresh hope for the future. After three new EFN students from around the world arrived in late August 2002 at the Yale School of Forestry and Environmental Studies, an e-mail message from the director of admissions to Shaun Martin described them as "born leaders. Reports from their classmates and our staff are unanimously outstanding. Don't know what magic you use but EFN certainly knows how to select the best!"[9] At about the same time, I picked up *Time* magazine's special environmental issue and found EFN participants highlighted as environmental heroes for their work in saving and restoring parts of the fast-disappearing Atlantic coastal forest of Brazil.[10]

As is obvious from these remarks, I have tremendous personal enthusiasm for EFN. It complements WWF's global conservation vision and

312 POLITICS, POLLUTION, AND PANDAS

my own long-standing personal interest. Of course, I have no management role in the program, but I attend as many meetings and meet as many of the grantees as I can. All net royalties that I receive from the sale of this book will go to the World Wildlife Fund, earmarked for EFN.*

*Any reader desiring to make a special tax-deductible contribution for this purpose may write a check payable to the World Wildlife Fund, specifying that it is for EFN, and mail it to WWF, 1250 24th Street, NW, Washington, DC 20037. All such contributors will receive periodic reports on the progress of EFN.

Chapter 17

The Eleventh Commandment

I N THE EARLY years of the 1990s, I played a role not only in WWF's overseas projects but also on a number of domestic fronts. Three such activities—a conference on religion and ecology, my involvement with the Clean Sites, Inc. program, and my work on the National Commission on the Environment—point out the range of this work and indicate something of the sobering state of environmental affairs, at least as I saw them, at the time.

I have long felt concern about the attitude of organized religion toward the environment—not because I am a particularly religious person but because religious institutions, along with families and schools, tend to be the principal transmitters of values in most societies around the world. And I am convinced that environmental protection must become a recognized and shared value of humanity.

Religion and Ecology

In 1990, WWF-US helped sponsor a Christian conference called the North American Conference on Religion and Ecology in Washington, D.C., and I addressed the participants at their closing dinner. I expressed puzzlement over what had seemed to me to be organized religion's almost total obliviousness to environmental issues. Here we had one of the most fundamental concerns to agitate human society within living memory— certainly in North America and Europe and increasingly around the globe. Here we had issues that went to the heart of the human condition, the quality of human life, even humanity's ultimate survival. Here we had problems that could be said to threaten the very integrity of Creation. "And yet," I said, "the churches and other institutions of organized religion have largely ignored the whole subject."[1] It was perhaps a bit of an overstatement, but not far off the mark.

After briefly outlining the world population problem as I saw it at the time, I went on to point out that Pope John Paul II was reported to have declared the previous week in Mexico, "If the possibility of conceiving a child is artificially eliminated in the conjugal act, couples shut themselves off from God and oppose His will."

I declared that I found it difficult to accept that it was the will of God that humanity should degrade, deface, desecrate, and ultimately perhaps destroy His Creation on the earth. "Yet," I continued, "that is the course on which we are embarked." Almost every significant threat to the environment, I pointed out, has been contributed to and compounded by human numbers. And whatever other adverse effects on the natural environment might result from the growth in sheer human numbers, such growth is necessarily accompanied by a reduction in space for other species, a reduction of opportunity for other forms of life. "Natural ecosystems," I said, "do not have the capacity to absorb infinite numbers of species."[2]

I did not suggest that the Christian church abandon its concern for humanity; instead, I suggested it give at least equal time to the rest of God's Creation—and do so not as a concern that is separate and apart but in recognition that the welfare of any part, including the human, is inseparable from the welfare of the whole.

I urged that the church assume major responsibility for teaching that we humans, individually and collectively, are part of the living community of the earth that nurtures and sustains us; that humanity as well as all life depends for its very being on the healthy functioning of the natural systems of the earth; that all living things, including humans, are interdependent; that we have the duty, collectively and individually, to care for God's Creation; and that in that relationship lie all the creative possibilities for life now and in the future. Taking a deep breath, I declared that "[these] are precepts that could provide the substance for an Eleventh Commandment: Thou shalt cherish and care for the Earth and all within it."[3]

If my language was at times a bit churchy—many in my audience were churchmen and churchwomen—it does express my continuing deep personal conviction as to the essential interrelationship of humanity and nature. The reaction of my audience was very positive, and I received at least one standing ovation—during my remarks on the human population issue. Moreover, I am glad to report that in the ensuing years there has been a definite increase in the attention of the church, as I know it, to environmental concerns, although there is still a long way to go.

From Religion to Superfund

If one abiding personal conviction has been the essential interrelationship of humanity and nature, another has been that, in the long run, the economy and the environment are not contending principles and there is much to be gained through fostering dialogue among various economic and environmental interests.

In May 1984, I undertook the chairmanship of Clean Sites, Inc., when the organization was founded, and I served in that capacity until 1993, when Bill Reilly took my place after he left the Environmental Protection Agency. Clean Sites was the product of discussions among members of the environmental community, industry, and government who sought a constructive dialogue and a nonadversarial approach to addressing the many problems associated with the cleanup of toxic waste dumps under the so-called Superfund legislation that was enacted in 1980. The discussions were held with the active encouragement of Bill Ruckelshaus and Lee Thomas while they were EPA administrators and were hosted by Reilly, who was then president of The Conservation Foundation. The whole effort was largely initiated by the Chemical Manufacturers Association, the members of which found themselves responsible for much of the cleanup effort under Superfund. Initial funding came mostly from members of the chemical industry.

The Clean Sites board was a remarkable group that reflected vividly the organization's commitment to bringing the different communities of interest together.[4] The organization was fortunate in having three outstanding presidents—Chuck Powers, Tom Grumbly, and Toby Clark—during the fourteen years of its existence.

Unfortunately, the effort to get the environmental community, industry, and government to work together to speed up substantially the cleanup process turned out to be less successful than hoped. There were some successes, but, however much the leaders of the organizations might see the benefits of cooperation, there were strong incentives, particularly at the staff level, not to cooperate.

Many businesses, disquieted by the potentially substantial cleanup costs, concluded that lawyers were cheaper than contractors. Not only might aggressive legal action reduce their ultimate financial responsibility, but also simply delaying the required expenditures had financial benefits. Significant growth in the number of Superfund lawyers reinforced these tendencies.

Some environmental organizations found that the public's concern about hazardous waste sites was a particularly effective issue in attracting new members and increased financial support. Some also appeared to consider the Superfund program as a way of punishing businesses for what they saw as the businesses' environmental transgressions.

On its part, government also had incentives not to cooperate. It could not give up the responsibilities it had been assigned under the law and the pace at which it carried out these responsibilities was often a major cause of the delay in cleaning up sites. And government had a financial interest in maintaining the program's high profile — a significant portion of EPA's budget came from the Superfund program.

Clean Sites was unable to moderate significantly these strong contrary incentives and it had no power to compel mediation. As a result, cleanups often continued to take decades to complete and to be conducted under conditions of substantial hostility and recrimination.

The effort to generate revenues was more successful. Clean Sites did develop some new and valuable services based on the principles of dispute resolution. One such service involved mediation efforts to determine the appropriate allocation of costs among the various companies responsible for paying for a cleanup. This was substantially more efficient than the previous practice of companies suing one another in order to have a judge determine the allocation. Another service provided neutral technical experts to oversee the cleanup efforts. In addition to ensuring that cleanups were conducted efficiently and according to plan, these experts were often able to soothe relations among the affected communities, the government agencies, and the companies conducting the cleanup.

Both of these services were sufficiently successful, as Toby Clark[5] has pointed out to me, that many commercial enterprises began offering them as well. This was exactly the model envisaged when Clean Sites was established. However, it also demonstrated a fallacy in the business plan.

Once the commercial sector began offering the services Clean Sites had developed, Clean Sites was under pressure to discontinue those services because it is considered inappropriate for a nonprofit organization to compete with for-profit companies. Thus, as soon as a service showed signs of being profitable, Clean Sites was expected to stop providing it, and this made it difficult for the organization to support itself from its own revenues.

Clean Sites' contribution in the public policy arena was unusual because it was based on two of the organization's unique characteristics — its hands-on experience in attempting to improve the cleanup program and its ability to bring together high-level representatives from the environmental, business, and regulatory communities to discuss public policy issues. Both of these characteristics made it a sought-after commentator on administrative and congressional initiatives to improve the program. For instance, Congress asked Clean Sites to testify at least half a dozen times when it was reauthorizing and amending the Superfund program during 1994 and 1995.

Ultimately, however, Congress did not enact the proposed legislation, and the program fell into a legislative limbo. Facing congressional deadlock and intense competition from commercial organizations for steadily declining work, the board of directors decided in 1998 that Clean Sites had accomplished as many of its original goals as it was likely to accomplish, and, consistent with the original intent, should be closed down.

Clean Sites was a bold, ambitious, and imaginative undertaking, and its history demonstrated both the strengths and weaknesses of taking such an approach to address public policy issues.

A National Commission on the Environment

In 1991, WWF sponsored the National Commission on the Environment to review U.S. environmental policy as it currently stood and develop strategies for addressing the environmental challenges of the future. I had suggested to President Ford that he create a group of this kind and may also have mentioned the idea to George H. W. Bush. In any event, I was apt to say that, since I had made the suggestion to several presidents and none of them had taken me up on it, I had decided to do it on my own.

The membership of the commission represented a broad spectrum of the interests involved in environmental issues — industry, science, economics, international finance, religion, environmental organizations (both national and grassroots), public health, and government. Four of the five former EPA administrators (excluding only Anne Gorsuch) were members, as was Gus Speth, former chairman of CEQ. No one employed at the time by the government was included. The administrator of EPA, Bill Reilly, was very supportive of our endeavor and addressed our opening meeting. Among the business leaders were Paul O'Neill, then chairman and chief executive officer of Alcoa (and, more recently, George W. Bush's first secretary of the Department of the Treasury), and A. W. "Tom" Clausen, former president of the World Bank and retired chairman and chief executive of the BankAmerica Corporation.[6]

The commission, which I chaired, met eight times, once in San Francisco, once in Racine, Wisconsin, and six times in Washington, D.C. Although WWF sponsored the commission, it studiously avoided trying to influence our recommendations. The commission's report was released in December 1992, though it was not published in book form until early the following year.[7]

The report could have been released in the early fall of 1992, in time to have played a part in the Bush-Clinton presidential election. Several members of the commission urged just that course, but I insisted on postponing the release until after the election. I believed the report would have greater credibility with the incoming administration, whoever won the presidency, if it had not been a political issue during the campaign. (Earlier, when asked to co-chair an environmental committee for Bush in the campaign, I had declined out of concern that my role as chairman of our bipartisan commission would thereby have been compromised.) As it turned out, the environmental issue played little or no role in the campaign and our later efforts to present the report to both President Bill Clinton and Vice President Al Gore were to no avail. Clinton had largely delegated environmental issues to Gore, and my sense is that the latter had little interest in independent, outside initiatives such as our report represented.

The natural processes that support life on the earth were increasingly at risk, we declared in the report, and by choosing to act or not to act to confront this risk, the nation would be choosing between two very different futures. If America continued down its current path, primarily reacting to environmental problems and trying to correct them, the quality of

our environment would continue to deteriorate, and eventually our economy would decline as well. If, however, our country pioneered new technologies, shifted to proactive environmental policies, made bold economic changes in the direction of sustainable development, and embraced
an ethic of environmentally responsible behavior, the future would be far
more likely to bring a higher quality of life, a healthier environment, and
a more vibrant economy for all Americans.

A central tenet of the report was that economic and environmental
well-being were mutually reinforcing goals that needed to be pursued
simultaneously if either was to be achieved. Such a premise reflects my
own long-standing belief. Economic growth cannot be sustained over the
long term if it continues to undermine the healthy functioning of the natural systems of the earth. By the same token, only healthy economies can
generate the resources necessary for investments in environmental protection. Poverty is the enemy of the environment. Environmental protection is not possible where poverty is pervasive and the quality of life is
degraded. For this reason, one of the principal objectives of environmental policy must be to ensure a decent standard of living for all.

We saw the choice between a deteriorating environment and sustainable development as one our nation shared with the rest of the world. It
was a choice that had to be addressed through international cooperation
and by U.S. commitment to action at home and leadership abroad. As the
world's single largest economy, the largest user of natural resources, the
largest producer and consumer of energy, and the largest producer of carbon dioxide pollution, the United States had a special responsibility to
exercise world leadership.

We pointed out that, over the previous twenty years, the United States
had put into place a large array of pollution control measures at every
level of government. The overall cost of environmental protection was
averaging about 2 percent of gross national product annually. As a result,
we had been in the fortunate position of not having to contend with the
blighted landscapes, polluted air and water, poisoned soils, and ravaged
public health at the acute levels that were common, for example, in central and eastern Europe.

At the same time, in a number of specific areas the United States was
losing ground: deterioration of air quality in those cities where improvements in automobile emission controls were being overwhelmed by the
sheer number of cars, by the miles driven, and by congestion; land devel-

opment that was displacing and undermining critical ecosystems, such as wetlands, and threatening rural landscapes, natural areas, and biological diversity; and depletion of the most important commercial fisheries by overfishing and pollution. Such problems would be compounded, we predicted, as economic activity and population increased in coming years. The continuing pursuit of politics as usual would almost certainly guarantee failure in achieving environmental goals.

The United Nations Conference on Environment and Development had just met, in June 1992, in Rio de Janeiro and had begun the process of establishing a new environmental agenda based on sustainable development. That concept now needed to be turned into a specific national action plan, we decided:

> There must be an end to U.S. ambivalence about the environment and a beginning of a steadfast commitment to improving the environment both nationally and internationally. *The United States must have a long-term strategy for pursuing the goal of sustainable development.*[8]

We urged that, by the close of the twentieth century, economic development and environmental protection be brought together in a new synthesis: a broad-based economic program accomplished in a manner that protects and restores the quality of the natural environment, improves the quality of life for individuals, and broadens the prospects for future generations.

Innovations made along these lines to achieve sustainable development would themselves bring major economic benefits, we agreed. The economic advantage of using materials and energy efficiently was self-evident. The most efficient way to achieve environmental progress, therefore, was to harness market forces. Here, the role of public policy was to send the right signals to the economy—"getting the prices right"—and make the marketplace work for, instead of against, environmental protection.

We had no illusion that market mechanisms alone could put the United States or the world on the road to sustainable development. There would still be a need for a strong regulatory system with strong enforcement. However, we were critical of the existing statutory and regulatory framework in the United States, which put most of its emphasis on "end-of-the-pipe" cleanup rather than prevention of pollution before the fact.

Following a new emphasis on pollution prevention, we saw an opportunity for the United States to develop a whole array of new technologies in which it could become the international leader. We saw this need (and opportunity) most acutely in the transportation and energy sectors. And there also was where our two most controversial proposals lay.

There must be a deep-seated change in the way our country produces and uses energy, we declared; no single area of activity was so closely interwoven with the environment. Were it not for the burning of fossil fuels, the problems of global warming, acid rain, and urban smog would be minor. Since the United States used in excess of one-quarter of the world's energy, it should be the leader in developing other energy sources. We urged a progressive shift away from fossil fuels as quickly as possible in both the energy and transportation sectors.

We recommended that a carbon tax be phased in to start moving the country away from carbon-rich fossil fuels. Second, we recommended a $1 increase in the federal tax on gasoline, to be phased in gradually over the ensuing five years. Even with an increase of this magnitude, the cost of gasoline in the country, in constant dollars, would be about the same as it had been in 1981.

Considerable emphasis in the report was placed on international aspects of environmental issues. Along with economic opportunities, we believed that a commitment to sustainable development could bring new political opportunities, particularly in foreign affairs:

> With the end of the Cold War and the Communist threat, the bond that held the United States and its allies together for half a century has loosened. The international community is breaking into national or (at best) regional groupings pursuing their own narrow self-interests. Prospects for sustainable development could shatter in such a divided world. We are convinced that the urgent need to put the world on the road to sustainability provides a common purpose that can and must unite the global community.[9]

It was our firm belief that the United States had a tremendous stake in effectively addressing global environmental problems. The threat of global climate change required national initiatives in the United States but could really be addressed only through a common worldwide effort. The continued destruction of forests would exacerbate global warming. The great potential for expanding trade with developing countries would not be realized unless those nations achieved sustainable development. Finally, U.S. national security interests would depend increasingly on achieving a level of international stability that could come only from sustainable development.

The report emphasized the need to curb human population growth, stressing not only the importance of supporting family planning but also the role of education and of improvement of the economic and social status of women. We saw these objectives as best pursued not only by a U.S. national effort but as part of an international community effort.

We also advocated effective land-use planning at the state and local levels based on federal criteria, much as had been twice proposed to Congress twenty years earlier by President Richard Nixon. We urged that environmental values be integrated into policy and decision making across the entire spectrum of government functions. To that end, we recommended the establishment of a Department of the Environment that would have the ability to formulate and oversee a National Environmental Strategy.

In a world increasingly without environmental borders, the commission emphasized that each individual and every nation has a fundamental ethical responsibility to respect nature and to care for the earth, protecting its life support systems, biological diversity, and beauty. It was only within such an ethical framework, we said, that the values to sustain and guide us would be found as we moved toward the goal of sustainable development. Schools, religious institutions, and the news media, as well as businesses, governments, and (perhaps above all) families, must share in the tasks of achieving this aim. We declared:

> We have a vision for the future: a vision of an America and a world in which humanity lives and prospers in harmonious, sustainable balance with the natural systems of the Earth. America has an opportunity to rise to the challenge of environmental leadership as it has to the causes of human liberty, equality, and free and open markets. The challenge starts at home.[10]

It was indeed a visionary report, but one that combined hardheaded realism with idealism. Whether or not individuals agree with each and every recommendation, I believe we succeeded in highlighting the important issues. Every member of the commission felt very real pride in our combined effort.

It is discouraging to recall how little public response there was to the issuance of the report. The *Wall Street Journal* published a brief story on our recommendation for a steep increase in the gasoline tax.[11] A press conference we held to outline the report was reasonably well attended but resulted in only modest coverage.[12] The incoming Clinton administration showed no interest. As chairman of the commission, it was my responsibility to secure reasonable press coverage and public attention. I clearly failed in that regard.

Nevertheless, in congressional testimony in 1993,[13] I was able to cite several actions then under way in Congress and the Clinton administration that would further the recommendations of the commission. Legislation to create a Department of the Environment had passed the Senate and was before the House. (It died.) A broad-based energy tax was part of the administration's economic package and had passed the House. (It died.) Congress passed a small gasoline tax increase. The secretary of Interior had instituted a national survey of biological diversity. The administration had reversed the so-called Mexico City policy of President Reagan, which precluded U.S. funding of international family planning organizations. (President George W. Bush has now reinstated the Reagan policy.) Clinton had also committed the United States to the terms of the Convention on Biological Diversity, commonly known as the Biodiversity Treaty, and to strong implementation of the United Nations Framework Convention on Climate Change, known as the Kyoto Protocol (both of which were reversed by the George W. Bush administration).

The concept of sustainable development has been quite widely accepted in the abstract. Various studies, conferences, and commissions, both domestic and international, as I have described earlier, have adopted the concept as the keystone of environmental policy. However, other than to give some currency to the concept, I am not certain that any of these initiatives have really produced any tangible results.

As I reread the report of our commission ten years after its adoption, I am struck by the fact that the issues we highlighted then are still very much with us and even more urgent today. Our call for an end to U.S. ambivalence about the environment and for a steadfast commitment to improving the environment both nationally and internationally rings more true than ever. Our insistence that U.S. *national security* increasingly depends upon sustainable development on an international scale is a lesson we surely need to take to heart in the aftermath of 9/11. There is a desperate need for leadership in this regard, and equivocation only compounds the problems.

Chapter 18

Ethics, Leadership, and the Environment

W HILE THE REPORT of the National Commission on the Environment emphasized the need for an environmental ethic, it did not spell out just what such an ethic meant. The question is not a simple one, and I have wrestled with it myself on more than one occasion.[1] It is an issue of compelling importance. If environmental protection is to be a core value of human society — as I believe it absolutely must — then it must have a strong ethical underpinning as do our other societal values.

Toward an Environmental Ethic

Likewise, if an environmental ethic is to have meaning and carry conviction for people around the world, whatever their ethnic, religious, or cultural backgrounds, as it must, such an ethic needs a strongly rational basis. The nearest thing to an environmental ethic that one is apt to hear in Judeo-Christian teaching is that we humans should be good stewards of the earth. We are never told why. Of course, being a good steward is far better than the reverse, but the concept risks missing the point. Advocacy of stewardship by itself is a teaching that tends to perpetuate the very anthropocentric view of the world that has gotten us into much of the environmental trouble we are in. It is a teaching premised on the concept that humanity has been given "dominion over the earth," and it implies that we are separate from and superior to the biotic process. From this concept, it has been an easy step to the conclusion that everything on the earth, both living and inanimate, exists for our benefit, for us to use and exploit at our will and pleasure.

What is needed, I am convinced, is for us to see ourselves, individually and collectively, as part of an interrelated, interdependent community: the community of living things, the world of nature. We may, indeed, usually be the dominant members of that community, but, dominant or not, we are at the same time totally dependent for our health, sustenance, and very existence on the other members of the community, from the plants, which absorb carbon and produce oxygen through the marvel of photosynthesis, to the lowly bacteria that fix nitrogen and maintain the fertility and productivity of the soil. Without the forests, our atmosphere would be very different, perhaps even incapable of supporting life. The oceans likewise sequester carbon, moderate the climate, and support (fast-diminishing) fishery resources. Wetlands provide habitat for aquatic life and waterfowl, filter toxic materials, and combat erosion. Coral reefs protect shorelines from erosion as well as maintaining rich reservoirs of biological diversity. Such benefits are almost infinite in number and, in their totality, are indispensable to a sustainable future for humanity.

We human beings are but a part of an infinitely complex natural system in which no part can be truly independent but in which all parts are interdependent. To accept this as a principle underlying our existence is, I believe, simply to accept scientific reality.

Aldo Leopold, the father of the science of wildlife management, in his *Sand County Almanac*,[2] speaks of the need for an ethical relationship between humanity and the land, defining the latter in such broad terms as to be, to all intents and purposes, synonymous with "nature." He urges that we stop looking at land as simply a commodity and start seeing it as a community, a community to which we all belong.

The traditional concept of community is social in character — the family, the village, the ethnic group, the nation. It was in that context, I believe, that our generally accepted moral or ethical values developed. As I grew up, I understood that rules of behavior, such as not to lie, steal, murder, or commit adultery, were mandated by commandments handed down by God. The same or very similar rules tend to be the norm in most human societies around the globe, whatever their religious beliefs. It seems likely, therefore, that such rules of behavior emerged from a common human experience over the many thousands of years during which our species evolved from small parties of hunter-gatherers into ever larger communities bound together by mutual self-interest.

Whether as hunter-gatherers or later as cultivators of crops, the banding together of individuals in social groups was critical to self-defense, to the acquisition and distribution of food, to the nurturing of children, and in countless other ways. If individuals within a group treated their fellows dishonestly, acted violently toward others in the group, failed to respect family bonds or to share in the common defense, those actions would have been highly disruptive of the social fabric of the group and therefore its stability, safety, and even continued existence. Such individual behavior would have been destructive to the community. Yet, at the same time, the individual could not survive and prosper outside the community. From the earliest times, therefore, adherence on the part of individuals to generally accepted rules of social behavior has been not only in the interest of the community but also in the individual's *self-interest*.* Communities, then, are bonded together in interdependence by the mutual self-interest of the community as a whole and of its individual members. Therein lies the clear, rational basis for ethical behavior on the part of each of us as a member of the human community. Hence the Golden Rule: to do unto others as we would have them do unto us.† And it is the need to protect the interests both of the individual and of the larger community and to maintain an effective balance between those interests that is the foundation of the rule of law in our society.

It is in a comparable framework that I see the need, indeed the imperative, for an environmental ethic, a shared set of environmental values to motivate our human society and its members. The relationship of humanity and nature is exactly the kind of interdependent relationship in which the social concept of community has evolved. We are an integral part of the natural world around us, and all parts of that natural world are interrelated and interdependent. Our well-being, our health, and our long-term survival depend on the continuing health of the natural systems of which we are a part. We are part of the community of living things, and,

---

*That such rules of behavior have their roots in humanity's distant, prehistorical past has been suggested to me in persuasive fashion by my observation in Tanzania of the behavior of troops of wild chimpanzees, who do, in fact, bond together in the defense of their territory, in the nurture and care of their offspring, and in the gathering of food, among other mutual interests. To be forced out of the troop is akin to a death sentence.
†Matthew 7:12, Luke 6:31.

as with socially responsible behavior, we have an ethical responsibility for building and sustaining the health of that community. To do so is clearly in our own self-interest. To fail to do so will ultimately exact tremendous penalties on the health, productivity, and even survival of ourselves, our children, and our children's children.

In the latter regard, the natural community of which we are a part exists not only in space but also in time. For us to take actions that reduce the long-term health of the natural systems of which our descendants will be a part is destructive of our own species and clearly unethical. Therefore, in my view, our own self-interest includes the well-being of our descendants.

While I believe that the case for an environmental ethic is clear and compelling, I recognize that the concept has emerged only recently on the human scene. Ethical social behavior has evolved in all probability over hundreds of thousands of years and, as such, is deeply embedded in our value system. To a great extent, socially responsible behavior has become almost second nature. Throughout most of that time, human influence on the environment has been relatively negligible,[3] which probably explains why the Bible and other early religious teachings have so little to say about the subject. Anti-environmental behavior by human groups did not seriously threaten human well-being. The group could always move if necessary. It is only in the past few hundred years that human numbers and technology have begun to threaten so seriously the natural world and, thereby, ourselves. Today, we have no place else to which to move.

It requires but little stretch of the mind and spirit to understand that the Golden Rule — to do unto others as we would have them do unto us — embraces in the word "others" not only our fellow humans but that whole community of life and nature of which we are so clearly an interdependent part.

Political Leadership and the Environment

Though the interdependence of humanity and nature is, in my opinion, intellectually unarguable, it is a fact that is unfortunately becoming increasingly obscure in our rapidly urbanizing world. Our food comes from the supermarket, our drinking water comes from a tap or a bottle, and much of the nature we do observe is by grace of our television sets.

Under such circumstances, it becomes increasingly difficult for us, as individuals, to recognize the connection between a healthy environment and our own well-being.

One of the realities we must face in this regard is that the relationship between human cause and natural effect is not always easy to recognize or comprehend. Driving a gas-guzzling sport utility vehicle may contribute to smog, increased respiratory ailments, and global warming (not to mention increased energy dependence on foreign sources, trade imbalances, and downward pressure on the dollar, among other effects). However, the only consequence immediately evident to the vehicle owner is the out-of-pocket expense of fuel for an energy-inefficient vehicle—an expense, but a modest one, thanks to tax-shy politicians. Similarly, the sulfur oxide emissions of a coal-fired power plant in the Midwest may make rivers on the New England coast toxic to spawning fish. Soil runoff from a farming community in the Central American uplands may flow into streams that will carry the silt to offshore coral reefs, smothering the reefs and destroying a wealth of marine life. The runoff of wastes from poultry operations and of fertilizer and pesticides from farms along the tributaries of Chesapeake Bay poses a serious threat to the bay's aquatic resources. The continued cutting of rain forests in the western Amazon basin could (in addition to the heavy loss of species) lead to a catastrophic loss of water for the densely populated São Paulo region of Brazil and, according to some experts, a major loss of rainfall in the agricultural areas of southern Africa. Such examples can be multiplied many times over.

These are not problems that we can shrug off as afflicting someone else. In this increasingly interdependent world, such problems have major impacts on the United States, either directly as, in the case of climate change, inadequately controlled sulfur oxide emissions, fuel-inefficient vehicles, and immigration pressures from countries no longer able to support their own growing populations, or indirectly, by spreading poverty and political instability abroad, leading to constant threats to foreign and domestic security. To address such problems aggressively is the ethical course, and it is also in the vital self-interest of the United States as well as the world community as a whole. Because the linkages between cause and effect are not always immediately apparent to the individual, because most of us have a tendency to deny the existence of problems whose solution could cause discomfort or entail sacrifice on our part, and because an isolationist streak exists among significant numbers of Americans, the need for powerful environmental leadership at the top level of our government is compelling. Our political leaders must understand that threats to our environment constitute threats to humanity.

In that regard, I have to admit to dismay that President George W. Bush and his White House have shown so little leadership on environmental issues and so little apparent understanding of these issues' overriding, long-term implications for the well-being of the American people as well as of the world at large.

The answers to many environmental issues are complex and often obscure, and it is not my purpose here to fault the Bush administration on the details or subtleties of environmental performance. Nor do I fault the Environmental Protection Agency, the Department of the Interior, or other responsible agencies because it has been clear from the beginning of the George W. Bush administration that it is the White House that is calling the tune. Moreover, it seems that the tune is being called not by program staff in the White House but by political operatives. I find it unacceptable that the current U.S. political leadership should demonstrate such disregard for and disinterest in values that are among the most crucial concerns of humanity today.

That disregard and disinterest have been demonstrated in numerous ways. At the outset of this administration, it was announced that the United States would ignore the Kyoto Protocol on climate change, an agreement reached by the global community only after much negotiation, in which the United States played an active role. Global climate change is an issue that deeply concerns governments and peoples around the world. The United States, by far the largest user of energy of any country, told the rest of the world, in effect, to go to hell.

There is much in the Kyoto Protocol with which one can disagree. Many Americans believe the exemption of developing countries from the treaty's rules to be unfair and the U.S. Senate would very likely reject the treaty in its present form. But that is no reason to give the back of our hand to an issue that poses such very real threats as rising sea levels, widespread loss of species, potentially catastrophic shifts in ocean currents, and radical changes in climate. The administration continues to suggest that the science behind the global warming problem is inadequate and uncertain, blatantly ignoring the fact that the overwhelming majority of atmospheric scientists around the world and our own National Academy of Sciences are in essential agreement on the facts of global warming and the significant contribution of human activity to that trend. Suggesting otherwise may be good domestic politics, but it is not playing square with the American people.

None of this is to say that we should necessarily have accepted the Kyoto Protocol in its present form. But we should have declared our intention to keep actively engaged internationally in the climate change issue, with the hope of ultimately forging an agreement that we could accept. Most important, we should have announced at the same time a U.S. commitment to significant reductions in our domestic energy demand and a program to accomplish that objective. We have done none of this.

Some attribute the Kyoto Protocol fiasco to diplomatic ineptitude and inexperience on the part of the new administration, and there may have been a share of that, but the overriding evidence is of an administration strongly biased in favor of special energy interests and against environmental concerns. The task force on energy convened by Vice President Dick Cheney in 2001 — although the White House has refused to permit public access to the record of its proceedings or even to the identity of those with whom it met — appears to have largely ignored environmental concerns.

The administration's fixation on opening the Arctic National Wildlife Refuge to oil development has been, in my opinion, another case of one-sided bias. As much as I would hate to see our last pristine wilderness lost to development, if the administration had proposed at the same time a major energy conservation initiative, such as a significant improvement in fuel economy of the nation's vehicle fleet, I would have thought the combined program at least worthy of serious consideration. Of course, it made no such proposal.[4]

The George W. Bush administration appears to view most issues as either black or white — that, for example, environmental protection and energy supply are mutually exclusive objectives. Such simplistic approaches may lend themselves to good sound bites or to easy political communication, but they do not serve us well in terms of developing effective solutions to the all-too-real problems that face this country and the world. Our modern society needs energy, and we need to produce it and utilize it in ways that do not damage the environment. That goal should be self-evident. To achieve it will not be easy or cheap, but the costs will be far less than the cost of the damage to our environment —

and us—if we fail to address the problem. The task cannot be done overnight. The need is to get on with it and to do so with meaningful timetables and measurable milestones.

On a broader scale, we need to recognize as a society that the economy and the environment are not antithetical to each other but are instead different sides of the same coin. Economic activity is to a great extent the conversion of the earth's environmental resources to human use and enjoyment—resources such as air, water, soils, plants (including forests), animals (including fisheries), energy, and minerals, together with all the myriad transactions involved in the conversion process. Environmental protection will not be achieved in a failing economy. At the same time, a healthy economy that is sustainable over the long term can be achieved only in the context of a healthy environment. The two must go hand in hand.

Many people thought of as political conservatives are often negative toward environmental protection policies and are apt to dismiss environmentalists as a lot of wild-eyed extremists. Government laws and regulations affecting the management of private land, in particular, may often seem overly intrusive, and every effort should be made in such situations to develop community-based consultative mechanisms to help bridge the communication gap. More understanding and acceptance of environmental ethics would surely help. And there are, of course, some wild-eyed types among environmentalists, just as there are among businessmen, politicians, or any other group. But the mainstream environmental movement has had an enormous and positive influence on the quality of our life—on safeguarding clean air and water, on regulating toxic substances, on conserving open space, and on protecting species, among many other environmental policy achievements.*

*Environmental leaders such as Patrick Noonan (recently retired as head of The Conservation Fund), Steve McCormick (CEO, The Nature Conservancy), Kathryn Fuller (CEO, World Wildlife Fund), Jonathan Lash (CEO, World Resources Institute), John Flicker (CEO, National Audubon Society), Roger Portney (CEO, Resources for the Future), and many others that I could name are sound, balanced, and thoroughly professional. Former EPA heads Bill Ruckelshaus, Bill Reilly, Carole Browner—all now chairs of major environmental organizations—fit into the same category; as does former CEO head Gus Speth, now dean of the Yale School of Forestry and Environmental Studies, and Doug Wheeler, former secretary of resources of California and now chair of the American Farmland Trust. There isn't a radical in the entire group. To claim otherwise is either an act of ignorance or an effort to polarize issues of vital importance to us all.

To my mind, to oppose environmental protection is not to be truly conservative. To put short-term financial gain ahead of the long-term health of the environment is a fundamentally radical policy, as well as being unethical. Conservation, which is essentially no more and no less than protection of the natural capital with which we have been endowed, should be seen as truly conservative. Of course, some environmental requirements can be unreasonable and impose costs out of all proportion to the benefits secured. Here again, I am not trying to make the case that every environmental argument need be accepted at face value. What I do say is that even conservatives should support environmental safeguards. If they oppose further government regulation of any sort in principle, then they should support other methods of achieving environmental protection objectives, such as the use of market incentives. There should be no argument over the goals, only over the methods of attaining those goals. I hasten to add that reliance on voluntary compliance is not an acceptable or effective alternative.

It was the farsighted leadership of Theodore Roosevelt that gave us our system of national forests and national wildlife refuges and did so much to build our national park system. In the early 1970s, it was the Republican administration of Richard Nixon, together with bipartisan support in Congress, that put into place the bulk of the programs that are the foundation of environmental protection in the United States today. And it was the leadership of the United States, both at home and abroad, that helped move the world through positive and cooperative engagement to new levels of environmental commitment and achievement. We need to find that road again; it is the only path to a sustainable future for humanity.

Epilogue

ANUARY 20, 1961, dawned bitterly cold in Washington, and an overnight snowfall blanketed the city. But, despite the weather, a sense of excitement and anticipation filled the air. John F. Kennedy was to be inaugurated at noon as the thirty-fifth president of the United States. Aileen and I had seats on the platform on the east front of the Capitol.

It was from that privileged vantage point that we watched Robert Frost, then in his eighties, stand at the podium, his wispy white hair blowing in the wind as he recited his poem "The Road Not Taken." Of course, the words of the poem were quickly overshadowed on that occasion by the eloquence of the young, new president.

I hardly knew Kennedy, though a number of Washington friends were on intimate terms with him. In June 1953, Aileen had attended the coronation of Queen Elizabeth II of England with Jacqueline Bouvier. The two of them had gone on to Paris and then flown back to the United States together. I was courting Aileen at the time, and I went to New York's Idlewild Airport to meet her flight. Also waiting in the gate area was Kennedy, then junior senator from Massachusetts, who was there to meet Jackie. He was pacing up and down, full of energy and impatience. We exchanged greetings but little more. On my first-ever visit to Idlewild, I had thus been in the company of the man for whom the airport would later be renamed. When Jack and Jackie married three months later, in September, Aileen was one of the bridesmaids.

Some ten years later, in 1963, when I was presiding at a U.S. Tax Court session in San Antonio, the president and Mrs. Kennedy were scheduled to pass by the courthouse in a motorcade. I recessed the court so that everyone who so wished could go out and view the event, myself included. I stood on a street corner as their open car passed a few feet away. Jackie saw me, smiled, and waved. The president was looking in the other direction. The next day, Jack Kennedy was shot to death in Dallas.

I recount all this ancient history because I never cease to be fascinated by the currents and crosscurrents that move through one's life and the interplay of events and people, seemingly fortuitous and coincidental at the time, that go to make up that life.

I do not pretend for a moment that the words Frost recited on that icy inaugural day so long ago have stayed with me through the years and somehow influenced life choices I have made. However, the fact is, in choosing an environmental career, I did, in the poet's words, take the road "less traveled by, / And that has made all the difference."

It has been a wonderful difference — challenging, rewarding, exciting, often frustrating. But it has almost always been fun, in the best sense of the word, even at times exhilarating, in feeling oneself on the cutting edge of a compelling new dimension to public policy. Today, as a nation we urgently need to develop the political will to overcome our avoidance of difficult environmental decisions. The problems will only get worse, and we have a long way to go.

I am reminded of a story that was a favorite of Kennedy's, who seems rather unexpectedly to have become central to this epilogue. A French marshal, so the story goes, told his gardener that he wished to have a certain tree planted in his garden. "But, *mon général,* that kind of tree will not mature for a hundred years," replied the gardener. "In that case," cried the marshal, "we must not delay. Plant the tree immediately!"

Notes

The initials RET indicate materials in the Russell E. Train Papers, Manuscript Division, Library of Congress.

PREFACE

1. John C. Whitaker, *Striking a Balance: Environment and Natural Resources Policy in the Nixon-Ford Years* (Washington, D.C.: American Enterprise Institute for Public Policy Research; Stanford, Calif.: Hoover Institution on War, Revolution and Peace, 1976).

2. J. Brooks Flippen, *Nixon and the Environment* (Albuquerque: University of New Mexico Press, 2000).

3. Russell E. Train, *A Memoir* (Washington, D.C.: privately published, 2000). Concurrently with that volume I also wrote and published *The Train Family* and *The Bowdoin Family*, the latter an account of the family of my wife, Aileen.

4. John McPhee, *Encounters with the Archdruid* (New York: Farrar, Straus and Giroux, 1971), p. 87.

5. *Audubon*, September 1982, p. 46.

PROLOGUE: HOW ONE THING LEADS TO ANOTHER

1. McCracken, an economics professor at Michigan State University, became chairman of the Council of Economic Advisors in the Nixon White House.

2. The following were the members of the task force: Edward A. Ackerman, executive officer, Carnegie Institution, Washington, D.C.; Stanley A. Cain, professor, Department of Resource Planning and Conservation, University of Michigan (formerly assistant secretary of Interior for fish and wildlife and parks); Charles H. Callison, executive vice president, National Audubon Society, New York; Joseph L. Fisher, president, Resources for the Future, Washington, D.C.; Loren V. Forman, vice president, Scott Paper Company, Philadelphia, Pennsylvania; Charles H. W. Foster, consultant, The Conservation Foundation (formerly commissioner, Department of Natural Resources, State of Massachusetts),

Washington, D.C.; Maurice K. Goddard, secretary, Department of Forests and Waters, Commonwealth of Pennsylvania, Harrisburg; Norman B. Livermore Jr., secretary, the Resources Agency, State of California, Sacramento; Charles F. Luce, chairman and chief executive officer, Consolidated Edison Company (formerly under secretary of Interior), New York; John H. Meier, executive aide, Hughes Nevada Operations, Las Vegas, Nevada; H. Byron Mock, attorney, Salt Lake City, Utah, and vice chairman, Public Land Law Review Commission; Bernard L. Orrell, vice president, Weyerhaeuser Company, Tacoma, Washington; Nathaniel P. Reed, conservation advisor to the governor of Florida, Tallahassee; S. Dillon Ripley, secretary, Smithsonian Institution, Washington, D.C.; Laurance S. Rockefeller, chairman, Citizens' Advisory Committee on Recreation and Natural Beauty, New York; Lelan F. Sillin Jr., president, Northeast Utilities, Hartford, Connecticut; John O. Simonds, landscape architect and past president, American Society of Landscape Architects, Pittsburgh, Pennsylvania; M. Frederik Smith, American Conservation Association (formerly vice president, Prudential Insurance Company of America), New York; Russell E. Train, president, The Conservation Foundation, Washington, D.C.; and John W. Tukey, professor and chairman, Department of Statistics, Princeton University, and executive director, Bell Laboratories, Princeton.

CHAPTER 1. WASHINGTON BEGINNINGS

1. David F. Trask, *The War with Spain in 1898* (New York: Free Press, 1981; reprint, Lincoln: University of Nebraska Press, 1996), pp. 72–76.
2. See Robert V. Remini, *Andrew Jackson and the Course of American Freedom, 1822–1832*, vol. 2 (New York: Harper and Row, 1981), pp. 169–170.

CHAPTER 2. FROM CLERK TO JUDGE

1. *Washington Post*, editorial, October 24, 1976.
2. *Congressional Record*, January 14, 1977.
3. Walter Cronkite, in his excellent memoir, *A Reporter's Life* (New York: Knopf, 1996), tells exactly the same story but attributes it to an English judge (p. 127).
4. My law clerks were as follows: Roger Quinnan (9/3/57–5/5/60); Willard I. Zucker (6/26/60–11/26/60); Edward Lee Rogers (8/26/57–3/31/61); John D. Totz (12/11/60–7/28/63); Herbert L. Chabot (4/10/61–1/31/65); Stephen L. Kadish (9/16/63–); Michael P. Oshatz (1/31/65–). Both Kadish and Oshatz served with me until I left the court.
5. My Memorandum Opinions fill seven volumes, and the published Tax Court Opinions of my cases fill another four volumes. My last opinion was filed on July 31, 1965.

CHAPTER 3. AFRICA: LAND OF THE SOUL

1. *New York Times*, January 30, 1970. Fourteen years later, on June 4, 1984 (my birthday), a *New York Times* profile by Philip Shabecoff titled "Mr. Conservation" said something very similar: "Russell Errol Train was converted to the cause of conservation on an African safari in 1956 when he shot an elephant, was

chased by a rhinoceros, and was so impressed by the experience that he founded the African Wildlife Leadership Foundation."

2. Joy Adamson, *Born Free: A Lioness of Two Worlds* (London: Pantheon Books, 1960); *Living Free: The Story of Elsa and Her Cubs* (New York: Harcourt, Brace & World, 1961); *Forever Free: Elsa's Pride* (London: Collins & Harvill Press, 1962).

CHAPTER 4. FIRST STEPS FOR WILDLIFE

1. Kermit Roosevelt, *A Sentimental Safari* (New York: Knopf, 1963).
2. The history of the African Wildlife Foundation (AWF) is told in *Thirty-Five Years of Conservation in Africa: A History of the African Wildlife Foundation* by Jacqueline Russell, with foreword by Russell E. Train (Washington, D.C.: African Wildlife Foundation, 1997).
3. This particular commitment was facilitated by James Hyde, an advisor to Rockefeller, a distinguished attorney, and president of the International Bar Association.

CHAPTER 5. FROM JUDGE TO CONSERVATIONIST

1. The WWF-US president was Ira Gabrielson, who had been director of the U.S. Fish and Wildlife Service and was president of the Wildlife Management Institute. I had consulted with him and his vice president, C. R. "Pink" Gutermuth, when I was drawing up the articles of incorporation for AWLF. Gutermuth became secretary of the WWF board. John I. Snyder was chairman but was soon replaced by John D. Murchison of Dallas. There were six in that group of founding directors, including Kermit Roosevelt and Harold J. Coolidge. The latter was probably the leading U.S. proponent of international conservation and he had been part of the international group that organized WWF. He was also an early AWLF trustee.
2. Fairfield Osborn, *Our Plundered Planet* (Boston: Little, Brown, 1948); Fairfield Osborn, *The Limits of the Earth* (London: Faber & Faber, 1954).
3. An excellent biography of Rockefeller is Robin W. Winks, *Laurance S. Rockefeller: Catalyst for Conservation* (Washington, D.C.: Island Press, 1997). Winks describes not only LSR's many contributions to conservation but also his philosophy of conservation and its evolution over time.
4. President Lyndon B. Johnson, Letter to RET, July 29, 1965.
5. *Congressional Record*, August 3, 1965, p. 18511.
6. RET, "America the Beautiful" (address by president of The Conservation Foundation to the 90th annual meeting of the American Forestry Association, held jointly with the National Council of State Garden Clubs, Jackson Lake Lodge, Grand Teton National Park, Wyoming, September 6, 1965).
7. Ian L. McHarg, *Design with Nature* (Garden City, N.Y.: Natural History Press, 1969; reprint, New York: Wiley, 1992).
8. CF's close association with the Senate Interior Committee on NEPA was due in large part to the suggestion of Wallace Bowman, a member of the Legislative Reference Service of the Library of Congress and former secretary of CF in New York.

CHAPTER 6. TO INTERIOR AS UNDER SECRETARY

1. *Congressional Record*, January 21, 1969.
2. Senate Committee on Interior and Insular Affairs, *Hearings before the Senate Committee on Interior and Insular Affairs*, 91st Cong., 1st sess., February 4, 1969 (Washington, D.C.: U.S. Government Printing Office, 1969), pp. 6–7.
3. RET, Memorandum for the Files, June 30, 1969.
4. RET, Memorandum to John Ehrlichman, January 16, 1970.
5. Senate Committee on Interior and Insular Affairs, *Hearings before the Senate Committee on Interior and Insular Affairs on the Status of the Proposed Trans-Alaska Pipeline*, 91st Cong., 1st sess., October 16, 1969 (Washington, D.C.: U.S. Government Printing Office, 1969), pp. 81–143.
6. William K. Wyant Jr., interview with RET, *St. Louis Post-Dispatch*, April 11, 1970.
7. RET, Memorandum to John Ehrlichman, "Everglades Jetport," September 8, 1969.
8. Veneman's daughter, Ann, is secretary of Agriculture in the George W. Bush administration.
9. Bureau of the Budget, later included in the Office of Management and Budget.
10. Senate Committee on Interior and Insular Affairs, *Hearing before the Senate Committee on Interior and Insular Affairs on S. 1075, S. 237, and S. 1752*, 91st Cong., 1st sess., April 16, 1969 (Washington, D.C.: U.S. Government Printing Office, 1969), pp. 73–76.
11. *Wall Street Journal*, June 18, 1969.
12. RET, Diary, September 16, 1969.
13. RET, Memorandum for the Files, October 29, 1969.
14. RET, Diary, September 17, 1969.
15. Among many press contacts were Stan Benjamin of the Associated Press; Gladwin Hill, Bob Semple, Phil Shabecoff, and Ned Kenworthy of the *New York Times*; Margot Hornblower and George Wilson of the *Washington Post*; Al Otten of the *Wall Street Journal*; Casey Bukro of the *Chicago Tribune*; William K. Wyant Jr. of the *St. Louis Post-Dispatch*; Howard Scarlett of the *Houston Post*; Roberta Hornig of the *Washington Star*; and Bob Cahn of the *Christian Science Monitor*. Among journalists who wrote for periodicals, there was Jim Bishop of *Newsweek*, Linda Ba Thung of the *Environmental Reporter*, and John Osborne of the *New Republic*. The latter was not an environmental reporter as such but was positive in his occasional coverage as part of his regular "Nixon Watch" column.

    Editorial board contacts were sporadic. *New York Times* editorials under the leadership of John Oakes and, later, Max Frankel gave considerable and helpful attention to environmental issues. At the *Washington Post*, Phil Geyelin was editorial editor from 1967 to 1979, and the editorial comment was almost always positive and constructive.

CHAPTER 7. THE CEQ YEARS

1. Richard M. Nixon, "Annual Message to the Congress on the State of the Union," January 22, 1971.

2. Ibid.
3. National Environmental Policy Act of 1969 (42 U.S.C. 4321).
4. Nixon, "Annual Message to the Congress on the State of the Union," January 22, 1971.
5. Richard M. Nixon, "Special Message to the Congress Proposing the 1971 Environmental Program," February 8, 1971.
6. See, for example, Richard Reeves, *President Nixon: Alone in the White House* (New York: Simon & Schuster, 2001), p. 261.
7. Ibid., pp. 172–173.
8. Ibid., p. 297.
9. RET, testimony before Senate Committee on Interior and Insular Affairs, February 5, 1970.
10. My formal designation as chairman was by presidential order on February 9, 1970.
11. *New York Times*, front-page article with photograph, January 30, 1970.
12. RET, Diary, February 7, 1970.
13. See Edmund Morris, *Theodore Rex* (New York: Random House, 2001), pp. 118, 156 (photograph).
14. *Washington Post*, September 5, 1970.
15. RET, Memorandum to the President, "Environmental Effects of the SST," July 29, 1970.
16. RET, Diary, February 5, 1970. One of my strongest allies in the matter was Senator Jim Buckley of New York, although his opposition to the SST was based primarily on economic grounds. A longtime personal friend, Buckley had strong conservative credentials and was a member of the Senate Public Works Committee, which had jurisdiction over most environmental legislation.
17. House Public Works Committee, *Hearings on H.R. 11896, H.R. 11895 to Amend the Federal Water Pollution Control Act*, 92nd Cong., 2nd sess., December 7, 1971 (Washington, D.C.: U.S. Government Printing Office, 1971); *Washington Post*, December 8, 1971.
18. J. Brooks Flippen, *Nixon and the Environment* (Albuquerque: University of New Mexico Press, 2000), pp. 181–183, presents a detailed history of these events, suggesting that Nixon was souring on the environment. Likewise, see John C. Whitaker, *Striking a Balance: Environment and Natural Resources Policy in the Nixon-Ford Years* (Washington, D.C.: American Enterprise Institute for Public Policy Research; Stanford, Calif.: Hoover Institution on War, Revolution and Peace, 1976), pp. 73–92.
19. John Quarles, who managed the permit program at EPA, has described this whole history in detail, including the administrative difficulties of putting the program into place. John Quarles, *Cleaning Up America: An Insider's View of the Environmental Protection Agency* (Boston: Houghton Mifflin, 1976), pp. 97–116.
20. CEQ submitted a report to the president recommending a 10-cent deposit on the purchase of each beverage container. RET, Memorandum to the President, April 30, 1970. After interagency discussions, the proposal was shelved. The issue was essentially left to state action.

21. Executive Order 11514, "Protection and Enhancement of Environmental Quality," March 5, 1970.
22. *New York Times*, front-page article, February 4, 1970; *Washington Post*, front-page article, February 4, 1970.
23. "Ten Years Ago," *Forbes*, April 7, 1986.
24. *New York Times*, September 12, 1972.
25. RET, Letter to John Whitaker, April 14, 1970; May 21, 1970.
26. RET, Letter to John Whitaker, December 1, 1970.
27. Executive Order 11643, "Environmental Safeguards on Activities for Animal Damage Control on Federal Lands," February 8, 1972.
28. "Environmental Teach-In," Harvard University Graduate School of Business Administration, April 22, 1970.
29. Inauguration of Chancellor James H. Meyer, April 24, 1970.
30. A thoughtful study describes Earth Day proper and analyzes the course of environmental issues since then: Mary Graham, *The Morning After Earth Day: Practical Environmental Politics* (Washington, D.C.: Brookings Institution Press, 1999).
31. CEQ's Legal Advisory Committee was one of several such groups established by CEQ during the years 1970–1973. These were the Advisory Committee on Alternative Automotive Power Systems (chaired by David O. Ragone, dean, Thayer School of Engineering, Dartmouth College); the Legal Advisory Committee (chaired by Whitney North Seymour Jr., U.S. attorney for the Southern District of New York); and the Tax Advisory Committee (chaired by Dan Throop Smith, former assistant secretary of Treasury for tax policy). In addition, the Citizen's Advisory Committee on Environmental Quality (chaired first by Laurance S. Rockefeller and later by Henry Diamond, former commissioner, New York State Department of Environmental Conservation) was advisory to both the president and CEQ.

    When I informed John Whitaker at the White House on March 10, 1970, of my intention to set up a CEQ Task Force (forerunner of the advisory group) on the Impact of Federal, State, and Local Tax Structures on Environmental Quality, I told him that I had checked with, and received an enthusiastic response from, Charls Walker (deputy secretary of Treasury); Edwin S. Cohen (commissioner, Internal Revenue Service); Paul McCracken (chairman, Council of Economic Advisors); Wilbur Mills (chairman, Ways and Means Committee); and John Byrnes (ranking Republican member, Ways and Means Committee). There is nothing more important than touching the bases in government!
32. RET, Letter to IRS Commissioner Randolph Thrower, September 30, 1970. The letter was published by the Senate Interior Committee on November 7, 1970, in a document titled *Law and the Environment — Selected Materials on Tax Exempt Status and Public Interest Litigation*. I was particularly gratified to see in the same document a letter on behalf of the Environmental Defense Fund signed by its general counsel, Edward Lee Rogers, who had been one of my law clerks when I was a judge of the United States Tax Court (see chapter 2).

33. Letter to RET from Mortimer Caplin, November 18, 1970.

34. In May 1972, in a related matter, I testified before the House Ways and Means Committee in support of legislation protecting the right of charitable organizations to spend at least a portion of their funds on lobbying activities without loss of their tax-exempt status.

35. RET, Memorandum to Department and Agency Heads, April 30, 1970.

36. P.L. 92-532, 86 Stat. 1052, 1972.

37. *New York Times*, January 18, 1972.

38. *Life*, August 28, 1970.

39. RET, Letter to John Irwin, December 2, 1970; *Washington Evening Star*, November 3, 1971; *Washington Post*, November 4, 1971; editorial, November 5, 1971; *New York Times*, November 4, 1971; *Newsweek*, November 15, 1971. The issue was front-paged by the *Sunday Times* in London on November 7, 1971.

40. Alvin Alm, Memorandum to Staff Group, "Need for an Institute of Environmental Studies and the Problems It Would Attack," May 27, 1970.

41. The Russell E. Train Papers in the Manuscript Division of the Library of Congress contain numerous documents relating to the original proposal for an environmental policy institute.

42. RET, Memorandum to Donald H. Rumsfeld, Assistant to the President, February 10, 1975.

43. RET, Memorandum to John Ehrlichman, March 23, 1970.

44. I addressed the issue of separating EPA so that there were no obvious internal conflicts (rather than putting the functions in a department such as Interior) at a symposium. Russell E. Train, "Improving the Management of Environmental Programs" (speech given at symposium, Improving Management for More Effective Government: 50th Anniversary Lectures of the United States General Accounting Office, 1921–1971, Washington, D.C., June 11, 1971).

45. RET, Letter to President George H. W. Bush, January 22, 1990.

46. *New York Times*, January 25, 1990.

47. See, for example, RET letter to the editor, *New York Times*, June 21, 2003.

48. RET, Letter to John Ehrlichman, April 27, 1970.

49. *New York Times*, August 11, 1970.

50. For a summary of the environmental accomplishments of the Nixon administration during the years 1969–1974, see Russell E. Train, "The Environmental Record of the Nixon Administration," *Presidential Studies Quarterly* 26, no. 1 (winter 1996): 185–196 (published by the Center for the Study of the Presidency, New York).

51. RET, Memorandum for the Files, February 26, 1973.

52. Fred Bosselman and David Callies, *The Quiet Revolution in Land-Use Control* (Washington, D.C.: U.S. Government Printing Office, December 1971).

53. Nixon, "Special Message to the Congress Proposing the 1971 Environmental Program," February 8, 1971.

54. Whitaker, *Striking a Balance*, pp. 147–173.

55. In early 1973, I had also recommended that the president announce a White

House Conference on Land Use in his State of the Union Address (RET, Memorandum to Richard Fairbanks, January 17, 1973). My purpose was to generate discussion and broaden public understanding of the issue. There was no follow-up by the administration, however.

56. Whitaker, *Striking a Balance*, p. 173.
57. RET, Memorandum for the Files, February 26, 1973.
58. This account of the Dan Schorr affair differs in some respects from the account given in *A Memoir* and is based, in large part, on notes I kept at the time, but of which I was unaware when writing *A Memoir*. Russell E. Train, *A Memoir* (Washington, D.C.: privately published, 2000).
59. John Whitaker, Memorandum to RET, March 3, 1972.
60. John Whitaker, Memorandum to RET, July 31, 1970.
61. RET, Memorandum for the Files, May 4, 1973.
62. *Washington Evening Star*, February 8, 1972; *New York Times*, February 9, 1972; editorial, February 11, 1972.
63. RET, Memorandum to Daniel P. Moynihan, March 9, 1970.
64. For an internal review of the CEQ record, see RET, Memorandum to CEQ Members and Staff, "CEQ Accomplishments," July 24, 1972. At the end of 1972, I sent a memo to the White House setting out at some length what I saw as CEQ's responsibilities and opportunities. RET, Memorandum to Frederick Malek, December 14, 1972 (in response to Malek's request for a discussion of the responsibilities of all presidential appointees).
65. *Washington Post*, September 12, 1972. For a divergent view, see James Rathlesberger, ed., *Nixon and the Environment: The Politics of Devastation*, a League of Conservation Voters report (New York: Taurus Communications, 1972).
66. RET, Memorandum to John Ehrlichman, "Environmental Strategy for 1972," December 2, 1971.
67. Ibid.
68. Ibid.

CHAPTER 8. U.S. ENVIRONMENTAL LEADERSHIP
1. Chris Herter's father was secretary of State in the Dwight D. Eisenhower administration, following John Foster Dulles. Among other State Department staff members I recall working with the most were Bill Salmon and Cameron Sanders, as well as Alan Berlin and John MacDonald.
2. President Richard Nixon, Letter to RET, September 18, 1973. President Gerald Ford renewed this directive in a letter to RET on October 17, 1974.
3. *New York Times*, April 16, 1972.
4. *Las Vegas Sun*, June 24, 1971; *Las Vegas Review-Journal*, June 24, 1971.
5. RET, Memorandum to the President, July 2, 1970.
6. RET, Memorandum to the President, April 16, 1970.
7. *New York Times*, June 11, 1971; *Washington Post*, June 11, 1971.
8. *U.S. News and World Report*, September 27, 1976, p. 51.

9. Theo Colburn, Dianne Dumanoski, and John Peterson Myers, *Our Stolen Future: Are We Threatening Our Fertility, Intelligence, and Survival? A Scientific Detective Story* (New York: Dutton, 1996).

10. RET, Letter to Henry Kissinger, October 28, 1971.

11. *Washington Post*, May 24, 1972.

12. RET, Memorandum to John Whitaker, September 1, 1972.

13. RET, Memorandum for the Files, September 11, 1972; I also issued a statement to the press about the agreement and the upcoming meeting in Moscow on September 15, 1972. I lunched again with Ambassador Dobrynin and briefed him on the status of the agreement and plans for its implementation on July 28, 1972.

14. RET, chairman, U.S. delegation, "Remarks on the Opening of the First Meeting of the US-USSR Joint Committee on Cooperation in the Field of Environmental Protection" (address given at House of Unions, Moscow, September 18, 1972).

15. RET, Memorandum for the Files, November 14, 1973 (the day of the meeting).

16. E. U. Curtis "Buff" Bohlen, Letter to RET, enclosing a copy of the convention, December 1, 1976.

17. Nixon then wrote to Podgorny, on October 16, 1972, informing him of my report on the trip.

18. RET, Memorandum for the Files, "Meeting with Soviet President Podgorny," November 19, 1976.

19. RET, Memorandum to the President, (1) "Meeting of US-USSR Joint Committee on Environmental Protection," and (2) "Meeting with Soviet President Podgorny," November 24, 1976. Acknowledged by letter to RET from General Brent Scowcroft on December 6, 1976.

20. RET, Memorandum to Henry Kissinger, February 8, 1973.

21. Gary R. Waxmonsky, executive secretary of the U.S.-Russian Federation Environment Committee, Letter to RET, May 24, 2002.

22. Barbara Ward co-authored, with René Dubos, *Only One Earth: The Care and Maintenance of a Small Planet* (New York: Norton, 1972), an unofficial report commissioned by the secretary-general of the United Nations Conference on the Human Environment and prepared with the assistance of the 152-member Committee of Corresponding Consultants in fifty-eight countries.

23. Later that autumn, George H. W. Bush, then U.S. representative to the United Nations, asked me to make Mrs. Black available to help with a U.S. "diplomatic offensive" at the United Nations: "She has terrific contacts with Ambassadors of the Developing Countries." George Bush, Letter to RET, October 25, 1972. I agreed and left it to the two of them to work the matter out. RET, Letter to George Bush, October 31, 1972.

24. John Ehrlichman, *Witness to Power: The Nixon Years* (New York: Simon and Schuster, 1982), pp. 317–320.

25. White House press release, June 20, 1972.

26. *New York Times*, August 30, 1972.

27. *New York Times*, July 24, 1982.
28. RET, op-ed piece on the World Heritage Trust, *New York Times*, November 6, 1971.
29. RET, address to the International Congress on Nature and Man, Amsterdam, April 29, 1967.
30. See, for example, Mark Swadling, ed., *Masterworks of Man and Nature: Preserving Our World Heritage*, published by UNESCO's World Heritage Committee and the IUCN (Patonga, Australia: Harper-MacRae, 1992), preface, p. 7. This massive tome provides a complete history of the World Heritage Trust (WHT), including an essay by me on pp. 377–379 and a listing and description of all WHT sites worldwide as of 1992. See also Carol Bittig Lutyk, ed., *Our World's Heritage* (Washington, D.C.: National Geographic Society, 1987). This large volume contains photographs and descriptions of the WHT sites as of 1987.
31. These statistics are as of May 2003.
32. RET, "The World Heritage: A Vision for the Future" (speech given in Venice, November 16, 2002). I was the keynote speaker at the twentieth-anniversary meeting of the World Heritage Convention in Phoenix and spoke again on its thirtieth anniversary in Venice. It was at the latter that I emphasized the pride people everywhere could take in sites regardless of the country in which they were located because they represent our common humanity. RET, "The World Heritage Convention: The First Twenty Years and Beyond" (speech given at meeting of the International World Heritage Committee, Santa Fe, New Mexico, December 7, 1992). I also addressed the subject at a conference on the World Heritage convened by the World Heritage Centre of UNESCO, the United Nations Foundation, and the National Geographic Society. RET, "The World Heritage: An Historical Perspective" (speech given at World Heritage conference, Washington, D.C., June 3, 2003).
33. On July 1, 2003, I attended and spoke at a celebration at the Interior Department of the thirtieth anniversary of the ratification of CITES by the United States.
34. There is a detailed diary of the entire trip, including stops in the USSR, Japan, and China (June 6–July 1, 1975), in my collected papers at the Library of Congress.
35. RET, Diary, June 24, 1975.
36. RET, Diary, June 26, 1975.
37. RET, Diary, June 30, 1975.
38. RET, Memorandum to the President, May 3, 1972.
39. President Richard Nixon, Letter to RET, January 14, 1971.
40. RET, "Statement on Chlorofluorocarbons at a Public Meeting, EPA Headquarters, Washington, D.C.," December 3, 1976.
41. F. A. Harris, Letter to RET, May 31, 1977, with enclosures.
42. Benedick recounts the history of the Montreal Protocol in *Ozone Diplomacy: New Directions in Safeguarding the Planet* (Cambridge, Mass.: Harvard University

Press, 1991), which was published in cooperation with the World Wildlife Fund, The Conservation Foundation, and the Institute for the Study of Diplomacy, Georgetown University.

43. For a detailed description of the CCMS operation in its early years, see Russell E. Train, "A New Approach to International Environmental Cooperation: The NATO Committee on the Challenges of a Modern Society," *Kansas Law Review* 22, no. 2 (winter 1974).

CHAPTER 9. EPA UNDER NIXON

1. *New York Times*, July 27, 1973; *Washington Star-News*, July 27, 1973.
2. Examples were editorials as follows: *Minneapolis Tribune*, July 29, 1973; *Minneapolis Evening Star*, July 30, 1973; *Los Angeles Times*, July 31, 1973; *Scranton Tribune*, July 31, 1973; *Washington Star-News*, August 2, 1973; *Denver Post*, August 5, 1973; *New York Times*, August 7, 1973; *Sacramento Bee*, August 7, 1973; *Wall Street Journal*, August 7, 1973; *Washington Post*, August 7, 1973; *Baltimore News American*, August 9, 1973; *Philadelphia Evening Bulletin*, August 13, 1973.
3. *Wall Street Journal*, July 27, 1973.
4. *Time*, August 6, 1973.
5. Senator William L. Scott, Letter to RET, August 6, 1973.
6. In *A Memoir*, I said that my confirmation was held up for three months, which is incorrect. At the time of that writing, I recalled that I was nominated in early June, but it was actually on July 26. Russell E. Train, *A Memoir* (Washington, D.C.: privately published, 2000), p. 197.
7. According to J. Brooks Flippen in *Nixon and the Environment* (Albuquerque: University of New Mexico Press, 2000), pp. 199–200, "environmental policy," Nixon told Train, "was moving into a new and difficult period of maturity. The earlier first blush of emotion and commitment" had passed and, as the new EPA administrator, his job was to "balance environmental protection with other pressing needs." The quoted language does not sound like Nixon as I remember him and I do not recall the statement. However, the thrust of the remark reasonably reflects what Nixon undoubtedly had on his mind.
8. RET, Speech to the Rotary Club of Washington, D.C., June 14, 1973.
9. RET, Memorandum for the Files, September 8, 1973.
10. *Washington Post*, September 9, 1973. The front-page, three-column headline proclaimed: "Clean Air Rules Must Be Eased, Nixon Declares."
11. RET, interview with *Business Week*, December 15, 1973.
12. RET, Handwritten Memorandum for the Files, November 6, 1973.
13. RET, Note on Cabinet Meeting, March 8, 1974.
14. William D. Ruckelshaus, conversation with author, July 27, 2002.
15. Administrator's decision, August 2, 1974.
16. Howard Scarlett, article in *Houston Post*, August 24, 1975.
17. For a discussion of automobile emission issues of the time, see John C. Whitaker, *Striking a Balance: Environment and Natural Resources Policy in the Nixon-*

Ford Years (Washington, D.C.: American Enterprise Institute for Public Policy Research; Stanford, Calif.: Hoover Institution on War, Revolution and Peace, 1976), pp. 95–105. See also Flippen, *Nixon and the Environment*, pp. 65–67, 108. For a detailed account of these issues up to August 1976, see Eric O. Stork (deputy assistant administrator for mobile source air pollution control, EPA), "The United States Experience with Imposing Automobile Emission Standards" (paper for the Australian Society of Automotive Engineers, Perth, Australia, September 22, 1976).

18. Whitaker, *Striking a Balance*, p. 99.

19. Senate Committee on Public Works, *Hearings on Compliance with Title II (Auto Emission Standards) of the Clean Air Act Before the Senate Committee on Public Works*, 93rd Cong., lst sess., November 6, 1973 (Washington, D.C.: U.S. Government Printing Office, 1973), pp. 431–436. See also Whitaker, *Striking a Balance*, p. 102.

20. RET, Memorandum for the Files, March 3, 1975.

21. "Mr. Train's Decision Is a Wise One," *Washington Post*, editorial, March 14, 1975.

22. *Arizona Republic*, August 1, 1976.

23. RET, Letter to Senator Barry Goldwater, August 18, 1976. Goldwater wrote a lengthy reply.

24. Barry Goldwater, Letter to RET, August 25, 1976.

25. *New York Times Magazine*, April 20, 1975, p. 60.

26. RET, Memorandum for the Files, March 14, 1975.

27. The Federal Energy Office was the commonly used name for the Energy Policy Office, which was established in the Executive Office of the President in June 1973 and terminated in March 1974.

28. *New York Times*, March 11, 1974.

29. *Wall Street Journal*, March 11, 1974.

30. *Business Week*, March 16, 1974.

31. *Washington Post*, March 11, 1974.

32. *San Francisco Chronicle*, March 11, 1974.

33. *Washington Star*, March 11, 1974.

34. *New York Times*, March 11, 1974; see also *Baltimore Sun*, editorial, April 7, 1974.

35. RET, Memorandum to the President, March 1, 1974.

36. *New York Times*, March 22, 1974.

37. *Washington Post*, March 23, 1974.

38. John Quarles, *Cleaning Up America: An Insider's View of the Environmental Protection Agency* (Boston: Houghton Mifflin, 1976), p. 141.

39. Robert L. Sansom, *The New American Dream Machine: Toward a Simpler Lifestyle in an Environmental Age* (Garden City, N.Y.: Anchor Press, 1976), p. 25.

40. Morton Keller and R. Shep Melnick, eds., *Taking Stock: American Government in the Twentieth Century* (Washington, D.C.: Woodrow Wilson Center Press, 1999).

41. *Wall Street Journal*, March 19, 1974. The *Journal* stated at the end of my letter,

"We regret having overstated Mr. Train's opposition to changes in the act. — Ed."

42. *Wall Street Journal*, March 22, 1974.

43. Rowland Evans and Robert Novak, *Washington Post*, March 31, 1974.

44. For an excellent discussion of this problem, see Quarles, *Cleaning Up America*, pp. 193–194, 203–204, 207, 210–211.

45. Merle Miller, *Plain Speaking: An Oral Biography of Harry S. Truman* (New York: Berkley Publishing Corporation, 1974).

46. John Whitaker, quoted in Flippen, *Nixon and the Environment*, p. 52.

47. RET, speech given at Economic Club of Chicago, July 1974.

48. RET, testimony before the Senate Committee on Public Works, July 16, 1993.

49. RET, Diary, August 2, 1976.

50. RET, Diary, February 19, 1976.

51. RET, Diary, February 26, 1976.

52. Whitaker, *Striking a Balance*, p. 333.

CHAPTER 10. EPA UNDER FORD

1. RET, Memorandum for the Files, October 17, 1974.

2. RET, Letter to Rogers Morton, secretary of Interior, August 13, 1974. After reading the letter, Harlow sent a copy to Rumsfeld, calling it "well done" (October 29, 1974). Rumsfeld replied to Harlow: "You're right! Russ Train letter to Rog was excellent. I have acted on a piece of it today" (November 5, 1974).

3. RET, Memorandum for the Files, October 17, 1974.

4. *Washington Post*, September 3, 1974.

5. *Wall Street Journal*, April 16, 1975.

6. RET, Memorandum for the Files, n.d.

7. *Wall Street Journal*, November 29, 1974.

8. *Washington Post*, October 12, 1974.

9. *Time*, October 21, 1974.

10. *St. Louis Post-Dispatch*, October 28, 1974. Wyant sent me a copy of his article and penned this note with it: "Dear Mr. Train — It is very painful for me to heap praise on a Princeton man, but I must say you continue to deserve it. — All the best — Bill Wyant."

11. RET, Memorandum for the Files, October 23, 1974.

12. The economy-versus-environment issue was one I addressed with some frequency. See, for example, my speech to the Economic Club of Chicago, reported as an op-ed article in the *Atlantic Journal* on June 15, 1974, and my speech to the New York Chamber of Commerce and Industry, reported as an op-ed article in the *Cincinnati Post* on October 31, 1974.

13. My notes for 1975, for example, indicate that, in addition to the Portland conference, I took part in such White House conferences in Peoria (August 19), Seattle (September 5), St. Louis (September 12), Omaha (October 1), Knoxville (October 7), and Philadelphia (November 18). A Denver friend, George Caulkins, has a clear recollection of me in a Pilgrim costume leading a parade down

a main street of Denver, ringing a large bell, and calling out, "Town meeting! Town meeting!" Perhaps that was an EPA-sponsored event.

14. Remarks of President Gerald Ford at the White House Conference on Domestic and Economic Affairs, Memorial Coliseum, Portland, Oregon, November 1, 1974.

15. RET, opening statement, White House Conference on Domestic and Economic Affairs, Memorial Coliseum, Portland, Oregon, November 1, 1974.

16. RET, Memorandum to the President, December 4, 1974.

17. *Washington Post*, March 6, 1974.

18. *Washington Post*, July 9, 1974.

19. *New York Times*, July 10, 1974.

20. *Washington Star*, editorial, July 21, 1974.

21. *Washington Post*, editorial, July 17, 1974.

22. RET, Memorandum for the Files, May 28, 1975.

23. I had previously set out my position to the president in a memorandum dated May 9, 1975.

24. RET, notes on a White House notepad, November 28, 1974.

25. RET, Memorandum for the Files, "Meeting with President Ford, Vail, Colorado, December 28–29, 1974," January 7, 1975.

26. Linda Ba Thung, typed copy of speech, n.p., 1975.

27. Ibid.

28. Thanks in part to the international date line, I had given a speech the day before, July 2, to the Chamber of Commerce of Japan, Tokyo, titled "Environmental Protection versus Economic Growth: A Global Dilemma."

29. *New York Times*, July 9, 1975.

30. White House press release, "Text of Remarks by the President to Be Delivered at the Dedication of the National Environmental Research Center, Cincinnati, Ohio," July 2, 1975.

31. RET, Memorandum for the Files, "Cabinet Meeting August 27, 1975," September 22, 1975.

32. RET, Memorandum for the Files, September 18, 1975.

33. Meldrim Thomson Jr., Letter to RET, April 23, 1974.

34. A report on this meeting, although not carrying these quotations, is found in *National Journal Reports*, March 29, 1975, p. 479.

35. Lynette Fromme, Letter to RET; copy in RET files, along with copies of reports to RET from Charles Jenkins, director, Security and Inspection Division, EPA, dated January 7 and 14, 1976.

36. The speech was carried live for one hour (including the question-and-answer session at the end) by 183 public broadcasting radio stations. There was television coverage on the evening news and wire service coverage by the Associated Press and United Press International. RET, Diary, February 26, 1976. That day's edition of the *New York Times* carried a lengthy article on the speech by Ned Kenworthy. The *Washington Post* also ran an editorial about the speech on February 28, 1976.

37. RET, speech given at National Press Club, February 26, 1976. Several years later, I was cast as the villain in a book that quoted from my Press Club speech and disputed my facts: Edith Efron, *The Apocalyptics: Cancer and the Big Lie* (New York: Simon and Schuster, 1984). The book dismissed the whole toxic substances issue as a "mythic drama" (p. 470).

38. RET, speech given at National Press Club, February 26, 1976.

39. Ibid.

40. RET, Diary, February 26 and 27, 1976.

41. For example, RET on the CBS report "The American Way of Cancer," October 15, 1975; RET on the *CBS Evening News*, commenting on toxic substances, November 19, 1975; RET, announcement of plans to eliminate PCBs on WTTG-TV, ABC, and *CBS Evening News*, December 22, 1975; same story, CBS, December 23, 1975; RET interviewed about toxic chemicals on the Public Broadcasting Service's *Evening Edition*; RET warning on spread of Kepone contamination in Chesapeake Bay seafood, NBC and WTOP *Eyewitness News*, August 17, 1976. These were in addition to extensive coverage in the print media.

CHAPTER 11. THE LAST FORD YEARS

1. *Sierra Club v. Ruckelshaus*, 344 F. Supp. 253, 4 Env't Rep. Cas. 1205 (D.D.C. 1972), *aff'd*, 4 Env't Rep. Cas. 1815 (D.C. Cir. 1972), *cert. granted*, 41 U.S.L.W. 3392 (U.S. Jan. 15, 1973), *aff'd by tie vote*, 41 U.S.J.W. 4825 (U.S. June 11, 1973).

2. RET, Diary, March 29, 1976.

3. RET, Diary, May 3, 1976.

4. RET, Diary, May 4, 1976.

5. RET, Diary, June 1, 1976.

6. RET, Diary, April 10, 1976.

7. RET, Diary, June 8, 1976. This account of the meeting differs in some respects from the account given in *A Memoir*, which was based entirely on my unaided recollection. Russell E. Train, *A Memoir* (Washington, D.C.: privately published, 2000).

8. RET, Memorandum to the President, July 19, 1976.

9. RET, Diary, November 2, 1976.

10. RET, Diary, August 11–12, 1976.

11. RET, Diary, September 7, 1976.

12. RET, Memorandum for the Files, January 29, 1998.

13. RET, Diary, October 21, 1976.

14. RET, Diary, August 30, 1976.

15. RET, Diary, September 28, 1976.

16. *Weekly Energy Report*, May 12, 1975, p. 2.

17. *Des Moines Register*, July 17, 1975.

18. For an industry view of EPA's effort to open dialogue with the agricultural community, see "The EPA Discovers Agriculture," *Agrichemical Age*, November–December 1976, p. 3.

19. RET, Diary, April 7, 8, 9, and 15, 1976; *Washington Post*, April 9, 1976; *Washington Star*, August 21, 1976.
20. RET, Diary, December 29, 1976.
21. RET, Diary, December 18 and 19, 1976.
22. RET, Diary, December 21, 1976.
23. RET, Diary, December 20, 1976.
24. RET, Diary, December 21, 1976.
25. RET, statement during a special hearing on the *Argo Merchant* oil spill, Boston, Massachusetts, December 22, 1976.
26. RET, Diary, December 6, 1976.
27. RET, Diary, November 30, 1976.
28. *New York Times*, December 19, 1976.
29. Ibid.
30. *Princeton Alumni Weekly*, November 8, 1976, pp. 9–12.
31. A remarkably comprehensive report of the accomplishments of EPA in the first six years of its existence was prepared under the direction of deputy administrator John Quarles. See *Pollution Control in the U.S.: Some Examples of Recent Accomplishments* (Washington, D.C.: U.S. Environmental Protection Agency, November 24, 1976).
32. According to my diary entry for January 11, 1977, I signed and sent a letter of resignation on that day, effective January 20.
33. Gregory P. Lennox, Letter to RET, February 11, 1976.
34. Environmental Protection Agency, *Alvin L. Alm: Oral History Interview*, Document No. EPA-202-K-94-005 (Washington, D.C.: Environmental Protection Agency, Public Information Center, January 1994), p. 6.
35. RET, Diary, September 11, 1976.
36. John Osborne, *White House Watch: The Ford Years* (Washington, D.C.: New Republic Books, 1977), p. 180.
37. Gerald Ford, *A Time to Heal* (New York: Harper and Row, 1979).
38. Noël Mostert, *Supership* (New York: Knopf, 1974).
39. RET, Diary, January 5, 1977; RET, Memorandum for the Files, January 10, 1977.
40. *New York Times*, January 21, 1977. See also *Baltimore Sun*, March 15, 1977.
41. RET, Diary, January 27, 1977.

CHAPTER 12. WORLD WILDLIFE FUND: TRANSITION YEARS

1. In addition, over time, I joined the boards of the Alliance to Save Energy, the German Marshall Fund, the American Conservation Association, the American Committee for International Conservation, and the Center for Law and Social Policy. I also (briefly) became a senior fellow of the International Institute for Environment and Development. I also undertook the chairmanship of Clean Sites, Inc., as described more fully in a later chapter. For many years, I was a member of the Washington National Monument Society, which was chartered by Congress to build the monument in 1834. I served as senior vice president (executive head) until my retirement in 2001.

2. Letter to H.R.H. Prince Saud al Faisal, Foreign Minister, signed by A. Karim Ahmed, David D. Comey, Denis Hayes, Alice Tepper Marlin, Robert E. Stein, Aileen B. Train, and Russell E. Train, May 4, 1977.

3. Energy Research and Development Administration, "LMFBR Program Review," April 6, 1977.

4. RET, "Proliferation Resistant Nuclear Power Technologies: Preferred Alternatives to the Plutonium Breeder, April 6, 1977, Additional Views," April 6, 1977.

5. Letter to RET on behalf of President Jimmy Carter, June 14, 1977, stating that he had "deferred indefinitely construction of the Clinch River Breeder Reactor."

6. Carroll L. Wilson, Letter to RET, October 12, 1978.

7. Carroll W. Wilson, proj. dir., *Coal — Bridge to the Future: A Report of the World Coal Study*, WOCOL (Cambridge, Mass.: Ballinger, 1980).

8. RET, Diary, January 9, 1982. Ironically, twenty years later, on January 8, 2002, the front page of the *New York Times* reported that "top regulators" from EPA and the Department of Energy were recommending to the White House a relaxation of the rules requiring old coal-fired power plants to upgrade their pollution controls when renovating their plants.

9. RESOLVE was merged into The Conservation Foundation three years later and then, with the latter, into WWF in 1985. It is now once again an independent organization under the continuing leadership of Gail Bingham.

10. RET, Diary, December 9, 1979.

11. RET, Diary, March 7, 1978.

12. Ruth Patrick, longtime president of the Academy of Natural Sciences in Philadelphia and an internationally recognized limnologist, was my principal sponsor for the prize.

13. RET, address to the Tyler Ecology Symposium, Los Angeles, March 31, 1978.

14. Frank Kellogg stepped down as non–executive president, and Godfrey Rockefeller left as executive vice president. The latter became chairman of the board of the Chesapeake Bay Foundation.

15. World Wildlife Fund–US, *Annual Report 1978* (Washington, D.C.: World Wildlife Fund–US, 1978), p. 1.

16. Nancy Hammond administered WWF's conservation program, managing the grants and keeping in touch with all the projects. Doris McClanahan handled our finances, Diana Kingsbury-Smith was in charge of fund-raising from individual major donors, and Janet Bohlen handled membership and direct-mail fund-raising.

17. World Wildlife Fund–US, *Annual Report 1978*, p. 1.

18. RET, Memorandum for the Files, December 12, 1978; RET, Diary, December 7, 1978.

19. RET, Activities Report to WWF Board, February 22, 1984.

20. RET, opening remarks at the World Conference on Sea Turtle Conservation, Department of State, Washington, D.C., November 26, 1979.

21. For a fuller account of this experience on a turtle nesting beach, see RET, Diary, July 6–10, 1981.

22. A marvelous book on all the cranes is Peter Matthiessen, *The Birds of Heaven: Travels with Cranes* (New York: North Point Press, 2001), which is illustrated with paintings and drawings by Robert Bateman.

CHAPTER 13. ENCOUNTERS WITH THREE PRESIDENTS

1. *New York Times*, December 20, 1980.
2. RET, Diary, Christmas 1978.
3. RET, Diary, March 3, 1979.
4. *Baltimore Sun*, editorial, November 14, 1980.
5. RET, Diary, January 6, 1981.
6. RET, Diary, January 13, 1981.
7. RET, Diary, June 22, 1981.
8. *Jackson Hole News*, September 10, 1981.
9. *Maine Sunday Telegram*, July 26, 1981.
10. *Wall Street Journal*, June 2, 1982.
11. For further comment on the OMB regulatory review process, see Environmental Protection Agency, *Alvin L. Alm: Oral History Interview*, Document No. EPA-202-K-94-005 (Washington, D.C.: Environmental Protection Agency, Public Information Center, January 1994).
12. See Russell E. Train, *A Memoir* (Washington, D.C.: privately published, 2000), p. 292. See also RET, Diary, April 15, 1981. The review process continued in the George H. W. Bush presidency under the Council on Competitiveness, chaired by Vice President Dan Quayle. During the Bill Clinton administration, the process was pretty much dismantled, although Vice President Al Gore headed a group called Reinventing Government, which had a broader mandate and did not focus on reviewing individual regulations.
13. *Washington Post*, April 10, 1981; *New York Times*, April 10, 1981.
14. RET, Diary, January 7, 1982.
15. RET, Diary, January 6 and 8, 1982.
16. *Washington Post*, February 2, 1982.
17. *New York Times*, February 7, 1982.
18. RET, Diary, March 2, 1982.
19. RET, Diary, February 23, 1983.
20. RET, Diary, March 13, 1983.
21. RET, Diary, March 17, 1983.
22. The winners of the 1984 Getty Prize were Alvaro Ugalde, director of the national park service of Costa Rica, and Mario Boza, Costa Rica's first national parks director.
23. White House press release, July 25, 1983.
24. These were Bill Reilly of The Conservation Foundation, Jay Hair of the National Wildlife Federation, Paul Pritchard of the National Parks and Conservation Association, Jack Lorenz of the Izaak Walton League of America, and me as head of WWF. Also present were Bill Ruckelshaus, then back at EPA; Jim Baker,

the president's chief of staff; Ed Meese, the attorney general; and the secretary of the Cabinet.

25. RET, handwritten notes, "RET Remarks at May 9 Meeting in VP's Office."

26. RET, Letter to Vice President George H. W. Bush, enclosing draft environmental speech, March 21, 1988; RET, Letter to Bush Advisor Charles W. Greenleaf Jr., April 12, 1988, suggesting certain changes in the draft after discussion with William Ruckelshaus.

27. George H. W. Bush, speech given at Seattle Chamber of Commerce, May 16, 1988.

28. See, for example, the *Washington Post* lead editorial, September 2, 1988.

29. This was a meeting in Cincinnati of the National Trust for Historic Preservation. RET, Handwritten Text of Remarks, six pages, autumn 1988.

30. RET, Letter to Vice President George H. W. Bush, October 31, 1988.

31. Ibid.

CHAPTER 14. OF OSTRICHES AND DINOSAURS

1. RET, testimony before the Senate Committee on Foreign Relations, May 5, 1976.

2. The Nairobi conference was called by the United Nations General Assembly and technically named a Session of Special Character of the Governing Council of the United Nations Environment Programme (UNEP).

3. World Commission on Environment and Development, *Our Common Future* (Oxford, England, and New York: Oxford University Press, 1987).

4. Lash had succeeded James Gustave (Gus) Speth in 1993 as head of the World Resources Institute.

5. Council on Environmental Quality and Department of State, *The Global 2000 Report to the President — Entering the Twenty-first Century: A Report*, 3 vols. (Washington, D.C.: U.S. Government Printing Office, 1980). The responsible officials were Gustave Speth, chairman of the Council on Environmental Quality, and Thomas Pickering, assistant secretary of State for oceans and international environmental and scientific affairs. The staff director was Gerald Barney.

6. Julian L. Simon and Herman Kahn, eds., *The Resourceful Earth: A Response to "Global 2000"* (Oxford, England, and New York: Basil Blackwell, 1984).

7. In addition to Anderson and me, the group consisted of Robert Blake, a retired Foreign Service officer and former ambassador who was active in environmental matters; Lester Brown, president of Worldwatch Institute; Walter Cronkite of CBS; Adrian DeWind, chairman of the Natural Resources Defense Council; Marian Heiskell, a member of several environmental boards; Hans Landsberg, an economist with Resources for the Future; Robert McNamara, president of the World Bank and former secretary of Defense; George Mitchell, chairman and chief executive officer of Mitchell Energy and Development Corporation; Roger Revelle, head of the Harvard Center for Population and Development Studies; S. Dillon Ripley, secretary of the Smithsonian Institution; William

Ruckelshaus, vice president of the Weyerhaeuser Corporation and former EPA administrator; Henry Schacht, chief executive officer of Cummins Engine Company; John Sewall, president of the Overseas Development Council; Cyrus Vance, recently retired as secretary of State; and George Zeidenstein, president of the Population Council.

8. RET, Diary, August 27, 1981. The meeting with Watt apparently took place at some time considerably prior to that date.

CHAPTER 15. WWF AROUND THE WORLD

1. A key player then and thereafter in these Nepal arrangements was Prabhakar S. J. B. Rana, a close friend of the prince and a member of the Rana family, which had in effect ruled Nepal for more than a hundred years, with the monarchy little more than a figurehead. Prabhakar was an astute businessman, manager of the modern Soaltee Oberoi Hotel in Kathmandu, where I often stayed, and he had many friends and contacts in the West. I found him uniformly helpful.

2. World Wildlife Fund–US, *Annual Report 1985* (Washington, D.C.: World Wildlife Fund–US, 1985).

3. Galen Rowell, "Annapurna: Sanctuary for the Himalaya," *National Geographic* 176, no. 3 (September 1981): 394–405. Tragically, Rowell and his wife, Barbara, died in a plane crash in California in 2002.

4. Our trek to Muktinath, as well as other aspects of this visit to Nepal, is recorded in RET, "Activities Report to the WWF-US Board of Directors," May 9, 1985.

5. In the United States, Hillary works closely with the American Himalayan Foundation, which the Dalai Lama also supports. The president of the foundation is Richard Blum, currently a member of the WWF-US board (and husband of Senator Dianne Feinstein of California). Until recently, they were close neighbors of Aileen and me at Kalorama Square in Washington, D.C. For a recent, beautifully illustrated account of Hillary and his relationship with the Sherpa people, see Cynthia Russ Ramsay, *Sir Edmund Hillary and the People of Everest*, with photographs by Anne B. Keiser (Kansas City, Mo.: Andrews McMeel, 2002). A considerable portion of the book is devoted to WWF vice president Mingma Norbu Sherpa.

6. *Dawn*, May 1, 1985.

7. Matthiesson, *The Birds of Heaven*, p. 142.

8. *The Nation*, Bangkok, November 23, 1986.

9. *Economist*, February 23, 2002, p. 48.

10. Sadly, Celso Roque died in Manila in 2002 after a long illness.

11. RET, Memorandum for the Files, November 12, 1984.

12. Thomas E. Lovejoy III, "Aid Debtor Nations' Ecology," *New York Times*, October 4, 1984. The concept had emerged in a conversation between Lovejoy and Rodney Wagner, a vice chairman of J.P. Morgan and a longtime member of the boards of WWF-US and WWF-International.

13. The description in this chapter of the Philippine debt swaps and the creation of the Foundation for the Philippine Environment is taken almost verbatim from

WWF's Center for Conservation Finance publication titled *Business Plan — Building Conservation Capital for the Future*. See also a publication by Barry Spergel of WWF's Center for Conservation Finance titled *Raising Revenues for Protected Areas: A Menu of Options*, ca. 2000.

14. Recognizing the increasingly important role conservation finance must play in future global conservation efforts, in 2000 WWF-US formally created its Center for Conservation Finance, directed by Bruce Bunting. The center is composed of top professionals from the conservation, legal, finance, and international development fields.

CHAPTER 16. EDUCATION AND NATURE: A GLOBAL VISION

1. Communal Areas Management Programme for Indigenous Resources.
2. David M. Olson and Eric Dinerstein, "The Global 200: A Representation Approach to Conserving the Earth's Most Biologically Valuable Ecoregions," *Conservation Biology* 12 (1998): 502–515.
3. Ibid.
4. The twenty-three ecoregions (always subject to change over time) are as follows:
    1. Western Congo Basin Moist Forests (Republic of the Congo, Cameroon, Central African Republic, Gabon, Democratic Republic of the Congo, Equatorial Guinea)
    2. Zambezian Woodlands and Savannas (Zambia, Tanzania, Malawi, Zimbabwe, Mozambique, Angola, Botswana, Burundi, Democratic Republic of the Congo)
    3. East African Marine Ecosystems (Somalia, Kenya, Tanzania, Mozambique)
    4. Madagascar Dry Forest and Spiny Desert (Madagascar)
    5. Western Himalayan Forests, Meadows, and Grasslands (Bhutan, India, Nepal, Myanmar, China)
    6. Tibetan Plateau Steppe (China, India, Pakistan)
    7. Southwestern China Temperate Forests (China)
    8. Forests of the Lower Mekong (Vietnam, Laos, Thailand, Cambodia)
    9. Sulu-Sulawesi Seas (Philippines, Malaysia, Indonesia)
    10. New Guinea Rain Forests (Papua New Guinea, Indonesia)
    11. Mesoamerican Caribbean Reef (Belize, Guatemala, Honduras, Mexico)
    12. Montane Forests of the Northern Andes (Ecuador, Colombia, Peru, Venezuela)
    13. Galápagos Islands (Ecuador)
    14. Southwestern Amazon Moist Forests (Brazil, Peru, Bolivia)
    15. Atlantic Forests (Brazil, Paraguay, Argentina)
    16. Valdivian Temperate Forests (Chile, Argentina)
    17. Gulf of California (Mexico)
    18. Bering-Beaufort-Chukchi Seas (United States, Canada, Russia)
    19. Klamath-Siskiyou Forests (California, Oregon)
    20. Chihuahuan Desert (United States, Mexico)
    21. Rivers and Streams of the American Southeast (United States)

22. Everglades and Florida Keys (southern Florida)

23. Northern High Plains (United States, Canada)

5. Kathryn Fuller, "The State of the Natural World" (speech given at Aspen Institute, Barcelona, Spain, May 29, 2002).

6. Ibid.

7. In 2003, Sant retired as chairman of the AES Corporation, an independent power company that he cofounded with Dennis Bakke in 1981. I served for a number of years on the AES board, retiring in 1997.

8. See, for example, Roger D. Stone and Claudia D'Andrea, *Tropical Forests and the Human Spirit: Journeys to the Brink of Hope* (Berkeley and Los Angeles: University of California Press, 2002). The authors see the involvement of local people as the principal hope for forest conservation around the world.

9. Emily McDiarmid, director of admissions, Yale School of Forestry and Environmental Studies, e-mail message to Shaun Martin, EFN director, WWF, August 23, 2002.

10. "Special Report: How to Save the Earth," *Time*, August 26, 2002, pp. A26–A27.

CHAPTER 17. AN ELEVENTH COMMANDMENT

1. RET, "Caring for Creation" (speech given at North American Conference on Religion and Ecology, Washington, D.C., May 18, 1990). Reprinted in *Vital Speeches of the Day*, August 15, 1990 (published by City News Publishing Company, Mount Pleasant, South Carolina).

2. Ibid.

3. Ibid.

4. The board included Peter Berle, president of the National Audubon Society; Doug Costle, former EPA administrator; Lou Fernandez, chairman of the Monsanto Company and a key figure in establishing the organization; Sandra Gardebring, chair of the Metropolitan Council of the Twin Cities; Ed Gee, director and former chairman and chief executive officer of the International Paper Company; Jay Hair, executive vice president of the National Wildlife Federation; Don Kennedy, president of Stanford University; Joshua Lederberg, president of Rockefeller University; H. Eugene McBrayer, executive vice president of the Exxon Chemical Company; Bill Reilly, then president of WWF and The Conservation Foundation; and Hank Schacht, chairman and chief executive officer of Cummins Engine Company. The first president of Clean Sites, Chuck Powers, was also a member of the board.

5. Edwin H. Clark II.

6. J. Clarence "Terry" Davies was executive director of the commission, and Amelia Salzman was its project director. A full list of the membership with affiliations as of 1992 is as follows: Russell E. Train, chairman; Peter A. A. Berle, president of the National Audubon Society and former commissioner of the New York State Department of Environmental Conservation; John E. Bryson, chairman and chief executive officer of Southern California Edison Company; A. W. Clausen, chairman of the executive committee of the BankAmerica Cor-

poration and former president of the World Bank; Douglas M. Costle, distinguished senior fellow of the Institute for Sustainable Communities and former EPA administrator; Madeleine May Kunin, president of the Institute for Sustainable Communities and former governor of Vermont; Gene E. Likens, vice president of the New York Botanical Garden and director of the Institute of Ecosystem Studies; Cruz A. Matos, environmental consultant and former chief technical advisor for the United Nations; Gilbert S. Omenn, professor and dean of the University of Washington's School of Public Health and Community Medicine; Paul H. O'Neill, chairman and chief executive officer of Alcoa; Alice M. Rivlin, senior fellow of the Brookings Institution's Economic Studies program and former director of the Congressional Budget Office; Priscilla Robinson, environmental consultant and former director and founder of the Southwest Environmental Service; Steven C. Rockefeller, professor of religion at Middlebury College; William D. Ruckelshaus, chairman and chief executive officer of Browning-Ferris Industries and former EPA administrator; Gloria R. Scott, president of Bennett College; James Gustave (Gus) Speth, president of the World Resources Institute and former chairman of the Council on Environmental Quality; Lee M. Thomas, chairman and chief executive officer of Law Companies Environmental Group and former EPA administrator; Victoria J. Tschinkel, senior consultant for Landers and Parsons and former secretary of the Florida Department of Environmental Regulation; and Robert M. White, president of the National Academy of Engineering and former administrator of the National Oceanic and Atmospheric Administration (NOAA).

7. National Commission on the Environment, *Choosing a Sustainable Future: The Report of the National Commission on the Environment* (Washington, D.C.: Island Press, 1993).

8. Ibid.

9. Ibid.

10. Ibid.

11. *Wall Street Journal*, December 9, 1992.

12. See, for example, *Washington Post*, December 10, 1992; *Philadelphia Inquirer*, December 10, 1992.

13. RET, testimony before the U.S. Senate Committee on Public Works, July 16, 1993.

CHAPTER 18. ETHICS, LEADERSHIP, AND THE ENVIRONMENT

1. See, for example, RET, "Caring for Creation" (speech given at North American Conference on Religion and Ecology, Washington, D.C., May 18, 1990); RET, "Toward an Environmental Ethic" (speech given at Humane Society of the United States, October 12, 1991); RET, Memorandum for the Files, "Environmental Ethics," October 24, 1991.

2. Aldo Leopold, *A Sand County Almanac* (New York: Oxford University Press, 1966).

3. For a more sophisticated explanation of the interaction of humans with their

environment over millennia, see Tim F. Flannery, *The Eternal Frontier: An Ecological History of North America and Its Peoples* (New York: Atlantic Monthly Press, 2001).

4. For a recent, innovative view of energy policy, see Timothy Wirth, C. Boyden Gray, and John Podesta, "An Energy Strategy for the Future," *Foreign Affairs* 82, no. 4 (July–August 2003): 132–155.

Acknowledgments

As I have tried to make clear from time to time in this book, I have been blessed throughout my career with associates whose outstanding qualities have been the principal factor in whatever success I have had. To all of them, I am eternally grateful.

In writing this book, I have contacted numerous associates (past and present), and I thank them one and all for their recollections of events and their insights. Among these are Alvin Alm, Gordon Binder, Harry C. Blaney III, E. U. Curtis "Buff" Bohlen, Janet Trowbridge Bohlen, Bruce Bunting, David Challinor, Edwin H. "Toby" Clark, J. Clarence "Terry" Davies III, Jared Diamond, Eric Dinerstein, William Dircks, Alan Eckart, William Eichbaum, Richard Fairbanks, Janet Fesler, Robert W. Fri, Kathryn Fuller, Boyd Gibbons, Christian A. Herter Jr., Craig Hoover, Joel Horn, Alan Kirk, James Leape, Shaun Martin, Steffen Plehn, David Pryor, John Quarles, Nathaniel P. Reed, William K. Reilly, William D. Ruckelshaus, David Sandalow, Mingma Norbu Sherpa, Randall Snodgrass, Eric Stork, Lee M. Talbot, and John Whitaker.

With respect to World Wildlife Fund subjects, I am particularly indebted to Eric Dinerstein for his advice and counsel on the subject of ecoregion conservation; to Toby Clark for his thoughts on the Clean Sites, Inc. experience; to Terry Davies and Amy Salzman for all the great work they put into the report on the National Commission on the Environment, from which I have drawn extensively; and to Shaun Martin and his staff for their suggestions for the "Education for Nature" section.

To Jonathan Cobb, my editor, for his patience, experience, encouragement, and understanding, my appreciation knows no bounds. The book has entailed a lot more work, in terms of both research and writing, than I ever envisaged at the outset. Jonathan has helped make it satisfying and fun from start to finish.

My copyeditor, Pat Harris, has astounded me with her ability to check and correct the smallest detail about people and events going back many years, as well as with her knowledge of proper usage of language in setting out those matters. I am extremely grateful to her.

Catherine Williams, my secretary for many years, has taken my original longhand script and converted it through various iterations to the final copy for my editor. It has been an enormous task, which she has performed with skill and patience. I give her my heartfelt thanks.

Finally, but most of all, I am grateful to my wife, Aileen, who not only has encouraged me in the writing of this book but also has been with me throughout the story I tell — at least for the past fifty years of it! She has been a true and valuable partner in all I have done.

Index